501 low-fat recipes

501 low-fat recipes

Editorial director Susan Tomnay
Creative director Hieu Chi Nguyen
Food director Pamela Clark
Food editor Cathie Lonnie
Editor Stephanie Kistner
Designer Corey Butler
Director of sales Brian Cearnes
Marketing manager Bridget Cody
Production manager Cedric Taylor

Chief executive officer Ian Law
Group publisher Pat Ingram
General manager Christine Whiston
Editorial director (WW) Deborah Thomas

Cover Thai basil chicken stir-fry, page 167
Photographer Ian Wallace
Stylist Sarah O'Brien

Page 1 Leek and asparagus risotto, page 228
Page 2 Mango lime syrup cake, page 295

Back cover (clockwise from top left) Pasta with fresh tomato sauce, page 246; Char-grilled polenta cakes with corn salsa, page 75; Mushroom, tomato and zucchini skewers with white bean puree, page 255; Leek and asparagus risotto, page 228; Poached eggs and asparagus with dill sauce, page 66; Pork rice paper rolls, page 194

Photographers Steve Brown, Ben Dearnley, Rowan Fotheringham, Louise Lister, Andre Martin, Brett Stevens, Ian Wallace
Stylists Wendy Berecry, Julz Beresford, Janelle Bloom, Marie-Helene Clauzon, Jane Hann, Sarah O'Brien

Produced by ACP Books, Sydney.
Printed by Everbest Printing Co. Ltd., China.
Published by ACP Magazines Ltd, 54 Park St, Sydney, NSW 2000, Australia;
GPO Box 4088, Sydney, NSW 2001, Australia. Ph: +61 2 9282 8618 Fax: +61 2 9267 9438
acpbooks@acpmagazines.com.au www.acpbooks.com.au

RIGHTS ENQUIRIES
Laura Bamford, Director ACP Books. lbamford@acpuk.com

AUSTRALIA Distributed by Network Services, GPO Box 4088, Sydney, NSW 1028.
Ph (02) 9282 8777 Fax (02) 9264 3278
UNITED KINGDOM Distributed by Australian Consolidated Press (UK),
Moulton Park Business Centre, Red House Rd, Moulton Park, Northhampton, NN3 6AQ
Ph (01604) 497 531 Fax (01604) 497 533 books@acpuk.com
CANADA Distributed by Whitecap Books Ltd, 351 Lynn Ave, North Vancouver, BC, V7J 2C4
Ph (604) 980 9852 Fax (604) 980 8197 customerservice@whitecap.ca www.whitecap.ca
NEW ZEALAND Distributed by Southern Publishers Group, 44 New North Road, Eden Terrace, Auckland. Ph (64 9) 309 6930 Fax (64 9) 309 6170 hub@spg.co.nz
SOUTH AFRICA Distributed by PSD Promotions (Pty) Ltd, PO Box 1175, Isando, 1600, Gauteng, Johannesburg, SA. Ph (011) 392 6065 Fax (011) 392 6079 orders@psdprom.co.za

Clark, Pamela
The Australian Women's Weekly 501 Low-fat Recipes
Includes index.
ISBN 978-1-86396-646-7
1. Low-fat diet – Recipes. I. Title.
641.56384

contents

low-fat eating

We all need fat in our diet – otherwise our hair would be brittle, our skin dry, our nails cracked. But if we eat too much of it, and especially if we eat saturated fats, we'll put on weight.

how to maintain your weight

CHOOSE NATURAL FOODS Limit packaged, takeaway and fast foods in your diet, they're mostly made with high amounts of fat. Avoid commercial cakes and biscuits too, they contain the twin evils of saturated fat and high amounts of sugar.

FORGET FRYING Especially deep-frying. Stir-fry in a wok or large frying pan instead, lightly spraying with cooking oil, or roast, poach, grill or steam.

SHED SKIN Scrap the skin from chicken and remove excess fat from meat.

SKIMMING FAT Make soups, sauces and casseroles a day ahead, refrigerate them overnight, then skim away the fat that solidifies on the surface before reheating.

USE GOOD OILS Use olive or canola oil whenever possible instead of butter.

DAIRY FOOD Go for low-fat, light or skim milk, sour cream and yogurt.

FISH Increase your consumption of fish, including canned fish such as tuna or salmon.

WHOLEMEAL Choose whole-grain breads, brown rice and wholemeal pasta whenever possible.

DOWNSIZE Cut down on portion sizes of high-fat food, but give yourself big servings of fresh fruit and vegetables – that way you won't be hungry.

SHOPPING Don't do your grocery shopping when you're hungry; you are much more likely to buy fatty food on impulse then.

THE PANTRY Keep only low-fat food in the house. That way if you must have a packet of chocolate biscuits you'll have to go out to get them.

WATER Drink water in preference to anything else and drink lots of it.

EXERCISE Moderate, regular exercise will not only help you lose weight, but also make you feel healthier and more alert.

LOW-FAT means 15g or less of fat per serving
MEDIUM-FAT means 15-30g of fat per serving
HIGH-FAT means more than 30g of fat per serving

These figures relate to a main course; starters and desserts should come in at less. To maintain weight you shouldn't eat any more than about 56g fat a day; less if you want to lose weight. In this book we've tried to keep main course recipes below 15g fat; many of them are well below, so if you use these recipes on a regular basis, you shouldn't have any trouble maintaining or even losing weight.

breakfast

untoasted muesli

PREPARATION TIME 10 MINUTES

2 cups (180g) rolled oats
½ cup (35g) all-bran
1 tablespoon sunflower seeds
⅓ cup (55g) sultanas
¼ cup (35g) finely chopped dried apricots
½ cup (80g) finely chopped seeded dried dates
3 cups (750ml) no-fat milk
½ cup (140g) low-fat yogurt

1. Combine oats, all-bran, seeds and dried fruit in large bowl.
2. Divide muesli and milk among serving bowls. Top with yogurt.

SERVES 6
per serving 4.3g total fat (0.7g saturated fat); 1139kj (272 cal); 11.4g protein; 47.3g carbohydrate; 6.2g fibre

toasted muesli

PREPARATION TIME 15 MINUTES COOKING TIME 45 MINUTES (PLUS COOLING TIME)

1 cup (90g) rolled oats
¼ cup (15g) unprocessed bran
¼ cup (35g) finely chopped dried apricots
¼ cup (20g) finely chopped dried apples
2 tablespoons sultanas
1 tablespoon honey
1 tablespoon water
1 cup (250ml) skim milk

1. Preheat oven to 150°C/130°C fan-forced.
2. Combine oats, bran and dried fruit in medium bowl; stir in combined honey and water.
3. Spread mixture onto oven tray; bake, uncovered, about 45 minutes or until toasted, stirring occasionally. Cool.
4. Serve muesli with milk, and fresh fruit, if desired.

SERVES 2
per serving 4.4g total fat (0.8g saturated fat); 1574kj (376 cal); 11.7g protein; 73.3g carbohydrate; 7.6g fibre
store muesli can be refrigerated in an airtight container for several weeks.

swiss muesli with grilled mangoes and blueberries

PREPARATION TIME 15 MINUTES (PLUS REFRIGERATION TIME) COOKING TIME 5 MINUTES

1½ cups (135g) traditional rolled oats
1 cup (250ml) low-fat milk
300g low-fat yogurt with honey
2 medium (860g) mangoes
1 medium (150g) apple, chopped finely
2 tablespoons lemon juice
100g fresh blueberries
2 tablespoons honey

1. Combine oats, half the milk and half the yogurt in large bowl; cover, refrigerate 20 minutes.
2. Meanwhile, cut through mangoes on both sides of seed; scoop out flesh in one piece with a large spoon. Cut mango halves into thick slices. Cook mango on heated grill plate (or grill or barbecue) until browned both sides.
3. Stir remaining milk, remaining yogurt, apple and juice into oat mixture. Top with blueberries and grilled mango, drizzle with honey.

SERVES 4
per serving 3.5g total fat (0.7g saturated fat); 1543kj (369 cal); 12.4g protein; 71g carbohydrate; 5.7g fibre

bircher muesli

PREPARATION TIME 15 MINUTES (PLUS REFRIGERATION TIME)

During the late 19th century, a Swiss nutritionist, Dr Max Bircher-Benner, developed a breakfast cereal for his patients. A staunch vegetarian, Bircher-Benner believed firmly that people should eat as little processed food as possible. Bircher muesli has become a very popular breakfast food and is now being made commercially by a few yogurt and cereal companies.

3 cups (270g) rolled oats
2 cups (500ml) fresh orange juice
400g yogurt
1 cup (160g) seeded dried dates, chopped coarsely
½ cup (85g) raisins
½ cup (150g) dried apricots, sliced thinly
⅓ cup (80ml) honey
1 cup (250ml) milk
1 large apple (200g), peeled, grated coarsely
⅓ cup (45g) toasted slivered almonds

1. Combine oats, juice and yogurt in large bowl. Cover tightly; refrigerate overnight.
2. Stir dates, raisins, apricot, honey, milk and apple into oat mixture. Cover; refrigerate 30 minutes.
3. Serve muesli in individual serving bowls; top with almonds.

SERVES 6
per serving 11.3g total fat (3.1g saturated fat); 2288kj (547 cal); 13.8g protein; 98.2g carbohydrate; 10.1g fibre
tips try to find plain full-cream yogurt, sometimes called country-style or greek-style, for this recipe. Other types, especially the low-fat kind, are not suitable.
Additional milk can be added if muesli is too thick.
Use a tart, crisp green apple, such as a granny smith, for this recipe.
serving suggestion serve muesli topped with a combination of fresh mixed berries.

porridge with sticky fruits

PREPARATION TIME 10 MINUTES COOKING TIME 20 MINUTES

1 cup (150g) dried apricots
2 tablespoons honey
1 cup (250ml) water
1 cinnamon stick
1 tablespoon finely grated lemon rind
1 cup (230g) fresh dates
2¼ cups (200g) traditional rolled oats
1.5 litres (6 cups) low-fat milk
1 tablespoon flaked almonds, toasted

1. Combine apricots, honey, the water, cinnamon and rind in small saucepan; bring to a boil. Reduce heat, simmer, uncovered, about 5 minutes or until syrup has thickened slightly; cool. Cut dates in half lengthways, discard seeds; add dates to apricot mixture.
2. Combine oats and milk in medium saucepan; cook, stirring, about 10 minutes or until mixture thickens.
3. Drain fruit over large bowl; reserve syrup. Spoon porridge into bowls; top with apricot mixture and nuts, drizzle with syrup.

SERVES 4
per serving 6.5g total fat (1.3g saturated fat); 2267kj (541 cal); 25.8g protein; 96.2g carbohydrate; 8.9g fibre

porridge with apple compote

PREPARATION TIME 10 MINUTES COOKING TIME 10 MINUTES

There can be few things as comforting or nutritious as a warming bowl of porridge. Here, it's given a natural flavour enhancer with the addition of gently cooked apples, tasting of cinnamon.

2 medium apples (300g)
¼ cup (55g) caster sugar
¼ teaspoon ground cinnamon
¼ cup (60ml) water
8 dried apricots
1 tablespoon sultanas
1 cup (90g) rolled oats
1 cup (250ml) skim milk
1½ cups (375ml) boiling water
2 tablespoons brown sugar

1. Peel, core and slice apples thickly. Cook apple, caster sugar, cinnamon and the water in medium saucepan, stirring, over low heat until sugar dissolves. Bring to a boil; reduce heat, simmer, uncovered, 5 minutes. Add apricots and sultanas; simmer, uncovered, about 5 minutes or until apple is tender.
2. Meanwhile, combine oats, milk and the boiling water in another medium saucepan; bring to a boil. Reduce heat, simmer, uncovered, stirring, about 5 minutes or until mixture thickens.
3. Serve porridge with apple compote, sprinkled with brown sugar.

SERVES 4
per serving 2.1g total fat (0.4g saturated fat); 1004kj (240 cal); 5.8g protein; 50.4g carbohydrate; 3.4g fibre
tip any other dried fruit, such as prunes, pears or peaches, could be used instead of the apricots.

quick banana bread

PREPARATION TIME 10 MINUTES COOKING TIME 20 MINUTES

You will need 1 large overripe banana for this recipe.

1¼ cups (185g) self-raising flour
1 teaspoon ground cinnamon
1 tablespoon low-fat margarine
½ cup (110g) sugar
1 egg, beaten lightly
¼ cup (60ml) low-fat milk
½ cup mashed banana

1. Preheat oven to 220°C/200°C fan-forced. Line base and sides of 14cm x 21cm loaf pan with baking paper.
2. Combine flour and cinnamon in large bowl; rub in margarine. Stir in sugar, egg, milk and banana; do not overmix, batter should be lumpy. Spoon mixture into prepared pan.
3. Bake, uncovered, about 20 minutes or until cooked when tested.

SERVES 4
per serving 4g total fat (1g saturated fat); 1374kj (328 cal); 7.2g protein; 66.8g carbohydrate; 2.4g fibre

breakfast with the lot

PREPARATION TIME 10 MINUTES COOKING TIME 25 MINUTES

2 large egg tomatoes (180g), quartered
4 eggs
4 slices multigrain bread
60g light ham
50g baby spinach leaves

1. Preheat oven to 220°C/200°C fan-forced. Line oven tray with baking paper.
2. Place tomato, cut-side up, on oven tray; roast, uncovered, about 25 minutes or until softened and lightly browned.
3. Meanwhile, place enough water in a large shallow frying pan to come halfway up the side; bring to a boil. Break eggs, one at a time, into small bowl, sliding each into pan; allow water to return to a boil. Cover pan, turn off heat; stand about 4 minutes or until a light film of egg white has set over each yolk.
4. Toast bread slices until lightly browned both sides.
5. Using slotted spoon, remove eggs, one at a time from pan; place spoon on absorbent-paper-lined saucer briefly to blot up any poaching liquid. Serve toast topped with ham, spinach, egg then tomato.

SERVES 4
per serving 7.2g total fat (2g saturated fat); 834kj (199 cal); 13.9g protein; 19.6g carbohydrate; 3g fibre

corn fritters with roasted tomato chilli jam

PREPARATION TIME 20 MINUTES COOKING TIME 1 HOUR 25 MINUTES

You will need 2 medium corn cobs, each weighing about 250g after being trimmed. Roasted tomato chilli jam is best made a day or two ahead to allow the flavours to develop.

1 cup (160g) wholemeal self-raising flour
½ teaspoon bicarbonate of soda
½ teaspoon hot paprika
¾ cup (180ml) no-fat milk
2 eggs, beaten lightly
2 cups (330g) fresh corn kernels
1 small red capsicum (150g), chopped finely
2 green onions, sliced thinly
2 tablespoons finely chopped fresh flat-leaf parsley

ROASTED TOMATO CHILLI JAM

2 medium tomatoes (380g)
1 small red onion (100g), chopped finely
1 clove garlic, crushed
2 teaspoons grated fresh ginger
¼ cup (60ml) lime juice
2 tablespoons brown sugar
2 fresh red thai chillies, chopped finely

1 Make roasted tomato chilli jam.

2 Sift flour, soda and paprika into medium bowl. Make well in centre of flour mixture, gradually whisk in combined milk and eggs until batter is smooth. Stir corn, capsicum, onion and parsley into batter.

3 Pour ¼ cup batter into heated large oiled frying pan; using spatula, spread batter to shape into a round. Cook about 2 minutes each side or until fritter is lightly browned and cooked through, remove from pan; cover to keep warm. Repeat with remaining batter.

4 Serve fritters with jam.

ROASTED TOMATO CHILLI JAM preheat oven to 220°C/200°C fan-forced. Halve tomatoes; place, cut-side up, on oiled oven tray. Roast, uncovered, 30 minutes; chop tomato coarsely. Combine tomato with remaining ingredients in small saucepan, stirring over low heat until sugar dissolves; bring to a boil. Reduce heat; simmer, uncovered, about 40 minutes or until thickened.

SERVES 4
per serving 4.7g total fat (1g saturated fat); 1327kj (317 cal); 15.6g protein; 52g carbohydrate; 10.4g fibre
tip you can make double the quantity of jam and keep it, covered, in the refrigerator for up to 4 weeks.
serving suggestion serve with baby spinach leaves.

morning trifles

PREPARATION TIME 20 MINUTES

You will need about 5 passionfruit for the recipe.

⅓ cup (20g) all-bran
⅓ cup (20g) special k
⅓ cup (20g) puffed wheat
250g strawberries, hulled
1 cup (280g) low-fat vanilla yogurt
⅓ cup (80ml) passionfruit pulp

1. Combine cereals in small bowl.
2. Cut six strawberries in half; reserve. Slice remaining strawberries thinly.
3. Divide half of the cereal mixture among four 1-cup (250ml) serving bowls; divide half of the yogurt, all the strawberry slices and half of the passionfruit pulp among bowls. Continue layering with remaining cereal and yogurt; top with reserved strawberry halves and remaining passionfruit pulp.

SERVES 4
per serving 0.7g total fat (0.2g saturated fat); 527kj (126 cal); 8.2g protein; 20.4g carbohydrate; 6.3g fibre

grilled figs with ricotta and honeycomb on toasted fruit bread

PREPARATION TIME 5 MINUTES COOKING TIME 10 MINUTES

Honeycomb is the structure made of beeswax that houses the honey; this edible chewy comb, saturated with honey, is available in health food stores and some supermarkets.

8 large fresh figs (about 650g), halved
1 tablespoon brown sugar
500g loaf fruit bread
2 cups (400g) ricotta cheese
150g honeycomb, sliced thickly
2 tablespoons honey

1. Preheat grill. Place figs, cut-side up, on oven tray; sprinkle with sugar. Cook under hot grill about 5 minutes or until sugar melts and figs are browned lightly.
2. Cut bread into 1cm slices; toast both sides under hot grill.
3. Divide toast among serving plates; top each with equal amounts of ricotta and honeycomb, then top with two fig halves and drizzle with honey.

SERVES 8
per serving 8.1g total fat (4g saturated fat); 1554kj (371 cal); 11.1g protein; 64.9g carbohydrate; 4.7g fibre
tip walnut or almond bread can be substituted for the fruit loaf, if you prefer.
serving suggestion serve with a bowl of chopped pineapple, apple and orange segments.

cheesy polenta muffins with tomato jam

PREPARATION TIME 25 MINUTES COOKING TIME 45 MINUTES

2 bacon rashers, chopped finely
1½ cups (225g) self-raising flour
1 cup (170g) polenta
½ teaspoon bicarbonate of soda
½ teaspoon salt
1 tablespoon caster sugar
3 green onions, chopped coarsely
¼ cup coarsely chopped fresh flat-leaf parsley
1 cup (125g) coarsely grated cheddar cheese
1 egg
1 cup (250ml) buttermilk

TOMATO JAM

5 small tomatoes (650g), chopped coarsely
2 medium brown onions (300g), chopped coarsely
3 fresh red thai chillies, chopped coarsely
4 cloves garlic, chopped coarsely
½ cup (125ml) malt vinegar
½ cup (100g) firmly packed brown sugar
1 tablespoon tomato paste

1 Make tomato jam.

2 Preheat oven to 180°C/160°C fan-froced. Oil 12-hole (⅓ cup/80ml) muffin pan.

3 Cook bacon, stirring, in heated medium frying pan until crisp; drain on absorbent paper.

4 Place bacon in large bowl with remaining muffin ingredients; stir until just combined (do not overmix). Spoon mixture evenly into pan.

5 Bake, uncovered, about 35 minutes. Serve muffins with tomato jam.

TOMATO JAM combine ingredients in medium saucepan; bring to a boil, stirring. Reduce heat, simmer, uncovered, stirring occasionally, about 45 minutes or until mixture thickens. Blend or process mixture until pureed.

SERVES 6
per serving 10.6g total fat (5.7g saturated fat); 1950kj (466 cal); 19g protein; 72.7g carbohydrate; 19g fibre
tip muffins can be made a day ahead and refrigerated, covered (you can also freeze them for up to three months). Wrap in foil and reheat briefly in a hot oven before serving. Tomato jam can be made three days ahead and refrigerated, covered.
serving suggestion serve with creamy scrambled eggs.

date and bran muffins

PREPARATION TIME 15 MINUTES (PLUS STANDING TIME) COOKING TIME 25 MINUTES

1½ cups (100g) unprocessed bran
1½ cups (375ml) no-fat milk
1¼ cups (185g) self-raising flour
½ cup (100g) firmly packed brown sugar
2 teaspoons ground cinnamon
⅓ cup (90g) low-fat dairy-free spread, melted
1 egg
1 cup (160g) finely chopped seeded dried dates

1. Preheat oven to 180°C/160°C fan-forced. Grease 12-hole (⅓ cup/80ml) muffin pan.
2. Combine bran and milk in large bowl; stand 5 minutes.
3. Stir flour, sugar and cinnamon into bran mixture until combined. Add remaining ingredients; stir until almost combined (do not overmix). Spoon mixture into pan.
4. Bake, uncovered, about 25 minutes. Turn muffins onto wire rack to cool.

MAKES 12 MUFFINS
per muffin 4g total fat (0.8g saturated fat); 742kj (177 cal); 4.9g protein; 31g carbohydrate; 5.6g fibre

blueberry muffins

PREPARATION TIME 10 MINUTES COOKING TIME 20 MINUTES

cooking-oil spray
1 cup (150g) self-raising flour
1 cup (160g) wholemeal self-raising flour
½ cup (100g) firmly packed brown sugar
1 cup (150g) fresh or frozen blueberries
2 egg whites, beaten lightly
⅓ cup (80ml) prepared apple sauce
¾ cup (180ml) skim milk

1. Preheat oven to 220°C/200°C fan-forced. Coat a 12-hole (⅓ cup/80ml) muffin pan with cooking-oil spray.
2. Sift flours into a large bowl; stir in sugar and blueberries.
3. Stir in egg whites, sauce and milk until almost combined (do not overmix); spoon into pan.
4. Bake, uncovered, about 20 minutes or until cooked when tested.

MAKES 12 MUFFINS
per muffin 0.7g total fat (0.1g saturated fat); 575kj (137 cal); 4.1g protein; 28.8g carbohydrate; 2.3g fibre
tip muffins can be made a day ahead and kept in an airtight container at room temperature, or frozen.

strawberry hotcakes with blueberry sauce

PREPARATION TIME 15 MINUTES COOKING TIME 20 MINUTES

1 egg, separated

2 egg whites, extra

½ cup (125ml) apple sauce

1 teaspoon vanilla essence

2 cups (560g) low-fat yogurt

1¾ cups (280g) wholemeal self-raising flour

250g strawberries, hulled, chopped coarsely

BLUEBERRY SAUCE

150g blueberries, chopped coarsely

2 tablespoons sugar

1 tablespoon water

1. Make blueberry sauce.
2. Beat all egg whites in small bowl with electric mixer until soft peaks form.
3. Combine egg yolk, sauce, essence, yogurt, flour and strawberries in large bowl; fold in egg whites.
4. Pour ¼ cup batter into heated large greased frying pan; using spatula, spread batter to shape into a round. Cook, over low heat, about 2 minutes or until bubbles appear on the surface. Turn hotcake; cook until lightly browned on other side. Remove from pan; cover to keep warm. Repeat with remaining batter. Serve with blueberry sauce.

BLUEBERRY SAUCE combine ingredients in small saucepan; bring to a boil, stirring constantly. Reduce heat, simmer 2 minutes. Remove from heat; cool. Blend or process until smooth.

SERVES 4

per serving 3.2g total fat (0.8g saturated fat); 1722kj (411 cal); 21.4g protein; 72.5g carbohydrate; 10.3g fibre

buttermilk pancakes with golden pears

PREPARATION TIME 15 MINUTES COOKING TIME 25 MINUTES

1 cup (150g) self-raising flour

1 cup (250ml) buttermilk

¼ cup (60ml) skim milk

1 egg white

GOLDEN PEARS

4 corella pears (665g), peeled and halved

¼ cup (60ml) golden syrup

1 cup (250ml) water

1 tablespoon lemon juice

3 teaspoons cornflour

1 tablespoon water, extra

1. Make golden pears.
2. Sift flour into large bowl; gradually stir in combined milks to make a smooth batter. Beat egg white with electric mixer until soft peaks form; fold lightly into batter.
3. Pour ½ cup batter mixture into heated large frying pan. Cook, over low heat, about 2 minutes or until bubbles appear on the surface. Turn hotcake; cook until lightly browned on other side. Remove from pan; cover to keep warm. Repeat with remaining batter. Serve pancakes with pears and syrup.

GOLDEN PEARS place pears in medium saucepan with golden syrup, the water and juice; bring to a boil. Reduce heat, simmer, uncovered, until pears are just tender. Remove pears from syrup; reserve syrup. Stir blended cornflour and the extra water into reserved syrup; stir over heat until mixture boils and thickens.

SERVES 4

per serving 1.9g total fat (0.9g saturated fat); 1298kj (310 cal); 8.3g protein; 65.6g carbohydrate; 3.7g fibre

tip cook recipe just before serving.

mini spinach frittata

PREPARATION TIME 10 MINUTES COOKING TIME 20 MINUTES

250g baby spinach leaves
½ teaspoon olive oil
1 small brown onion (80g), sliced thinly
1 tablespoon water
pinch ground nutmeg
2 egg whites
2 tablespoons skim milk
½ teaspoon olive oil, extra

1. Steam or microwave spinach until tender. Drain; chop roughly.
2. Heat oil in medium saucepan; cook onion and the water, covered, until onion is soft. Combine spinach, onion mixture, nutmeg, egg whites and milk in bowl.
3. Oil four egg rings with a little of the extra oil; heat remaining extra oil in large frying pan. Place egg rings in pan; fill with egg mixture. Cook until mixture is set; remove egg rings. Turn frittatas, cook until lightly browned underneath.
4. Serve frittatas with a green salad, if desired.

SERVES 2
per serving 2.7g total fat (0.3g saturated fat); 304kj (73 cal); 7.8g protein; 4.2g carbohydrate; 3.9g fibre
tip cook recipe just before serving.

buckwheat pancakes with caramelised banana

PREPARATION TIME 10 MINUTES (PLUS REFRIGERATION TIME) COOKING TIME 20 MINUTES

The seeds of the buckwheat plant are ground into the flour that is the essential ingredient in Japanese soba, Russian blini and delicious pancakes such as these.

¼ cup (35g) self-raising flour
¼ cup (35g) buckwheat flour
1 tablespoon caster sugar
¼ teaspoon ground cinnamon
1 egg
¾ cup (180ml) skim milk
20g butter
¼ cup (50g) firmly packed brown sugar
4 medium bananas (800g), sliced thickly
2 tablespoons water

1. Combine flours, caster sugar and cinnamon in medium bowl; gradually whisk in combined egg and milk until batter is smooth. Cover; refrigerate 30 minutes.
2. Meanwhile, melt butter in large frying pan; cook brown sugar, stirring, until dissolved. Add banana and the water; cook, uncovered, stirring occasionally, about 2 minutes or until banana is caramelised.
3. Pour ¼ cup batter into heated 20cm frying pan; cook pancake until browned both sides. Repeat with remaining batter, to make four pancakes in total. Cover to keep warm.
4. Just before serving, halve each pancake; divide halves among serving plates. Spoon banana mixture onto each half, fold to enclose filling, drizzle with caramel.

SERVES 4
per serving 5.9g total fat (3.2g saturated fat); 1280kj (306 cal); 7.5g protein; 57.1g carbohydrate; 3.5g fibre
tips fresh strawberries may be used as a filling instead of caramelised bananas. Dust pancakes with icing sugar before serving.
serving suggestion these pancakes also make a lovely dessert.

roast garlic mushrooms with crispy ham

PREPARATION TIME 10 MINUTES COOKING TIME 25 MINTUES

200g button mushrooms
150g flat mushrooms, halved
100g swiss brown mushrooms
1 medium red onion (170g), sliced thinly
1 clove garlic, crushed
1 tablespoon lemon juice
coarsely ground black pepper
cooking-oil spray
200g shaved light leg ham
½ small french stick, sliced thickly
8 basil leaves, torn

1 Preheat oven to 220°C/200°C fan-forced.
2 Combine mushrooms, onion, garlic, juice and pepper in baking dish; spray lightly with cooking-oil spray. Roast, uncovered, about 20 minutes or until mushrooms are tender, stirring occasionally.
3 Meanwhile, spread ham on oven tray; bake, uncovered, about 15 minutes or until crisp.
4 Toast bread on both sides; stir basil through mushroom mixture. Serve bread topped with ham and mushroom.

SERVES 2
per serving 7.8g total fat (1.7g saturated fat); 1443kj (345 cal); 32.8g protein; 35g carbohydrate; 8.9g fibre
tip cook recipe just before serving.

roast garlic mushrooms with crispy ham

egg-white omelette

egg-white omelette

PREPARATION TIME 10 MINUTES COOKING TIME 15 MINUTES

150g light ham
200g button mushrooms, sliced thinly
12 egg whites
¼ cup finely chopped fresh chives
2 medium tomatoes (380g), chopped coarsely
½ cup (45g) coarsely grated low-fat cheddar cheese
8 slices wholemeal bread

1. Trim and discard any fat from ham; cut into thin strips. Cook ham in heated large frying pan, stirring, until lightly browned. Remove from pan. Cook mushrooms in same pan, stirring, until lightly browned.
2. Beat 3 of the egg whites in small bowl with electric mixer until soft peaks form; fold in a quarter of the chives. Preheat grill. Pour egg-white mixture into heated oiled 20cm frying pan; cook, uncovered, over low heat until just browned underneath. Place pan under hot grill; cook until top just sets. Place a quarter of the tomato on one half of the omelette; return to grill, cook until tomato is hot and top is lightly browned. Gently place a quarter of each of the cheese, ham and mushroom on tomato half of omelette; fold over to enclose filling. Carefully transfer omelette to serving plate; cover to keep warm.
3. Repeat step 2 with remaining egg whites, chives and fillings to make four omelettes in total.
4. Toast bread until lightly browned both sides. Serve omelettes with toast.

SERVES 4
per serving 4.9g total fat (1.4g saturated fat); 1276kj (305 cal); 31.2g protein; 33.2g carbohydrate; 7.4g fibre

mushroom and parsley omelette

PREPARATION TIME 10 MINUTES COOKING TIME 10 MINUTES

4 eggs, beaten lightly
6 egg whites
500g swiss brown mushrooms, sliced thinly
⅓ cup loosely packed, coarsely chopped fresh flat-leaf parsley

1. Whisk beaten egg with egg whites in medium bowl.
2. Cook mushrooms in lightly oiled heated 20cm frying pan, stirring, until tender. Place mushrooms in small bowl with parsley.
3. Return pan to heat, add a quarter of the egg mixture; cook, tilting pan, over medium heat until almost set. Place a quarter of the mushroom mixture evenly over half of the omelette; fold omelette over to enclose filling, slide onto serving plate.
4. Repeat with remaining egg and mushroom mixtures to make four omelettes in total.

SERVES 4
per serving 5.4g total fat (1.6g saturated fat); 514kj (123 cal); 16.2g protein; 2.2g carbohydrate; 3.4g fibre
tip basil can be substituted for parsley.
serving suggestion serve with thick slices of toasted sourdough.

fruit salad with honey yogurt

PREPARATION TIME 15 MINUTES

We have the Greeks to thank for the serendipitous combination of yogurt and honey, and the benevolence of the Australian tropics for the combination of fruits. You need only small quantities of pineapple and rockmelon for this recipe, so buy the smallest ones you can find. Two passionfruit will supply the right amount of pulp.

¾ cup (210g) low-fat yogurt
2 tablespoons honey
200g peeled, coarsely chopped pineapple
200g seeded, peeled, coarsely chopped rockmelon
250g strawberries, halved
250g blueberries
1 large banana (230g), sliced thinly
2 tablespoons passionfruit pulp
2 teaspoons lime juice
12 fresh mint leaves

1. Combine yogurt and honey in small bowl.
2. Just before serving, combine remaining ingredients in large bowl; serve with honey yogurt.

SERVES 4
per serving 0.4g total fat (0g saturated fat); 716kj (171 cal); 6g protein; 35.5g carbohydrate; 5.6g fibre
tips lime juice not only adds flavour to this recipe but also prevents the banana from discolouring.
Honey yogurt can be made a day ahead; store, covered, in refrigerator.

bagels with scrambled eggs and smoked salmon

PREPARATION TIME 10 MINUTES COOKING TIME 10 MINUTES

2 eggs, beaten lightly
10 egg whites
2 tablespoons finely chopped fresh chives
2 bagels
1 small green cucumber (130g), sliced thinly
200g sliced smoked salmon

1 Whisk egg, egg whites and chives together in medium bowl. Cook egg mixture in oiled medium frying pan, gently stirring, over low heat until almost set.

2 Split bagels in half; toast both sides. Top bagel halves with cucumber, eggs and salmon.

SERVES 4
per serving 5.5g total fat (1.3g saturated fat); 1097kj (262 cal); 28.4g protein; 24.4g carbohydrate; 1.6g fibre

eggs with asparagus, grilled ham and onion jam

PREPARATION TIME 10 MINUTES COOKING TIME 20 MINUTES

2 medium red onions (340g), sliced thinly
2 tablespoons balsamic vinegar
⅓ cup (75g) firmly packed brown sugar
2 tablespoons chicken stock
100g shaved leg ham
500g asparagus, trimmed
4 eggs

1 Heat oiled medium frying pan; cook onion, stirring, until almost soft. Stir in vinegar and sugar; cook, stirring, until sugar dissolves. Stir in stock; simmer, uncovered, about 15 minutes or until onion caramelises, cool.

2 Preheat grill. Place ham, in single layer, on oven tray; cook under hot grill until browned lightly.

3 Boil, steam or microwave asparagus until just tender; drain.

4 Heat oiled large frying pan; fry eggs until cooked as desired. Serve eggs with asparagus, ham and onion jam.

SERVES 4
per serving 5.8g total fat (1.8g saturated fat); 839kj (200 cal); 13.3g protein; 24.2g carbohydrate; 2.4g fibre
tips we used 48g eggs for this recipe.

light meals

lemon-fetta couscous with steamed vegetables

PREPARATION TIME 20 MINUTES COOKING TIME 10 MINUTES

You will need about half a butternut pumpkin for this recipe. Preserved lemons, a North African specialty, are quartered and preserved in salt and lemon juice. To use, remove and discard pulp, squeeze juice from rind, rinse rind well then use. Sold in jars or in bulk by delicatessens; once opened, store preserved lemon in the refrigerator.

600g butternut pumpkin, chopped coarsely
2 small green zucchini (180g), chopped coarsely
2 small yellow zucchini (180g), chopped coarsely
300g spinach, trimmed, chopped coarsely
2 cups (500ml) prepared vegetable stock
2 cups (400g) couscous
¼ cup (60ml) lemon juice
⅓ cup coarsely chopped fresh basil
200g low-fat fetta cheese, chopped coarsely
¼ cup (50g) finely chopped preserved lemon rind
6 green onions, sliced thinly

1 Boil, steam or microwave pumpkin, green and yellow zucchini and spinach, separately, until tender; drain.
2 Meanwhile, bring stock to a boil in large saucepan. Add couscous, remove from heat, cover; stand about 5 minutes or until liquid is absorbed, fluffing with fork occasionally.
3 Place couscous and vegetables in large bowl with remaining ingredients; toss gently to combine.

SERVES 4
per serving 9.2g total fat (5.4g saturated fat); 2374kj (568 cal); 31.7g protein; 87.7g carbohydrate; 4.8g fibre

niçoise salad

PREPARATION TIME 15 MINUTES COOKING TIME 5 MINUTES

100g green beans, trimmed
2 x 180g cans tuna in springwater, drained
1 small red onion (100g), sliced thinly
2 green onions, sliced thinly
250g cherry tomatoes, halved
100g mesclun
2 teaspoons finely grated lemon rind
½ cup (125ml) lemon juice
1 tablespoon wholegrain mustard
2 cloves garlic, crushed
2 teaspoons sugar

1. Boil, steam or microwave beans until just tender; cool. Cut beans in half.
2. Place beans in large bowl with tuna, onions, tomato and mesclun.
3. Whisk remaining ingredients in small bowl. Add dressing to salad; toss gently to combine.

SERVES 4
per serving 2.2g total fat (0.7g saturated fat); 545kj (130 cal); 19.5g protein; 6.8g carbohydrate; 3.1g fibre

thai-style stir-fried prawn salad

PREPARATION TIME 35 MINUTES COOKING TIME 15 MINUTES

500g uncooked medium prawns
1 clove garlic, crushed
2 tablespoons lime juice
1 tablespoon mild sweet chilli sauce
1½ teaspoons fish sauce
1 tablespoon chopped fresh coriander leaves
1 tablespoon chopped fresh lemon grass
250g asparagus
1 tablespoon peanut oil
500g baby buk choy, chopped
1 medium yellow capsicum (200g), chopped
1 cup (80g) snow pea sprouts
1 tablespoon shredded fresh basil leaves

1. Shell and devein prawns, leaving tails intact. Combine prawns, garlic, 1 tablespoon of the juice, chilli sauce, ½ teaspoon of the fish sauce, coriander and lemon grass in large bowl. Cover, refrigerate several hours or overnight.
2. Drain prawns; discard marinade. Cut asparagus into 5cm lengths. Add asparagus to large pan of boiling water, drain immediately, rinse under cold water; drain.
3. Heat oil in wok; stir-fry prawns until tender. Remove from wok. Stir-fry asparagus, buk choy and capsicum until just tender. Add remaining juice, remaining fish sauce, sprouts and basil; stir-fry until sprouts are just wilted. Serve vegetables topped with prawns.

SERVES 4
per serving 5.6g total fat (1g saturated fat); 676kj (161 cal); 17.9g protein; 9.3g carbohydrate; 3.9g fibre
tips marinade can be prepared a day ahead; stir-fry just before serving.

sweet chilli prawn salad

PREPARATION TIME 10 MINUTES COOKING TIME 10 MINUTES

250g rigatoni
24 large cooked shelled prawns (about 1kg), tails intact
2 green onions, chopped finely
1 tablespoon coarsely chopped fresh watercress
1 tablespoon coarsely chopped fresh coriander leaves
1 lebanese cucumber (130g), chopped coarsely
½ cup (125ml) sweet chilli sauce
1 teaspoon sesame oil
1 tablespoon lime juice

1. Cook pasta in large saucepan of boiling water, uncovered, until tender; drain. Rinse under cold water; drain.
2. Place pasta in large bowl with prawns, onion, watercress, coriander, cucumber and combined remaining ingredients; toss gently to combine.

SERVES 4
per serving 3.6g total fat (0.7g saturated fat); 1705kj (408 cal); 37.2g protein; 55.1g carbohydrate; 3.7g fibre
tip we used thai sweet chilli sauce; if you use a less sweet, more concentrated chilli sauce, we suggest you use far less, tasting as you go.

prawn noodle salad with mint, basil and coriander

PREPARATION TIME 30 MINUTES

Bean thread noodles, also known as bean thread vermicelli, or cellophane or glass noodles, are very fine, almost transparent noodles. They look similar to dried rice vermicelli but are tougher. Soak the noodles just long enough to soften them – any longer and they become soggy and start to break up.

200g bean thread noodles
18 medium cooked prawns (450g)
2 teaspoons fish sauce
1 tablespoon light soy sauce
2 tablespoons lime juice
1 tablespoon sugar
1 red thai chilli, chopped finely
1 lebanese cucumber (130g), halved lengthways, seeded, sliced thinly
250g cherry tomatoes, quartered
¼ cup loosely packed, coarsely chopped fresh mint
¼ cup loosely packed, coarsely chopped fresh coriander
¼ cup loosely packed, coarsely chopped fresh basil

1. Place noodles in large heatproof bowl; cover with boiling water. Stand until just tender; drain. Rinse noodles under cold water; drain well. Chop noodles coarsely.
2. Shell and devein prawns; halve lengthways.
3. Combine sauces, juice, sugar and chilli in small bowl.
4. Place noodles, prawns and sauce mixture in large bowl with cucumber, tomato and herbs; toss gently to combine.

SERVES 4
per serving 0.7g total fat (0.1g saturated fat); 1108kj (265 cal); 14.6g protein; 49.9g carbohydrate; 1.8g fibre
tip for a milder version of this salad, remove and discard seeds from the chillies before chopping.

vietnamese prawn salad

PREPARATION TIME 20 MINUTES COOKING TIME 10 MINUTES

Noodles are an integral part of the Vietnamese diet that are enjoyed, in some form, at practically every meal. This recipe combines noodles with prawns – another popular ingredient in Vietnam. Ensure the prawns are cooked just before serving.

24 large uncooked prawns (1kg)
1 teaspoon sambal oelek
1 tablespoon grated fresh ginger
2 cloves garlic, crushed
2 tablespoons coarsely chopped fresh coriander
2 tablespoons coarsely chopped fresh mint
1 tablespoon peanut oil
¼ cup (60ml) light soy sauce
¼ cup (60ml) oyster sauce
250g rice vermicelli

1 Shell and devein prawns, leaving tails intact. Combine prawns with sambal oelek, ginger, garlic, and half of the fresh herbs in a large bowl.
2 Heat oil in large wok; cook prawn mixture, in batches, stirring over high heat until prawns just change colour. Add half of the combined sauces; stir-fry until hot.
3 Place noodles in medium heatproof bowl; cover with boiling water. Stand until just tender; drain.
4 Combine noodles with remaining sauce mixture, coriander and mint. Serve noodle mixture with prawns.

SERVES 4
per serving 6.4g total fat (1g saturated fat); 1540kj (368 cal); 31g protein; 45.2g carbohydrate; 1.6g fibre
tip you can substitute bean thread noodles, also known as cellophane noodles, for rice vermicelli if you wish.
serving suggestion serve accompanied by a bowl of soy or fish sauce.

prawn, snow pea and wild rice salad

PREPARATION TIME 20 MINUTES COOKING TIME 20 MINUTES

24 medium uncooked king prawns (1kg)
1½ cups (300g) white and wild rice blend
150g snow peas, trimmed, halved lengthways
1 small red onion (100g), sliced thinly
½ cup coarsely chopped fresh flat-leaf parsley
150g snow pea tendrils

RASPBERRY VINEGAR DRESSING
⅓ cup (80ml) raspberry vinegar
2 tablespoons olive oil
1 tablespoon dijon mustard
2 cloves garlic, crushed
2 tablespoons lemon juice
2 teaspoons sugar

1 Shell and devein prawns, leaving tails intact.
2 Make raspberry vinegar dressing.
3 Cook rice in large saucepan of boiling water, uncovered, until tender; drain.
4 Meanwhile, boil, steam or microwave peas until just tender.
5 Cook prawns on heated lightly oiled grill plate (or grill or barbecue) until changed in colour.
6 Place rice, peas and prawns in large bowl with onion, parsley, tendrils and dressing; toss gently to combine.

RASPBERRY VINEGAR DRESSING place ingredients in screw-top jar; shake well.

SERVES 4
per serving 10.6g total fat (1.5g saturated fat); 2024kj (496 cal); 33.9g protein; 64.6g carbohydrate; 2.4g fibre

tortellini and smoked salmon salad

PREPARATION TIME 15 MINUTES (PLUS COOLING TIME) COOKING TIME 10 MINUTES

500g cheese and spinach tortellini
200g smoked salmon
1 tablespoon drained capers
1 tablespoon chopped fresh dill

DILL YOGURT DRESSING

¼ cup (60ml) low-fat yogurt
2 tablespoons chopped fresh dill
1 tablespoon honey
2 teaspoons dijon mustard
1 clove garlic, crushed
2 teaspoons lemon juice

1 Cook tortellini in large pan of boiling water, uncovered, until just tender; drain, cool.
2 Cut salmon into strips lengthways, roll up. Make dill yogurt dressing.
3 Place tortellini, salmon rolls and dressing in large bowl with capers and dill; toss gently to combine.
4 Serve tortellini mixture over salad leaves, if desired.

DILL YOGURT DRESSING combine all ingredients in bowl; mix well.

SERVES 4
per serving 7.9g total fat (3.7g saturated fat); 1450kj (347 cal); 22.9g protein; 43.7g carbohydrate; 2.2g fibre
tip this recipe can be made up to 3 hours ahead. Store, covered, in refrigerator.

chilli and lime chicken salad

PREPARATION TIME 20 MINUTES (PLUS COOLING TIME) COOKING TIME 10 MINUTES

1 cup (250ml) water
1 cup (250ml) chicken stock
340g chicken breast fillets
1 small carrot (70g)
1 small red capsicum (150g), sliced thinly
½ small wombok (200g), shredded finely
2 green onions, chopped finely
¾ cup (60g) bean sprouts
½ cup firmly packed fresh coriander leaves
100g watercress, trimmed

CHILLI LIME DRESSING

¼ cup (60ml) lime juice
2 tablespoons sweet chilli sauce
1 clove garlic, crushed
1 tablespoon oyster sauce
1 teaspoon sesame oil

1 Combine the water and stock in large saucepan; bring to a boil. Reduce heat, add chicken, simmer about 10 minutes or until chicken is cooked through. Allow chicken to cool in poaching liquid; drain, discarding liquid. Slice chicken thinly.
2 Meanwhile, halve carrot crossways, cut each half into 2mm-wide lengths; cut lengths into matchstick-thin strips.
3 Make chilli lime dressing.
4 Place chicken, carrot and dressing in large bowl with capsicum, wombok, onion, sprouts, coriander and watercress; toss gently to combine.

CHILLI LIME DRESSING place ingredients in screw-topped jar; shake well.

SERVES 4
per serving 3.6g total fat (0.8g saturated fat); 610kj (146 cal); 22.5g protein; 5.2g carbohydrate; 2.9g fibre

herbed potatoes

PREPARATION TIME 15 MINUTES COOKING TIME 1 HOUR 20 MINUTES

2 large desiree potatoes (600g)

FILLING

1 small carrot (70g), chopped finely

75g broccoli, chopped finely

150g reduced-fat ricotta cheese

1 tablespoon finely chopped fresh chives

1. Preheat oven to 180°C/160°C fan-forced.
2. Wash and dry potatoes; prick all over with a skewer. Bake for 1 hour. Cut tops off potatoes; scoop out flesh leaving 1cm shell. Reserve flesh for filling.
3. Increase oven to 220°C/200°C fan-forced. Place potato shells on oven tray; bake for 10 minutes.
4. Make filling.
5. Return oven to 180°C/160°C fan-forced. Spoon filling into shells. Bake for about 10 minutes or until hot. Serve with fresh green salad, if desired.

FILLING boil, steam or microwave carrot and broccoli until soft; drain. Beat cheese in small bowl until smooth; stir in reserved potato flesh, carrot mixture and chives.

SERVES 2
per serving 7g total fat (4.2g saturated fat); 1221kj (292 cal); 16.4g protein; 39.7g carbohydrate; 6.9g fibre

tuna and white bean salad

PREPARATION TIME 15 MINUTES COOKING TIME 5 MINUTES

Canned cooked white beans can have one of several different names on the label such as cannellini, butter or haricot. There is little difference in taste or texture among any of these small, slightly kidney-shaped white beans, and any would be suitable for this salad.

2 x 300g cans white beans, rinsed, drained

425g can tuna chunks in springwater, drained, flaked

1 medium red onion (170g), sliced thinly

½ cup chopped fresh flat-leaf parsley

1 tablespoon chopped fresh oregano

250g cherry tomatoes, quartered

2 tablespoons olive oil

1 tablespoon white vinegar

2 teaspoons finely grated lemon rind

2 tablespoons lemon juice

2 cloves garlic, crushed

1 long loaf turkish bread

1. Combine beans, tuna, onion, herbs and tomato in large bowl with combined oil, vinegar, rind, juice and garlic; toss gently to combine.
2. Quarter bread crossways; slice pieces in half horizontally. Cut bread again, on the diagonal, to make 16 triangles; toast triangles, cut-side up.
3. Place one triangle, toasted-side up, on each serving plate; top with salad, then remaining triangles.

SERVES 8
per serving 10.8g total fat (4.2g saturated fat); 1062kj (254 cal); 15.2g protein; 23.7g carbohydrate; 3g fibre

cabbage, fennel and carrot salad with orange-herb dressing

PREPARATION TIME 20 MINUTES

You will need to buy a quarter of a medium red cabbage and a medium wombok for this recipe.

4 trimmed celery stalks (400g)
2 medium carrots (240g)
2 small fennel (400g), trimmed, sliced thinly
4 trimmed red radishes (60g), sliced thinly
1½ cups (120g) finely shredded red cabbage
5 cups (400g) coarsely shredded wombok
1 cup loosely packed fresh basil leaves
1 cup loosely packed fresh mint leaves
¼ cup (40g) pepitas

ORANGE-HERB DRESSING

1 tablespoon finely chopped fresh flat-leaf parsley
4 green onions, chopped coarsely
½ teaspoon finely grated orange rind
⅓ cup (80ml) orange juice
2 tablespoons raspberry vinegar
2 cloves garlic, crushed
1 tablespoon peanut oil

1 Make orange-herb dressing.

2 Cut celery and carrot into 6cm lengths; using vegetable peeler, slice celery and carrot into ribbons.

3 Place ribbons in large bowl with fennel, radish, cabbage, wombok, herbs and dressing; toss gently to combine. Sprinkle with pepitas.

ORANGE-HERB DRESSING place ingredients in screw-top jar; shake well.

SERVES 4
per serving 9.9g total fat (1.6g saturated fat); 698kj (167 cal); 6.7g protein; 12.7g carbohydrate; 10g fibre

zucchini lentil pasties

PREPARATION TIME 20 MINUTES (PLUS REFRIGERATION TIME) COOKING TIME 40 MINUTES (PLUS COOLING TIME)

1 cup (160g) plain wholemeal flour
50g polyunsaturated or monounsaturated margarine
¼ cup (60ml) cold water, approximately
1 medium brown onion (150g), chopped finely
2 cloves garlic, crushed
1 teaspoon curry powder
½ teaspoon grated fresh ginger
¼ teaspoon sambal oelek
¼ cup (50g) red lentils
⅔ cup (160ml) water, extra
1 medium zucchini (120g), grated finely
1 egg white

CHILLI AND CORIANDER SAUCE

2 large tomatoes (500g), chopped coarsely
¼ cup (60ml) water
⅓ cup (80ml) lime juice
¼ cup (50g) brown sugar
1 teaspoon fish sauce
⅓ cup (80ml) sweet chilli sauce
2 tablespoons finely chopped fresh coriander leaves

1. Place flour and chopped margarine in food processor; process until combined. With motor operating, add enough of the water until mixture just forms a ball. Lightly knead on a floured surface until smooth; cover. Refrigerate for 20 minutes.
2. Meanwhile, cook onion, garlic, curry powder, ginger and sambal in large saucepan for 1 minute. Stir in lentils and the extra water, bring to a boil. Reduce heat, simmer, uncovered, for about 10 minutes or until all liquid is absorbed. Remove from heat; stir in zucchini.
3. Preheat oven to 200°C/180°C fan-forced.
4. Roll pastry out on floured surface until 5mm thick. Cut out six rounds using 12cm cutter; divide filling among rounds. Brush edges with egg white, fold rounds to enclose filling; pinch edges together to seal. Brush with egg white; place on baking paper-lined oven tray.
5. Bake, uncovered, about 25 minutes or until well browned.
6. Make chilli and coriander sauce; serve with pasties.

CHILLI AND CORIANDER SAUCE combine tomato, the water, juice, sugar and sauces in medium saucepan; stir over low heat until sugar dissolves. Bring to a boil; simmer, uncovered, about 10 minutes or until sauce thickens. Remove from heat, cool; stir in coriander.

MAKES 6
per pasty 6.8g total fat (1.2g saturated fat); 970kj (232 cal); 7.5g protein; 35g carbohydrate; 5.9g fibre
tip uncooked pasties can be made a day ahead; store, covered, in the refrigerator or freezer.

vegetable salad

PREPARATION TIME 10 MINUTES COOKING TIME 25 MINUTES

1 large red onion (300g)
8 medium egg tomatoes (600g)
8 baby eggplant (480g)
4 medium zucchini (480g)
4 medium yellow patty-pan squash (120g), halved
2 medium red capsicums (400g), sliced thickly

DRESSING

¼ cup (60ml) extra virgin olive oil
¼ cup (60ml) balsamic vinegar
1 clove garlic, crushed

1. Cut onion and tomatoes into eight wedges each; thinly slice eggplant and zucchini lengthways.
2. Cook onion, tomato, eggplant, zucchini, squash and capsicum, in batches, on heated oiled grill plate (or grill or barbecue) until vegetables are browned and just tender.
3. Make dressing.
4. Place vegetables in large bowl or on serving platter, drizzle with dressing; toss gently to combine.

DRESSING place ingredients in screw-top jar; shake well.

SERVES 8
per serving 7.3g total fat (1g saturated fat); 447kj (107 cal); 3.3g protein; 6.9g carbohydrate; 4.1g fibre

roasted pumpkin, sesame and rocket salad

PREPARATION TIME 15 MINUTES COOKING TIME 25 MINUTES

You will need a piece of pumpkin weighing about 750g for this recipe; we used butternut, but you can use any pumpkin variety you like.

600g trimmed pumpkin
cooking-oil spray
1 tablespoon honey
1 tablespoon sesame seeds
500g asparagus, halved
150g baby rocket leaves
1 small red onion (100g), sliced thinly
1 tablespoon sesame oil
1 tablespoon cider vinegar
1 teaspoon honey, extra

1. Preheat oven to 240°C/220°C fan-forced.
2. Cut pumpkin into 1.5cm wide strips.
3. Place pumpkin, in single layer, in baking dish lined with baking paper; spray lightly with cooking-oil spray. Roast, uncovered, about 20 minutes or until pumpkin is just tender. Drizzle with honey, sprinkle with seeds; roast a further 5 minutes, uncovered, or until seeds are browned lightly.
4. Meanwhile, boil, steam or microwave asparagus until just tender; drain. Rinse under cold water; drain.
5. Combine pumpkin, asparagus, rocket and onion in large bowl. Drizzle with combined remaining ingredients; toss gently to combine.

SERVES 6
per serving 5.3g total fat (0.9g saturated fat); 497kj (119 cal); 4.9g protein; 13.3g carbohydrate; 2.9g fibre
tip reserve any seeds or honey from pumpkin pan and add to dressing.
serving suggestion serve with warmed or toasted turkish bread.

watercress salad

PREPARATION TIME 25 MINUTES COOKING TIME 2 MINUTES

We used corella pears for this recipe. You will need a bunch of watercress weighing about 350g in total to yield the leaves required for this salad.

3 small pears (540g), sliced thinly
1 teaspoon finely grated orange rind
½ cup (125ml) orange juice
300g snow peas, trimmed
100g watercress leaves

CHEESE BALLS

150g low-fat ricotta cheese
100g low-fat fetta cheese
¼ cup (30g) finely grated cheddar cheese
1 tablespoon finely chopped fresh flat-leaf parsley
1 tablespoon finely chopped fresh chives
2 teaspoons finely chopped fresh thyme
1 teaspoon curry powder
1 teaspoon sweet paprika

1. Combine pear, rind and juice in large bowl. Cover; refrigerate 15 minutes.
2. Boil, steam or microwave snow peas until just tender; drain. Rinse under cold water; drain.
3. Make cheese balls.
4. Add snow peas and watercress to pear mixture; toss gently to combine. Serve topped with cheese balls.

CHEESE BALLS combine cheeses, parsley, chives and thyme in small bowl. Roll level teaspoons of mixture into balls. Combine curry powder and paprika in small bowl; gently toss half of the cheese balls in curry mixture to coat.

SERVES 6
per serving 7g total fat (4.3g saturated fat); 681kj (163 cal); 11.7g protein; 13.9g carbohydrate; 3.6g fibre
serving suggestion serve as an appetiser before grilled or barbecued steak or lamb.

rice noodle salad

PREPARATION TIME 20 MINUTES

You will need about half a medium red cabbage for this recipe.

150g rice stick noodles
¼ cup (60ml) lime juice
¼ cup (60ml) sweet chilli sauce
1 tablespoon light soy sauce
1 tablespoon sugar
6 cups (480g) finely shredded red cabbage
1 large carrot (180g), sliced thinly
1 lebanese cucumber (130g), seeded, sliced thinly
3 medium egg tomatoes (225g), seeded, sliced thinly
1 medium yellow capsicum (200g), sliced thinly
½ cup firmly packed fresh coriander leaves
½ cup firmly packed fresh mint leaves
½ cup firmly packed fresh thai basil leaves

1 Place noodles in large heatproof bowl; cover with boiling water. Stand until just tender; drain.
2 Combine juice, sauces and sugar in small bowl; stir until sugar dissolves.
3 Place noodles in large bowl with juice mixture and remaining ingredients; toss gently to combine.

SERVES 4
per serving 1.3g total fat (0.1g saturated fat); 928kj (222 cal); 7.4g protein; 44g carbohydrate; 8.9g fibre
tip rice stick noodles and dried rice noodles are virtually the same thing, except that rice stick noodles are thicker. The two can easily be interchanged in recipes.

oven-roasted potato wedges with tomato relish

PREPARATION TIME 15 MINUTES COOKING TIME 40 MINUTES

1kg large new potatoes
cooking-oil spray
1 teaspoon salt
1 teaspoon freshly ground black pepper
4 medium tomatoes (760g), chopped finely
1 small brown onion (80g), chopped finely
2 tablespoons brown sugar
2 tablespoons red wine vinegar
1 teaspoon mustard powder

1 Preheat oven to 240°C/220°C fan-forced.

2 Halve potatoes lengthways; cut each half into wedges. Place wedges, in single layer, in large shallow baking dish; spray with oil, sprinkle with salt and pepper. Bake, uncovered, about 30 minutes or until browned and crisp, turning occasionally.

3 Meanwhile, heat tomato, onion, sugar, vinegar and mustard in medium saucepan; bring to a boil. Reduce heat, simmer, uncovered, 30 minutes or until relish thickens. Serve potato wedges with relish.

SERVES 6
per serving 1.1g total fat (0.1g saturated fat); 631kj (151 cal); 5.4g protein; 28.9g carbohydrate; 4.2g fibre

beef salad with garlic dressing

PREPARATION TIME 25 MINUTES (PLUS REFRIGERATION TIME) COOKING TIME 1 HOUR

500g piece lean beef rump steak
1 teaspoon cracked black pepper
2 tablespoons red wine vinegar
2 teaspoons chopped fresh thyme
2 teaspoons wholegrain mustard
cooking-oil spray
1 medium butter lettuce
1 cup (50g) firmly packed fresh watercress sprigs
250g cherry tomatoes, halved
1 small green cucumber (130g), sliced
1 small red onion (100g), sliced

GARLIC DRESSING

3 medium bulbs garlic (210g)
1 teaspoon balsamic vinegar
½ cup (125ml) chicken stock
2 tablespoons low-fat sour cream

1 Combine beef, pepper, vinegar, thyme and mustard in large bowl, cover; refrigerate overnight.

2 Preheat oven to 180°C/160°C fan-forced; make garlic dressing.

3 Coat griddle pan with cooking-oil spray; cook beef until well browned on both sides and tender. Stand beef 5 minutes before slicing thinly.

4 Serve beef on lettuce leaves with remaining ingredients; drizzle with dressing.

GARLIC DRESSING place whole unpeeled garlic bulbs in small baking dish, coat with cooking-oil spray. Bake, uncovered, about 50 minutes or until bulbs are soft; wrap in foil, cool. Squeeze garlic from cloves – you will need 2 tablespoons of garlic puree for this recipe. Blend or process garlic, vinegar, stock and cream until smooth.

SERVES 4
per serving 6.6g total fat (3g saturated fat); 961kj (230 cal); 34.2g protein; 7.3g carbohydrate; 9.2g fibre
tip dressing can be made a day ahead; store, covered, in the refrigerator.

caesar salad

PREPARATION TIME 10 MINUTES COOKING TIME 15 MINUTES

4 slices white bread
4 slices prosciutto (40g)
¼ cup (70g) low-fat yogurt
¼ cup (75g) low-fat mayonnaise
2 cloves garlic, quartered
5 anchovy fillets, drained
½ teaspoon worcestershire sauce
½ teaspoon dijon mustard
1½ tablespoons lemon juice
4 baby cos lettuces
¼ cup (20g) finely grated parmesan cheese

1. Preheat oven to 180°C/160°C fan-forced.
2. Remove crusts from bread; cut bread into 1cm cubes. Place on oven tray; bake, uncovered, about 5 minutes or until croutons are just toasted lightly.
3. Meanwhile, cook prosciutto, uncovered, stirring, in medium heated frying pan until browned and crisp; chop coarsely.
4. Blend or process yogurt, mayonnaise, garlic, anchovy, sauce, mustard and juice until almost smooth.
5. Combine croutons, prosciutto and yogurt mixture in large bowl with lettuce leaves and cheese; toss gently to combine.

SERVES 8
per serving 4.1g total fat (1.1g saturated fat); 439kj (105 cal); 5.3g protein; 11.5g carbohydrate; 2g fibre

smoked chicken salad

PREPARATION TIME 15 MINUTES

Smoked chicken has already been cooked during the curing process, making this a simple salad to put together at short notice. You can keep a smoked chicken in your freezer; just thaw before slicing.

400g smoked chicken breast
200g baby spinach leaves
1 medium yellow capsicum (200g), sliced thinly
1 medium red onion (170g), sliced thinly
1 cup firmly packed fresh purple basil leaves
2 teaspoons finely grated lime rind
¼ cup (60ml) lime juice
2 tablespoons coarsely chopped fresh coriander
2 fresh red thai chillies, chopped finely
2 teaspoons peanut oil
1 teaspoon sugar

1. Remove and discard any skin from chicken; slice flesh thinly.
2. Combine chicken in large bowl with spinach, capsicum, onion and basil.
3. Combine remaining ingredients in screw-top jar; shake well.
4. Pour dressing over salad; toss gently to combine.

SERVES 8
per serving 4.8g total fat (1.2g saturated fat); 456kj (109 cal); 13.7g protein; 2.6g carbohydrate; 1.5g fibre
serving suggestion serve with corn bread or flour tortillas.

caesar salad

vegetable burgers

vegetable burgers

PREPARATION TIME 20 MINUTES COOKING TIME 40 MINUTES

You will need to cook ½ cup (100g) long-grain white rice for this recipe.

1 tablespoon vegetable oil
1 large brown onion (200g), chopped finely
300g button mushrooms, chopped coarsely
1 medium red capsicum (200g), chopped finely
1 clove garlic, crushed
1 cup (200g) red lentils
2 cups (500ml) vegetable stock
1½ cups cooked rice
2 tablespoons finely chopped fresh flat-leaf parsley
⅓ cup (50g) plain flour
2 medium carrots (240g), grated coarsely
6 small wholemeal bread rolls
225g can sliced beetroot, drained
1½ cups (60g) alfalfa
2 medium tomatoes (380g), sliced thinly
200g low-fat yogurt
1 tablespoon finely chopped fresh mint
1 teaspoon sugar

1. Heat oil in large frying pan; cook onion, mushrooms, capsicum, garlic and lentils, stirring, until vegetables soften. Add stock; bring to a boil. Reduce heat, simmer, uncovered, stirring occasionally, about 10 minutes or until lentils are tender and stock is absorbed. Remove from heat. Add rice, parsley, flour and half of the carrot; stir to combine.
2. When lentil mixture is cool enough to handle, use hands to shape into six burger-shaped patties. Cook, in batches, in large heated oiled frying pan until burgers are browned both sides and heated through.
3. Meanwhile, split bread rolls in half; toast, cut-side up, until browned lightly. Just before serving, sandwich patties with remaining carrot, beetroot, alfalfa, tomato and combined yogurt, mint and sugar in rolls.

SERVES 6
per serving 6.4g total fat (1.2g saturated fat); 1530kj (366 cal); 20g protein; 57.1g carbohydrate; 11.8g fibre

thai beef salad

PREPARATION TIME 15 MINUTES (PLUS STANDING TIME) COOKING TIME 15 MINUTES

500g beef fillet
3 medium green cucumbers (510g), peeled, sliced thickly
4 red thai chillies, sliced thinly
3 green onions, sliced thinly
½ cup loosely packed fresh mint leaves
½ cup loosely packed fresh coriander leaves

LEMON GRASS DRESSING

1 clove garlic, crushed
2 teaspoons finely chopped fresh lemon grass
2 teaspoons finely chopped fresh coriander root
1 tablespoon lime juice
2 tablespoons light soy sauce
½ teaspoon fish sauce
2 teaspoons brown sugar

1. Cook beef on heated oiled grill plate (or grill or barbecue) until browned all over and cooked as desired. Stand 5 minutes; slice thinly.
2. Make lemon grass dressing.
3. Place beef and dressing in large bowl with cucumber, chilli, onion and herbs; toss gently to combine.

LEMON GRASS DRESSING combine ingredients in small bowl.

SERVES 4
per serving 4.9g total fat (2g saturated fat); 765kj (183 cal); 28.8g protein; 5.5g carbohydrate; 2.7g fibre

tortilla beef cones

PREPARATION TIME 45 MINUTES (PLUS CHILLING TIME) COOKING TIME 35 MINTUES

1 medium red capsicum (200g)
1 medium green capsicum (200g)
8 x 20cm flour tortillas
8 lettuce leaves, shredded
⅓ cup (80ml) low-fat sour cream
1 tablespoon chopped fresh parsley

PATTIES

310g can red kidney beans, rinsed, drained
500g very lean minced beef
1 small onion (80g), chopped finely
35g packet taco seasoning mix
cooking-oil spray

SALSA

1 small onion (80g), chopped
4 medium egg tomatoes (300g), chopped
1 tablespoon chopped fresh flat-leaf parsley
1 tablespoon mild sweet chilli sauce

1. Make patties. Make salsa.
2. Quarter capsicums, remove seeds and membranes. Grill capsicums, skin-side up, until skin blisters and blackens. Peel away skin; slice capsicums.
3. Reduce oven to 180°C/160°C fan-forced. Heat tortillas in microwave on HIGH (100%) for 30 seconds. Shape tortillas into cones; secure with toothpicks. Place on oven tray; heat in oven, uncovered, about 5 minutes or until crisp.
4. Fill each tortilla with lettuce, capsicums, patties, salsa and 2 teaspoons sour cream, sprinkle with parsley.

PATTIES mash half the beans. Place beef, all the beans, onion and seasoning mix in bowl; mix well. Shape mixture into eight patties. Place on oven tray coated with cooking-oil spray; cover, refrigerate 1 hour. Preheat oven to 200°C/180°C fan-forced. Bake, uncovered, 25 minutes or until firm.

SALSA combine ingredients in medium bowl.

MAKES 8
per serving 9g total fat (3.5g saturated fat); 1078kj (258 cal); 18.9g protein; 25.1g carbohydrate; 4.1g fibre
tips patties and salsa can fbe made a day ahead. Store separately, covered, in refrigerator.

chicken tandori pockets with raita

PREPARATION TIME 10 MINUTES COOKING TIME 10 MINUTES

400g chicken tenderloins
1 tablespoon lime juice
⅓ cup (100g) tandoori paste
¼ cup (70g) low-fat yogurt
8 large flour tortillas
60g snow pea tendrills

RAITA

1 cup (280g) low-fat yogurt
1 lebanese cucumber (130g), halved, seeded, chopped finely
1 tablespoon finely chopped fresh mint

1. Combine chicken, juice, paste and yogurt in medium bowl.
2. Cook chicken mixture, in batches, on heated oiled grill plate (or grill or barbecue) until cooked through. Stand 5 minutes; slice thickly.
3. Meanwhile, heat tortillas according to manufacturer's instructions.
4. Make raita.
5. Place equal amounts of each of the chicken, tendrils and raita on a quarter section of each tortilla; fold tortilla in half and then in half again to enclose filling and form triangle-shaped pockets.

RAITA combine ingredients in small bowl.

MAKES 8
per pocket 8.3g total fat (1.6g saturated fat); 1024kj (245 cal); 17.8g protein; 24g carbohydrate; 2.9g fibre

baked ricotta with roasted capsicum salad

PREPARATION TIME 15 MINUTES COOKING TIME 30 MINUTES (PLUS STANDING TIME)

200g low-fat ricotta cheese
2 tablespoons finely grated parmesan cheese
1 egg, beaten lightly
1 teaspoon coarsely chopped fresh sage
3 fresh bay leaves, chopped coarsely
2 medium red capsicums (400g)
2 medium yellow capsicums (400g)
250g mesclun
¼ cup (60ml) balsamic vinegar
1 tablespoon olive oil
1 tablespoon honey

1. Preheat oven to 160°C/140°C fan-forced. Oil eight holes of a 12-hole (⅓ cup/80ml) muffin pan.
2. Combine cheeses and egg in small bowl. Divide ricotta mixture among prepared holes; sprinkle with combined herbs.
3. Place muffin pan in large baking dish; add enough boiling water to come halfway up side of pan. Bake, uncovered, about 30 minutes or until set. Stand 10 minutes before turning ricottas out.
4. Meanwhile, quarter capsicums; remove and discard seeds and membranes. Roast under grill, skin-side up, until skin blisters and blackens. Cover capsicum pieces with plastic or paper 5 minutes. Peel away skin; slice capsicum thickly.
5. Place capsicum and mesclun in large bowl with combined remaining ingredients, divide among serving plates; top each with a baked ricotta.

SERVES 8
per serving 5.9g total fat (2.3g saturated fat); 435kj (104 cal); 5.8g protein; 7g carbohydrate; 1.6g fibre
tip dried bay leaves and ¼ teaspoon crumbled dried sage can be substituted for the fresh varieties.
serving suggestion serve as a starter before a pasta main course.

rice and chickpea salad

PREPARATION TIME 15 MINTUES COOKING TIME 10 MINUTES (PLUS STANDING TIME)

Doongara rice has a lower glycaemic index than most other types of rice, and can be found at your local supermarket.

1 cup (200g) doongara rice
1¾ cups (430ml) water
300g can chickpeas, rinsed, drained
¼ cup (40g) sultanas
¼ cup (35g) dried apricots, chopped finely
2 green onions, sliced thinly
2 tablespoons toasted pine nuts

BALSAMIC ORANGE DRESSING

1 teaspoon finely grated orange rind
⅓ cup (80ml) orange juice
1 tablespoon balsamic vinegar
1 clove garlic, crushed
1 teaspoon grated fresh ginger

1 Place rice and the water in medium heavy-based saucepan; bring to a boil. Reduce heat, simmer, covered, about 8 minutes or until rice is tender. Remove from heat; stand, covered, 10 minutes. Fluff rice with fork; cool. Refrigerate, covered, until cold.
2 Make balsamic orange dressing.
3 Combine rice with dressing and remaining ingredients in large bowl; toss gently to combine.

BALSAMIC ORANGE DRESSING place ingredients in screw-topped jar; shake well.

SERVES 6
per serving 4.3g total fat (0.3g saturated fat); 911kj (218 cal); 5.3g protein; 39.6g carbohydrate; 3g fibre

grilled vegetable salad with creamy dressing

PREPARATION TIME 35 MINUTES (PLUS STANDING TIME) COOKING TIME 30 MINUTES

2 medium potatoes (400g)
1 large kumara (500g)
200g medium flat mushrooms
cooking-oil spray
1 teaspoon cajun seasoning
250g spinach
1 medium green oak leaf lettuce

CREAMY DRESSING

¼ cup (15g) sun-dried tomatoes without oil
½ cup (125ml) low-fat milk
½ cup (125ml) low-fat sour cream
2 teaspoons chopped fresh oregano
1 clove garlic, crushed
2 teaspoons balsamic vinegar

1 Make creamy dressing.
2 Cut potatoes and kumara into 1cm slices. Boil, steam or microwave potatoes and kumara until just tender; pat dry with absorbent paper.
3 Coat potatoes, kumara and mushrooms with cooking-oil spray; sprinkle with seasoning.
4 Cook vegetables in batches on heated grill pan (or grill or barbecue) until browned and tender. Serve vegetables with torn spinach and lettuce leaves; drizzle with creamy dressing.

CREAMY DRESSING cover tomatoes with boiling water in small heatproof bowl, stand 20 minutes or until soft. Drain tomatoes, chop finely. Whisk milk and sour cream in bowl, stir in tomatoes, oregano and garlic; whisk in vinegar.

SERVES 4
per serving 8.3g total fat (4.1g saturated fat); 1141kj (273 cal); 12.4g protein; 36.1g carbohydrate; 9.9g fibre
tip recipe best made just before serving.

white bean salad with coriander, mint and lemon grass

PREPARATION TIME 15 MINUTES

2 x 400g cans cannellini beans, rinsed, drained
150g baby spinach leaves
1 small red onion (100g), sliced thinly
1 clove garlic, crushed
1 tablespoon coarsely chopped fresh coriander
1 tablespoon coarsely chopped fresh mint
1 tablespoon thinly sliced fresh lemon grass
1cm piece fresh ginger (5g), grated finely
2 tablespoons sesame oil
2 tablespoons soy sauce
2 tablespoons sweet chilli sauce
2 tablespoons lime juice
1 teaspoon honey
2 fresh small red thai chillies, sliced thinly

1. Combine beans with spinach and onion in large bowl.
2. Combine garlic, herbs, lemon grass, ginger, oil, sauces, juice and honey in screw-top jar; shake well.
3. Just before serving, drizzle dressing over salad; toss gently to combine, then sprinkle with chilli.

SERVES 4
per serving 10.5g total fat (1.3g saturated fat); 1028kj (246 cal); 12.3g protein; 25.1g carbohydrate; 12.3g fibre

cajun beef roll

PREPARATION TIME 10 MINUTES COOKING TIME 25 MINUTES

500g beef rump steak, sliced thinly
1 medium brown onion (150g), sliced thinly
1 medium red capsicum (200g), sliced thinly
2 tablespoons cajun seasoning
3 medium tomatoes (570g)
1 long french bread stick

1 Heat oiled large frying pan; cook beef, in batches, until beef is browned and cooked as desired.

2 Cook onion, capsicum and seasoning in same pan, stirring, until onion is browned lightly. Cut each tomato into 8 wedges, add to pan; simmer, uncovered, about 15 minutes or until mixture thickens. Return beef to pan; toss gently to combine with tomato mixture.

3 Trim ends from bread stick; quarter stick then split pieces almost all the way through. Line bread with lettuce leaves, if desired. Divide beef mixture among bread pieces just before serving.

SERVES 4
per serving (excluding lettuce) 6.6g total fat (1.8g saturated fat); 1743kj (417 cal); 39.1g protein; 49.1g carbohydrate; 5.5g fibre

warm minted lamb salad

PREPARATION TIME 25 MINUTES COOKING TIME 45 MINUTES

400g lean lamb fillets
1 clove garlic, crushed
2 tablespoons lemon juice
⅓ cup (80ml) chicken stock
½ cup (100g) couscous
cooking-oil spray
3 medium tomatoes (390g), peeled, seeded
1 small green cucumber (130g)
150g mixed salad leaves
2 tablespoons chopped fresh mint leaves

DRESSING

¾ cup (180g) low-fat yogurt
3 teaspoons lemon juice
¼ cup (60ml) water
pinch ground cumin
1 clove garlic, crushed
1 teaspoon low-salt soy sauce

1 Combine lamb, garlic and juice in bowl; cover, refrigerate several hours or overnight.

2 Bring stock to a boil in saucepan, add couscous; remove pan from heat, stir, cover, stand 5 minutes or until stock is absorbed.

3 Heat frying pan, coat with cooking-oil spray, add couscous; cook, stirring, until grains are separated. Remove from pan, cool.

4 Slice tomatoes thinly. Slice cucumber thinly with vegetable peeler.

5 Coat heated grill pan (or grill or barbeuce) with cooking-oil spray; cook lamb, turning, until cooked as desired. Cut lamb into thin slices.

6 Make dressing.

7 Place salad leaves, cucumber, tomatoes and lamb on serving plate; drizzle with dressing, sprinkle with mint and couscous.

DRESSING place ingredients in small bowl; mix well.

SERVES 4
per serving 4.9g total fat (2.2g saturated fat); 1141kj (273 cal); 29.4g protein; 26g carbohydrate; 2.6g fibre
tip recipe can be prepared a day ahead. Store separately, covered, in refrigerator.

mushroom, eggplant and zucchini pizza

PREPARATION TIME 10 MINUTES COOKING TIME 25 MINUTES

2 medium zucchini (240g)
1 baby eggplant (60g)
200g button mushrooms, sliced thinly
2 large pittas
½ x 140g tub pizza sauce
½ cup (60g) finely grated low-fat cheddar cheese
2 teaspoons finely chopped fresh thyme

1 Preheat oven to 240°C/220°C fan-forced.

2 Slice zucchini and eggplant lengthways. Cook mushroom, zucchini and eggplant, in batches, on heated oiled grill plate (or grill or barbecue) until browned lightly and just tender.

3 Place pittas on oven trays, spread evenly with pizza sauce. Sprinkle ¼ of the cheese over each pitta, top with mushroom, zucchini and eggplant; sprinkle with remaining cheese, then thyme. Bake, uncovered, about 10 minutes or until pizzas are browned and crisp.

SERVES 4
per serving 4.8g total fat (2.4g saturated fat); 727kj (174 cal); 10.6g protein; 21.9g carbohydrate; 4g fibre

chilli seafood pizza

PREPARATION TIME 35 MINUTES COOKING TIME 20 MINUTES

400g whole small calamari
400g baby octopus
400g medium uncooked prawns
2 cloves garlic, crushed
1 tablespoon chopped fresh flat-leaf parsley
1 teaspoon olive oil
1 tablespoon polenta
2 x 30cm-round prepared pizza bases
⅔ cup (180g) tomato pizza sauce
4 fresh red thai chillies, sliced thinly
4 green onions, sliced thinly
1 medium red onion (170g), sliced thinly

1 Clean calamari by gently pulling head and tentacles from body. Remove clear backbone (quill) from inside body. Remove fins and skin with salted fingers, rinse body. Cut into thin rings.

2 To prepare octopus, remove and discard head; push black beak from centre of tentacles, discard beak. Cut tentacles into quarters.

3 Peel and devein prawns. Combine calamari rings, octopus, prawns, garlic and parsley in medium bowl.

4 Preheat oven to 240°C/220°C fan-forced. Brush two 30cm-round pizza trays with oil; sprinkle with polenta. Place pizza bases on trays, spread bases with pizza sauce.

5 Divide seafood mixture between pizzas. Top with chilli and green and red onions. Bake, uncovered, 10 minutes.

6 Reduce oven to 180°C/160°C fan-forced. Slide pizzas from trays onto oven racks; bake further 10 minutes or until bases are crisp. Serve sprinkled with extra parsley, if desired.

SERVES 6
per serving 9.2g total fat (1.5g saturated fat); 2107kj (504 cal); 44.5g protein; 44.5g carbohydrate; 5.8g fibre

potato and rosemary pizza

PREPARATION TIME 8 MINUTES COOKING TIME 15 MINUTES

For this recipe we used packaged pizza bases, which measure 15cm across and come in packs of two, but any fresh or frozen variety would also be suitable.

4 x 112g pizza bases
1½ cups (120g) finely grated parmesan cheese
3 tiny new potatoes (120g)
1 tablespoon coarsely chopped fresh rosemary
3 cloves garlic, sliced thinly

1. Preheat oven to 220°C/200°C fan-forced. Place pizza bases on oven tray. Divide half of the cheese into four portions; sprinkle a portion over each pizza base.
2. Slice potatoes thinly using vegetable peeler; divide into four portions. Layer a portion of potato over cheese-topped base in circular pattern until covered; repeat with remaining potato and bases. Divide rosemary and garlic among bases. Sprinkle remaining cheese evenly over pizzas.
3. Bake, uncovered, 15 minutes or until pizza tops are browned lightly and bases are crisp.

SERVES 4
per serving 14.1g total fat (6.8g saturated fat); 1973kj (472 cal); 22.3g protein; 63.5g carbohydrate; 5g fibre
tip you could use one large packaged pizza base instead of making individual servings.
serving suggestion serve with a tossed green salad.

lamb lavash with crunchy chilli glaze

PREPARATION TIME 20 MINUTES COOKING TIME 40 MINUTES

½ cup (125ml) sweet chilli sauce
3 cloves garlic, crushed
¼ cup (60ml) beef stock
¼ cup (35g) unsalted roasted peanuts, chopped coarsely
300g lamb eye of loin
4 pieces lavash bread
4 cos lettuce leaves
1 green onion, sliced thinly
1 cup (80g) bean sprouts

1. Combine sauce, garlic, stock and peanuts in small pan; simmer, uncovered, about 5 minutes or until mixture has thickened to a glaze.
2. Meanwhile, cook lamb in heated oiled medium pan until browned all over and cooked as desired. Remove lamb from pan, cover, rest 5 minutes; cut into thin slices.
3. Spread 1 piece lavash with a little chilli glaze, top with lettuce leaf. Sprinkle ¼ of the onion and ¼ of the sprouts across one short end of lavash, top with ¼ of the sliced lamb, roll lavash to enclose filling; cut in half. Repeat process with remaining ingredients. Serve lavash rolls with remaining chilli glaze.

SERVES 4
per serving 8.7g total fat (2.1g saturated fat); 1647kj (394 cal); 26.4g protein; 51.7g carbohydrate; 4.6g fibre

couscous tabbouleh sandwich

PREPARATION TIME 10 MINUTES COOKING TIME 5 MINUTES

2 tablespoons couscous
2 tablespoons boiling water
½ cup finely chopped fresh parsley leaves
1 small tomato (130g), seeded, chopped finely
½ small red onion (50g), chopped finely
1 tablespoon lemon juice
1 teaspoon finely chopped fresh mint leaves
4 slices black rye bread (210g)
½ medium avocado (125g), sliced thinly

1. Combine couscous and the boiling water in small bowl. Stir with fork until the water is absorbed; cool.
2. Combine couscous in medium bowl with parsley, tomato, onion, juice and mint. Divide couscous mixture between 2 bread slices; top with avocado and remaining bread.

SERVES 2
per serving 12.6g total fat (2.5g saturated fat); 1802kj (431 cal); 14.1g protein; 64.2g carbohydrate; 9.7g fibre
tip tabbouleh can be made a day ahead. Store, covered, in refrigerator.

chicken tikka wrap

PREPARATION TIME 20 MINUTES (PLUS REFRIGERATION TIME) COOKING TIME 15 MINUTES

2 single chicken breast fillets (340g)
1 tablespoon tikka masala curry paste
2½ cups (700g) low-fat yogurt
2 lebanese cucumbers (260g), seeded, chopped finely
⅓ cup coarsely chopped fresh mint
1 small red onion (100g), chopped finely
4 large pitta
100g mesclun

1. Cut each chicken fillet in half horizontally. Combine chicken, curry paste and 2 tablespoons of the yogurt in large bowl; cover, refrigerate 3 hours or overnight.
2. Cook chicken mixture, in batches, on heated oiled grill plate (or grill or barbecue) until browned all over and cooked through. Stand 5 minutes; slice thinly.
3. Meanwhile, combine cucumber, mint, onion and remaining yogurt in medium bowl.
4. Just before serving, spread yogurt mixture over whole of each piece of bread; top with equal amounts of mesclun then chicken. Roll to enclose filling.

SERVES 4
per serving 8.7g total fat (2.9g saturated fat); 1902kj (455 cal); 36.3g protein; 55.3g carbohydrate; 4.5g fibre

lamb and tabbouleh wrap

PREPARATION TIME 35 MINUTES COOKING TIME 10 MINUTES

Sumac, a purple-red astringent spice, can be teamed with almost anything – from fish to meat. It is also great sprinkled over vegetables. You can find sumac at any Middle-Eastern food store.

½ cup (80g) burghul
1 cup (250ml) water
300g can chickpeas, drained, rinsed
⅓ cup (95g) low-fat yogurt
1 teaspoon finely grated lemon rind
1 tablespoon lemon juice
3 green onions, sliced thinly
2 medium tomatoes (380g), seeded, chopped finely
1 lebanese cucumber (130g), seeded, chopped finely
1 cup coarsely chopped fresh flat-leaf parsley
½ cup coarsely chopped fresh mint
1 tablespoon lemon juice, extra
250g lean lamb strips
2 tablespoons sumac
8 slices lavash bread

1. Combine burghul and the water in small bowl; stand 30 minutes. Drain; squeeze burghul with hands to remove excess water.
2. Meanwhile, blend or process chickpeas, yogurt, rind and juice until hummus is smooth.
3. Place burghul in large bowl with onion, tomato, cucumber, herbs and extra juice; toss gently to combine tabbouleh.
4. Combine lamb and sumac in medium bowl; cook, in batches, on heated lightly oiled grill plate (or grill or barbecue) until browned both sides and cooked as desired.
5. Just before serving, spread hummus equally over half of each slice of the bread, top with equal amounts of lamb and tabbouleh; roll to enclose filling. Cut into pieces, if desired, to serve.

MAKES 8 WRAPS
per wrap 3.5g total fat (0.9g saturated fat); 1237kj (296 cal); 17g protein; 48.1g carbohydrate; 6.2g fibre

chicken and pickled cucumber pitta

PREPARATION TIME 10 MINUTES (PLUS STANDING TIME) COOKING TIME 15 MINUTES

250g chicken breast fillet
1 medium green cucumber (170g)
1 tablespoon cider vinegar
2 teaspoons sugar
1 fresh red thai chilli, chopped finely
1 teaspoon soy sauce
1 small butter lettuce
4 pocket pittas

1. Cook chicken on heated oiled grill plate (or grill or barbecue) until browned both sides and cooked through; cool. Slice chicken thinly.
2. Meanwhile, slice cucumber into long, thin strips with a vegetable peeler. Combine cucumber, vinegar, sugar, chilli and sauce in medium bowl; stand 10 minutes.
3. Serve chicken, pickled cucumber and lettuce in pittas.

SERVES 4
per serving 3.5g total fat (0.6g saturated fat); 1308kj (313 cal); 22.7g protein; 46.8g carbohydrate; 3.4g fibre

gourmet chicken sandwiches

PREPARATION TIME 20 MINUTES COOKING TIME 15 MINUTES

Black cumin seeds, also sold as jeera kala, are darker and sweeter than ordinary cumin and are sometimes confused with kalonji (nigella seeds). Used extensively in Indian and Moroccan-style cooking, the nutty flavour of black cumin seeds is brought out by toasting.

600g chicken breast fillets
2 cups (500ml) prepared chicken stock
1½ cups (375ml) water
⅓ cup (50g) drained sun-dried tomatoes
1 tablespoon coarsely chopped fresh rosemary
2 tablespoons prepared chicken stock, extra
½ long loaf turkish bread
½ small red onion (50g), sliced thinly
1 lebanese cucumber (130g), sliced thinly
60g baby rocket leaves
⅓ cup (95g) yogurt
½ teaspoon toasted black cumin seeds

1. Combine chicken, stock and the water in large saucepan; bring to a boil. Reduce heat, simmer, uncovered, about 10 minutes or until cooked through. Cool chicken in poaching liquid 10 minutes. Remove chicken from pan; discard poaching liquid (or reserve for another use). Slice chicken thinly.
2. Meanwhile, drain tomatoes on absorbent paper; pressing firmly to remove as much oil as possible. Quarter tomatoes; blend or process with rosemary and extra stock until tomato mixture forms a paste.
3. Halve bread, slice pieces horizontally; toast both sides. Spread cut sides of bread with tomato paste; top with chicken, onion, cucumber and rocket. Serve with combined yogurt and seeds.

SERVES 4
per serving 8.6g total fat (1.9g saturated fat); 1722kj (412 cal); 41.8g protein; 23.3g carbohydrate; 2.5g fibre

eggplant tahini

PREPARATION TIME 10 MINUTES COOKING TIME 25 MINUTES

1 medium eggplant (300g)
1 tablespoon tahini paste
1 clove garlic, crushed
1½ tablespoons lemon juice
4 slices wholemeal bread (180g)
1 cup coarsely shredded lettuce
1 tablespoon finely chopped fresh mint leaves

1. Preheat oven to 200°C/180°C fan-forced.
2. Halve eggplant; place on oven tray. Bake, uncovered, about 25 minutes or until soft; cool. Remove skin; blend or process eggplant, paste, garlic and juice until well combined. You will have about 1 cup of mixture.
3. Spread 2 bread slices each with 2 tablespoons of eggplant mixture. Top with lettuce and mint, then remaining bread. Keep remaining mixture for future use.

SERVES 2
per serving 8.4g total fat (1g saturated fat); 974kj (233 cal); 10.2g protein; 28.4g carbohydrate; 9.4g fibre
tip eggplant mixture can be made 3 days ahead. Store, covered, in refrigerator.

steak sandwich

PREPARATION TIME 15 MINUTES COOKING TIME 15 MINUTES

Mesclun is a mixture of various baby salad leaves; substitute any single lettuce variety if you prefer. Beef rib-eye is also called scotch fillet by some butchers.

2 small leeks (400g), sliced thinly
1 tablespoon brown sugar
¼ cup (60ml) dry white wine
1 tablespoon seeded mustard
2 medium zucchini (240g), sliced thinly
2 baby eggplants (120g), sliced thinly
2 medium tomatoes (380g), sliced thickly
4 x 100g beef rib-eye steaks
8 slices white bread
50g mesclun

1. Cook leek, with about 2 tablespoons of water to prevent it sticking, in medium frying pan over low heat, stirring, until softened. Add sugar, wine and mustard; cook, stirring, about 10 minutes or until leek is browned and liquid evaporates.
2. Meanwhile, cook zucchini, eggplant and tomato on heated oiled grill plate (or grill or barbecue) until vegetables are browned all over and just tender. Keep warm.
3. Cook beef on heated oiled grill plate (or grill or barbecue) until browned both sides and cooked as desired.
4. Toast bread lightly. Sandwich each steak, with a quarter each of the vegetables and mesclun, between two pieces of toast.

SERVES 4
per serving 6.7g total fat (2.2g saturated fat); 1442kj (345 cal); 31.4g protein; 36.9g carbohydrate; 5.9g fibre
tip leek may be cooked longer to caramelise it if you prefer.
serving suggestion serve with oven-baked potato wedges.

beef fajitas

PREPARATION TIME 30 MINUTES COOKING TIME 20 MINUTES

You will need a small iceberg lettuce for this recipe and two packets of small flour tortillas (sometimes labelled "fajita tortillas" on the package).

800g trimmed beef rump steak

1 large red capsicum (350g), sliced thinly

1 large green capsicum (350g), sliced thinly

1 large yellow capsicum (350g), sliced thinly

1 large red onion (300g), sliced thinly

16 small flour tortillas (16cm diameter)

3 cups finely shredded iceberg lettuce

1¼ cups (155g) coarsely grated low-fat cheddar cheese

FRESH TOMATO SALSA

3 medium tomatoes (570g), seeded, chopped finely

1 medium red onion (170g), chopped finely

1 tablespoon finely chopped drained jalapeño chillies

¼ cup firmly packed, finely chopped fresh coriander

1 tablespoon lemon juice

1. Heat large lightly oiled grill plate (or grill or barbecue). Sear beef both sides until browned and cooked as desired. Cover; stand 10 minutes. Slice thinly.
2. Meanwhile, on same grill plate, cook capsicums and onion, in batches, until vegetables are browned all over.
3. Heat tortillas according to manufacturer's instructions.
4. Make fresh tomato salsa.
5. Divide beef slices and vegetables among tortillas on serving plates. Top each with lettuce and cheese; roll to enclose filling. Serve with separate bowl of salsa.

FRESH TOMATO SALSA combine ingredients in small bowl.

SERVES 8

per serving 10.2g total fat (4.4g saturated fat); 1446kj (346 cal); 35.7g protein; 27.2g carbohydrate; 4.3g fibre

vegetable cheese puffs

PREPARATION TIME 30 MINUTES COOKING TIME 40 MINUTES

cooking-oil spray
2 teaspoons vegetable oil
60g pumpkin, chopped finely
1 small red onion (100g), chopped
½ small carrot (40g), grated
¼ small red capsicum (40g), chopped
½ small zucchini (50g), grated
15g butter or margarine
1 tablespoon plain flour
⅓ cup (80ml) low-fat milk
¼ cup (20g) grated parmesan cheese
2 eggs, separated
1 egg white

1. Preheat oven to 220°C/200°C fan-forced. Coat four ¾-cup (180ml) soufflé dishes with cooking-oil spray.
2. Heat oil in small saucepan; cook vegetables, covered, until pumpkin is tender. Process vegetables until combined.
3. Melt butter in medium saucepan, add flour; cook, stirring, over heat until bubbling. Remove from heat, gradually stir in milk. Return to heat, stir until mixture boils and thickens; transfer to large bowl. Stir in vegetable mixture, cheese and egg yolks.
4. Beat all egg whites in small bowl until soft peaks form; fold into vegetable mixture in two batches. Spoon mixture into dishes, place on oven tray.
5. Bake, uncovered, 10 minutes. Reduce oven to 180°C/160°C fan-forced. Bake, uncovered, further 15 minutes or until puffed. Serve immediately.

SERVES 4
per serving 9.8g total fat (4.2g saturated fat); 614kj (147 cal); 8.4g protein; 6.3g carbohydrate; 1.2g fibre
tip recipe must be made just before serving.

pumpkin gnocchi

PREPARATION TIME 50 MINUTES COOKING TIME 50 MINUTES

16 medium egg tomatoes (1.2kg), quartered
1.6kg butternut pumpkin
1 egg
2 tablespoons finely chopped fresh flat-leaf parsley
2 tablespoons finely chopped fresh basil
2 cups (300g) plain flour
1 cup (150g) self-raising flour
2 teaspoons olive oil
1 small leek (200g), sliced thinly
1.5kg spinach, chopped coarsely
2 tablespoons olive paste
½ cup (40g) shaved parmesan cheese

1. Preheat oven to 220°C/200°C fan-forced.
2. Place tomato in large baking dish; bake, uncovered, about 20 minutes or until browned lightly and softened.
3. Meanwhile, peel pumpkin; chop coarsely. Boil, steam or microwave until tender; drain. Blend or process cooled pumpkin and egg until smooth; transfer to large bowl.
4. Using hand, mix herbs and flours into pumpkin mixture. Turn dough onto floured surface; knead lightly for about 2 minutes or until smooth. Roll heaped teaspoons of dough into gnocchi-shaped ovals; press lightly against back of fork tines. Place gnocchi on tray. Cover; refrigerate 30 minutes.
5. Heat oil in large frying pan; cook leek, stirring, until softened. Add spinach; cook, stirring, until spinach is just wilted.
6. Cook gnocchi, uncovered, in large saucepan of boiling water until all gnocchi float to surface. Carefully remove gnocchi from pan using slotted spoon; drain. Serve gnocchi on spinach-leek mixture; top with tomato, paste and cheese.

SERVES 8
per serving 5.7g total fat (2g saturated fat); 1442kj (345 cal); 16.1g protein; 56.3g carbohydrate; 9.3g fibre

spinach and cheese quesadillas

PREPARATION TIME 20 MINUTES COOKING TIME 10 MINUTES

Quesadillas are filled tortillas which are grilled or fried and served with fresh salsa. We used small flour tortillas measuring about 16cm in diameter (sometimes labelled "fajita tortillas" on the package).

⅔ cup (130g) low-fat cottage cheese
100g spinach leaves, trimmed
1 medium avocado (230g), chopped finely
1 cup (200g) canned mexican-style beans, drained
125g can corn kernels, drained
2 medium tomatoes (380g), seeded, chopped finely
1 small red onion (100g), chopped finely
2 medium zucchini (240g), grated coarsely
16 small flour tortillas
1½ cups (150g) coarsely grated low-fat mozzarella cheese

1. Blend or process cottage cheese and spinach until smooth.
2. Combine avocado, beans, corn, tomato, onion and zucchini in bowl.
3. Place eight tortillas on oiled oven tray; divide spinach mixture among tortillas, leaving 2cm border around edge. Sprinkle avocado mixture among tortillas; top each with one of the remaining tortillas.
4. Preheat grill. Sprinkle mozzarella over quesadilla stacks; place under grill until cheese just melts and browns lightly.

SERVES 8
per serving 11.6g total fat (3.9g saturated fat); 1162kj (278 cal); 15.1g protein; 28.7g carbohydrate; 4.6g fibre

carrot and zucchini rice paper rolls

PREPARATION TIME 20 MINUTES

1 cup loosely packed, coarsely grated carrot
1⅓ cups loosely packed, coarsely grated zucchini
2 green onions, chopped finely
1 tablespoon light soy sauce
1 tablespoon sweet chilli sauce
½ teaspoon sesame oil
½ teaspoon grated fresh ginger
8 x 22cm rice paper sheets

1. Combine carrot, zucchini, onion, sauces, oil and ginger in medium bowl.
2. Place one sheet of rice paper in medium bowl of warm water until softened slightly; lift sheet carefully from water. Place on board; pat dry with absorbent paper.
3. Divide carrot mixture into eight portions; place one portion in centre of rice paper sheet. Roll to enclose filling, folding in sides after first complete turn of the roll. Repeat with remaining rice sheets and filling.

SERVES 4
per serving 0.9g total fat (0.1g saturated fat); 213kj (51 cal); 1.8g protein; 8.7g carbohydrate; 1.7g fibre
tip you can also use fresh rice noodle sheets, cut into 14cm x 16cm rectangles, to enclose the filling.
serving suggestion serve with a snow pea sprout salad.

spinach and cheese quesadillas

roasted vegetable fillo tart

roasted vegetable fillo tart

PREPARATION TIME 20 MINUTES COOKING TIME 45 MINUTES

6 medium egg tomatoes (450g), quartered
1 small red onion (100g), sliced thickly
2 small yellow capsicums (300g)
2 small red capsicums (300g)
100g low-fat fetta cheese, crumbled
1 tablespoon finely shredded fresh basil
9 sheets fillo pastry
cooking-oil spray

1 Preheat oven to 200°C/180°C fan-forced.
2 Combine tomatoes and onion in baking dish; roast, uncovered, about 30 minutes or until onion softens.
3 Meanwhile, quarter capsicums; remove and discard seeds and membranes. Roast under grill or in very hot oven, skin-side up, until skin blisters and blackens; cover capsicum pieces with plastic or paper 5 minutes. Peel away skin; slice capsicum thinly. Add capsicum, cheese and basil to tomato mixture; stir gently to combine.
4 Stack sheets of fillo; spray with cooking-oil spray every third sheet. Carefully fold over all four edges of the stack to create 18cm x 30cm tart "shell".
5 Fill tart shell with vegetable mixture, spreading it to an even thickness; bake, uncovered, about 15 minutes or until pastry is browned lightly.

SERVES 6
per serving 4.7g total fat (1.8g saturated fat); 577kj (138 cal); 8.3g protein; 15.5g carbohydrate; 2.4g fibre
tip keep fillo covered with a damp tea towel to prevent the sheets from drying out before use.

light-white frittata

PREPARATION TIME 15 MINUTES COOKING TIME 20 MINUTES

A frittata, Italian in origin, is a type of omelette cooked either in a frying pan, on top of the stove, or in the oven until set. It makes great picnic fare or a welcome addition to the antipasto plate. You will need 200g of fresh peas in their pods for this recipe.

½ cup (80g) fresh shelled peas
1 medium yellow capsicum (200g), sliced thinly
1 small kumara (250g), grated coarsely
12 egg whites
½ cup (120g) light sour cream
1 cup loosely packed fresh basil leaves
¼ cup (20g) finely grated parmesan cheese

1 Cook peas, capsicum and kumara in heated oiled 20cm frying pan, stirring, until vegetables are just tender.
2 Whisk egg whites and cream in medium bowl; stir in basil.
3 Pour egg-white mixture over vegetables; cook, covered, over low heat about 10 minutes or until frittata is almost set.
4 Preheat grill. Sprinkle cheese over frittata; place under grill until frittata is set and top is browned lightly.

SERVES 4
per serving 7.8g total fat (4.9g saturated fat); 803kj (192 cal); 16.8g protein; 13.5g carbohydrate; 2.9g fibre
tips frittata can be served hot or at room temperature. You can freeze the yolks, in packages of two or four, for future use when baking or when making custard. Frozen peas can be substituted for fresh peas, if you prefer.

baked spinach and mushroom frittata

PREPARATION TIME 15 MINUTES COOKING TIME 40 MINUTES

1 teaspoon olive oil
3 cloves garlic, crushed
1 small leek (200g), sliced thinly
400g button mushrooms, sliced thickly
200g baby spinach leaves
2 eggs
6 egg whites
½ cup (125ml) skim milk
⅓ cup (40g) coarsely grated low-fat cheddar cheese

1. Preheat oven to 160°C/140°C fan-forced. Oil deep 23cm-round cake pan; line base with baking paper.
2. Heat oil in medium frying pan; cook garlic and leek, stirring, until leek softens. Add mushrooms; cook, stirring, until mushrooms are just tender. Add spinach; cook, stirring, until spinach just wilts. Drain; discard any liquid.
3. Whisk whole eggs, egg whites, milk and cheese in large bowl; stir in vegetable mixture. Pour egg mixture into prepared pan. Bake, uncovered, about 30 minutes or until just set.
4. Preheat grill. Place frittata under grill until browned. Top with baby spinach, if desired.

SERVES 4
per serving 6.8g total fat (2.5g saturated fat); 656kj (157 cal); 18.5g protein; 5.2g carbohydrate; 5.1g fibre
tip use swiss brown mushrooms as an alternative to button mushroom.

kumara, leek and sage frittata

PREPARATION TIME 20 MINUTES COOKING TIME 50 MINUTES

cooking-oil spray
2 medium kumara (800g)
1 small leek, sliced (200g)
1 clove garlic, crushed
1 tablespoon chopped fresh sage leaves
3 eggs
3 egg whites
½ cup (125ml) low-fat milk
⅓ cup (40g) grated low-fat cheddar cheese
1 tablespoon chopped fresh parsley

1. Preheat oven to 180°C/160°C fan-forced. Coat 25cm round flan dish (1.5 litre/6 cup) with cooking-oil spray.
2. Cut kumara into 5mm slices. Boil, steam or microwave kumara until tender; drain.
3. Heat frying pan, coat with cooking-oil spray; cook leek and garlic, covered, over low heat until leek is tender, stirring occasionally. Stir in half the sage.
4. Place half the kumara over base of dish, top with leek mixture, then remaining kumara. Pour combined eggs, egg whites, milk, cheese and parsley over kumara, sprinkle with remaining sage. Bake, uncovered, about 35 minutes or until frittata is firm.

SERVES 6
per serving 4.6g total fat (1.9g saturated fat); 706kj (169 cal); 11.1g protein; 21g carbohydrate; 3.1g fibre
tip recipe can be made a day ahead. Store, covered, in refrigerator.

kumara and corn frittata

PREPARATION TIME 20 MINUTES COOKING TIME 1 HOUR 10 MINUTES

1 medium kumara (400g)
1 fresh corn cob (400g)
1 large brown onion (200g), chopped coarsely
1 tablespoon raw sugar
4 eggs, beaten lightly
3 egg whites, beaten lightly
½ cup (125ml) low-fat milk
½ cup (60g) grated low-fat cheddar cheese

1 Preheat oven to 240°C/220°C fan-forced. Line deep 19cm-square cake pan with baking paper.

2 Chop kumara into 2cm pieces. Discard husk, silk and ends from cob; cut corn kernels from cob.

3 Combine kumara, onion and sugar in oiled small baking dish; shake dish to coat vegetables with sugar and oil. Bake, uncovered, 20 minutes. Stir in corn, bake further 20 minutes or until kumara and onion are tender. [Can be made ahead to this stage. Cover, refrigerate until required.]

4 Combine kumara mixture with remaining ingredients in large bowl; mix well. Pour mixture into pan; bake, uncovered, about 30 minutes or until frittata is cooked through.

SERVES 4
per serving 8.5g total fat (3.6g saturated fat); 1145kj (274 cal); 17.6g protein; 31.6g carbohydrate; 5.4g fibre

tuna and asparagus frittata

PREPARATION TIME 10 MINUTES COOKING TIME 30 MINUTES

5 medium potatoes (1kg), sliced thinly
250g asparagus, trimmed, chopped coarsely
1 medium brown onion (150g), sliced thinly
1 clove garlic, crushed
425g can tuna in spring water, drained
4 eggs, beaten lightly
4 egg whites, beaten lightly
2 tablespoons finely chopped fresh flat-leaf parsley
cooking-oil spray

1 Boil, steam or microwave potatoes and asparagus, separately, until almost tender.

2 Cook onion and garlic in heated oiled small frying pan, stirring, until onion softens.

3 Combine potato and onion mixture in large bowl with asparagus, tuna, egg, egg white and parsley.

4 Preheat grill.

5 Reheat same pan; spray lightly with cooking-oil spray. Spoon frittata mixture into pan, press down firmly; cook, uncovered, over low heat until almost set. Remove from heat; place under grill until frittata sets and top is browned lightly.

SERVES 4
per serving 7.9g total fat (2.5g saturated fat); 1542kj (369 cal); 37.8g protein; 35.3g carbohydrate; 5.4g fibre
tip substitute well-drained canned asparagus for the fresh, if desired.
serving suggestion serve with a salad of baby rocket leaves drizzled with balsamic vinegar.

tandoori lamb naan

PREPARATION TIME 15 MINUTES (PLUS REFRIGERATION TIME) COOKING TIME 10 MINUTES

250g lamb fillets
1 tablespoon tandoori paste
¾ cup (180ml) low-fat yogurt
4 naan bread
2 tablespoons chopped fresh mint leaves
1 tablespoon lime juice
100g curly endive
1 lebanese cucumber (130g), seeded, sliced finely

1. Combine lamb, paste and ¼ cup (60ml) of the yogurt in medium bowl; cover, refrigerate 10 minutes.
2. Cook lamb mixture on heated oiled grill plate (or grill or barbecue) until browned all over and cooked as desired; slice lamb.
3. Meanwhile, heat naan according to manufacturer's directions.
4. Blend or process remaining yogurt, mint and juice until smooth.
5. Place lamb, endive, cucumber and yogurt mixture in centre of naan; roll to enclose filling.

SERVES 4
per serving 10.4g total fat (5.2g saturated fat); 1552kj (292 cal); 20.6g protein; 28g carbohydrate; 2.7g fibre

creamy corn cake with salsa

PREPARATION TIME 20 MINUTES COOKING TIME 30 MINUTES

The energy and fat counts on this pared-down version of an omelette prove that they don't have to be kilojoule-laden to be deliciously satisfying.

1 egg yolk
½ cup (75g) self-raising flour
420g can corn kernels, rinsed, drained
310g can creamed corn
2 egg whites

AVOCADO SALSA
500g cherry tomatoes, quartered
1 small avocado (200g), chopped coarsely
1 small red onion (100g), chopped finely
2 tablespoons coarsely chopped fresh coriander
2 tablespoons coarsely chopped fresh mint
¼ cup (60ml) lime juice

1. Preheat oven to 220°C/200°C fan-forced. Oil deep 23cm-round cake pan; line base and side with baking paper.
2. Combine egg yolk, flour, corn kernels and creamed corn in medium bowl. Beat egg whites in small bowl with electric mixer until soft peaks form; fold into yolk mixture.
3. Spread mixture into prepared pan; bake, uncovered, about 30 minutes or until browned lightly and cooked through.
4. Make avocado salsa. Cut cake into eight wedges; serve with salsa.

AVOCADO SALSA place ingredients in small bowl; toss gently to combine.

SERVES 8
per serving 5.7g total fat (1.2g saturated fat); 669kj (160 cal); 5g protein; 21.7g carbohydrate; 4.3g fibre
tip if you omit the avocado from the salsa, the fat count will be significantly lower.
serving suggestion serve with sambal oelek or add some finely chopped chilli to the salsa for a bit more spice.

salmon patties with baby spinach

PREPARATION TIME 30 MINUTES COOKING TIME 45 MINUTES

Baby spinach leaves, along with baby rocket, are the greens of choice for many people today. And why not? They can be used in everything from salads to stir-fries to soups, with no preparation or pre-cooking required; they're full of nutrients; and their respective singular flavours add something special to the dishes in which they are used.

5 medium potatoes (1kg), chopped coarsely
415g can red salmon, drained, flaked
6 green onions, chopped finely
2 trimmed sticks celery (150g), grated coarsely
1 teaspoon finely grated lemon rind
⅓ cup (80ml) lemon juice
2 egg whites
2 tablespoons water
2 cups (200g) packaged breadcrumbs
1 teaspoon vegetable oil
230g can sliced water chestnuts, drained
600g baby spinach leaves
1 tablespoon light soy sauce
¼ cup (60ml) mirin
2 teaspoons sugar

1. Boil, steam or microwave potato until tender; drain. Mash potato in large bowl until smooth; cool slightly. Stir in salmon, onion, celery, rind and half of the juice.
2. Using floured hands, shape fish mixture into 16 patties. Dip patties, one at a time, in combined egg white and water, then in breadcrumbs. Place patties on lightly oiled oven tray. Cover; refrigerate 30 minutes.
3. Preheat oven to 240°C/220°C fan-forced.
4. Bake patties, uncovered, about 30 minutes or until golden brown and heated through.
5. Meanwhile, heat oil in wok; stir-fry water chestnuts 1 minute. Add spinach, remaining juice, sauce, mirin and sugar; stir-fry until spinach just wilts. Divide spinach mixture among serving plates; top with salmon patties.

SERVES 8
per serving 7.1g total fat (1.6g saturated fat); 1170kj (280 cal); 18.4g protein; 34.6g carbohydrate; 5.8g fibre
serving suggestion accompany patties and spinach with tomato or sweet onion relish and sliced light rye bread.

felafel rolls with tabbouleh

PREPARATION TIME 1 HOUR 45 MINUTES (PLUS STANDING TIME) COOKING TIME 40 MINTUES

cooking-oil spray
250g frozen broad beans
310g can chickpeas, rinsed, drained
2 cloves garlic, crushed
6 green onions, chopped
1 teaspoon ground cumin
½ teaspoon ground coriander
¼ cup coarsely chopped fresh flat-leaf parsley
¼ cup coarsely chopped fresh mint
2 tablespoons polenta, approximately
1 small green cucumber (130g)
8 cos lettuce leaves
400g packet wholemeal lebanese bread

TABBOULEH

2 tablespoons burghul
⅔ cup coarsely chopped fresh flat-leaf parsley
2 green onions, chopped finely
1 medium tomato (130g), chopped
1 teaspoon lemon juice
2 teaspoons olive oil

YOGURT SAUCE

1 cup (250g) low-fat yogurt
1 clove garlic, crushed
2 teaspoons lemon juice
1 teaspoon low-salt soy sauce
2 teaspoons coarsely chopped fresh mint

1. Preheat oven to 220°C/200°C fan-forced. Coat oven tray with cooking-oil spray.
2. Place beans in bowl, cover with boiling water, stand 5 minutes. Drain, remove skins; drain beans on absorbent paper.
3. Blend or process beans with chickpeas, garlic, onions, cumin, coriander and herbs until combined. Shape level tablespoons of mixture into patties, roll in polenta; place on oven tray. Coat felafel with cooking-oil spray.
4. Bake, uncovered, about 40 minutes or until browned.
5. Make tabbouleh. Make yogurt sauce.
6. Using a vegetable peeler, cut cucumber into strips lengthways. Divide lettuce, tabbouleh, cucumber, felafel and yogurt sauce among bread; fold over filling.

TABBOULEH place burghul in small bowl, cover with boiling water. Stand 10 minutes, drain; blot dry with absorbent paper. Combine burghul with remaining ingredients in bowl; mix well.

YOGURT SAUCE combine ingredients in bowl; mix well.

SERVES 4
per serving 8.7g total fat (1.7g saturated fat); 2053kj (491 cal); 21.9g protein; 80g carbohydrate; 15.1g fibre
tip felafel can be made a day ahead. Store, covered, in refrigerator.

polenta with tomato, asparagus and watercress

PREPARATION TIME 25 MINUTES (PLUS REFRIGERATION TIME) COOKING TIME 25 MINUTES

2 cups (500ml) low-fat milk
1 cup (170g) polenta
⅓ cup (25g) finely grated parmesan cheese
1 medium zucchini (120g), sliced finely
2 baby eggplants (120g), sliced finely
4 medium tomatoes (760g), chopped coarsely
250g asparagus, trimmed, halved lengthways
100g watercress

1 Heat milk in medium saucepan, without boiling. Stir in polenta; cook, stirring, about 10 minutes or until milk is absorbed and polenta is soft, stir in cheese. Spread polenta into oiled 22cm slab pan, cover; refrigerate until firm. Using 8.5cm round cutter, cut polenta into 4 circles. [Can be made ahead to this stage. Cover, refrigerate until required.]

2 Heat oiled medium saucepan; cook zucchini and eggplant, stirring, until vegetables are tender. Stir in tomato; simmer, uncovered, about 5 minutes or until tomato softens.

3 Meanwhile, preheat grill. Place asparagus on oiled oven tray; place under grill until browned lightly and just tender. Place polenta on oiled oven tray; place under grill until hot and browned lightly.

4 Serve polenta with tomato mixture, asparagus and watercress.

SERVES 4
per serving 3.5g total fat (1.5g saturated fat); 1104kj (264 cal); 15.4g protein; 41.5g carbohydrate; 5.7g fibre

polenta with quick spinach sauté

PREPARATION TIME 30 MINUTES (PLUS CHILLING TIME) COOKING TIME 35 MINTUES

1 litre (4 cups) chicken stock
1½ cups (255g) polenta
½ cup (40g) grated parmesan cheese
¼ cup chopped fresh parsley
2 teaspoons olive oil
1 clove garlic, crushed
1 bunch spinach (500g)

TOMATO MUSHROOM SAUCE
½ cup (125ml) water
1 medium onion (150g), chopped finely
1 clove garlic, crushed
400g can low-salt tomatoes
1 tablespoon no-salt tomato paste
250g button mushrooms, halved

1 Line 20cm x 30cm lamington pan with baking paper.

2 Bring stock to a boil in saucepan, stir in polenta; cook, stirring, about 10 minutes or until polenta is soft and thick. Stir in cheese and parsley. Spread mixture evenly into pan, cover; refrigerate 2 hours or until firm. Turn polenta out, cut into 16 triangles.

3 Make tomato mushroom sauce.

4 Preheat grill. Place polenta on oiled oven tray; place under grill until lightly browned on both sides.

5 Heat oil in large saucepan; cook garlic and spinach, stirring, until spinach is just wilted. Serve polenta and spinach with sauce.

TOMATO MUSHROOM SAUCE combine water, onion and garlic in saucepan; cook, stirring, until onion is soft and water evaporated. Add undrained crushed tomatoes, paste and mushrooms; simmer, stirring, 5 minutes or until thickened.

SERVES 4
per serving 8.5g total fat (3.1g saturated fat); 1488kj (356 cal); 17.2g protein; 52.3g carbohydrate; 7.5g fibre
tip polenta and sauce can be made a day ahead. Store separately, covered, in refrigerator.

starters and soups

roasted eggplants with capsicum and pesto

PREPARATION TIME 50 MINUTES (PLUS STANDING TIME) COOKING TIME 40 MINUTES

1 large red capsicum (350g)
14 finger eggplants (840g)
coarse cooking salt
4 slices wholemeal bread
2 tablespoons shaved parmesan cheese

MARINADE

⅓ cup (80ml) lemon juice
1 tablespoon balsamic vinegar
3 teaspoons mild sweet chilli sauce
2 teaspoons sugar
2 cloves garlic, crushed
2 teaspoons olive oil

PESTO

1½ cups loosely packed basil leaves
2 tablespoons fresh oregano
⅔ cup (130g) low-fat ricotta cheese
2 tablespoons water

1. Quarter capsicums; remove and discard seeds and membranes. Roast under grill or in very hot oven, skin-side up, until skin blisters and blackens; cover capsicum pieces with plastic or paper 5 minutes. Peel away skin; slice capsicum.
2. Cut eggplants into 4 slices lengthways, sprinkle with salt, stand 20 minutes. Rinse eggplants; drain, pat dry with absorbent paper.
3. Make marinade. Combine marinade and eggplant in medium bowl, cover; refrigerate 30 minutes.
4. Preheat grill. Drain eggplants; reserve marinade. Place eggplant under grill, brushing with some of the reserved marinade, on both sides until tender.
5. Make pesto.
6. Remove crusts from bread, toast bread. Place toast on serving plates, top with eggplant, capsicum, cheese and pesto.

MARINADE combine ingredients in bowl; mix well.

PESTO blend or process ingredients with ¼ cup (60ml) of reserved marinade until smooth.

SERVES 4
per serving 7.9g total fat (3g saturated fat); 880kj (210 cal); 11.1g protein; 23g carbohydrate; 7.5g fibre
tip pesto can be made up to 2 days ahead. Store, covered, in refrigerator.

tomato tarte tatin

PREPARATION TIME 20 MINUTES COOKING TIME 1 HOUR (PLUS STANDING TIME)

The French sisters Tatin, who are credited with the invention of the apple version of this upside-down tart, would no doubt approve of their recipe's savoury incarnation.

2 large red onions (400g), sliced thinly
2 cups (440g) raw sugar
½ cup (125ml) balsamic vinegar
12 medium egg tomatoes (900g), halved
1 tablespoon water
2 sheets ready-rolled puff pastry with canola oil

1. Preheat oven to 200°C/280°C fan-forced. Oil eight 10cm pie dishes.
2. Heat large oiled frying pan; cook onion, stirring, until onion softens. Add 1 tablespoon of the sugar and vinegar to pan; cook, stirring, until onion caramelises.
3. Place tomatoes, cut-side up, in single layer on oven tray; roast, uncovered, about 20 minutes or until softened and browned lightly.
4. Meanwhile, combine remaining sugar with the water in large heavy-based saucepan; stir over low heat to combine. Cook, shaking pan constantly and stirring occasionally, until mixture crystallises. Continue cooking, stirring occasionally until mixture turns to a thick, dark syrup. Divide sugar mixture among pie dishes. Arrange three tomato halves, cut-side down, in each dish; top with onion mixture.
5. Cut four 10cm-rounds from each pastry sheet; top each dish with pastry round. Bake, uncovered, about 15 minutes or until pastry is browned lightly; stand tarts for 2 minutes before turning onto serving plates.

SERVES 8

per serving 9.6g total fat (0.7g saturated fat); 1664kj (397 cal); 4.2g protein; 75.2g carbohydrate; 2.8g fibre

tip don't worry when the sugar and water mixture turns to dry crystals. As you continue cooking, it will liquefy and become a toffee-like mixture.

poached eggs and asparagus with dill sauce

PREPARATION TIME 5 MINUTES COOKING TIME 20 MINUTES

20g butter

¼ teaspoon saffron threads

1 teaspoon dijon mustard

1 tablespoon plain flour

1 cup (250ml) prepared salt-reduced vegetable stock

2 tablespoons finely chopped fresh dill

750g asparagus, trimmed

4 eggs

1 Melt butter with saffron in small saucepan over medium heat; stir in mustard. Add flour; cook, stirring, until mixture thickens and bubbles. Gradually add stock; stir until mixture boils and thickens. Stir in dill.

2 Boil, steam or microwave asparagus until just tender, drain; cover to keep warm.

3 Half-fill a large shallow frying pan with water; bring to a boil. Break eggs into cup then slide into pan, one at a time. When all eggs are in pan, allow water to return to a boil. Cover pan, turn off heat; stand about 4 minutes or until a light film of egg white sets over yolks. Using slotted spoon, remove eggs, one at a time, and place on absorbent-paper-lined saucer to blot up poaching liquid.

4 Divide asparagus among serving plates; top with eggs, drizzle with dill sauce.

SERVES 4
per serving 9.6g total fat (4.4g saturated fat); 612kj (146 cal); 10.7g protein; 4.5g carbohydrate; 2.1g fibre

steamed garlic and herb mussels

PREPARATION TIME 30 MINUTES COOKING TIME 25 MINUTES

80 medium black mussels (about 2kg)

2 tablespoons olive oil

8 cloves garlic, crushed

4 fresh red thai chillies, chopped finely

1 tablespoon finely grated lemon rind

1 cup (250ml) lemon juice

1 cup (250ml) dry white wine

½ cup finely chopped fresh flat-leaf parsley

⅓ cup finely chopped fresh basil leaves

1 Scrub mussels; remove beards.

2 Heat oil in large saucepan; cook garlic, chilli and rind, stirring, about 2 minutes or until fragrant. Add mussels, juice and wine; bring to a boil. Cook, covered, about 5 minutes or until mussels open (discard any that do not). Remove mussels from pan.

3 Return liquid in pan to a boil; cook, uncovered, about 10 minutes or until mixture thickens slightly. Stir in parsley and basil.

4 Return mussels to pan; simmer, stirring, until heated through.

SERVES 8
per serving 5.6g total fat (0.9g saturated fat); 483kj (115 cal); 6.5g protein; 3.7g carbohydrate; 0.9g fibre
serving suggestion serve with steamed jasmine or basmati rice.

thai pork and corn cakes

PREPARATION TIME 30 MINUTES COOKING TIME 25 MINUTES

500g lean pork and veal mince
1 tablespoon red curry paste
1 egg, beaten lightly
6 green onions, chopped finely
130g can corn kernels, drained
½ cup (35g) stale wholemeal breadcrumbs
¼ cup chopped fresh coriander leaves

DIPPING SAUCE
½ cup (125ml) mild sweet chilli sauce
½ small green cucumber (65g), chopped finely

1. Preheat oven to 220°C/200°C fan-forced.
2. Combine mince, paste, egg, onion, corn, breadcrumbs and coriander in large bowl. Roll rounded tablespoons of mixture into balls, shape into patties; place on oven tray.
3. Bake, uncovered, about 25 minutes or until browned, turn halfway during cooking.
4. Make dipping sauce; serve with cakes.

DIPPING SAUCE combine ingredients in small bowl; mix well.

MAKES 16
per cake 3.3g total fat (1.1g saturated fat); 328kj (78 cal); 7.6g protein; 4.4g carbohydrate; 0.9g fibre
tip cakes can be prepared a day ahead. Store, covered, in refrigerator.

japanese-style tuna with red-maple radish

PREPARATION TIME 25 MINUTES

Tuna sold as sashimi has to meet stringent guidelines regarding its handling and treatment after leaving the water. Nevertheless, it is best to seek local advice from authorities before eating any raw seafood. The combination of daikon and chilli treated in this way is commonly known in Japan as "red-maple radish". It can be used as an accompaniment to any Japanese dish using raw fish.

600g piece sashimi tuna
⅓ cup (80ml) rice vinegar
½ small daikon (200g), peeled
4 dried long red chillies, chopped finely
2 tablespoons mirin
1 teaspoon sesame oil
1 teaspoon black sesame seeds
1 sheet toasted seaweed (nori), shredded finely

1. Slice tuna as thinly as possible; place, in single layer, on large platter, drizzle with vinegar. Cover; refrigerate until required.
2. Meanwhile, finely grate daikon. Place daikon and chilli in fine sieve set over small bowl; stir with small wooden spoon to combine then press with back of spoon to extract as much daikon liquid as possible.
3. Drain vinegar from tuna. Divide tuna among serving plates; drizzle with combined mirin and oil, sprinkle with seeds. Serve tuna with red-maple radish and seaweed.

SERVES 4
per serving 10.2g total fat (3.7g saturated fat); 1089kj (260 cal); 38.5g protein; 2.3g carbohydrate; 1.4g fibre

garlic prawns and buk choy

PREPARATION TIME 20 MINUTES COOKING TIME 15 MINUTES

Traditional garlic prawns are given a South-East Asian tweak in this stir-fry.

36 medium uncooked prawns (1kg)
6 cloves garlic, crushed
2 teaspoons finely chopped fresh coriander
3 fresh red thai chillies, chopped finely
⅓ cup (80ml) lime juice
1 teaspoon sugar
1 tablespoon peanut oil
1kg baby buk choy, quartered lengthways
6 green onions, sliced thinly
1 tablespoon sweet chilli sauce

1. Shell and devein prawns, leaving tails intact.
2. Combine prawns in large bowl with garlic, coriander, chilli, juice and sugar.
3. Heat half of the oil in wok; stir-fry prawn mixture, in batches, until just changed in colour.
4. Heat remaining oil with pan liquids in wok; stir-fry buk choy, onion and sauce, in batches, until just tender. Combine buk choy mixture and prawns in wok; stir-fry until hot.

SERVES 6
per serving 4.5g total fat (0.7g saturated fat); 611kj (146 cal); 22.5g protein; 3.1g carbohydrate; 5.9g fibre

tofu cakes with sweet chilli dipping sauce

PREPARATION TIME 15 MINUTES (PLUS STANDING TIME) COOKING TIME 15 MINUTES

You will need to cook about ⅓ cup basmati rice for this recipe.

300g fresh firm tofu
1 cup (150g) cooked basmati rice
3 teaspoons red curry paste
2 green onions, chopped finely
1 tablespoon coarsely chopped fresh coriander
1 egg, beaten lightly

SWEET CHILLI DIPPING SAUCE

¼ cup (60ml) white vinegar
½ cup (110g) caster sugar
½ teaspoon salt
¾ cup (180ml) water
½ small red onion (50g), chopped finely
½ small carrot (35g), chopped finely
½ small lebanese cucumber (65g), seeded, chopped finely
2 tablespoons coarsely chopped fresh coriander
⅓ cup (80ml) sweet chilli sauce

1 Press tofu between two chopping boards or trays, place weight on top; elevate boards slightly to allow tofu liquid to drain away. Stand 20 minutes; chop coarsely. Blend or process tofu until smooth.

2 Preheat oven to 200°C/180°C fan-forced. Line oven tray with baking paper.

3 Combine tofu in medium bowl with rice, paste, onion, coriander and egg. Shape level tablespoons of the tofu mixture into rounds; place on oven tray, press lightly with fork to flatten.

4 Bake, uncovered, 10 minutes or until lightly browned and heated through.

5 Make sweet chilli dipping sauce; serve with tofu cakes.

SWEET CHILLI DIPPING SAUCE place vinegar, sugar, salt and the water in small saucepan; bring to a boil. Boil, stirring, about 2 minutes or until sugar dissolves. Pour vinegar mixture over remaining ingredients in medium heatproof bowl; stir to combine.

MAKES 20
per cake 1.7g total fat (0.3g saturated fat); 325kj (78 cal); 2.8g protein; 12.8g carbohydrate; 0.8g fibre

char-grilled baby octopus salad

PREPARATION TIME 20 MINUTES (PLUS REFRIGERATION TIME) COOKING TIME 10 MINUTES

1kg baby octopus
1 clove garlic, crushed
1 teaspoon grated fresh ginger
2 teaspoons dry sherry
1 teaspoon brown sugar
1 teaspoon malt vinegar
½ teaspoon sesame oil
2 teaspoons kecap manis
2 teaspoons sweet chilli sauce
¼ cup (60ml) tomato sauce
250g cherry tomatoes, halved
1 small red onion (100g), sliced thinly
150g mesclun
2 lebanese cucumbers (260g), seeded, sliced thinly
⅓ cup coarsely chopped fresh coriander

DRESSING

¼ cup (60ml) sweet chilli sauce
1 tablespoon soy sauce
1 clove garlic, crushed
1 tablespoon lime juice

1. Remove and discard heads and beaks from octopus; cut each octopus in half.
2. Combine octopus in large bowl with garlic, ginger, sherry, sugar, vinegar, oil and sauces. Cover; refrigerate 3 hours or overnight.
3. Just before cooking octopus, combine tomato, onion, mesclun, cucumber and coriander in large bowl. Make dressing.
4. Char-grill (or barbecue or pan-fry) undrained octopus mixture, in batches, until browned all over and cooked through. Add octopus to salad bowl with dressing; toss gently to combine.

DRESSING place ingredients in a screw-top jar; shake well.

SERVES 4

per serving 3.8g total fat (0.7g saturated fat); 1014kj (242 cal); 36.5g protein; 14.1g carbohydrate; 4.2g fibre

steamed scallops with asian flavours

PREPARATION TIME 15 MINUTES COOKING TIME 15 MINUTES

3cm piece fresh ginger (15g)
20 scallops (800g), in half shell, roe removed
2 tablespoons thinly sliced fresh lemon grass
4 green onions, sliced thinly
1 tablespoon sesame oil
¼ cup (60ml) kecap manis
¼ cup (60ml) soy sauce

1 Slice ginger thinly; cut slices into thin strips.
2 Place scallops, in batches, in single layer in large bamboo steamer; top with ginger, lemon grass and onion. Steam, covered, about 5 minutes or until scallops are tender and cooked as desired.
3 Divide scallops among serving plates; top with combined oil, kecap manis and sauce.

SERVES 4
per serving 5.2g total fat (0.8g saturated fat); 404kj (97 cal); 10.5g protein; 1.9g carbohydrate; 0.3g fibre
tip you can also use scallops with the roe attached, if you prefer.

chilli scallops

PREPARATION TIME 15 MINUTES COOKING TIME 15 MINUTES

1 tablespoon peanut oil
32 small scallops
4 cloves garlic, sliced thinly
10cm piece fresh ginger (50g), peeled, sliced thinly
2 fresh red thai chillies, chopped finely
3 green onions, sliced thinly
⅓ cup (80ml) sweet chilli sauce
1 teaspoon fish sauce
2 teaspoons brown sugar
½ cup (125ml) chicken stock
¼ cup chopped fresh coriander

1 Heat half of the oil in wok; stir-fry scallops, in batches, until just changed in colour.
2 Heat remaining oil in wok; stir-fry garlic, ginger, chilli and onion until onion is soft. Stir in combined sauces, sugar and stock; bring to a boil. Return scallops to wok; stir until heated through.
3 Serve scallops sprinkled with coriander.

SERVES 4
per serving 6.1g total fat (1.2g saturated fat); 585kj (140 cal); 13.2g protein; 7.9g carbohydrate; 2.2g fibre
tip if you buy scallops in their shell, don't discard the shell – they are great (washed and dried) to use as serving "dishes" for the chilli scallops.

salt and pepper scallops with cherry tomato salsa

PREPARATION TIME 20 MINUTES (PLUS REFRIGERATION TIME) COOKING TIME 10 MINUTES

1kg scallops
2 teaspoons sea salt
½ teaspoon cracked black pepper
2 cloves garlic, crushed
2 teaspoons peanut oil

CHERRY TOMATO SALSA

400g cherry tomatoes, quartered
2 lebanese cucumbers (260g), seeded, chopped finely
1 medium red onion (170g), chopped finely
4 green onions, sliced thinly
2 tablespoons lemon juice
2 fresh small red thai chillies, chopped finely

1 Combine scallops with salt, pepper and garlic in medium bowl; use fingers to sprinkle salt mixture evenly over each scallop. Cover; refrigerate 15 minutes.

2 Heat oil in wok; stir-fry scallops, in batches, until salt-pepper coating is lightly browned and scallops are cooked as desired. Add scallops to cherry tomato salsa; toss gently to combine.

CHERRY TOMATO SALSA combine ingredients in large bowl.

SERVES 4
per serving 4.3g total fat (0.9g saturated fat); 823kj (196 cal); 30.7g protein; 8g carbohydrate; 3.3g fibre

spicy squid salad

PREPARATION TIME 35 MINUTES (PLUS REFRIGERATION TIME) COOKING TIME 15 MINUTES

Mizuna, a mild-tasting, crinkled salad leaf, is usually one of the greens found in mesclun, which can also be used in this recipe.

900g squid hoods
2 tablespoons finely chopped fresh lemon grass
½ cup (125ml) sweet chilli sauce
1 clove garlic, crushed
2 tablespoons peanut oil
¼ cup (60ml) lemon juice
100g mizuna
1 cup (80g) bean sprouts
⅓ cup firmly packed fresh mint leaves
3 medium tomatoes (570g), seeded, chopped finely

1 Cut squid hoods down centre to open out, cut into three triangles; lightly score the inside of each squid triangle in a diagonal pattern. Combine in medium bowl with lemon grass, sauce, garlic, oil and juice. Cover; refrigerate 3 hours or overnight.

2 Drain squid over small saucepan; reserve marinade. Cook squid, in batches, on heated oiled grill plate (or grill or barbecue) until browned all over and cooked through. Cover to keep warm.

3 Meanwhile, place mizuna, sprouts, mint and tomato in large bowl; toss gently to combine. Bring reserved marinade to a boil; boil, uncovered, 1 minute.

4 Serve salad topped with squid; drizzle with hot marinade.

SERVES 6
per serving 8.6g total fat (1.8g saturated fat); 873kj (208 cal); 26.4g protein; 5.8g carbohydrate; 2.5g fibre

salt and pepper scallops with cherry tomato salsa

char-grilled polenta cakes with corn salsa

char-grilled polenta cakes with corn salsa

PREPARATION TIME 15 MINUTES (PLUS REFRIGERATION TIME) COOKING TIME 20 MINUTES

cooking-oil spray
1 litre (4 cups) water
1 teaspoon salt
1 cup (170g) polenta
2 tablespoons wholegrain mustard

CORN SALSA

2 trimmed corn cobs (500g)
1 medium red capsicum (200g), chopped finely
1 medium red onion (170g), chopped finely
1 lebanese cucumber (130g), seeded, chopped finely
¼ cup coarsely chopped fresh flat-leaf parsley
1 teaspoon finely grated lime rind
⅓ cup (80ml) lime juice
2 tablespoons olive oil
3 cloves garlic, crushed
1 tablespoon sweet chilli sauce

1. Lightly spray 23cm-square slab cake pan with cooking-oil spray.
2. Bring the water and salt to a boil in large saucepan. Stir in polenta; cook, stirring, about 10 minutes or until polenta thickens. Stir in mustard until combined; spread polenta into pan. Cover; refrigerate about 30 minutes or until firm.
3. Meanwhile, make corn salsa.
4. Turn polenta onto board; cut into six rectangles. Heat large lightly oiled frying pan; cook polenta, in batches, until browned both sides. Serve polenta cakes with corn salsa. Top with baby rocket, if desired.

CORN SALSA boil, steam or microwave corn until just tender. Drain; cool. Using sharp knife, remove kernels from cob. Combine corn in medium bowl with remaining ingredients.

SERVES 6
per serving 8.2g total fat (1.1g saturated fat); 992kj (237 cal); 6.3g protein; 33.8g carbohydrate; 5.2g fibre
tip you can reduce preparation and cooking times by substituting the fresh corn with a 420g can of drained corn kernels.
serving suggestion serve with a salad of rocket or mixed baby greens.

grilled asparagus, prosciutto and peach salad

PREPARATION TIME 25 MINUTES COOKING TIME 10 MINUTES

3 large peaches (660g)
6 slices prosciutto (90g)
500g asparagus, trimmed
2 tablespoons lemon juice
2 teaspoons extra virgin olive oil
100g mizuna

1. Preheat oven to 220°C/200°C fan-forced.
2. Cut peaches in half, remove seed, cut each half in half again. Cut each slice of prosciutto in half. Wrap peach quarters in prosciutto, place on oven tray; bake, uncovered, about 10 minutes or until prosciutto is crisp.
3. Meanwhile, cook asparagus on heated oiled grill plate (or grill or barbecue) until browned and just tender; drizzle with combined juice and oil.
4. Divide mizuna among serving plates, top with asparagus and prosciutto-wrapped peaches.

SERVES 4
per serving 3.8g total fat (0.8g saturated fat); 466kj (111 cal); 7.8g protein; 10.6g carbohydrate; 3.7g fibre

pureed parsnip and bean soup

PREPARATION TIME 15 MINUTES COOKING TIME 30 MINUTES

Many varieties of already cooked white beans are available canned, among them cannellini, butter and haricot beans; any of theses are suitable for this salad. We used small cannellini beans in this recipe.

2 large parsnips (700g), chopped coarsely
1 cup (250ml) water
1 clove garlic, crushed
20g butter
2 x 400g cans white beans, drained, rinsed
1 litre (4 cups) chicken stock
1 cup (250ml) buttermilk

1 Preheat oven to 220°C/200°C fan-forced.

2 Combine parsnip, the water, garlic and butter in medium baking dish; roast, uncovered, about 15 minutes or until parsnip is tender.

3 Transfer parsnip mixture to large saucepan. Add beans and stock; bring to a boil. Reduce heat, simmer, uncovered, 10 minutes.

4 Blend or process soup, in batches, until smooth. Return soup to same cleaned pan, add buttermilk; stir over low heat until hot.

SERVES 8
per serving 3.7g total fat (2.1g saturated fat); 629kj (150 cal); 8.5g protein; 20.3g carbohydrate; 6.2g fibre
serving suggestion sprinkle soup with finely chopped chives and serve with warmed sourdough bread.

thai fish cakes with noodle salad

PREPARATION TIME 15 MINUTES COOKING TIME 10 MINUTES

⅔ cup loosely packed fresh coriander leaves
½ cup loosely packed fresh mint leaves
4 fresh red thai chillies, quartered
600g firm white fish fillets, chopped coarsely
1 clove garlic, quartered
1 egg white, beaten lightly
250g rice vermicelli
2 teaspoons sugar
¼ cup (60ml) lime juice
1 tablespoon sambal oelek
1 lebanese cucumber (130g), seeded, chopped finely
100g snow peas, sliced thinly

1 Blend or process half of the coriander, half of the mint, half of the chilli, fish, garlic and egg white until mixture forms a paste; using one hand, shape into 12 patties.

2 Cook patties, in batches, in heated large frying pan until browned both sides and cooked through.

3 Meanwhile, place noodles in large heatproof bowl; cover with boiling water. Stand until just tender; drain. Keep warm.

4 Combine sugar, juice and sambal in small saucepan; bring to a boil. Reduce heat, simmer, stirring, until sugar dissolves.

5 Meanwhile, chop remaining coriander, mint and chilli finely. Add to large bowl with noodles, sugar mixture, cucumber and snowpeas; toss to combine.

6 Serve fish cakes on noodle salad.

SERVES 4
per serving 4.4g total fat (1.1g saturated fat); 1567kj (374 cal); 36.7g protein; 45.6g carbohydrate; 3.2g fibre
tip fish cakes can be made ahead and frozen; defrost in refrigerator.
serving suggestion som tum, the thai spicy-sour green pawpaw salad, is a good, low-kilojoule accompaniment to the fish cakes.

tomato and borlotti bean soup

PREPARATION TIME 15 MINUTES COOKING TIME 30 MINUTES

2 medium brown onions (300g), chopped coarsely
2 cloves garlic, crushed
11 large egg tomatoes (1kg), chopped coarsely
2 cups (500ml) chicken stock
1 tablespoon worcestershire sauce
2 tablespoons finely chopped fresh parsley
2 x 400g cans borlotti beans, rinsed, drained

1 Heat oiled large saucepan; cook onion and garlic, stirring, until onion softens. Stir in tomato; cook, stirring, about 3 minutes or until tomato softens. Add stock and sauce to pan, bring to a boil. Reduce heat, simmer, covered, 15 minutes.

2 Blend or process tomato mixture, in batches, until almost smooth. Return tomato mixture to same cleaned pan, stir in parsley and beans; simmer, uncovered, about 5 minutes or until hot.

SERVES 4
per serving 1.4g total fat (0.4g saturated fat); 777kj (186 cal); 13.4g protein; 30.2g carbohydrate; 12.9g fibre

roasted tomato and capsicum soup with tortilla strips

PREPARATION TIME 20 MINUTES COOKING TIME 35 MINUTES

2 large red capsicums (700g)
5 large vine-ripened tomatoes (1.2kg), halved
1 tablespoon olive oil
1 medium brown onion (150g), chopped coarsely
2 cloves garlic, crushed
4 fresh long red chillies, chopped coarsely
2 cups (500ml) water
2 cups (500ml) prepared vegetable stock
2 corn tortillas, cut into 1cm strips
cooking-oil spray
2 tablespoons light sour cream
2 tablespoons finely chopped fresh chives

1 Preheat oven to 240°C/220°C fan-forced. Oil oven trays.

2 Quarter capsicums, discard seeds and membranes. Roast capsicum, skin-side up, and tomato, cut-side up, on oven trays, uncovered, about 15 minutes or until capsicum skin blisters and blackens, and tomato softens. Cover capsicum pieces with plastic or paper for 5 minutes; peel away skin, cover to keep warm. Cool tomato 5 minutes; peel away skin.

3 Heat oil in large saucepan; cook onion, garlic and chilli, stirring, until onion softens. Add capsicum and tomato; cook, stirring, 5 minutes. Add the water and stock; bring to a boil. Reduce heat, simmer, uncovered, 10 minutes.

4 Meanwhile, preheat grill. Place tortilla strips, in single layer, on oiled oven tray; spray with cooking-oil spray. Place under grill until browned lightly and crisp.

5 Blend or process tomato mixture, in batches, until smooth, then pass through food mill (mouli) or fine sieve into large saucepan; discard solids.

6 Divide soup among serving bowls; top with sour cream and chives. Serve with tortilla strips.

SERVES 4
per serving 8.8g total fat (2.4g saturated fat); 816kj (195 cal); 8.5g protein; 19.7g carbohydrate; 6.9g fibre
tip warm any remaining corn tortillas in your microwave oven and serve them with the soup.

chicken-miso broth

PREPARATION TIME 20 MINUTES (PLUS STANDING TIME) COOKING TIME 2 HOURS 10 MINUTES

Udon is available fresh and dried, and these Japanese broad white wheat noodles are similar to the ones in homemade chicken noodle soup. Nori are sheets of paper-thin dried black seaweed used in Japanese cooking as a flavouring, garnish or for sushi; miso, a paste made from cooked, mashed, salted and fermented soy beans, is a common ingredient in soups, sauces and dressings. You can buy these ingredients at Asian food stores and selected supermarkets.

1.5kg chicken bones
5 litres (20 cups) water
2 medium carrots (240g), chopped coarsely
2 trimmed sticks celery (150g), chopped coarsely
4 black peppercorns
2 bay leaves
2 medium brown onions (300g), chopped coarsely
10 dried shiitake mushrooms
¼ cup (65g) white miso paste
50g piece ginger, sliced thinly
¼ cup (60ml) soy sauce
600g fresh udon noodles
1 large carrot (180g), sliced finely, extra
4 green onions, sliced finely
2 sheets toasted nori, sliced finely

1. Combine bones, the water, carrot, celery, peppercorns, bay leaves and brown onion in large saucepan; bring to a boil. Reduce heat, simmer, uncovered, 2 hours; strain through muslin-lined strainer into large bowl. Reserve stock; discard bones and vegetables.
2. Meanwhile, place mushrooms in medium heatproof bowl; cover with boiling water. Stand about 20 minutes or until just tender; drain. Discard stems; slice caps thinly.
3. Bring stock to a boil. Add miso, ginger and sauce; simmer, uncovered, 5 minutes.
4. Just before serving, stir noodles and mushroom into broth; simmer, uncovered, until noodles are just tender. Stir in extra carrot and green onion; sprinkle with nori.

SERVES 6
per serving 2g total fat (0.3g saturated fat); 1339kj (320 cal); 13.2g protein; 61.8g carbohydrate; 6.7g fibre
tips chicken stock can be made a day ahead. Store, covered, in refrigerator. You can also freeze stock for up to six months; store in 1- or 2-cup portions, then thaw only the amount you need for other soups and casseroles.
Dried udon, boiled until tender, can be used, but the cooking time will be longer.
serving suggestion serve with vegetable and prawn tempura.

pea and potato soup

PREPARATION TIME 10 MINUTES COOKING TIME 30 MINUTES (PLUS COOLING TIME)

Leek and potato are natural allies when teamed in a satisfying soup. Take care to wash the leeks well under cold water to remove any grit.

3 cups (750ml) chicken stock
2 medium leeks (700g), sliced thinly
1 clove garlic, crushed
2 medium potatoes (400g), chopped coarsely
4 cups (500g) frozen peas
3 cups (750ml) water
2 tablespoons finely shredded fresh mint leaves

1 Heat 2 tablespoons of the stock in large saucepan, add leek and garlic; cook, stirring, about 10 minutes or until leek is soft.

2 Add remaining stock, potato, peas and the water to pan; bring to a boil. Reduce heat, simmer, covered, about 15 minutes or until vegetables are tender. Cool 10 minutes.

3 Blend or process soup, in batches, until smooth. Return soup to same cleaned pan; stir over heat until hot. Stir in mint just before serving.

SERVES 4
per serving 1.8g total fat (0.4g saturated fat); 746kj (178 cal); 13.6g protein; 26.7g carbohydrate; 12g fibre
serving suggestion herb scones or damper make a good accompaniment to this soup.

carrot and lentil soup with caraway toast

PREPARATION TIME 20 MINUTES COOKING TIME 1 HOUR

1.125 litres (4½ cups) vegetable stock
2 large (400g) brown onions, chopped finely
2 cloves garlic, crushed
1 tablespoon ground cumin
6 large carrots (1kg), chopped coarsely
2 sticks celery, chopped coarsely
2 cups (500ml) water
½ cup (100g) brown lentils
8 slices ciabatta bread (200g)
⅓ cup (25g) finely grated parmesan cheese
2 cloves garlic, crushed, extra
1 teaspoon caraway seeds
2 tablespoons finely chopped fresh parsley
½ cup (125ml) buttermilk

1 Heat ½ cup of the stock in large saucepan, add onion, garlic and cumin; cook, stirring, until onion softens. Add carrot and celery; cook, stirring, 5 minutes. Add remaining stock and water, bring to a boil. Reduce heat, simmer, uncovered, about 20 minutes or until carrot softens.

2 Blend or process soup, in batches, until smooth. Return soup to same pan; add lentils, simmer, uncovered, about 20 minutes or until lentils are tender. [Can be made ahead to this stage. Cover, refrigerate until required.]

3 Preheat grill. Place ciabatta, in single layer, on oven tray; toast under grill until browned. Sprinkle combined cheese, extra garlic, seeds and parsley over untoasted sides of ciabatta; grill until topping is browned lightly and cheese is melted. Cut in half.

4 Stir buttermilk into hot soup; serve with caraway toast.

SERVES 4
per serving 6g total fat (2.6g saturated fat); 1479kj (353 cal); 20.7g protein; 53.9g carbohydrate; 13.9g fibre

lentil and spinach soup

PREPARATION TIME 15 MINUTES COOKING TIME 20 MINUTES

2 tablespoons peanut oil
2 large brown onions (400g), chopped finely
2 cloves garlic, crushed
2 teaspoons ground cumin
1 teaspoon ground turmeric
1 teaspoon ground coriander
3 cups (600g) red lentils
1.25 litres (5 cups) chicken stock
1 litre (4 cups) water
500g spinach, trimmed, chopped finely

1. Heat oil in large saucepan; cook onion and garlic, stirring, until onion is soft. Add spices; cook, stirring, until fragrant.
2. Add lentils to pan; stir to combine with spice mixture. Add stock and the water; bring to a boil. Reduce heat, simmer, uncovered, about 20 minutes or until lentils are tender.
3. Blend or process soup, in batches, until smooth. Return soup to same cleaned pan, add spinach; stir over heat until hot.

SERVES 8
per serving 6.9g total fat (1.4g saturated fat); 1131kj (270 cal); 21.5g protein; 32.6g carbohydrate; 11.9g fibre

lentil vegetable soup

PREPARATION TIME 15 MINUTES COOKING TIME 30 MINUTES

1 teaspoon olive oil
1 clove garlic, crushed
1 small brown onion (80g), chopped finely
2 small carrots (140g), chopped finely
2 trimmed sticks celery (150g), chopped finely
½ cup (100g) red lentils
1½ cups (375ml) water
1½ cups (375ml) chicken stock
1 bay leaf
½ x 410g can tomatoes
2 teaspoons tomato paste
1 tablespoon finely chopped fresh parsley

1. Heat oil in large saucepan; cook garlic, onion, carrot and celery, until onion is soft.
2. Stir in lentils, the water, stock, bay leaf, undrained crushed tomatoes and paste; bring to a boil. Reduce heat, simmer, covered, for about 20 minutes or until lentils are soft.
3. Discard bay leaf. Sprinkle with parsley just before serving.

SERVES 2
per serving 4.5g total fat (0.9g saturated fat); 952kj (227 cal); 16.8g protein; 31.2g carbohydrate; 12.1g fibre
store soup can be made 2 days ahead and refrigerated, covered, or frozen.

pumpkin soup

PREPARATION TIME 20 MINUTES COOKING TIME 35 MINUTES

40g butter

1 large brown onion (200g), chopped coarsely

3 bacon rashers (210g), chopped coarsely

1.5kg pumpkin, chopped coarsely

2 large potatoes (600g), chopped coarsely

1.5 litres (6 cups) chicken stock

1. Melt butter in large saucepan; cook onion and bacon, stirring, until onion softens. Stir in pumpkin, potato and stock; bring to a boil. Reduce heat, simmer, uncovered, about 20 minutes or until pumpkin is soft.
2. Blend or process soup, in batches, until pureed. Return to same cleaned pan; stir until heated through.

SERVES 6

per serving 8.6g total fat (5.1g saturated fat); 1050kj (251 cal); 14.7g protein; 28.5g carbohydrate; 4.3g fibre

tip the smoothest consistency for this soup can be achieved by using a blender, stab mixer or mouli.

lamb and spinach soup with risoni

PREPARATION TIME 20 MINUTES COOKING TIME 40 MINUTES

½ cup (110g) risoni pasta

1 large red capsicum (350g)

cooking-oil spray

350g lean lamb fillets, sliced thinly

½ cup (125ml) water

1 small leek (200g), sliced

2 cloves garlic, crushed

1 teaspoon chopped fresh rosemary

1 tablespoon no-salt tomato paste

1½ cups (375ml) vegetable stock

1.5 litres (6 cups) water, extra

1 chicken stock cube

1 small zucchini (90g), halved, sliced

4 silverbeet leaves (320g), shredded

1. Cook risoni in large saucepan of boiling water, uncovered, until just tender; drain.
2. Quarter capsicums; remove and discard seeds and membranes. Roast under grill or in very hot oven, skin-side up, until skin blisters and blackens; cover capsicum pieces with plastic or paper 5 minutes. Peel away skin; cut capsicum into 1cm strips.
3. Coat large saucepan with cooking-oil spray; cook lamb, in batches, until browned all over.
4. Place water, leek, garlic and rosemary in same pan; cook, stirring, until almost all the water has evaporated. Add paste, stock, extra water and crumbled stock cube; boil, uncovered, 10 minutes. Reduce heat, simmer, covered, 10 minutes.
5. Return lamb to pan, add zucchini; simmer, covered, until zucchini is tender. Add silverbeet, risoni and capsicum, stir until hot.

SERVES 6

per serving 3.5g total fat (1.2g saturated fat); 735kj (176 cal); 18.1g protein; 17.6g carbohydrate; 4.4g fibre

tip recipe can be made a day ahead. Store, covered, in refrigerator.

kumara and coriander soup

PREPARATION TIME 10 MINUTES COOKING TIME 35 MINUTES

1 teaspoon peanut oil
2 medium leeks (700g), chopped coarsely
3 cloves garlic, quartered
2 medium kumara (800g), chopped coarsely
1 litre (4 cups) chicken stock
⅔ cup (160ml) light evaporated milk
⅓ cup finely chopped fresh coriander

1. Heat oil in large saucepan; cook leek and garlic, stirring, until leek softens. Add kumara and stock; bring to a boil. Reduce heat, simmer, covered, about 15 minutes or until kumara softens.
2. Blend or process soup, in batches, until smooth. Return to same cleaned pan. Simmer, uncovered, until soup thickens slightly.
3. Stir in evaporated milk and coriander; stir over heat, without boiling, until heated through. Top with fresh coriander leaves, if desired.

SERVES 4
per serving 2.9g total fat (0.8g saturated fat); 880kj (210 cal); 11.7g protein; 34.6g carbohydrate; 6.8g fibre
tip the smoothest consistency for this soup will be achieved by using a blender, stab mixer or mouli.

minted lamb and vermicelli soup

PREPARATION TIME 10 MINUTES COOKING TIME 25 MINUTES

100g bean thread vermicelli
1 tablespoon peanut oil
600g lamb fillets, sliced thinly
2 teaspoons bottled chopped chilli
2 tablespoons finely chopped fresh lemon grass
2 tablespoons grated fresh ginger
4 cloves garlic, crushed
⅓ cup (80ml) fish sauce
1.5 litres (6 cups) chicken stock
1 tablespoon sugar
500g asparagus, trimmed, chopped
¼ cup chopped fresh coriander leaves
⅓ cup chopped fresh mint leaves
8 green onions, chopped finely
4 medium tomatoes (760g), seeded, sliced

1. Place vermicelli in large heatproof bowl, cover with boiling water, stand until just tender; drain.
2. Meanwhile, heat half of the oil in large saucepan; cook lamb, in batches, until browned all over.
3. Heat remaining oil in same pan; cook chilli, lemon grass, ginger and garlic, stirring, until fragrant. Add sauce, stock and sugar; cook, stirring, until mixture boils. Add asparagus; simmer, uncovered, until asparagus is just tender. Add herbs, onion, tomato, vermicelli and lamb; stir until soup is hot.

SERVES 6
per serving 8g total fat (2.7g saturated fat); 983kj (235 cal); 28.1g protein; 12.5g carbohydrate; 3.1g fibre

mussel chowder

PREPARATION TIME 20 MINUTES COOKING TIME 30 MINUTES

The name chowder came from the French word, chaudière, for the cauldron in which fishermen made their stews fresh from the sea. The Americans adopted this thick chunky soup as their own – New England chowders are made with milk or cream, while in Manhattan they use tomatoes for the base.

1kg mussels

1 teaspoon olive oil

1 small leek (200g), sliced thinly

2 large potatoes (600g), chopped finely

2 trimmed sticks celery (150g), chopped finely

½ cup (125ml) dry white wine

2 cups (500ml) fish stock

2 cups (500ml) water

30g butter

2 tablespoons plain flour

1 cup (250ml) skim milk

1 tablespoon finely chopped fresh flat-leaf parsley

1 tablespoon finely chopped fresh chives

1. Scrub mussels under cold running water; remove beards.
2. Heat oil in large saucepan; cook leek, potato and celery, stirring, until leek softens. Add wine; boil, uncovered, until wine reduces by half. Add stock and the water; bring to a boil. Reduce heat, simmer, uncovered, about 20 minutes or until potato is tender.
3. Meanwhile, melt butter in small saucepan; cook flour, stirring, 1 minute. Add milk; bring to a boil. Reduce heat, simmer, stirring, until sauce thickens.
4. Blend or process half of the chowder mixture, in batches, until smooth. Return to pan with remaining chowder; stir in sauce.
5. Add mussels to pan; bring to a boil. Reduce heat; simmer chowder, covered, about 5 minutes or until all mussels open (discard any that do not). Serve in bowls; sprinkle with herbs.

SERVES 6
per serving 5.9g total fat (3.1g saturated fat); 773kj (184 cal); 9.5g protein; 19.6g carbohydrate; 2.6g fibre
serving suggestion serve with a warm baguette, sliced, for dunking in the soup.

spicy seafood bouillabaisse

PREPARATION TIME 40 MINUTES COOKING TIME 30 MINUTES

500g boneless white fish fillets
300g medium uncooked prawns
16 small mussels (230g)
½ teaspoon olive oil
4 medium tomatoes (520g), peeled, chopped roughly
1 large red onion (300g), sliced
2 cloves garlic, crushed
2 fresh small red chillies, chopped finely
⅓ cup (65g) basmati rice
10cm strip orange rind
2 cups (500ml) fish stock
2 cups (500ml) water
1 cup (250ml) dry white wine
pinch saffron powder
1 tablespoon chopped fresh dill

1 Cut fish into 5cm pieces. Shell and devein prawns, leaving heads and tails intact. Scrub mussels under cold running water; remove beards.

2 Heat oil in large saucepan; cook tomatoes, onion, garlic and chillies, stirring, about 5 minutes or until onion is soft.

3 Add rice to pan with rind, stock, water, wine and saffron; boil, uncovered, stirring occasionally, about 10 minutes or until rice is tender.

4 Add fish and prawns, simmer, uncovered, about 3 minutes or until seafood is almost tender. Add mussels and dill; cook, covered, about 2 minutes or until mussels open (discard any that do not). Discard orange rind.

SERVES 6
per serving 3g total fat (0.7g saturated fat); 1055kj (252 cal); 31.3g protein; 17.5g carbohydrate; 3g fibre
tip recipe best made just before serving.

scallop mousse ravioli in star anise broth

PREPARATION TIME 40 MINUTES COOKING TIME 20 MINTUES

80g dried egg noodles
300g scallops, roe removed
2 tablespoons coarsely chopped fresh coriander
2 teaspoons finely chopped fresh lemon grass
1cm piece fresh ginger (5g), grated coarsely
2 tablespoons fish sauce
2 egg whites
1 litre (4 cups) chicken stock
1½ cups (375ml) fish stock
2 star anise
40 wonton wrappers
1 green onion
1 tablespoon drained sliced pink pickled ginger
1 fresh red thai chilli, sliced finely
⅓ cup firmly packed coriander leaves

1. Cook noodles in medium saucepan of boiling water until just tender; drain. Using kitchen scissors, chop noodles into random lengths; reserve.
2. Blend or process scallops, chopped coriander, lemon grass, fresh ginger, sauce and egg whites until mixture forms a smooth paste.
3. Bring stocks and star anise to a boil in large saucepan. Reduce heat, simmer, covered, while making ravioli.
4. Place a level tablespoon of the scallop mixture in centre of one wrapper; brush around edges with water. Top with another wrapper; press edges together to seal. Repeat process with remaining wrappers and filling to make 20 ravioli in total.
5. Trim onion; cut crossways into quarters, cut each quarter lengthways into thin strips. Cut pickled ginger slices into thin strips. Divide onion, pickled ginger, noodles, chilli and coriander leaves among soup bowls.
6. Cook ravioli, in two batches, in same cleaned medium saucepan of boiling water, uncovered, until ravioli float to the surface and are cooked through. Drain; divide among serving bowls. Discard star anise from hot stock; ladle over ravioli.

SERVES 4
per serving 3.4g total fat (1.1g saturated fat); 1352kj (323 cal); 23.4g protein; 48.9g carbohydrate; 2.8g fibre

fish and fennel soup

PREPARATION TIME 30 MINUTES COOKING TIME 35 MINUTES

We used ling here, but you can use any fish you like as long as it's firm enough not to break up during cooking.

1 tablespoon olive oil
1 large brown onion (200g), chopped coarsely
1 medium fennel bulb (300g), trimmed, chopped coarsely
2 cloves garlic, crushed
3 cups (750ml) fish stock
1 cup (250ml) dry white wine
6 medium tomatoes (900g), peeled, chopped finely
500g firm white fish fillets
¼ cup coarsely chopped fresh flat-leaf parsley

1 Heat oil in medium saucepan; cook onion, fennel and garlic, stirring occasionally, until vegetables soften. Add stock, wine and about two-thirds of the tomato; bring to a boil. Reduce heat, simmer soup, uncovered, stirring occasionally, 10 minutes.

2 Add fish to soup; simmer, covered, about 15 minutes or until cooked through. Remove fish from soup; flake fish with fork, divide among serving bowls.

3 Blend or process soup, in batches, until smooth. Reheat soup in same cleaned pan; stir in parsley. Ladle soup into serving bowls, over fish; top with remaining tomato.

SERVES 4
per serving 8g total fat (1.7g saturated fat); 1178kj (281 cal); 31.3g protein; 9.9g carbohydrate; 5g fibre

tofu in miso broth

PREPARATION TIME 10 MINUTES COOKING TIME 15 MINUTES

Wakame is a bright green lobe-leafed seaweed used in Japanese soups and salads. Miso is fermented soybean paste. White miso is a sweet variety used in salad dressings, sauces and soups. Red miso is saltier, often quite bitter in taste and popular for winter soups. Japanese pepper is also known as sansho.

1½ teaspoons dashi granules
1.25 litres (5 cups) boiling water
3½ tablespoons white miso paste
2 tablespoons red miso paste
1 tablespoon light soy sauce
1 tablespoon sake
150g firm tofu
30g fresh wakame
6 fresh shiitake mushrooms, sliced thinly
½ teaspoon japanese pepper
3 green onions, sliced thinly
1 teaspoon drained pickled ginger, sliced thinly

1 Combine granules and the water in large heatproof bowl; stir until dissolved. Combine miso pastes and ⅔ cup (160ml) of the hot stock in small heatproof bowl; stir until blended.

2 Simmer remaining stock in medium saucepan with sauce and sake; stir in miso mixture. Do not boil; remove from heat as soon as hot.

3 Cut tofu into 1cm cubes. Divide wakame, mushrooms, pepper and tofu evenly among serving bowls. Ladle broth into serving bowls; sprinkle with equal amounts of onion and ginger.

SERVES 4
per serving 4.7g total fat (0.7g saturated fat); 483kj (115 cal); 9.6g protein; 9g carbohydrate; 4g fibre
tip boiling the stock after miso has been added will give this soup an unappetising, cloudy appearance.
serving suggestion sushi would be a good appetiser to serve before this soup.

udon soup

PREPARATION TIME 10 MINUTES COOKING TIME 10 MINUTES

400g fresh udon noodles
1.5 litres (6 cups) water
1½ teaspoons instant dashi
400g chicken breast fillets, sliced thinly
100g oyster mushrooms, halved
300g baby buk choy, chopped coarsely
1 cup (80g) bean sprouts
1 tablespoon light soy sauce
2 green onions, sliced thinly

1 Rinse noodles under hot water; drain. Transfer to large bowl; separate noodles with fork.

2 Combine the water and dashi in large saucepan; bring to a boil. Add chicken; simmer, uncovered, until chicken is cooked through.

3 Add noodles to pan with mushrooms, buk choy, sprouts and sauce; bring to a boil. Reduce heat; simmer, uncovered, until buk choy just wilts. Sprinkle with onion to serve.

SERVES 4
per serving 3.8g total fat (0.9g saturated fat); 1645kj (393 cal); 34.8g protein; 53.7g carbohydrate; 4.7g fibre
tip udon noodles are available either fresh or dried; these broad Japanese wheat noodles are similar to the ones in homemade chicken noodle soup. You can substitute your favourite noodles, but be sure to check the manufacturer's instructions regarding their preparation.

gazpacho

PREPARATION TIME 25 MINUTES (PLUS REFRIGERATION TIME)

3 cups (750ml) tomato juice
8 medium egg tomatoes (600g), chopped coarsely
1 medium red onion (170g), chopped coarsely
1 clove garlic, quartered
1 lebanese cucumber (130g), chopped coarsely
1 small red capsicum (150g), chopped coarsely
2 teaspoons tabasco
4 green onions, chopped finely
½ lebanese cucumber (65g), extra, seeded, chopped finely
½ small yellow capsicum (75g), chopped finely
2 teaspoons olive oil
1 tablespoon vodka
2 tablespoons finely chopped fresh coriander

1 Blend or process juice, tomato, onion, garlic, coarsely chopped cucumber and red capsicum, in batches, until pureed. Strain through sieve into large bowl, cover; refrigerate 3 hours.

2 Combine remaining ingredients in small bowl. Divide soup among serving bowls; top with vegetable mixture.

SERVES 4
per serving 2.6g total fat (0.3g saturated fat); 517kj (123 cal); 4.7g protein; 17.1g carbohydrate; 5.1g fibre
tip gazpacho can be made a day ahead. Store, covered, in refrigerator.

vietnamese prawn soup

PREPARATION TIME 30 MINUTES COOKING TIME 25 MINUTES

12 uncooked medium king prawns (540g)
4cm piece fresh ginger (20g), sliced thinly
1 teaspoon black peppercorns
2 cloves garlic, crushed
2 fresh long red chillies, sliced thinly
10cm stick (20g) fresh lemon grass, chopped coarsely
3 litres (12 cups) water
400g fresh rice noodles
¼ cup (60ml) lemon juice
⅓ cup (80ml) fish sauce, approximately
2 green onions, sliced thinly
⅓ cup firmly packed fresh coriander leaves
¼ cup firmly packed fresh mint leaves

1. Peel and devein prawns; discard heads. Place prawn shells, ginger, peppercorns, garlic, half of the chilli, lemon grass and the water in large saucepan. Bring to a boil, reduce heat; simmer, uncovered, 20 minutes. Strain stock, discard solids, then return liquid to clean saucepan.
2. Add prawns to stock; simmer, covered, until prawns have changed colour.
3. Meanwhile, pour boiling water over rice noodles in medium bowl; drain well.
4. Add juice to stock; gradually add sauce to taste. Divide prawns and noodles evenly among serving bowls; top with stock, green onion, herbs and remaining chilli.

SERVES 6
per serving 0.7g total fat (0.1g saturated fat); 508kj (121 cal); 11.9g protein; 16g carbohydrate; 1.4g fibre

meatball pho

PREPARATION TIME 20 MINUTES COOKING TIME 15 MINUTES

Pho, the well-known Vietnamese noodle soup, is usually eaten for breakfast – but we like to eat it at any time of the day.

400g lean beef mince
2 tablespoons finely chopped fresh lemon grass
2 green onions, chopped finely
1 clove garlic, crushed
1 egg white
1½ litres (6 cups) beef stock
2 star anise
1 stick cinnamon
185g dried rice stick noodles
1 cup (80g) bean sprouts
1 cup loosely packed fresh coriander leaves
2 fresh long red chillies, sliced thinly
4 green onions, extra, sliced thinly

1 Using hand, combine beef, lemon grass, chopped onion, garlic and egg white in medium bowl; roll level tablespoons of the mixture into balls.

2 Heat stock, star anise and cinnamon in large saucepan; bring to a boil. Reduce heat, simmer, uncovered, 5 minutes. Add meatballs; return to a boil. Reduce heat, simmer, uncovered, about 5 minutes or until meatballs are cooked through. Discard star anise and cinnamon from pan.

3 Meanwhile, place noodles in large heatproof bowl, cover with boiling water, stand until just tender; drain.

4 Divide noodles, meatballs and stock among serving bowls; top with combined sprouts, coriander, chilli and sliced onion. Serve with lime wedges, if desired.

SERVES 4
per serving 8.4g total fat (3.3g saturated fat); 1387kj (331 cal); 29.8g protein; 33.5g carbohydrate; 2.7g fibre

hot and sour soup

PREPARATION TIME 10 MINUTES COOKING TIME 15 MINUTES

2cm piece fresh galangal (10g), chopped coarsely
10cm stick (20g) fresh lemon grass, chopped coarsely
2 green onions, chopped coarsely
3 kaffir lime leaves
1 clove garlic, quartered
2 teaspoons peanut oil
1½ cups (375ml) vegetable stock
1.125 litres (4½ cups) water
2cm piece fresh ginger (10g), sliced thinly
2 fresh red thai chillies, sliced thinly
425g canned straw mushrooms, drained, rinsed
2 teaspoons sugar
⅓ cup (80ml) lime juice
2 teaspoons soy sauce
2 tablespoons coarsely chopped fresh coriander

1. Blend or process galangal, lemon grass, onion, lime leaves and garlic until chopped finely.
2. Heat oil in large saucepan; cook galangal mixture, stirring, until fragrant.
3. Add stock and the water to pan; bring to a boil. Reduce heat, simmer, covered, 10 minutes. Strain stock mixture into large bowl; discard solids. Return stock mixture to same pan.
4. Return stock mixture to heat, add ginger, chilli, mushrooms, sugar, juice and sauce; cook, uncovered, until hot. Just before serving, stir coriander through soup.

SERVES 4
per serving 3g total fat (0.6g saturated fat); 242kj (58 cal); 3.6g protein; 3.6g carbohydrate; 2.5g fibre
tips for a milder flavour, remove seeds from the chillies. Straw mushrooms are usually sold canned in brine – canned champignons or fresh baby button mushrooms can be substituted.
The broth can be made ahead and frozen until required.
serving suggestion accompany soup with jasmine rice and wilted asian greens.

chicken and corn soup

PREPARATION TIME 10 MINUTES COOKING TIME 20 MINUTES

2 teaspoons peanut oil
2 green onions, sliced thinly
1 clove garlic, crushed
1 litre (4 cups) chicken stock
1 litre (4 cups) water
170g chicken breast fillets, chopped finely
310g can creamed corn
310g can corn kernels
1 tablespoon cornflour
¼ cup (60ml) water, extra
1 egg, beaten lightly

1. Heat oil in large saucepan; cook onion and garlic, stirring constantly, until onion softens.
2. Add stock and the water to onion mixture; bring to a boil. Reduce heat, add chicken; simmer, uncovered, about 5 minutes or until chicken is cooked through.
3. Add creamed corn and kernels, and cornflour blended with the extra water; cook, stirring, until mixture boils and thickens slightly. Gradually add egg, in a thin stream, to simmering soup.

SERVES 4
per serving 6.8g total fat (1.7g saturated fat); 1008kj (241 cal); 18.1g protein; 26.8g carbohydrate; 5.5g fibre

hot and sour soup

chunky vegetable and pasta soup

chunky vegetable and pasta soup

PREPARATION TIME 15 MINUTES COOKING TIME 20 MINUTES

1 tablespoon olive oil
2 medium brown onions (300g), chopped finely
2 cloves garlic, crushed
4 trimmed celery stalks (400g), chopped finely
2 medium carrots (240g), chopped finely
410g can tomato puree
⅓ cup (90g) tomato paste
420g can red kidney beans, rinsed, drained
3 litres (12 cups) chicken stock
500g penne pasta
¼ cup finely chopped fresh flat-leaf parsley

1. Heat oil in large saucepan; cook onion, garlic, celery and carrot, stirring, until onion softens.
2. Stir in puree and paste to pan with beans and stock; bring to a boil. Add pasta; boil, uncovered, until pasta is tender. Serve sprinkled with parsley.

SERVES 6
per serving 6.5g total fat (1.6g saturated fat); 1942kj (464 cal); 20.8g protein; 79.3g carbohydrate; 12.1g fibre
tip the pasta will absorb the liquid as it stands. If preparing ahead, more stock may need to be added on reheating.

pea and ham soup with sourdough croutons

PREPARATION TIME 35 MINUTES COOKING TIME 2 HOURS

2 thick slices sourdough bread
cooking-oil spray
800g ham hock
2 cups (400g) green split peas
2 medium brown onions (300g), chopped finely
2 medium potatoes (400g), chopped coarsely
2.5 litres (10 cups) cold water
2 cups (250g) frozen peas
1 cup (250ml) water, extra

1. Preheat oven to 220°C/200°C fan-forced. Coat baking dish with cooking-oil spray.
2. Cut bread into large cubes, place in baking dish; coat with cooking-oil spray. Bake, uncovered, turning occasionally, about 10 minutes or until crisp; cool. [Can be made ahead to this stage. Store cold croutons in an airtight container.]
3. Remove and discard rind and fat from hock. Rinse split peas under cold water until water runs clear; drain.
4. Heat oiled large saucepan; cook onion, stirring, about 2 minutes or until soft. Add hock, split peas and potato; cook, stirring, 2 minutes. Add water, bring to a boil; simmer, covered, skimming surface occasionally, 1½ hours.
5. Remove hock from soup, shred half the ham. Discard hock; keep remaining ham for another purpose. Stir frozen peas into hot soup, cook, covered, about 5 minutes or until peas have softened. Blend or process soup, in batches, until smooth. Return to same pan, stir in shredded ham and extra water, bring to a boil; simmer, covered, 5 minutes. Serve with sourdough croutons.

SERVES 4
per serving 7.5g total fat (1.8g saturated fat); 2371kj (566 cal); 48.9g protein; 75.8g carbohydrate; 18g fibre

combination wonton soup

PREPARATION TIME 30 MINUTES COOKING TIME 10 MINUTES

150g chicken mince
1 green onion, sliced thinly
2 tablespoons light soy sauce
16 wonton wrappers
24 uncooked medium prawns (600g)
1.5 litres (6 cups) chicken stock
100g chinese barbecued pork, sliced thinly
100g fresh shiitake mushrooms, sliced thinly
150g baby buk choy, chopped coarsely
4 green onions, sliced thinly, extra

1 Combine chicken, onion and half of the sauce in small bowl. Place heaped teaspoons of chicken mixture in centre of each wonton wrapper; brush edges with a little water, pinch edges together to seal.
2 Shell and devein prawns, leaving tails intact.
3 Bring stock to a boil in large saucepan, add wontons; cook, uncovered, about 3 minutes or until wontons are just cooked through. Add prawns, remaining sauce, pork and mushrooms; cook, uncovered, until prawns just change colour. Add buk choy and extra onion; cook, uncovered, until buk choy just wilts.

SERVES 4
per serving 9.5g total fat (3.4g saturated fat); 1265kj (302 cal); 36.4g protein; 17.5g carbohydrate; 2.7g fibre
tip uncooked wontons are suitable to freeze for up to three months. You don't have to defrost them; just remove them from the freezer and simmer in stock until cooked through.

chicken broth with rice noodles

PREPARATION TIME 15 MINUTES COOKING TIME 25 MINUTES (PLUS COOLING TIME)

You'll find a version of this popular soup in most Asian cuisines; this one has a Thai accent.

1.5 litres (6 cups) chicken stock
2 cups (500ml) water
50g piece ginger, sliced thinly
350g chicken breast fillets
500g fresh rice noodles
¼ cup (60ml) lime juice
1 tablespoon fish sauce
4 green onions, chopped coarsely
2 fresh red thai chillies, sliced thinly
2 tablespoons coarsely chopped fresh coriander leaves
1 cup (80g) bean sprouts

1 Bring stock, the water and ginger to a boil in large saucepan. Add chicken, return to a boil. Reduce heat, simmer, covered, about 15 minutes or until chicken is cooked through. Remove chicken; cool 10 minutes, then shred coarsely.
2 Return broth mixture to a boil; add noodles, juice and sauce. Reduce heat, simmer, stirring, until noodles are just tender.
3 Add chicken and remaining ingredients to broth; stir over heat until hot.

SERVES 4
per serving 4.6g total fat (1.3g saturated fat); 1631kj (390 cal); 30.1g protein; 55.6g carbohydrate; 2.6g fibre
tips coarsely chopped leafy green asian vegetables, such as choy sum or water spinach, can be added to this broth.
Dried rice noodles, or the thicker rice stick noodles, can be substituted for fresh noodles; they need to be soaked in boiling water for about 5 minutes and drained before being added to the stock.
serving suggestion serve with wedges of lime and follow with a selection of tropical fruit.

chicken wonton soup

PREPARATION TIME 20 MINUTES (PLUS REFRIGERATION TIME) COOKING TIME 2 HOURS 10 MINUTES

The wontons in this southern Chinese speciality make the soup short as distinct from long soup which contains noodles.

2kg chicken bones
2 medium brown onions (300g), chopped coarsely
2 trimmed sticks celery (150g), chopped coarsely
2 medium carrots (240g), chopped coarsely
3 bay leaves
2 teaspoons black peppercorns
5 litres (20 cups) water
2 tablespoons dark soy sauce
1 clove garlic, crushed
1 teaspoon grated fresh ginger
500g baby buk choy, chopped coarsely
2 green onions, sliced thinly

CHICKEN WONTONS

300g chicken mince
1 tablespoon dark soy sauce
1 clove garlic, crushed
1 teaspoon sesame oil
4 green onions, chopped finely
40 wonton wrappers

1. Combine bones, brown onion, celery, carrot, bay leaves, peppercorns and the water in large saucepan; bring to a boil. Reduce heat, simmer, uncovered, 2 hours, skimming occasionally.
2. Strain stock through muslin-lined strainer into large bowl; discard bones and other solids. Cover stock; refrigerate 3 hours or overnight.
3. Make chicken wontons.
4. Remove and discard fat from surface of stock. Return stock to large saucepan with sauce, garlic and ginger; bring to a boil. Reduce heat, add chicken wontons; simmer, uncovered, about 5 minutes or until wontons float to surface. Just before serving soup, stir in remaining ingredients.

CHICKEN WONTONS combine chicken, sauce, garlic, oil and onion in medium bowl. Brush edge of each wonton wrapper with water. Place rounded teaspoon of chicken mixture in centre of wrapper; pinch edges together to seal. Repeat with remaining wrappers and chicken mixture.

SERVES 8
per serving 4.6g total fat (1.2g saturated fat); 772kj (184 cal); 12.5g protein; 22.8g carbohydrate; 3.7g fibre
tip stock and wontons can be made in advance and frozen, separately.
serving suggestion accompany with a mixture of finely chopped fresh red thai chillies, coriander and mint.

mains
seafood

seafood skewers with radicchio and fennel salad

PREPARATION TIME 25 MINUTES (PLUS REFRIGERATION TIME) COOKING TIME 10 MINUTES

You will need to soak 8 bamboo skewers in water for at least an hour before use to prevent splintering and scorching. Any firm white fish fillet, such as ling or blue-eye, can be used in this recipe.

8 uncooked large king prawns (560g)
8 cleaned baby octopus (720g)
400g firm white fish fillets
8 scallops (200g), roe removed
2 teaspoons fennel seeds
2 teaspoons dried green peppercorns
2 tablespoons white wine vinegar
2 cloves garlic, crushed
1 tablespoon olive oil
2 medium radicchio (400g)
2 small fennel (400g), trimmed, sliced thinly
1 cup firmly packed fresh flat-leaf parsley leaves

MUSTARD DRESSING
¼ cup (60ml) white wine vinegar
½ teaspoon mustard powder
1 tablespoon olive oil
1 teaspoon sugar
4 green onions, chopped coarsely

1 Shell and devein prawns, leaving tails intact. Remove heads and beaks from octopus. Cut fish into 2.5cm pieces. Combine seafood in large bowl.

2 Using mortar and pestle, coarsely crush seeds and peppercorns, add to seafood with vinegar, garlic and oil; toss gently to combine. Cover; refrigerate 3 hours or overnight.

3 Make mustard dressing.

4 Thread seafood, alternating varieties, on skewers; cook on heated lightly oiled grill plate (or grill or barbecue) until seafood is just changed in colour and cooked as desired.

5 Meanwhile, discard dark outer leaves of radicchio, tear inner leaves roughly. Place radicchio in medium bowl with fennel, parsley and dressing; toss gently to combine. Serve seafood skewers on salad.

MUSTARD DRESSING place ingredients in screw-top jar; shake well.

SERVES 4
per serving 13.8g total fat (2.2g saturated fat); 2019kj (483 cal); 82.1g protein; 5.7g carbohydrate; 5g fibre
tip use green peppercorns in brine if you can't find the dried variety; rinse then drain them thoroughly before using.

stir-fried seafood with asian greens

PREPARATION TIME 20 MINUTES COOKING TIME 20 MINUTES

20 uncooked medium prawns (500g)
500g squid hoods
500g firm white fish fillets
1 tablespoon peanut oil
5 green onions, chopped coarsely
2 cloves garlic, sliced thinly
10cm piece fresh ginger (50g), sliced thinly
500g baby buk choy, chopped coarsely
500g choy sum, chopped coarsely
2 tablespoons soy sauce
2 tablespoons oyster sauce
1 tablespoon mild chilli sauce

1. Shell and devein prawns, leaving tails intact. Cut squid in half lengthways; score inside surface of each piece, cut into 5cm-wide strips. Cut fish into 3cm pieces.
2. Heat half of the oil in wok; stir-fry seafood, in batches, until browned lightly.
3. Heat remaining oil in wok; stir-fry onion, garlic and ginger until onion softens.
4. Return seafood to wok. Add buk choy, choy sum and combined sauces; stir-fry until greens are just wilted and heated through.

SERVES 4
per serving 8.1g total fat (1.6g saturated fat); 1430kj (342 cal); 58.8g protein; 7.5g carbohydrate; 4.4g fibre

seafood salad with gremolata dressing

PREPARATION TIME 30 MINUTES (PLUS REFRIGERATION TIME) COOKING TIME 20 MINUTES

1kg uncooked large prawns
500g squid hoods
500g cleaned baby octopus
⅓ cup (80ml) olive oil
2 tablespoons finely chopped fresh lemon rind
2 cloves garlic, chopped finely
1 lebanese cucumber (130g)
100g mesclun
2 tablespoons lemon juice
2 tablespoons chopped fresh flat-leaf parsley

1. Shell and devein prawns, leaving tails intact. Cut squid in half lengthways; score inside surface of each piece, cut into 5cm-wide strips. Remove and discard heads from octopus.
2. Combine seafood in large bowl with 1 tablespoon of the oil, 1 teaspoon of the rind and half of the garlic, cover; refrigerate 3 hours or overnight.
3. Cook seafood, in batches, on heated oiled grill plate (or grill or barbecue) until prawns are just changed in colour and squid and octopus are cooked through.
4. Using vegetable peeler, slice cucumber into ribbons. Combine cucumber with mesclun in medium bowl.
5. Place juice and parsley with remaining oil, rind and garlic in screw-top jar; shake well.
6. Serve seafood on cucumber-mesclun mixture; drizzle with dressing.

SERVES 6
per serving 15.2g total fat (2.4g saturated fat); 1463kj (350 cal); 51.2g protein; 1.8g carbohydrate; 1g fibre

stir-fried seafood with chilli and ginger

PREPARATION TIME 20 MINUTES COOKING TIME 20 MINUTES

300g squid hoods
300g uncooked medium king prawns
500g large black mussels
1½ cups (300g) jasmine rice
2 teaspoons sesame oil
4cm piece fresh ginger (20g), grated
1 tablespoon sambal oelek
250g cleaned baby octopus
350g buk choy, chopped coarsely
400g gai lan, chopped coarsely
¼ cup (60ml) kecap manis
4 fresh kaffir lime leaves, shredded finely

1 Cut squid down centre to open out, score inside in diagonal pattern then cut into strips. Shell and devein prawns, leaving tails intact. Scrub mussels under cold water; discard beards.
2 Cook rice in large saucepan of boiling water, uncovered, until just tender; drain. Cover to keep warm.
3 Meanwhile, heat oil in wok; stir-fry ginger, sambal and seafood, in batches, until seafood changes colour and mussels open (discard any that do not).
4 Return all seafood to wok. Add buk choy, gai lan and kecap manis; stir-fry until vegetables just wilt. Remove from heat; stir in lime leaves. Serve with rice.

SERVES 4
per serving 5.6g total fat (1.1g saturated fat); 2086kj (499 cal); 47.1g protein; 63.7g carbohydrate; 5.6g fibre

shellfish paella

PREPARATION TIME 30 MINUTES COOKING TIME 45 MINUTES

24 uncooked medium prawns (600g)
16 large black mussels (500g)
200g salmon fillet
3 cups (750ml) chicken stock
3 cups (750ml) water
½ cup (125ml) dry white wine
4 saffron threads, toasted, crushed
1 large red capsicum (350g)
2 large tomatoes (500g)
1 cup (125g) frozen peas
1 tablespoon olive oil
1 large brown onion (200g), chopped finely
2 cloves garlic, crushed
1½ cups (300g) arborio rice

1 Shell and devein prawns, leaving tails intact. Scrub mussels under cold water; remove beards. Heat small lightly oiled frying pan; cook salmon until browned both sides and just cooked through.
2 Combine stock, the water, wine and saffron in large saucepan; bring to a boil. Reduce heat, simmer, covered, over low heat.
3 Meanwhile, cut capsicum in half lengthways. Discard seeds and membranes; chop capsicum finely. Peel tomatoes; seed and chop finely. Rinse peas under hot water; drain.
4 Heat oil in large saucepan; cook onion, garlic and capsicum, stirring, until onion softens. Add rice; stir to coat in onion mixture. Stir in 1-cup batches of the hot stock mixture; cook, stirring, until liquid is absorbed after each addition. Total cooking time should be about 35 minutes or until rice is just tender and all the liquid has been absorbed.
5 Add prawns and mussels; cook, stirring, until prawns change in colour and mussels open (discard any that do not). Add tomato, peas and flaked salmon; stir gently until risotto is heated through.

SERVES 4
per serving 10.6g total fat (2.1g saturated fat); 2362kj (565 cal); 40.2g protein; 71g carbohydrate; 5.6g fibre

seafood risoni paella

PREPARATION TIME 30 MINUTES COOKING TIME 30 MINUTES

Paella is traditionally made by Spaniards using short-grain white rice but, for an interesting alternative, try risoni, a tiny short pasta that adds a smoother texture to the finished dish.

12 uncooked medium king prawns (540g)
250g small mussels
300g piece ling
2 tablespoons olive oil
1 small brown onion (80g), chopped finely
4 cloves garlic, crushed
500g risoni pasta
pinch saffron threads
6 small tomatoes (780g), seeded, chopped coarsely
1 cup (250ml) dry white wine
2 tablespoons tomato paste
1 teaspoon finely grated orange rind
4 sprigs fresh marjoram
1 litre (4 cups) vegetable stock, warmed
1½ cups (185g) frozen peas
150g calamari rings

1. Shell and devein prawns, leaving tails intact. Scrub mussels under cold water; remove beards. Cut ling into 3cm pieces.
2. Heat oil in large deep frying pan; cook onion and garlic, stirring, until onion softens. Add risoni and saffron; stir to coat in onion mixture. Stir in tomato, wine, paste, rind and marjoram; cook, stirring, until wine has almost evaporated.
3. Add 1 cup of the stock, stirring, until absorbed. Add remaining stock; cook, stirring, until risoni is almost tender.
4. Place peas and seafood on top of risoni mixture; do not stir to combine. Cover pan, reduce heat; simmer about 10 minutes or until seafood has changed in colour and mussels have opened (discard any that do not).

SERVES 4
per serving 13.5g total fat (2.4g saturated fat); 3348kj (801 cal); 58.4g protein; 98.6g carbohydrate; 12.3g fibre
tip this recipe can be made in a traditional paella pan if you have one; otherwise a deep frying pan or wok with a tight-fitting lid will suffice. Serve the paella straight from the pan at the table.

seafood casserole with pasta

PREPARATION TIME 15 MINUTES COOKING TIME 35 MINUTES

Any type of pasta can be used instead of spaghetti.

12 uncooked small prawns (250g)
12 mussels (380g)
2 teaspoons olive oil
1 large brown onion (200g), chopped finely
2 cloves garlic, crushed
400g can tomatoes
¼ cup (60ml) dry red wine
¼ cup (60ml) tomato paste
2 teaspoons brown sugar
2 teaspoons balsamic vinegar
¼ cup (60ml) water
200g spaghetti
350g flathead fillets, chopped coarsely
250g squid hoods, sliced thickly
1 tablespoon coarsely chopped fresh oregano
⅓ cup firmly packed basil leaves, chopped coarsely

1. Peel and devein prawns, leaving tails intact. Clean mussels under cold water; discard beards.
2. Heat oil in large saucepan; cook onion and garlic, stirring, until onion is soft. Add undrained crushed tomatoes, wine, paste, sugar, vinegar and the water; bring to a boil. Reduce heat, simmer, uncovered, for about 20 minutes or until sauce thickens.
3. Meanwhile, cook spaghetti in large saucepan of boiling water, uncovered, until just tender; drain.
4. Add prawns, mussels, fish and squid to tomato sauce; simmer, uncovered, for about 10 minutes or until seafood is cooked through and mussels have opened (discard any that do not). Stir in spaghetti, oregano and basil just before serving.

SERVES 4
per serving 5.3g total fat (1.2g saturated fat); 1768kj (423 cal); 45.4g protein; 44.6g carbohydrate; 5.4g fibre
tip tomato sauce can be made a day ahead. Store, covered, in refrigerator or freezer. Add seafood when reheating.

prawn, asparagus and sesame stir-fry

PREPARATION TIME 30 MINUTES COOKING TIME 15 MINUTES

2 teaspoons sesame seeds
1 tablespoon peanut oil
1 teaspoon finely grated fresh ginger
2 cloves garlic, crushed
1 medium brown onion (150g), sliced thinly
300g asparagus, trimmed, chopped
2 teaspoons sesame oil
1kg uncooked large prawns, peeled, deveined, tails intact
1 fresh large red chilli, sliced thinly
2 tablespoons rice wine
¼ cup (60ml) soy sauce
2 teaspoons brown sugar

1. Dry-fry sesame seeds in heated wok, stirring, until browned lightly and fragrant. Remove from wok.
2. Heat half of the peanut oil in wok; stir-fry ginger, garlic and onion until fragrant. Add asparagus; stir-fry until just tender, remove from wok.
3. Heat remaining oils in wok; stir-fry prawns, in batches, until just changed in colour. Return asparagus mixture and prawns to wok with chilli and combined remaining ingredients; stir-fry until hot.
4. Serve sprinkled with sesame seeds.

SERVES 4
per serving 8.5g total fat (1.4g saturated fat); 920kj (220 cal); 28.7g protein; 4.7g carbohydrate; 1.7g fibre

prawn and basil risotto

PREPARATION TIME 15 MINUTES COOKING TIME 45 MINUTES

You will need to cook about ½ cup (100g) brown rice for this recipe.

500g uncooked medium prawns
3 cups (750ml) chicken stock
1 cup (250ml) dry white wine
1 stick celery, chopped finely
1 small onion (100g), chopped finely
1 cup (250ml) water
1 cup (200g) arborio rice
1 cup cooked brown rice
2 medium tomatoes (260g), peeled, seeded, chopped finely
2 tablespoons finely chopped fresh basil leaves
2 tablespoons finely chopped fresh parsley

1. Shell and devein prawns, leaving tails intact.
2. Combine stock and wine in medium saucepan; bring to a boil. Reduce heat, simmer, covered, over low heat.
3. Meanwhile, combine celery, onion and the water in large saucepan; cook, stirring occasionally, about 10 minutes or until water has evaporated. Add arborio rice; cook, stirring, 1 minute. Stir in ⅔ cup (160ml) hot stock mixture; cook, stirring, over low heat until liquid is absorbed. Continue adding stock mixture in 1-cup batches, stirring, until absorbed after each addition. Total cooking time should be about 35 minutes.
4. Add prawns and brown rice after last addition of stock mixture; cook, stirring, until prawns are just tender. Stir in tomato and herbs.

SERVES 4
per serving 2g total fat (0.6g saturated fat); 1580kj (378 cal); 20.9g protein; 58g carbohydrate; 2.7g fibre
tip recipe best made just before serving.

chilli prawn noodle salad

PREPARATION TIME 20 MINUTES COOKING TIME 10 MINUTES

250g cooked medium prawns
¼ cup (60ml) lime juice
2 tablespoons sweet chilli sauce
1 fresh long red chilli, sliced
1 long green chilli, sliced
2 teaspoons sugar
200g bean thread noodles
2 tablespoons shredded fresh mint leaves

1 Shell and devein prawns, leaving tails intact. Combine prawns in large bowl with juice, sauce, chillies and sugar.

2 Place noodles in large heatproof bowl, cover with boiling water, stand until tender; drain.

3 Add noodles to prawn mixture with mint; toss gently to combine.

SERVES 4
per serving 1g total fat (0.1g saturated fat); 840kj (201 cal); 8.4g protein; 38.5g carbohydrate; 1g fibre

spicy prawns

PREPARATION TIME 20 MINUTES (PLUS REFRIGERATION TIME) COOKING TIME 15 MINUTES

1kg uncooked medium prawns
2 teaspoons peanut oil

SPICY MARINADE
2 cloves garlic, crushed
2 teaspoons grated fresh ginger
2 teaspoons finely chopped lemon grass
½ teaspoon ground cumin
½ teaspoon ground coriander
1 tablespoon teriyaki sauce
2 teaspoons honey
4 green onions, chopped
½ teaspoon sambal oelek

1 Shell and devein prawns, leaving tails intact. Make spicy marinade.

2 Combine prawns and marinade in large bowl. Cover; refrigerate 3 hours or overnight.

3 Heat oil in large frying pan; cook prawn mixture, in batches, until just changed in colour.

SPICY MARINADE place ingredients in bowl; mix well.

SERVES 6
per serving 2.1g total fat (0.4g saturated fat); 418kj (100 cal); 17.5g protein; 2.6g carbohydrate; 0.4g fibre
tip prawns are best cooked just before serving.

stir-fried prawns with pineapple and chilli salad

PREPARATION TIME 25 MINUTES COOKING TIME 10 MINUTES

1.5kg uncooked large king prawns
1 clove garlic, crushed
2cm piece fresh ginger (10g), grated
4 green onions, sliced thinly
1 tablespoon sesame oil

PINEAPPLE AND CHILLI SALAD

1 small fresh pineapple (800g)
2 medium mangoes (860g)
¼ cup (30g) coarsely chopped roasted unsalted peanuts
1 fresh long red chilli, sliced thinly
2 green onions, sliced thinly
1 tablespoon finely chopped vietnamese mint
¼ cup finely chopped fresh coriander
2 tablespoons lime juice
1 tablespoon fish sauce
2 teaspoons sugar

1. Shell and devein prawns, leaving tails intact. Combine prawns with garlic, ginger and onion in medium bowl.
2. Make pineapple and chilli salad.
3. Heat oil in wok; stir-fry prawn mixture, in batches, until just changed in colour.
4. Divide salad among serving plates; top with prawns.

PINEAPPLE AND CHILLI SALAD slice pineapple and mango thinly; cut slices into 5mm matchsticks. Combine fruit in large bowl with nuts, chilli, onion and herbs. Add combined remaining ingredients; toss gently to combine.

SERVES 4
per serving 9.8g total fat (1.3g saturated fat); 1634kj (391 cal); 43.7g protein; 31.1g carbohydrate; 5.9g fibre

cajun prawns with bean and coriander salad

PREPARATION TIME 30 MINUTES COOKING TIME 15 MINUTES

You will need three limes for this recipe.

24 uncooked medium king prawns (1kg)
1 tablespoon hot paprika
1 teaspoon chilli powder
1 teaspoon ground ginger
2 teaspoons ground cumin
1 teaspoon ground cardamom
1 teaspoon ground coriander
1 tablespoon vegetable oil
1 medium red onion (150g), chopped coarsely
1 clove garlic, crushed
1 teaspoon vegetable oil, extra
1 tablespoon lime juice
1 lime, cut into wedges

BEAN AND CORIANDER SALAD

400g green beans, halved crossways
1 cup loosely packed fresh coriander leaves
4 small vine-ripened tomatoes (120g), quartered
1 medium red onion (150g), sliced thinly
1 teaspoon coarsely grated lime rind
2 tablespoons lime juice
1 clove garlic, crushed
1 teaspoon sugar

1. Shell and devein prawns, leaving tails intact.
2. Blend or process spices, oil, onion and garlic until mixture forms a paste.
3. Make bean and coriander salad.
4. Heat extra oil in wok; stir-fry prawns, in batches, until just changed in colour.
5. Cook paste, stirring, in same wok about 2 minutes or until fragrant. Return prawns to wok with juice; stir-fry until prawns are heated through. Serve with salad and lime wedges.

BEAN AND CORIANDER SALAD boil, steam or microwave beans until just tender; drain. Rinse under cold water; drain. Combine beans in medium bowl with coriander, tomato and onion. Whisk rind, juice, garlic and sugar in small jug to combine, pour over salad; toss gently to combine.

SERVES 4
per serving 6.9g total fat (0.9g saturated fat); 915kj (219 cal); 30g protein; 7.9g carbohydrate; 5.6g fibre

stir-fried prawns and noodles

PREPARATION TIME 15 MINUTES COOKING TIME 20 MINUTES

500g uncooked medium prawns
200g dried rice noodles
1 clove garlic, crushed
2 tablespoons soy sauce
2 tablespoons fish sauce
1 teaspoon sambal oelek
1 cup (80g) bean sprouts
¼ cup fresh coriander leaves

1 Shell and devein prawns, leaving tails intact.
2 Place noodles in large heatproof bowl, cover with boiling water, stand until just tender; drain. Cover to keep warm.
3 Heat lightly oiled wok; stir-fry prawns and garlic until prawns are just changed in colour. Add noodles, sauces and sambal; stir-fry until hot. Stir in sprouts and coriander.

SERVES 4
per serving 1.1g total fat (0.1g saturated fat); 907kj (217 cal); 17.8g protein; 33.2g carbohydrate; 1.8g fibre

hokkien noodles with prawns

PREPARATION TIME 20 MINUTES COOKING TIME 10 MINUTES

24 uncooked large prawns (1.2kg)
300g baby buk choy
500g hokkien noodles
2 teaspoons peanut oil
1 fresh red thai chilli, chopped finely
1 clove garlic, crushed
¼ cup (60ml) water
2 tablespoons sesame oil
½ cup (125ml) kecap manis
¼ cup (60ml) light soy sauce
½ cup coarsely chopped fresh coriander

1 Shell and devein prawns, leaving tails intact. Cut buk choy lengthways into quarters.
2 Place noodles in large heatproof bowl; cover with boiling water. Use fork to separate noodles; drain. Rinse again by pouring boiling water over noodles in colander; drain.
3 Heat half of the peanut oil in wok; stir-fry chilli and garlic, until just fragrant. Add prawns, in batches; stir-fry over high heat until just changed in colour.
4 Heat remaining peanut oil in wok; stir-fry noodles and buk choy over high heat until buk choy just wilts.
5 Return prawns to wok with the water, sesame oil, kecap manis, sauce and coriander; stir-fry over high heat until just hot.

SERVES 4
per serving 12.9g total fat (1.9g saturated fat); 1714kj (410 cal); 39.3g protein; 32.9g carbohydrate; 3.7g fibre

prawn curry

PREPARATION TIME 15 MINUTES COOKING TIME 15 MINUTES

1kg uncooked medium prawns
2 tablespoons tikka masala paste
2 tablespoons mango chutney
⅓ cup (80ml) vegetable stock
½ cup (125g) low-fat yogurt
½ cup coarsely chopped fresh coriander leaves
2 teaspoons lime juice

1 Shell and devein prawns, leaving tails intact.
2 Heat paste and chutney in large saucepan; cook prawns, stirring, until just changed in colour. Add remaining ingredients; stir until combined.
3 Serve curry with pappadums, rice noodles and lime wedges, if desired.

SERVES 4
per serving 5g total fat (0.9g saturated fat); 815kj (195 cal); 28.2g protein; 8.8g carbohydrate; 1.8g fibre

prawn phad thai

PREPARATION TIME 15 MINUTES COOKING TIME 10 MINUTES

600g uncooked medium prawns
1 teaspoon grated fresh ginger
2 cloves garlic, crushed
1 fresh red thai chilli, sliced thinly
1½ tablespoons finely chopped palm sugar
¼ cup (60ml) soy sauce
2 tablespoons sweet chilli sauce
1 tablespoon fish sauce
1½ tablespoons tomato paste
250g angel hair pasta
1 tablespoon sesame oil
6 green onions, sliced thinly
2 cups (160g) bean sprouts
½ cup loosely packed fresh coriander leaves

1 Shell and devein prawns, leaving tails intact. Place prawns in large bowl with ginger, garlic and chilli; toss to combine. Combine sugar, sauces and paste in screw-top jar; shake well.
2 Cook pasta in large saucepan of boiling water, uncovered, until just tender; drain.
3 Meanwhile, heat oil in wok or large frying pan; stir-fry prawn mixture, in batches, until prawns just change in colour. Return prawns to wok, add sauce mixture; stir-fry about 1 minute or until sugar melts. Remove from heat; add onion, sprouts, coriander and pasta, toss gently to combine.

SERVES 4
per serving 6g total fat (0.9g saturated fat); 1609kj (385 cal); 25.6g protein; 56g carbohydrate; 5.7g fibre

crisp-skinned thai chilli snapper

PREPARATION TIME 15 MINUTES (PLUS REFRIGERATION TIME) COOKING TIME 45 MINUTES

1.2kg whole snapper
4 cloves garlic, crushed
¼ cup chopped fresh lemon grass
¼ cup chopped fresh coriander
2 fresh red thai chillies, chopped finely
2 tablespoons sweet chilli sauce
1 tablespoon grated fresh ginger
1 tablespoon thai red curry paste
2 tablespoons lime juice
2 tablespoons sweet chilli sauce, extra

1. Make four deep slits diagonally across both sides of fish; place fish in shallow non-metallic ovenproof dish.
2. Combine remaining ingredients, except extra chilli sauce, in medium bowl. Pour over fish, cover; refrigerate up to 3 hours.
3. Preheat oven to 180°C/160°C fan-forced. Cover dish with a lid or foil; bake about 35 minutes or until fish is almost cooked through.
4. Preheat grill. Brush fish with extra chilli sauce; place under grill 10 minutes or until skin is browned and crisp. Serve with lime wedges, if desired.

SERVES 4
per serving 4.5g total fat (1.2g saturated fat); 865kj (207 cal); 9.6g protein; 31.2g carbohydrate; 1.2g fibre

barramundi with kipflers and roasted capsicum

PREPARATION TIME 25 MINUTES COOKING TIME 40 MINUTES

We used a whole barramundi for this recipe, but any whole, firm, white-fleshed large fish can be used.

½ cup (125ml) vegetable stock
1 tablespoon lemon juice
700g kipfler potatoes, halved lengthways
1 tablespoon finely grated lemon rind
⅓ cup coarsely chopped fresh oregano
1.2kg whole barramundi, cleaned
1 large red capsicum (350g), sliced thinly
1 large yellow capsicum (350g), sliced thinly
2 cloves garlic, crushed

1. Preheat oven to 180°C/160°C fan-forced.
2. Combine stock, juice and potatoes in large baking dish; roast, uncovered, 10 minutes.
3. Meanwhile, combine rind and oregano in small bowl. Score fish both sides; press rind mixture into cuts and inside cavity.
4. Place fish in oiled large baking dish; roast, uncovered, about 30 minutes.
5. Meanwhile, add capsicums and garlic to potato mixture; stir to combine. Roast, uncovered, further 30 minutes or until potato is tender.
6. Serve fish with vegetables, drizzled with any pan juices; sprinkle fish with oregano leaves, if desired.

SERVES 4
per serving 2.5g total fat (0.7g saturated fat); 1271kj (304 cal); 38.9g protein; 30g carbohydrate; 5.7g fibre

cajun-spiced fish with roasted corn salsa

PREPARATION TIME 15 MINUTES COOKING TIME 25 MINUTES

1 clove garlic, crushed
1 tablespoon low-fat dairy-free spread, melted
2 teaspoons sweet paprika
½ teaspoon ground cumin
1 teaspoon ground white pepper
¼ teaspoon cayenne pepper
4 x 200g firm white fish fillets
3 trimmed fresh corn cobs (750g)
1 small red onion (100g), chopped coarsely
1 medium avocado (250g), chopped coarsely
250g cherry tomatoes, halved
2 tablespoons lime juice
¼ cup coarsely chopped fresh coriander

1. Preheat oven to 220°C/200°C fan-forced.
2. Combine garlic and spread in small jug; combine spices in small bowl.
3. Place fish on oven tray, brush both sides with garlic spread, sprinkle with combined spices. Roast, uncovered, about 15 minutes or until browned both sides and cooked as desired.
4. Meanwhile, roast corn on heated lightly oiled grill plate (or grill or barbecue) until browned all over. When corn is just cool enough to handle, cut kernels from cobs with a small, sharp knife.
5. Combine kernels in medium bowl with onion, avocado, tomatoes, juice and coriander. Serve fish with salsa.

SERVES 4
per serving 14.8g total fat (2.8g saturated fat); 1777kj (425 cal); 46.8g protein; 25.2g carbohydrate; 8.3g fibre

garfish with sweet cucumber peanut sauce

PREPARATION TIME 15 MINUTES COOKING TIME 15 MINUTES

¼ cup (55g) caster sugar
½ cup (125ml) water
¼ cup (60ml) lime juice
1 tablespoon fish sauce
2 fresh medium red chillies, sliced
1 teaspoon grated fresh ginger
18 whole garfish (1.5kg), cleaned
cooking-oil spray
1 lebanese cucumber (130g), peeled, seeded, chopped
1 green onion, sliced thinly
1 tablespoon coarsely chopped fresh coriander
1 tablespoon coarsely chopped roasted unsalted peanuts

1. Combine sugar and the water in small saucepan; cook, stirring, without boiling, until sugar dissolves. Bring to a boil; simmer, uncovered, until reduced by half.
2. Remove syrup from heat, stir in juice, fish sauce, chilli and ginger; cool.
3. Meanwhile, spray garfish on each side with cooking-oil spray. Cook garfish, in batches, on heated oiled grill plate (or grill or barbecue) until browned and cooked through.
4. Just before serving, stir remaining ingredients into sauce.
5. Serve garfish with sauce and, if desired, thick char-grilled lime slices.

SERVES 6
per serving 3.3g total fat (0.7g saturated fat); 744kj (178 cal); 26.7g protein; 10.2g carbohydrate; 0.6g fibre
tip the sweet cucumber and peanut sauce can be made 4 days ahead. Store, covered, in refrigerator.

cajun-spiced fish with roasted corn salsa

fish and oven-roasted chips

fish and oven-roasted chips

PREPARATION TIME 20 MINUTES COOKING TIME 45 MINUTES

Yes, it's true! You can make delicious fish and chips without using an extravagant amount of oil. We used bream fillets here but you can use other firm white fish fillets, such as whiting or john dory.

5 large potatoes (1.5kg)

1 teaspoon sea salt

½ teaspoon cracked black pepper

cooking-oil spray

6 x 120g white fish fillets

2 tablespoons drained baby capers

1 tablespoon finely chopped fresh dill

1 teaspoon finely grated lemon rind

⅓ cup (80ml) lemon juice

1. Preheat oven to 220°C/200°C fan-forced.
2. Halve unpeeled potatoes lengthways; cut each half into six wedges. Combine potato, in single layer, in large baking dish with salt and pepper; spray lightly with cooking-oil spray. Roast, uncovered, about 45 minutes or until lightly browned and tender.
3. Meanwhile, cook fish, uncovered, in large heated lightly oiled frying pan until browned both sides and cooked as desired.
4. Just before serving, drizzle combined remaining ingredients over fish. Serve with lemon wedges, if desired.

SERVES 6

per serving 1.8g total fat (0.2g saturated fat); 1104kj (264 cal); 26.3g protein; 33.8g carbohydrate; 5.1g fibre

serving suggestion serve with individual garden salads in a light lemony vinaigrette.

sumac and sesame-grilled blue-eye with fattoush

PREPARATION TIME 30 MINUTES COOKING TIME 10 MINUTES

Sumac is used extensively in kitchens from the eastern Mediterranean through to Pakistan. Both in cooking and as a condiment, sumac's tart astringency adds a delightful piquancy to food without the heat of a chilli. We used blue-eye cutlets, but any firm white fish can be used for this recipe.

4 x 200g blue-eye cutlets
1 tablespoon sesame seeds
2 teaspoons dried chilli flakes
1 tablespoon sumac
2 teaspoons sea salt flakes
1 lemon, cut into wedges

FATTOUSH

6 pocket pitta
4 small tomatoes (520g), chopped coarsely
1 large green capsicum (350g), chopped coarsely
2 lebanese cucumbers (260g), seeded, chopped coarsely
4 red radishes (140g), sliced thinly
4 green onions, sliced thinly
1½ cups firmly packed fresh flat-leaf parsley leaves
½ cup coarsely chopped fresh mint
1 tablespoon olive oil
¼ cup (60ml) lemon juice
2 cloves garlic, crushed

1. Preheat oven to 200°C/180°C fan-forced; make fattoush.
2. Meanwhile, combine fish, seeds, chilli, sumac and salt in large bowl.
3. Cook fish mixture on heated oiled grill plate (or grill or barbecue) until cooked as desired. Serve fish with lemon and fattoush.

FATTOUSH split pitta in half horizontally, cut halves into 2.5cm pieces; place on oven tray. Toast, uncovered, in oven until browned lightly. Place pitta in large bowl with tomato, capsicum, cucumber, radish, onion and herbs. Add combined oil, juice and garlic; toss gently to combine.

SERVES 4
per serving 10.2g total fat (1.4g saturated fat); 2437kj (583 cal); 65.4g protein; 54.9g carbohydrate; 14g fibre

grilled dukkah-spiced blue-eye with pilaf

PREPARATION TIME 20 MINUTES COOKING TIME 45 MINUTES

Dukkah is an Egyptian nut, seed and spice mixture used similarly to Lebanese za'atar, Moroccan ras al honout and Indian garam masala. It adds exotically complex, uniquely aromatic flavours to various grilled, baked or barbecued seafood, meat and poultry dishes. Each blend is slightly different, depending on the individual cook. Dukkah can also be used in a dip or sprinkled over a finished dish just before serving.

2 tablespoons hazelnut meal
2 tablespoons almond meal
1 tablespoon sesame seeds
1 tablespoon coriander seeds, crushed
1 tablespoon ground cumin
1 tablespoon sweet paprika
2 teaspoons ground turmeric
2 large red onions (600g)
800g flat mushrooms, quartered
6 cloves garlic
2 tablespoons olive oil
100g vermicelli, broken roughly
2 cups (400g) long-grain white rice
1 litre (4 cups) boiling water
8 x 150g blue-eye fillets
200g low-fat yogurt
1 tablespoon coarsely chopped fresh coriander
1 tablespoon lemon juice

1. Preheat oven to 200°C/180°C fan-forced.
2. Dry-fry nuts, seeds and spices in medium frying pan, stirring, until dukkah mixture is fragrant.
3. Cut each onion into six wedges; combine onion in large baking dish with mushrooms, garlic and half of the oil. Roast, uncovered, about 30 minutes or until vegetables are just tender.
4. Meanwhile, heat remaining oil in large saucepan with tight-fitting lid; cook vermicelli and rice, stirring, about 5 minutes or until vermicelli is golden brown and rice almost translucent. Add the water; bring to a boil. Reduce heat, simmer, covered, about 20 minutes or until liquid is absorbed and pilaf is cooked as desired.
5. While pilaf is cooking, coat fish all over in dukkah; cook, in batches, on heated oiled grill plate (or grill or barbecue) until browned both sides and cooked as desired.
6. Serve pilaf with fish and roasted vegetables; drizzle with combined yogurt, coriander and juice.

SERVES 8
per serving 9.7g total fat (1.4g saturated fat); 1981kj (474 cal); 40.8g protein; 54.7g carbohydrate; 5.1g fibre

pan-fried blue-eye cutlets with potato crisps and gingered carrots

PREPARATION TIME 25 MINUTES COOKING TIME 40 MINUTES

We used Pontiac potatoes here because they are excellent for baking. You can use any firm white-fleshed fish for this recipe. Green ginger wine is an alcoholic beverage with the taste of fresh ginger. In cooking, you can substitute it with a dry (white) vermouth, if you prefer.

6 medium potatoes (1.2kg)
cooking-oil spray
4 large carrots (720g)
10cm piece ginger (50g)
2 bunches chives
2 tablespoons olive oil
2 cloves garlic, crushed
6 x 250g blue-eye cutlets
⅓ cup (50g) plain flour
¾ cup (180ml) lemon juice
¼ cup (60ml) green ginger wine
2½ cups (625ml) fish stock

1. Preheat oven to 220°C/200°C fan-forced. Oil oven trays.
2. Cut potatoes into 5mm-thick slices. Place, in single layer, on oven trays; coat with cooking-oil spray. Roast, uncovered, about 40 minutes or until browned lightly.
3. Meanwhile, cut carrots and ginger into 2mm-wide lengths, then into thin strips. Cut chives in half.
4. Heat half of the oil in large frying pan; cook carrot, ginger and garlic, in batches, stirring, about 2 minutes or until carrot is just tender. Stir chives into carrot mixture; cover to keep warm.
5. Coat fish in flour; shake off excess. Heat remaining oil in same pan; cook fish, in batches, until browned lightly and cooked as desired. Drain oil from pan; add juice, wine and stock. Bring to a boil; simmer, uncovered, about 10 minutes or until sauce thickens.
6. Divide potato slices among serving plates. Top with gingered carrots then fish; drizzle with sauce.

SERVES 6
per serving 9.2g total fat (1.3g saturated fat); 2103kj (503 cal); 57.9g protein; 42.8g carbohydrate; 8.4g fibre
tip tuna and swordfish are both excellent substitutes for blue-eye.
serving suggestion serve with warmed bread rolls and olives.

pepper-crusted swordfish with bean and potato salad

PREPARATION TIME 15 MINUTES COOKING TIME 15 MINUTES

300g small red-skinned potatoes, halved
1 teaspoon ground white pepper
2 teaspoons cracked black pepper
½ cup (35g) stale breadcrumbs
4 x 200g swordfish fillets
200g green beans
200g yellow beans
¼ cup (60ml) lime juice
1 tablespoon olive oil
1 clove garlic, crushed

1. Boil, steam or microwave potato until just tender; drain. Cover to keep warm.
2. Meanwhile, combine peppers and breadcrumbs in small bowl; press mixture onto one side of each fish fillet. Cook fish, crumbed-side down, in heated lightly oiled large non-stick frying pan, until browned lightly and crisp; turn, cook until browned lightly and cooked as desired.
3. Meanwhile, boil, steam or microwave beans until just tender; drain.
4. Place juice, oil and garlic in screw-top jar; shake well.
5. Place potato, beans and dressing in large bowl; toss gently to combine. Serve fish with salad.

SERVES 4
per serving 6.4g total fat (0.9g saturated fat); 1317kj (315 cal); 44.8g protein; 18.3g carbohydrate; 4.7g fibre

vine-leaf-wrapped swordfish with tomato-olive salsa

PREPARATION TIME 20 MINUTES COOKING TIME 15 MINUTES

16 large fresh grapevine leaves
4 x 200g swordfish steaks

TOMATO-OLIVE SALSA
3 cloves garlic, crushed
1 cup loosely packed fresh flat-leaf parsley leaves
¼ cup coarsely chopped fresh chives
3 small tomatoes (390g), chopped coarsely
½ cup (75g) seeded kalamata olives, quartered lengthways
2 tablespoons drained capers, rinsed
2 tablespoons lemon juice
2 teaspoons olive oil

1. Trim vine leaves. Using metal tongs, dip, one at a time, in medium saucepan of boiling salted water. Rinse immediately under cold water; drain on absorbent paper.
2. Overlap four vine leaves slightly to form a rectangle large enough to wrap each piece of fish; fold leaves around fish to enclose completely. Place fish parcels in large steamer fitted over large saucepan of boiling water; steam, covered, about 15 minutes or until cooked as desired.
3. Meanwhile, make tomato-olive salsa.
4. Place fish parcels in serving bowls; pull back vine leaves to uncover fish, top with salsa.

TOMATO-OLIVE SALSA combine ingredients in medium bowl.

SERVES 4
per serving 3.9g total fat (0.6g saturated fat); 970kj (232 cal); 41g protein; 7.1g carbohydrate; 2.6g fibre
tip if you are unable to find fresh grapevine leaves, buy those that come cryovac-packed in brine; they can be found in most Greek or Middle-Eastern food stores. Be sure to rinse them in cold water and dry with absorbent paper before using.

lemon grass and lime fish parcels

PREPARATION TIME 10 MINUTES COOKING TIME 20 MINUTES

The lemon grass in this dish is not eaten, but it produces an amazing aroma and flavour simply by being close to the fish during cooking.

2 x 10cm sticks (20g) fresh lemon grass
½ cup coarsely chopped fresh coriander leaves
2 teaspoons grated fresh ginger
3 cloves garlic, crushed
4 spring onions (100g), sliced thinly
2 fresh red thai chillies, chopped finely
4 x 250g firm white fish fillets
1 lime, sliced thinly
1 tablespoon peanut oil

1. Cut each lemon grass stick in half lengthways.
2. Combine coriander, ginger, garlic, onion and chilli in small bowl.
3. Divide lemon grass among four pieces of foil; place fish on top. Top fish with coriander mixture and lime slices; drizzle with oil. Fold foil around fish to completely enclose.
4. Cook parcels on heated grill plate (or grill or barbecue) about 15 minutes or until fish is cooked through.
5. To serve, remove fish from foil and discard lemon grass. Serve with steamed rice and lime slices, if desired.

SERVES 4
per serving 6.2g total fat (1.1g saturated fat); 978kj (234 cal); 42.6g protein; 1g carbohydrate; 1.3g fibre
tips the fish can be wrapped in blanched banana leaves instead of foil, if desired. Fish can also be cooked in oven at 180°C/160°C fan-forced for 15 minutes or until cooked through.

fish fillets with coriander chilli sauce

PREPARATION TIME 10 MINUTES COOKING TIME 25 MINUTES

12 x 70g ocean perch fillets
1 medium brown onion (150g), sliced thinly
1 cup (250ml) water
½ cup (125ml) dry vermouth
⅓ cup (80ml) lime juice
2 fresh red thai chillies, chopped finely
⅓ cup (75g) sugar
2 teaspoons cornflour
2 tablespoons finely chopped fresh coriander
1 medium red capsicum (200g), sliced thinly
4 green onions, cut into 5cm lengths
½ cup firmly packed fresh coriander leaves

1. Preheat oven to 180°C/160°C fan-forced.
2. Place fish, in single layer, in shallow ovenproof dish; top with brown onion. Pour over combined water, vermouth and half of the juice.
3. Bake, covered, about 15 minutes or until fish is cooked as desired. Remove fish; keep warm. Strain and reserve liquid.
4. Place reserved liquid, chilli, sugar and combined cornflour and remaining juice in small saucepan. Stir over heat until sugar dissolves; bring to a boil. Reduce heat, simmer until mixture thickens. Stir in chopped coriander.
5. Arrange fish, capsicum, green onion and coriander leaves on serving plate; drizzle with sauce.

SERVES 4
per serving 1.5g total fat (0.2g saturated fat); 1212kj (290 cal); 37g protein; 24.3g carbohydrate; 1.7g fibre

fish with paprika and pimiento sauce

PREPARATION TIME 10 MINUTES COOKING TIME 10 MINUTES

Char-grilled, peeled and sliced red capsicums can be used instead of pimientos.

2 x 200g blue-eye fillets
½ x 390g can pimientos, drained
½ cup firmly packed fresh flat-leaf parsley leaves

PAPRIKA AND PIMIENTO SAUCE
2 teaspoons olive oil
1 small brown onion (80g), chopped finely
1 clove garlic, crushed
2 teaspoons paprika
¾ cup water (180ml)
2 teaspoons lemon juice
1 teaspoon sugar

1. Poach, steam or microwave fish until tender; drain.
2. Cut half the pimientos into strips; reserve remaining pimientos for sauce.
3. Make paprika and pimiento sauce.
4. Serve fish on a bed of parsley leaves, topped with sauce and pimiento strips.

PAPRIKA AND PIMIENTO SAUCE chop reserved pimientos. Heat oil in medium saucepan; cook onion and garlic until soft. Stir in paprika; cook for 30 seconds. Stir in pimiento with remaining ingredients; bring to a boil. Simmer, uncovered, for 3 minutes. Blend or process mixture until smooth.

SERVES 2
per serving 7.3g total fat (1.1g saturated fat); 1559kj (373 cal); 69.2g protein; 6.9g carbohydrate; 2.9g fibre
tip fish is best cooked close to serving time. Sauce can be made a day ahead; store, covered, in refrigerator.

lime and chilli fish baked in banana leaves

PREPARATION TIME 25 MINUTES COOKING TIME 15 MINUTES

2 large banana leaves
4 x 10cm sticks (20g) fresh lemon grass
4 fresh red thai chillies, sliced thinly
4 cloves garlic, crushed
1 tablespoon finely grated lime rind
⅓ cup (80ml) lime juice
2cm piece fresh ginger (10g), grated
1 cup coarsely chopped fresh coriander
1 cup (250ml) light coconut milk
8 x 150g ling fillets
cooking-oil spray
2 cups (400g) jasmine rice
4 green onions, sliced thinly

1. Preheat oven to 220°C/200°C fan-forced.
2. Trim each banana leaf into four 30cm squares. Using metal tongs, dip one square at a time into large saucepan of boiling water; remove immediately. Rinse under cold running water; pat dry with absorbent paper. Banana leaf squares should be soft and pliable.
3. Halve lemon grass. Combine chilli, garlic, rind, juice, ginger, coriander and coconut milk in small bowl. Centre each fillet on banana leaf square. Top with lemon grass; drizzle with chilli mixture. Fold square over fish to enclose; secure each parcel with kitchen string.
4. Place parcels, in single layer, in large baking dish; coat with cooking-oil spray. Roast in hot oven about 10 minutes or until fish is cooked as desired.
5. Meanwhile, cook rice, uncovered, in large saucepan of boiling water until tender; drain. Stir onion through rice; serve with fish parcels.

SERVES 8
per serving 5.7g total fat (3.7g saturated fat); 1505kj (360 cal); 33.8g protein; 42.2g carbohydrate; 1.3g fibre
tips foil can be used if banana leaves are unavailable. Banana leaves can be ordered from fruit and vegetable stores. Cut with a sharp knife close to the main stem; leaves must be immersed in hot water so they will be pliable.

slow-roasted ocean trout and asian greens

PREPARATION TIME 15 MINUTES COOKING TIME 20 MINUTES

8 x 100g ocean trout fillets
2 kaffir lime leaves, shredded finely
10cm stick (20g) fresh lemon grass, chopped finely
1 teaspoon sesame oil
250g baby buk choy, quartered
250g choy sum, chopped coarsely
2 teaspoons light soy sauce
⅓ cup (80ml) sweet chilli sauce
¼ cup (60ml) lime juice

1 Preheat oven to 150°C/130°C fan-forced.

2 Place four fish fillets, skin-side down, on board; sprinkle with lime leaves and lemon grass. Top with remaining fish fillets, skin-side up; tie with kitchen string. Place in large shallow baking dish; roast, uncovered, 15 minutes.

3 Just before serving, heat oil in wok; stir-fry buk choy, choy sum and soy sauce until vegetables just wilt.

4 Serve fish with stir-fried asian greens; drizzle with combined chilli sauce and juice.

SERVES 4
per serving 9.2g total fat (2g saturated fat); 1212kj (290 cal); 40.6g protein; 10.1g carbohydrate; 1.7g fibre

balti fish curry

PREPARATION TIME 15 MINUTES COOKING TIME 25 MINUTES

There is some controversy over the origin of Balti cooking, but regardless of whether it was Indian, Pakistani or Bangladeshi, the method is the same. Traditionally, a cast-iron wok-like pan, called a karahi, is used to quickly stir-fry ingredients. A wok or large frying pan is a perfect substitute.

800g white fish fillets
1 tablespoon vegetable oil
3 medium white onions (450g), sliced thinly
2 cloves garlic, crushed
1 tablespoon grated fresh ginger
1 fresh red thai chilli, chopped finely
2 teaspoons ground turmeric
1 teaspoon sweet paprika
1 teaspoon ground cumin
2 x 400g cans crushed tomatoes
¼ cup (60ml) coconut cream
¼ cup finely chopped fresh coriander
1 tablespoon finely chopped fresh mint

1 Cut fish into 2cm pieces.

2 Heat oil in wok; stir-fry onion, garlic, ginger, chilli and spices until onion softens.

3 Add undrained tomatoes to onion mixture; bring to a boil. Reduce heat, simmer, uncovered, about 10 minutes or until sauce thickens slightly.

4 Add fish and coconut cream; bring to a boil. Reduce heat, simmer, uncovered, about 10 minutes or until fish is cooked through. Just before serving, stir in coriander and mint.

SERVES 4
per serving 9.5g total fat (3.5g saturated fat); 1191kj (285 cal); 37.4g protein; 12.1g carbohydrate; 4.9g fibre
tip if you don't like hot flavours, seed the chilli; if you like your food spicy, then pop in an extra chilli.
serving suggestion serve with warm naan and steamed basmati rice (or a pilaf) garnished with mint.

grilled fish cutlets with tangy salsa

PREPARATION TIME 10 MINUTES COOKING TIME 10 MINUTES

We used blue-eye cutlets for this recipe.

2 lebanese cucumbers (260g), seeded, chopped finely
2 red radishes (70g), chopped finely
4 medium egg tomatoes (300g), seeded, chopped finely
1 medium yellow capsicum (200g), seeded, chopped finely
½ teaspoon Tabasco sauce
1 tablespoon sherry vinegar
4 x 175g small fish cutlets, bone removed

1 Combine cucumber, radish, tomato, capsicum, Tabasco and vinegar in small bowl.

2 Cook fish on heated oiled grill plate (or grill or barbecue) until browned both sides and cooked as desired. Serve fish with salsa.

SERVES 4
per serving 4.1g total fat (1.2g saturated fat); 869kj (208 cal); 37.5g protein; 4.7g carbohydrate; 2.2g fibre

fish kebabs with chilli sauce

PREPARATION TIME 15 MINUTES (PLUS REFRIGERATION TIME) COOKING TIME 15 MINUTES

You will need to cook about ⅓ cup (65g) long-grain white rice for this recipe. Soak 4 bamboo skewers in cold water for at least 1 hour before use to prevent them splintering and scorching.

300g tuna steaks, cut into 3cm pieces
1 tablespoon salt-reduced soy sauce
1 clove garlic, crushed
¼ teaspoon grated fresh ginger
1 medium red capsicum (200g), chopped coarsely
1 medium green capsicum (200g), chopped coarsely
2 teaspoons vegetable oil
1 cup cooked long-grain white rice

CHILLI SAUCE

1 fresh red thai chilli, chopped finely
2 cloves garlic, crushed
1 tablespoon finely chopped fresh coriander leaves
1 tablespoon fish sauce
1 tablespoon lime juice
1½ tablespoons brown sugar
1 tablespoon mirin
⅓ cup (80ml) water

1. Combine fish with sauce, garlic and ginger in large bowl. Cover; refrigerate 1 hour.
2. Make chilli sauce.
3. Preheat grill.
4. Thread fish and capsicum alternately onto four skewers. Brush with oil; cook under hot grill until fish is tender. Serve kebabs on rice topped with sauce.

CHILLI SAUCE grind chilli, garlic and coriander to a smooth paste. Add fish sauce, juice, sugar, mirin and the water. Transfer mixture to small saucepan; stir until sugar is dissolved and sauce heated through.

SERVES 2

per serving 13.8g total fat (4g saturated fat); 1977kj (473 cal); 42.3g protein; 43.9g carbohydrate; 3.1g fibre

tip fish can be marinated a day ahead. Store, covered, in refrigerator.

cantonese steamed ginger snapper

PREPARATION TIME 10 MINUTES COOKING TIME 30 MINUTES

8cm piece fresh ginger (40g), peeled
4 x 300g whole snappers
¼ cup (60ml) vegetable stock
4 green onions, sliced thinly
½ cup firmly packed fresh coriander leaves
⅓ cup (80ml) salt-reduced light soy sauce
1 teaspoon sesame oil

1. Cut ginger into thin strips lengthways; cut strips into matchstick-sized pieces.
2. Score fish three times on each side; place each fish on a separate large sheet of foil. Sprinkle with ginger, then drizzle with half of the stock; fold foil loosely to enclose fish.
3. Place fish in large bamboo steamer; steam fish, covered, over wok of simmering water about 30 minutes or until cooked through.
4. Transfer fish to serving dish; sprinkle with onion and coriander, then drizzle with combined remaining stock, sauce and oil. Serve with steamed broccoli and baby corn, if desired.

SERVES 4
per serving 3.7g total fat (1.1g saturated fat); 715kj (171 cal); 32.1g protein; 1.6g carbohydrate; 0.9g fibre

lemony fish fillets with poached leeks

PREPARATION TIME 15 MINUTES COOKING TIME 20 MINUTES

We used barramundi fillets for this recipe.

2 medium leeks (700g), sliced thickly
3 cups (750ml) chicken stock
3 star anise
½ cup finely chopped fresh lemon grass
2 fresh red thai chillies, chopped finely
3 dried kaffir lime leaves, chopped finely
4 x 300g fish fillets
cooking-oil spray

1. Preheat oven to 220°C/200°C fan-forced.
2. Combine leek, stock and star anise in medium saucepan, bring to a boil. Reduce heat, simmer, uncovered, until leek is just tender. Drain over heatproof medium bowl; reserve poaching liquid.
3. Meanwhile, combine lemon grass, chilli and lime leaves in small bowl. Place fish on oven tray, press lemon grass mixture onto fish; coat with cooking-oil spray. Bake, uncovered, about 15 minutes or until fish is cooked as desired.
4. Serve fish on poached leek; drizzle with a little reheated reserved liquid.

SERVES 4
per serving 6g total fat (1.7g saturated fat); 1438kj (344 cal); 67.2g protein; 5g carbohydrate; 2.8g fibre

tuna with char-grilled vegetables

PREPARATION TIME 10 MINUTES COOKING TIME 30 MINUTES

3 medium potatoes (600g)
2 medium lemons (280g)
2 pickled baby dill cucumbers, sliced thinly
4 x 150g tuna steaks
2 teaspoons drained green peppercorns
2 teaspoons drained baby capers

1. Boil, steam or microwave potatoes until just tender; cut each potato into four slices.
2. Cut each lemon into six slices. Cook lemon, potato and cucumber, in batches, on heated oiled grill plate (or grill or barbecue) until browned and just tender; cover to keep warm.
3. Cook tuna on same grill plate until browned both sides and cooked as desired; cover to keep warm.
4. Heat peppercorns and capers on same grill plate until hot.
5. Divide potato among plates, then top with tuna, lemon and cucumber. Sprinkle with peppercorns and capers.

SERVES 4
per serving 8.8g total fat (3.5g saturated fat); 1421kj (340 cal); 41.6g protein; 20.9g carbohydrate; 3.9g fibre

crumbed fish with warm tomato salad

PREPARATION TIME 15 MINUTES COOKING TIME 25 MINUTES

cooking-oil spray
1 medium red onion (170g)
250g cherry tomatoes
¼ cup (60ml) white wine vinegar
2 cloves garlic, crushed
⅓ cup (55g) corn flake crumbs
1 teaspoon ground cumin
1 teaspoon sweet paprika
1 teaspoon ground turmeric
4 x 180g firm white fish fillets
¼ cup (35g) plain flour
2 egg whites, beaten lightly
150g baby spinach leaves
¼ cup (50g) drained capers

1. Preheat oven to 220°C/200°C fan-forced. Coat oven tray lightly with cooking-oil spray.
2. Cut onion into thin wedges. Place onion and tomatoes on oven tray; drizzle with combined vinegar and garlic. Roast, uncovered, about 20 minutes or until tomatoes are softened.
3. Combine crumbs and spices in small bowl.
4. Meanwhile, coat fish in flour; shake away excess. Dip fish in egg white, coat in crumb mixture. Spray fish both sides with cooking-oil spray; cook, uncovered, in heated large non-stick frying pan until browned both sides and cooked through.
5. Combine spinach and capers in large bowl with tomato and onion mixture; serve with fish.

SERVES 4
per serving 2.3g total fat (0.8g saturated fat); 1216kj (291 cal); 43.6g protein; 22.5g carbohydrate; 3.8g fibre
tips you can use flathead, snapper, ling, bream or any other firm white fish in this recipe. Fish can be coated in crumb mixture 2 hours before cooking time; store, covered, in refrigerator.

salmon and dill tortellini salad

PREPARATION TIME 10 MINUTES COOKING TIME 10 MINUTES

You can use a flavoured tortellini of your choice. Mild flavours such as ham and cheese or cheese and spinach are the most suitable.

375g spinach and ricotta tortellini
½ cup (125g) low-fat yogurt
2 teaspoons wholegrain mustard
¼ cup (60ml) oil-free italian dressing
2 teaspoons finely chopped fresh dill
2 tablespoons water
1 teaspoon sugar
415g can red salmon, drained
1 tablespoon drained capers
2 trimmed celery stalks (200g), sliced
1 lebanese cucumber (130g), sliced thinly

1. Cook pasta in large saucepan of boiling water, uncovered, until just tender; drain. Rinse under cold water; cool.
2. Meanwhile, whisk yogurt, mustard, dressing, dill, water and sugar in small bowl until smooth.
3. Place pasta in large bowl with flaked salmon, capers, celery and cucumber. Just before serving, drizzle with dressing; toss gently to combine.

SERVES 4
per serving 14.9g total fat (5.6g saturated fat); 1659kj (397 cal); 28.3g protein; 35.3g carbohydrate; 1g fibre

grilled tuna with soba noodles

PREPARATION TIME 15 MINUTES COOKING TIME 10 MINUTES

Soba noodles are Japanese noodles made from buckwheat and are similar in appearance to spaghetti. They are available dried from Asian food stores and some supermarkets.

4 x 200g tuna steaks
½ cup (125ml) mirin
2 teaspoons wasabi paste
½ cup (125ml) japanese soy sauce
1 sheet toasted seaweed (nori)
300g soba noodles
6 green onions, sliced thinly
2 fresh long red chillies, chopped finely

1. Combine tuna with 2 tablespoons of the mirin, half of the wasabi and half of the sauce in large bowl. Cover; refrigerate 10 minutes.
2. Meanwhile, using scissors, cut seaweed into four strips; cut each strip crossways into thin pieces.
3. Cook noodles in large saucepan of boiling water, uncovered, until just tender; drain. Rinse under cold water; drain.
4. Meanwhile, cook tuna on heated lightly oiled grill plate (or grill or barbecue) until browned both sides and cooked as desired.
5. Combine noodles in medium bowl with onion, chilli and combined remaining mirin, wasabi and sauce. Serve noodles with tuna and seaweed.

SERVES 4
per serving 12.3g total fat (4.8g saturated fat); 2408kj (576 cal); 60.8g protein; 52.8g carbohydrate; 3.3g fibre

atlantic salmon with herb crumble

PREPARATION TIME 10 MINUTES COOKING TIME 10 MINUTES

⅓ cup (35g) stale white breadcrumbs
1 tablespoon lemon juice
1 tablespoon finely chopped fresh parsley
1 tablespoon finely chopped fresh chives
1 clove garlic, crushed
2 x 200g salmon fillets

1 Preheat grill.
2 Combined breadcrumbs, juice, herbs and garlic.
3 Cook fish, skin-side up, under grill for 5 minutes. Turn over, sprinkle with crumb mixture; cook for about 5 minutes or until cooked through and lightly browned. Serve with tossed salad, if desired.

SERVES 2
per serving 14.9g total fat (3.3g saturated fat); 1463kj (350 cal); 41.6g protein; 12g carbohydrate; 1.2g fibre
tip recipe best made just before serving.

salmon patties with capsicum yogurt sauce

PREPARATION TIME 20 MINUTES (PLUS REFRIGERATION AND STANDING TIME) COOKING TIME 20 MINUTES

You will need to cook about 2 medium potatoes (400g) for this recipe.

415g can red salmon, drained
1 cup (220g) mashed potato
1 small brown onion (80g), grated coarsely
½ teaspoon finely grated lemon rind
1 tablespoon finely chopped fresh chives
1 teaspoon finely chopped fresh dill
1 egg white
⅓ cup (55g) polenta, approximately
cooking-oil spray

CAPSICUM YOGURT SAUCE

1 large red capsicum (350g)
¼ cup (60ml) no-oil herb and garlic dressing
1 teaspoon sugar
¼ cup (60g) low-fat yogurt

1 Combine salmon, potato, onion, rind, chives, dill and egg white in bowl; mix well. Shape mixture into eight patties; coat with polenta. Refrigerate, covered, 30 minutes.
2 Meanwhile, make capsicum yogurt sauce.
3 Coat patties with cooking-oil spray. Cook in heated large frying pan about 5 minutes on each side or until lightly browned. Serve with sauce, and steamed asparagus and zucchini ribbons, if desired.

CAPSICUM YOGURT SAUCE quarter capsicum; remove seeds and membrane. Cook under grill or in very hot oven, skin-side up, until skin blisters and blackens. Cover capsicum pieces in plastic or paper for 5 minutes. Peel away skin; chop capsicum. Blend or process capsicum, dressing and sugar until smooth; add yogurt. Process until combined.

SERVES 4 (MAKES 8)
per patty 6.8g total fat (1.8g saturated fat); 669kj (160 cal); 12.1g protein; 12.5g carbohydrate; 1.2g fibre
tip patties and sauce can be made a day ahead. Store, covered separately, in refrigerator. Uncooked patties may be frozen.

char-grilled tuna salad

PREPARATION TIME 10 MINUTES COOKING TIME 5 MINUTES

600g piece tuna
¼ cup (60ml) mirin
1 tablespoon light soy sauce
1 clove garlic, crushed
1 fresh red thai chilli, chopped finely
1 green onion, chopped finely
2 medium red capsicums (400g), sliced thinly
200g mesclun

1. Cook tuna on heated oiled grill plate (or grill or barbecue) until browned both sides and cooked as desired. Cover, rest 2 minutes; cut into thick slices.
2. Meanwhile, combine mirin, sauce, garlic, chilli and onion in screw-top jar; shake well.
3. Combine tuna and dressing in large bowl with capsicum and mesclun; toss gently to combine.

SERVES 4
per serving 8.9g total fat (3.5g saturated fat); 1087kj (260 cal); 40g protein; 4g carbohydrate; 2.1g fibre

penne with tomato salsa and tuna

PREPARATION TIME 15 MINUTES COOKING TIME 20 MINUTES

The Italian name of this pasta means quills, a reference to the nib-like, pointy ends of each piece of pasta. Penne comes in both smooth (lisce) or ridged (rigate) versions, and a variety of sizes.

375g penne pasta
3 medium tomatoes (570g), seeded, chopped finely
1 medium red onion (170g), chopped finely
2 cloves garlic, crushed
¼ cup firmly packed torn fresh basil leaves
425g can tuna in brine, drained, flaked
¼ cup (60ml) balsamic vinegar

1. Cook pasta in large saucepan of boiling water, uncovered, until just tender; drain, keep warm.
2. Place pasta in large bowl with tomato, onion, garlic, basil, tuna and vinegar; toss to combine.

SERVES 4
per serving 3.3g total fat (1g saturated fat); 1877kj (449 cal); 32.1g protein; 70.1g carbohydrate; 7.1g fibre
tip you can substitute any pasta for the penne in this recipe.
serving suggestion serve with ciabatta bread and a mixed green salad.

farfalle with baked salmon, caperberries and dill

PREPARATION TIME 25 MINUTES COOKING TIME 30 MINUTES

Farfalle is a classic short, dense pasta that is called bow ties or butterflies in English. Its frilled edges and soft pleats help contain sauce; substitute orecchiette (little ears) or fusilli (spirals or corkscrews) if preferred.

2 large red onions (600g)
1 cup (160g) caperberries, rinsed, drained
cooking-oil spray
1 fresh red thai chilli, chopped finely
¼ cup finely chopped fresh dill
2 teaspoons olive oil
1kg piece skinless salmon fillet
500g farfalle pasta
⅔ cup (150ml) dry white wine
2 tablespoons lemon juice
½ cup (125ml) light cream
250g baby rocket leaves, trimmed

1. Preheat oven to 200°C/180°C fan-forced.
2. Cut each onion into eight wedges; place, in single layer, in large baking dish with caperberries. Spray lightly with cooking-oil spray; roast, uncovered, about 25 minutes or until onion is just softened.
3. Meanwhile, combine chilli and half of the dill in small bowl with olive oil. Place salmon on large baking-paper lined oven tray; brush salmon both sides with chilli mixture. Roast, uncovered, about 10 minutes or until salmon is just tender and cooked as desired.
4. Cook pasta in large saucepan of boiling water, uncovered, until just tender.
5. While pasta is cooking, combine wine and juice in small saucepan; bring to a boil. Reduce heat, simmer, uncovered, about 5 minutes or until liquid reduces by half. Add cream and remaining dill.
6. Place pasta, flaked salmon, onion mixture and dill cream sauce in large bowl with baby rocket leaves; toss gently to combine.

SERVES 8
per serving 15.6g total fat (5.1g saturated fat); 2057kj (492 cal); 33.9g protein; 50g carbohydrate; 4.9g fibre
serving suggestions sprinkle with freshly ground pepper and finely chopped chives.

salmon and herb soufflés

PREPARATION TIME 10 MINUTES COOKING TIME 20 MINUTES

210g can red salmon, drained, flaked
1 tablespoon finely chopped fresh chives
1 tablespoon chopped fresh flat-leaf parsley
pinch cayenne pepper
20g butter
1 tablespoon plain flour
½ cup (125ml) milk
2 egg whites

1. Preheat oven to 180°C/160°C fan-forced. Oil two 1 cup (250ml) soufflé dishes.
2. Combine salmon, herbs and cayenne in medium bowl; mix well.
3. Heat butter in small saucepan, stir in flour; cook until bubbling, remove from heat. Gradually stir in milk; stir over heat until sauce boils and thickens. Stir sauce into salmon mixture.
4. Beat egg whites with elextric beaters until soft peaks form; fold into salmon mixture. Spoon mixture into dishes. Bake, uncovered, about 20 minutes or until risen and well browned. Serve immediately.

SERVES 2
per serving 17.3g total fat (4.2g saturated fat); 1208kj (289 cal); 7.7g protein; 25.6g carbohydrate; 0.2g fibre

farfalle with baked salmon, caperberries and dill

char-grilled tuna with mixed vegetable stir-fry

char-grilled tuna with mixed vegetable stir-fry

PREPARATION TIME 15 MINUTES (PLUS REFRIGERATION TIME) COOKING TIME 10 MINUTES

¼ cup (60ml) sweet chilli sauce
¼ cup (60ml) lime juice
1 tablespoon coarsely chopped fresh coriander
6 x 200g tuna steaks
2 tablespoons finely grated lime rind
1 fresh red thai chilli, chopped finely
1 clove garlic, crushed
2 medium zucchini (240g)
2 medium carrots (240g)
2 medium red capsicums (400g), sliced thinly
1 medium yellow capsicum (200g), sliced thinly
1 small red onion (100g), sliced thinly

1. Combine sauce, 2 teaspoons of the juice and coriander in small bowl.
2. Combine remaining juice in large bowl with tuna, rind, chilli and garlic. Cover; refrigerate 1 hour.
3. Meanwhile, cut zucchini and carrots into very thin slices lengthways; cut slices into matchstick-sized pieces.
4. Drain tuna; cook, in batches, on heated oiled grill plate (or grill or barbecue) until browned and cooked as desired.
5. Meanwhile, heat oiled wok or large non-stick frying pan; cook 1 tablespoon of the chilli sauce mixture, zucchini, carrot, capsicums and onion, in batches, until vegetables are just tender.
6. Serve tuna on vegetables, drizzled with remaining chilli sauce mixture.

SERVES 6
per serving 11.8g total fat (4.6g saturated fat); 1517kj (363 cal); 52.6g protein; 10.7g carbohydrate; 2.9g fibre

salmon with dill and caper dressing

PREPARATION TIME 5 MINUTES COOKING TIME 10 MINUTES

2 tablespoons low-fat sour cream
1 tablespoon drained baby capers
2 teaspoons coarsely chopped fresh dill
2 teaspoons horseradish cream
1 teaspoon lime juice
4 x 150g salmon fillets

1. Combine sour cream, capers, dill, horseradish and juice in small bowl.
2. Heat oiled large frying pan; cook salmon until browned both sides and cooked as desired. Serve salmon with dill and caper dressing.

SERVES 4
per serving 13g total fat (3.9g saturated fat); 1007kj (241 cal); 29.7g protein; 1.2g carbohydrate; 0.1g fibre

stir-fried octopus with fettuccine

PREPARATION TIME 20 MINUTES (PLUS REFRIGERATION TIME) COOKING TIME 20 MINUTES

1kg baby octopus
2 tablespoons mango chutney
⅓ cup (80ml) lemon juice
¼ cup (60ml) no-oil french dressing
2 cloves garlic, crushed
2 tablespoons honey
2 tablespoons chopped fresh coriander leaves
4 green onions, chopped
500g fettuccine pasta
2 teaspoons vegetable oil
2 tablespoons chopped fresh parsley

1. Remove and discard heads and beaks from octopus. Combine octopus, chutney, juice, dressing, garlic, honey, coriander and onions in large bowl. Cover; refrigerate several hours or overnight.
2. Drain octopus; reserve marinade. Cook pasta in large saucepan of boiling water, uncovered, until just tender; drain.
3. Heat oil in wok; stir-fry octopus, in batches, over high heat 3 minutes or until tender. Return octopus to wok with reserved marinade, pasta and parsley; stir until marinade boils.

SERVES 6
per serving 5.4g total fat (1g saturated fat); 2261kj (541 cal); 49.1g protein; 72.3g carbohydrate; 4.9g fibre
tip recipe best made close to serving.

greek barbecued octopus seafood salad

PREPARATION TIME 10 MINUTES (PLUS REFRIGERATION TIME) COOKING TIME 10 MINUTES (PLUS COOLING TIME)

1kg cleaned baby octopus, halved
⅓ cup (80ml) lemon juice
1 tablespoon honey
4 cloves garlic, crushed
¼ teaspoon cayenne pepper
100g baby spinach leaves
1 small red onion (100g), sliced thinly
250g cherry tomatoes, halved
1 tablespoon shredded fresh mint
1 tablespoon shredded fresh basil
100g fetta cheese, chopped coarsely

1. Combine octopus, juice, honey, garlic and cayenne in large bowl. Cover; refrigerate 3 hours or overnight.
2. Drain octopus over large bowl; reserve marinade. Cook octopus, in batches, on heated oiled grill plate (or barbecue) until tender.
3. Meanwhile, place reserved marinade in small saucepan; bring to a boil. Reduce heat, simmer, uncovered, about 5 minutes or until marinade reduces slightly; cool.
4. Just before serving, place octopus and marinade in large bowl with remaining ingredients; toss gently to combine.

SERVES 4
per serving 10.3g total fat (4.8g saturated fat); 1689kj (404 cal); 65.2g protein; 11.6g carbohydrate; 2.6g fibre
tip you can substitute rocket or any other salad green for the spinach.

scallop and goat cheese salad

PREPARATION TIME 15 MINUTES COOKING TIME 10 MINUTES

8 slices white bread
12 large scallops (360g)
1 medium cos lettuce, torn
1 small red onion (100g), sliced finely
150g firm goat cheese, chopped
200g low-fat yogurt
¼ cup (60ml) lemon juice
1 tablespoon wholegrain mustard
1 clove garlic, crushed

1. Discard crusts from bread; cut bread into 2cm squares. Heat oiled large frying pan; cook bread, stirring, until browned all over. Remove from pan.
2. Cook scallops in same pan until browned both sides and cooked as desired.
3. Combine bread and scallops in large bowl with lettuce, onion and cheese; drizzle with combined yogurt, juice, mustard and garlic.

SERVES 4
per serving 9.6g total fat (4.9g saturated fat); 1404kj (336 cal); 26g protein; 35g carbohydrate; 6.4g fibre

scallops with sugar snap pea salad

PREPARATION TIME 20 MINUTES COOKING TIME 5 MINUTES

250g sugar snap peas, trimmed
20 scallops on the half shell (800g), roe removed
100g cherry tomatoes, halved
1 medium lebanese cucumber (130g), seeded, sliced thinly
½ cup loosely packed fresh mint leaves

BALSAMIC DRESSING
1 teaspoon finely grated lemon rind
2 tablespoons lemon juice
1 clove garlic, crushed
1 tablespoon olive oil
2 teaspoons balsamic vinegar

LEMON DRESSING
1 tablespoon finely grated lemon rind
¼ cup (60ml) lemon juice
1 clove garlic, crushed
1 tablespoon olive oil

1. Make balsamic dressing. Make lemon dressing.
2. Boil, steam or microwave peas until just tender; drain.
3. Remove scallops from shell; reserve shells. Place scallops, in single layer, in large steamer fitted over large saucepan of boiling water; steam scallops, covered, about 4 minutes or until cooked as desired.
4. Meanwhile, rinse and dry scallop shells.
5. Place peas in medium bowl with tomato, cucumber, mint and balsamic dressing; toss gently to combine.
6. Return scallops to shells; drizzle with lemon dressing. Serve scallops with salad.

BALSAMIC DRESSING place ingredients in screw-top jar; shake well.

LEMON DRESSING place ingredients in screw-top jar; shake well.

SERVES 4
per serving 10g total fat (1.5g saturated fat); 681kj (163 cal); 11.5g protein; 6.3g carbohydrate; 3.1g fibre

tagliatelle puttanesca

PREPARATION TIME 10 MINUTES COOKING TIME 20 MINUTES

2 teaspoons vegetable oil
1 large brown onion (200g), sliced thickly
3 cloves garlic, crushed
4 fresh red thai chillies, chopped finely
600ml bottled tomato pasta sauce
¼ cup (40g) drained capers
1 cup (160g) kalamata olives, seeded
8 drained anchovies, halved
½ cup coarsely chopped fresh flat-leaf parsley
375g tagliatelle pasta

1. Heat oil in large frying pan; cook onion, garlic and chilli, stirring, until onion softens. Add sauce, capers, olives and anchovies; bring to a boil. Reduce heat, simmer, uncovered, about 5 minutes or until sauce thickens slightly. Stir in parsley.
2. Cook pasta in large saucepan of boiling water, uncovered, until just tender; drain. Serve pasta with sauce.

SERVES 4
per serving 6g total fat (0.9g saturated fat); 2107kj (504 cal); 16.6g protein; 95.3g carbohydrate; 10.1g fibre

mussels with asian flavours

PREPARATION TIME 20 MINUTES COOKING TIME 15 MINUTES

1.5kg black mussels
1¼ cups (250g) jasmine rice
1 tablespoon sesame oil
4cm piece fresh ginger (20g), grated
1 tablespoon finely chopped fresh lemon grass
3 fresh red thai chillies, chopped finely
⅓ cup (80ml) sweet sherry
2 teaspoons cornflour
½ cup (125ml) water
2 tablespoons mirin
1 tablespoon soy sauce
12 green onions, sliced thinly
¼ cup coarsely chopped fresh mint
¼ cup coarsely chopped fresh coriander

1. Scrub mussels under cold water; discard beards.
2. Cook rice in medium saucepan of boiling water, uncovered, until just tender; drain. Cover to keep warm.
3. Meanwhile, heat oil in wok; stir-fry ginger, lemon grass and chilli until fragrant. Add mussels and sherry; cook, covered, about 5 minutes or until mussels open (discard any that do not).
4. Blend cornflour with the water, mirin and soy sauce in small jug; add to wok, stir-fry until mixture boils and thickens slightly. Remove from heat; stir in onion and herbs. Serve mussels with rice.

SERVES 4
per serving 6.4g total fat (1.1g saturated fat); 1547kj (370 cal); 14.1g protein; 58.4g carbohydrate; 2.7g fibre

citrus-ginger steamed bream

PREPARATION TIME 20 MINUTES COOKING TIME 15 MINUTES

We used whole bream for this recipe, but any fairly small white-fleshed fish can be used. You will need four 80cm-long sheets of foil to wrap the fish.

1 medium lemon (140g)
2 medium oranges (480g)
2 cloves garlic, crushed
2cm piece fresh ginger (10g), grated
4 x 250g whole bream, cleaned
2 cups (400g) jasmine rice
⅓ cup loosely packed torn fresh basil leaves

1. Using vegetable peeler, peel rind carefully from lemon and one orange; cut rind into thin strips. Squeeze juice of both oranges and lemon into large bowl; stir in rind, garlic and ginger. Score fish both sides; add to bowl, coat in marinade.
2. Fold 80cm-long piece of foil in half crossways; place one fish on foil, spoon a quarter of the marinade onto fish. Fold foil over fish to tightly enclose. Repeat process with remaining fish and marinade.
3. Place fish parcels in large steamer fitted over large saucepan of boiling water; steam, covered, about 15 minutes or until cooked as desired.
4. Meanwhile, cook rice in large saucepan of boiling water, uncovered, until just tender; drain. Divide rice among serving plates; top with fish, drizzle with cooking juices, sprinkle with basil.

SERVES 4
per serving 7.1g total fat (2.4g saturated fat); 2286kj (547 cal); 32.3g protein; 86.6g carbohydrate; 3.5g fibre
tip use a zester, if you have one, to remove orange and lemon rind.

chilli crab

PREPARATION TIME 25 MINUTES COOKING TIME 25 MINUTES

8 uncooked medium blue swimmer crabs (6kg)
1 tablespoon peanut oil
4 cloves garlic, crushed
2 tablespoons grated fresh ginger
4 fresh red thai chillies, chopped finely
1 tablespoon fish sauce
⅓ cup (80ml) tomato sauce
¼ cup (60ml) sweet chilli sauce
2 tablespoons brown sugar
1 cup (250ml) fish stock
1 cup (250ml) water
¼ cup coarsely chopped fresh coriander

1. Holding crab firmly, slide sharp knife under top of shell at back; lever off shell. Remove and discard gills and mustard-coloured gut. Rinse crab body under cold running water; quarter crab. Remove claws; using nutcracker or meat mallet, crack both sections of claws.
2. Heat oil in wok; stir-fry garlic, ginger and chilli until fragrant. Add sauces, sugar, stock and the water; bring to a boil. Boil, stirring constantly, for 5 minutes. Reserve two-thirds of the sauce in medium heatproof jug.
3. Place claws in wok with remaining sauce; stir-fry about 4 minutes or until changed in colour. Remove from wok; cover to keep warm.
4. Place half of the reserved sauce and half of the crab body pieces in wok; stir-fry about 5 minutes or until changed in colour. Remove from wok; cover to keep warm. Repeat with remaining reserved sauce and crab body pieces.
5. Serve crab immediately, sprinkled with coriander.

SERVES 8
per serving 3.6g total fat (0.7g saturated fat); 744kj (178 cal); 24.5g protein; 12g carbohydrate; 0.8g fibre

mains
poultry

mexican chicken with black bean and barley salad

PREPARATION TIME 10 MINUTES COOKING TIME 45 MINUTES

Black beans, also known as turtle beans, are Cuban or Latin American rather than Chinese in origin. Jet black with a tiny white eye, black beans can be found, either packaged or loose, in most greengrocers and delicatessens.

½ cup (100g) dried black beans
2 cups (500ml) chicken stock
1 litre (4 cups) water
¾ cup (165g) pearl barley
680g single chicken breast fillets
35g packet taco seasoning mix
⅓ cup (80ml) chicken stock, extra
1 large red capsicum (350g), chopped finely
1 clove garlic, crushed
¼ cup (60ml) lime juice
2 teaspoons olive oil
½ cup loosely packed fresh coriander leaves

1. Preheat oven to 200°C/180°C fan-forced.
2. Combine beans with half of the stock and half of the water in medium saucepan; bring to a boil. Reduce heat, simmer, uncovered, about 45 minutes or until tender, drain. Rinse under cold water; drain.
3. Meanwhile, combine barley with remaining stock and remaining water in medium saucepan; bring to a boil. Reduce heat, simmer, uncovered, until just tender; drain. Rinse under cold water; drain.
4. Combine chicken in medium bowl with blended seasoning and extra stock. Drain chicken; reserve marinade.
5. Place chicken, in single layer, on metal rack in large shallow baking dish; bake, uncovered, about 30 minutes or until cooked through, brushing with reserved marinade halfway through cooking time. Cover; stand 5 minutes then slice thickly.
6. Place beans and barley in large bowl with remaining ingredients; toss gently to combine. Divide salad among serving plates; top with chicken.

SERVES 4
per serving 8.4g total fat (1.9g saturated fat); 1835kj (439 cal); 50.8g protein; 38.6g carbohydrate; 11.5g fibre

moroccan grilled chicken with beetroot puree and couscous

PREPARATION TIME 30 MINUTES COOKING TIME 1 HOUR 15 MINUTES

Pureed beetroot takes on potato mash as one of the great accompaniments. You can also stir a bit more yogurt and a pinch of nutmeg into the beetroot puree to make a delectable dip for pitta crisps.

8 x 170g chicken breast fillets
1 tablespoon olive oil
2 teaspoons finely grated lemon rind
2 tablespoons lemon juice
2 cloves garlic, crushed
1 tablespoon ground coriander
1 tablespoon ground cumin
2 teaspoons ground cardamom
1 teaspoon sweet paprika
1 teaspoon ground turmeric
½ cup finely chopped fresh flat-leaf parsley
¼ cup finely chopped fresh coriander
6 medium beetroots (1kg), trimmed
½ cup (140g) low-fat yogurt
2 cups (400g) couscous
2 cups (500ml) boiling water
¼ cup finely chopped fresh mint

1. Preheat oven to 180°C/160°C fan-forced.
2. Combine chicken, oil, rind, juice, garlic, spices, parsley and coriander in large bowl. Cover; refrigerate 1 hour.
3. Meanwhile, wrap unpeeled beetroot in foil; place on oven tray. Roast about 1 hour or until tender. When cool enough to handle, peel beetroot; chop coarsely then blend or process until pureed. Stir in yogurt; cover to keep warm.
4. Combine couscous and the water in large heatproof bowl. Cover; stand about 5 minutes or until the water is absorbed, fluffing couscous with fork occasionally to separate grains. Add mint; toss gently with fork to combine.
5. Cook undrained chicken, in batches, in large heated lightly oiled frying pan until browned both sides and cooked through. Serve chicken on couscous; top with beetroot puree.

SERVES 8
per serving 7.1g total fat (1.6g saturated fat); 1931kj (462 cal); 49.2g protein; 49.2g carbohydrate; 4.4g fibre
serving suggestion serve with a simple mixed green salad.

spanish-style chicken

PREPARATION TIME 20 MINUTES COOKING TIME 45 MINUTES

Chicken drumettes are drumsticks with the end of the bone chopped off. They are also sold as "lovely legs".

2 teaspoons olive oil
1 large brown onion (200g), chopped coarsely
2 cloves garlic, crushed
2 medium green capsicums (400g), chopped coarsely
16 chicken drumettes (2kg)
410g can tomato puree
1 teaspoon hot paprika
1 tablespoon ground coriander
1 tablespoon ground cumin
½ teaspoon cayenne pepper
2 cups (320g) fresh corn kernels
½ cup (125ml) dry red wine
1 cup (250ml) chicken stock
2 bay leaves
1½ cups (300g) long-grain white rice
2 tablespoons finely chopped fresh flat-leaf parsley

1 Preheat oven to 200°C/180°C fan-forced.

2 Heat oil in large flameproof baking dish with tight-fitting lid; cook onion, garlic and capsicum, stirring, until vegetables just soften. Remove vegetables, leaving as much oil in dish as possible. Add chicken, in batches, to dish; cook until browned all over.

3 Return chicken and vegetables to dish with puree, spices, corn, wine, stock, bay leaves and rice; bring to a boil. Cover tightly; cook in oven about 30 minutes or until rice is tender and chicken cooked through. Sprinkle with parsley just before serving.

SERVES 8
per serving 10.4g total fat (3g saturated fat); 1839kj (440 cal); 42.3g protein; 41g carbohydrate; 3.9g fibre
serving suggestion serve with plenty of warmed crunchy bread rolls.

lemon thyme chicken with spinach and pea pilaf

PREPARATION TIME 10 MINUTES COOKING TIME 50 MINUTES

680g single chicken breast fillets
1 tablespoon coarsely chopped fresh thyme
2 teaspoons finely grated lemon rind
1 tablespoon lemon juice
1 tablespoon olive oil
1 large brown onion (200g), sliced thinly
1 clove garlic, crushed
1½ cups (300g) long-grain brown rice
2½ cups (625ml) water
3 cups (750ml) chicken stock
150g baby spinach leaves
1 cup (125g) frozen peas, thawed
2 teaspoons coarsely chopped fresh thyme, extra
1 tablespoon finely grated lemon rind, extra

1 Combine chicken, thyme, rind, juice and half of the oil in medium bowl. Cover; refrigerate 10 minutes.

2 Meanwhile, heat remaining oil in large deep frying pan; cook onion and garlic, stirring, until onion softens. Add rice; cook, stirring, 1 minute. Add the water and stock; bring to a boil. Reduce heat, simmer, covered, about 45 minutes or until liquid is absorbed and rice is cooked as desired.

3 Meanwhile, cook chicken on heated oiled grill plate (or grill or barbecue) until browned both sides and cooked through. Cover; stand 5 minutes. Slice chicken thickly.

4 Stir spinach, peas, extra thyme and extra rind into pilaf. Divide pilaf among serving plates; top with chicken.

SERVES 4
per serving 5.9g total fat (1.5g saturated fat); 1601kj (383 cal); 45.3g protein; 36.4g carbohydrate; 8.1g fibre

grilled chicken with barley pilaf

PREPARATION TIME 10 MINUTES COOKING TIME 55 MINUTES

1 cup (215g) pearl barley
2 cups (500ml) water
2 cups (500ml) chicken stock
250g cherry tomatoes
150g yellow teardrop tomatoes
4 x 170g chicken breast fillets
½ teaspoon coarsely ground black pepper
½ cup coarsely chopped fresh basil
2 green onions, sliced thinly
1 tablespoon dijon mustard

1. Preheat oven to 220°C/200°C fan-forced. Line baking oven tray with baking paper.
2. Cook barley with the water and stock in medium saucepan, uncovered, over low heat, about 50 minutes or until most of the liquid is absorbed, stirring occasionally.
3. Meanwhile, place tomatoes on oven tray; roast, uncovered, 20 minutes or until just browned and softened.
4. Cook chicken on heated oiled grill plate (or grill or barbecue) until browned both sides and cooked through.
5. Stir tomatoes, pepper, basil and onion gently into barley. Serve chicken, dolloped with mustard, with pilaf.

SERVES 4
per serving 5.9g total fat (1.5g saturated fat); 1601kj (383 cal); 45.3g protein; 36.4g carbohydrate; 8.1g fibre

chicken and fresh pea risoni

PREPARATION TIME 15 MINUTES COOKING TIME 30 MINUTES

Risoni is a small rice-shaped pasta very similar to orzo. You will need 400g of fresh peas in their pods for this recipe.

400g chicken breast fillets
1 litre (4 cups) chicken stock
300g sugar snap peas, trimmed
1 cup (160g) fresh shelled peas
1 tablespoon olive oil
1 small leek (200g), sliced thinly
1 clove garlic, crushed
500g risoni pasta
½ cup (125ml) dry white wine
1 tablespoon white wine vinegar
1 tablespoon finely chopped fresh tarragon

1. Combine chicken and stock in medium frying pan; bring to a boil. Reduce heat; simmer, uncovered, about 10 minutes or until cooked through. Cool chicken in poaching liquid 10 minutes. Remove chicken from pan; reserve liquid. Slice chicken thinly.
2. Meanwhile, boil, steam or microwave peas, separately, until just tender; drain.
3. Heat oil in large saucepan; cook leek and garlic, stirring, until leek softens. Add risoni; stir to coat in leek mixture. Add wine; stir until wine is almost absorbed. Add reserved liquid; bring to a boil. Reduce heat, simmer, uncovered, stirring occasionally, until stock is absorbed and risoni is just tender. Stir in vinegar; remove from heat. Gently stir in chicken, peas and tarragon.

SERVES 4
per serving 9.7g total fat (2g saturated fat); 2867kj (686 cal); 44.6g protein; 98.2g carbohydrate; 11.1g fibre

creole chicken and dirty rice

PREPARATION TIME 20 MINUTES COOKING TIME 45 MINUTES

This chicken recipe originated in the southern United States, where European cuisine merged with Haitian and African-American fare to create Creole dishes – the spicy, rich cooking style of Louisiana. As for the dirty rice, this classic recipe from the Deep South is so delicious that both Cajun and Creole cooks claim it as their own.

1 medium brown onion (150g), chopped coarsely
1 clove garlic, crushed
2 bay leaves
1 teaspoon hot paprika
½ teaspoon cayenne pepper
½ teaspoon cracked black pepper
1 medium green capsicum (200g), chopped coarsely
3 trimmed sticks celery (225g), chopped coarsely
100g fresh okra, sliced thinly
2 x 400g cans crushed tomatoes
500g chicken breast fillets, chopped coarsely

DIRTY RICE

1⅔ cups (330g) long-grain white rice
400g lean pork fillet
1 small green capsicum (150g), chopped finely
1 small brown onion (80g), chopped finely
1 trimmed stick celery (75g), chopped finely
1 teaspoon hot paprika
½ teaspoon mustard powder
¼ teaspoon ground cumin
1 teaspoon finely chopped fresh thyme
1 teaspoon finely chopped fresh oregano
1 cup (250ml) water
1 cup (250ml) chicken stock

1. Heat large oiled frying pan; cook onion, garlic, bay leaves and spices, stirring, until onion softens. Add capsicum, celery and okra; cook, stirring, until vegetables are just tender. Add undrained tomatoes; bring to a boil. Reduce heat, simmer, uncovered, stirring occasionally, about 25 minutes or until vegetable mixture thickens slightly.
2. Make dirty rice.
3. Add chicken to vegetable mixture; cook, uncovered, about 15 minutes or until chicken is cooked through.
4. Serve creole chicken with dirty rice.

DIRTY RICE cook ⅔ cup of the rice, uncovered, in medium saucepan of boiling water, until tender. Drain; keep warm. Chop pork into fine slivers (or blend or process). Cook pork in large heated oiled frying pan with capsicum, onion, celery, spices and herbs, stirring, until onion softens. Add remaining rice, the water and stock; bring to a boil. Reduce heat, simmer, covered, about 15 minutes or until rice is tender. Add cooked rice; toss gently until just combined.

SERVES 6
per serving 4.4g total fat (1.2g saturated fat); 1735kj (415 cal); 40.7g protein; 52.2g carbohydrate; 4.8g fibre

mushroom, chicken and asparagus risotto

PREPARATION TIME 20 MINUTES COOKING TIME 1 HOUR

320g chicken breast fillets
1 trimmed stick celery (75g), chopped finely
1 green onion, chopped
½ small carrot (35g), chopped
½ teaspoon black peppercorns
250g asparagus
1 litre (4 cups) chicken stock
2 cups (500ml) water, approximately
2 teaspoons olive oil
1 clove garlic, crushed
1 large onion (200g), chopped
250g button mushrooms, sliced
100g fresh shiitake mushrooms, sliced finely
2½ cups (500g) quick-cook brown rice
100g enoki mushrooms
1 tablespoon finely chopped fresh flat-leaf parsley

1. Combine chicken, celery, onion, carrot and peppercorns in saucepan, add enough water to cover chicken; simmer, uncovered, about 15 minutes or until chicken is tender. Remove chicken from pan, strain poaching liquid; reserve liquid. Cut chicken into thin strips.
2. Boil, steam or microwave asparagus until just tender, cut into 4cm pieces.
3. Combine reserved liquid, stock and enough of the water to make 2 litres (8 cups) of liquid in large heavy-based saucepan, bring to a boil; simmer to keep hot.
4. Heat oil in another saucepan; cook garlic, onion, button and shiitake mushrooms, stirring, until onion is soft. Stir in rice to coat.
5. Stir ⅔ cup (160ml) hot stock mixture into rice mixture; cook, stirring, over low heat until liquid is absorbed. Continue adding stock mixture in 1-cup batches, stirring, until absorbed between each addition. Total cooking time should be about 35 minutes or until rice is tender.
6. Stir in chicken, asparagus, enoki mushrooms and parsley, stir until hot.

SERVES 6
per serving 5.7g total fat (1.3g saturated fat); 1818kj (435 cal); 24.2g protein; 71.1g carbohydrate; 6.6g fibre
tip recipe best made just before serving.

chicken and wild rice paella

PREPARATION TIME 25 MINUTES COOKING TIME 45 MINUTES

8 uncooked medium prawns (300g)
8 small mussels
⅓ cup (60g) wild rice
560g skinless chicken thigh cutlets
1 small leek (200g), chopped
2 cloves garlic, crushed
1 medium yellow capsicum (200g), chopped coarsely
1 medium red capsicum (200g), chopped coarsely
1 teaspoon sambal oelek
2 tablespoons chopped fresh thyme
1 cup (200g) basmati rice
¼ cup (60ml) dry white wine
½ teaspoon saffron threads
2 cups (500ml) chicken stock
2 tablespoons drained capers
2 medium yellow zucchini (240g), chopped coarsely
1 cup coarsely chopped fresh flat-leaf parsley

1. Shell and devein prawns, discarding heads and leaving tails intact. Scrub mussels under cold water; remove beards.
2. Cook wild rice in saucepan of boiling water, uncovered, about 20 minutes or until tender; drain, rinse, drain well.
3. Cook chicken in large frying pan, both sides, until browned but not cooked through. Remove from pan; drain on absorbent paper. Remove bones from chicken; slice chicken.
4. Drain all but 1 tablespoon of drippings from pan; cook leek, garlic, capsicums, sambal and thyme, stirring, 5 minutes. Add basmati rice, wine, saffron, stock and chicken; cook, covered, about 12 minutes or until rice is just tender. Add seafood, capers, zucchini and wild rice; cook, covered, further 5 minutes or until seafood is tender. Serve sprinkled with parsley.

SERVES 6
per serving 5.9g total fat (1.7g saturated fat); 1551kj (371 cal); 24.8g protein; 52.3g carbohydrate; 2.9g fibre
tip recipe best made just before serving.

chicken breasts poached with ham and herbs

PREPARATION TIME 30 MINUTES COOKING TIME 15 MINUTES

4 x 170g chicken breast fillets
¼ cup finely chopped fresh chives
¼ cup finely chopped fresh basil
2 cloves garlic, crushed
2 teaspoons finely grated lemon rind
1 teaspoon olive oil
200g thinly sliced leg ham
4 green onions, sliced thinly

LEMON MUSTARD DRESSING

3 teaspoons olive oil
¼ cup (60ml) lemon juice
1 teaspoon dijon mustard

1 Pound chicken between sheets of plastic wrap until 1cm thick. Combine herbs, garlic, rind and oil in small bowl. Divide herb mixture among chicken fillets; top with ham.

2 Starting from one long side, roll chicken pieces tightly; enclose in plastic wrap, twisting ends to seal. Enclose each roll in one more layer of plastic wrap to secure.

3 Bring large frying pan of water to a boil; add rolls. Reduce heat, simmer, covered, about 15 minutes or until chicken is cooked through. Remove rolls from poaching liquid; cool rolls 5 minutes. Discard liquid.

4 Meanwhile, make lemon mustard dressing.

5 Remove plastic wrap from rolls; slice thinly. Divide slices among serving plates; sprinkle with onion, drizzle with dressing and serve with steamed green beans, if desired.

LEMON MUSTARD DRESSING place ingredients in screw-top jar; shake well.

SERVES 4
per serving 10.4g total fat (2.3g saturated fat); 1615kj (295 cal); 48.3g protein; 1.2g carbohydrate; 0.7g fibre

grilled paprika chicken with raisin and coriander pilaf

PREPARATION TIME 20 MINUTES (PLUS REFRIGERATION TIME) COOKING TIME 45 MINUTES

4 x 165g skinless chicken thigh cutlets
2 tablespoons lemon juice
3 cloves garlic, crushed
½ teaspoon hot paprika
1 teaspoon sweet paprika
1 teaspoon ground cinnamon
¾ cup (200g) yogurt
1 tablespoon olive oil
1 medium brown onion (150g), chopped finely
2 cups (200g) basmati rice
1 litre (4 cups) chicken stock
½ cup (85g) chopped raisins
¾ cup chopped fresh coriander

1 Combine chicken, juice, garlic and spices in large bowl. Cover; refrigerate 3 hours or overnight.

2 Cook chicken mixture, in batches, on heated oiled grill plate (or grill or barbecue), brushing with a little of the yogurt, until browned and cooked through.

3 Meanwhile, heat oil in medium saucepan; cook onion, stirring, until softened. Add rice; stir to coat in onion mixture. Add stock; bring to a boil. Reduce heat, simmer, covered, stirring occasionally, about 25 minutes or until rice is almost tender. Stir in raisins; cook, covered, 5 minutes.

4 Stir coriander into pilaf off the heat just before serving. Top pilaf with chicken and remaining yogurt.

SERVES 4
per serving 16g total fat (4.9g saturated fat); 2140kj (512 cal); 31g protein; 60.7g carbohydrate; 2.9g fibre

honeyed chicken stir-fry

PREPARATION TIME 10 MINUTES (PLUS REFRIGERATION TIME) COOKING TIME 15 MINUTES

600g chicken breast fillets, sliced thinly
2 tablespoons salt-reduced soy sauce
¼ cup honey (60ml)
1 clove garlic, crushed
1 teaspoon finely chopped fresh ginger
100g shiitake mushrooms, sliced thinly
1 medium red capsicum (200g), chopped finely
160g snake beans, cut into 8cm lengths
425g can baby corn, drained

1 Combine chicken, sauce, honey, garlic and ginger in large bowl. Cover; refrigerate several hours or overnight.
2 Stir-fry chicken mixture, in batches, in heated wok until chicken is tender.
3 Add mushroom, capsicum, beans and corn to wok; stir-fry for 5 minutes or until beans are just tender.
4 Return chicken to wok; stir-fry about 2 minutes or until chicken is hot.

SERVES 4
per serving 3.8g total fat (0.9g saturated fat); 1200kj (287 cal); 37.9g protein; 25.5g carbohydrate; 4.4g fibre
tip cook recipe just before serving.

thai-style steamed chicken with noodles

PREPARATION TIME 15 MINUTES COOKING TIME 30 MINUTES

4 large silver beet leaves
4 x 170g chicken breast fillets
2 kaffir lime leaves, shredded finely
2 fresh red thai chillies, sliced thinly
1 tablespoon finely chopped lemon grass
500g fresh rice noodles

SWEET CHILLI DRESSING
¼ cup (60ml) sweet chilli sauce
2 teaspoons fish sauce
1 tablespoon lime juice
1 clove garlic, crushed
2 tablespoons finely chopped fresh coriander

1 Drop silver beet into a pan of boiling water, drain immediately, then dip into a bowl of iced water until cold; drain well.
2 Place a chicken fillet on a silver beet leaf, sprinkle with lime leaves, chilli and lemon grass. Wrap silver beet around chicken to enclose.
3 Line a bamboo steamer with baking paper or a heatproof plate. Place chicken in steamer over wok of simmering water. Steam, covered, about 15 minutes or until cooked through.
4 Meanwhile, place noodles in large heatproof bowl, cover with hot water and stand for 5 minutes; drain.
5 Make sweet chilli dressing.
6 Toss half of the dressing through noodles. Serve sliced chicken with noodles and remaining sweet chilli dressing.

SWEET CHILLI DRESSING combine ingredients in small bowl.

SERVES 4
per serving 5.3g total fat (1.1g saturated fat); 1965kj (470 cal); 45.2g protein; 58.9g carbohydrate; 4.3g fibre

balsamic-glazed chicken breasts with tomato and basil couscous

PREPARATION TIME 20 MINUTES COOKING TIME 30 MINUTES

8 medium tomatoes (1.5kg)
8 cloves garlic, sliced thinly
1 tablespoon olive oil
8 x 175g chicken breast fillets
½ cup (125ml) balsamic vinegar
2 tablespoons honey
¼ cup (60ml) dry sherry
2 tablespoons wholegrain mustard
1 litre (4 cups) boiling water
4 cups (800g) couscous
20g butter
1 cup finely shredded fresh basil

1 Preheat oven to 180°C/160°C fan-forced.
2 Cut each tomato into eight wedges. Combine tomato, in single layer, with garlic and half of the oil in large shallow baking dish; roast, uncovered, 30 minutes.
3 Meanwhile, heat remaining oil in large frying pan; cook chicken, in batches, until lightly browned all over.
4 Place vinegar, honey, sherry and mustard in same pan; bring to a boil, return chicken to pan. Reduce heat, simmer, uncovered, about 10 minutes or until chicken is cooked through.
5 Bring the water to a boil in medium saucepan; stir in couscous and butter. Remove from heat; stand, covered, about 5 minutes or until liquid is absorbed, fluffing with fork occasionally. Stir in tomato mixture and basil; toss with fork to combine. Serve chicken on couscous; drizzle with remaining pan juices.

SERVES 8
per serving 9.3g total fat (2.8g saturated fat); 2771kj (663 cal); 54.5g protein; 86.2g carbohydrate; 3.6g fibre

rosemary, brie and sun-dried tomato chicken with corn mash

PREPARATION TIME 30 MINUTES COOKING TIME 15 MINUTES

30g sun-dried tomatoes in oil, drained, chopped finely
1 tablespoon finely chopped fresh rosemary
4 x 170g chicken breast fillets
60g firm brie, quartered
1kg medium new potatoes, quartered
2 cloves garlic, crushed
2 tablespoons milk
2 tablespoons sour cream
310g can creamed corn

1 Combine tomato and rosemary in small bowl.
2 Using a small sharp knife, slit a pocket in one side of each chicken fillet, taking care not to cut all the way through. Divide tomato mixture and brie among pockets; secure with toothpicks.
3 Cook chicken on heated oiled grill plate (or grill or barbecue) until browned both sides and cooked through; cover to keep warm.
4 Meanwhile, boil, steam or microwave potatoes until tender; drain. Mash potato in large bowl with garlic, milk and sour cream; fold in corn. Serve chicken with mash.

SERVES 4
per serving 13.9g total fat (6.8g saturated fat); 2207kj (528 cal); 50.3g protein; 48.9g carbohydrate; 8.9g fibre

balsamic-glazed chicken breasts with tomato and basil couscous

thai chicken in lettuce-leaf cups

thai chicken in lettuce-leaf cups

PREPARATION TIME 20 MINUTES (PLUS REFRIGERATION TIME)

You will need to purchase a large barbecued chicken weighing approximately 900g for this recipe.

8 large iceberg lettuce leaves
4 cups (400g) shredded chicken
1 large zucchini (150g), grated coarsely
1 medium carrot (120g), grated coarsely
2 green onions, sliced thinly
1 medium red capsicum (200g), sliced thinly
1 tablespoon finely chopped fresh mint
2 tablespoons coarsely chopped fresh coriander
1 tablespoon kecap manis
1 teaspoon sesame oil
1 tablespoon lime juice
2 tablespoons sweet chilli sauce

1. Trim lettuce-leaf edges with scissors. Place leaves in large bowl of iced water; refrigerate.
2. Meanwhile, combine chicken, zucchini, carrot, onion, capsicum, mint and half the coriander in large bowl with combined kecap manis, oil and juice in large bowl; toss gently to combine.
3. Dry lettuce; divide leaves among serving plates. Fill with chicken mixture; drizzle with combined sweet chilli sauce and remaining coriander.

SERVES 4
per serving 9.7g total fat (2.5g saturated fat); 1099kj (263 cal); 30.6g protein; 12.9g carbohydrate; 3.4g fibre

herb-coated chicken

PREPARATION TIME 20 MINUTES COOKING TIME 30 MINUTES

cooking-oil spray
1 cup (70g) stale breadcrumbs
1 clove garlic, crushed
½ teaspoon cajun seasoning
1 teaspoon finely chopped fresh thyme
1 teaspoon finely chopped fresh oregano
2 teaspoons finely chopped fresh basil
6 x 45g chicken tenderloins
⅓ cup (80g) low-fat yogurt

1. Preheat oven to 180°C/160°C fan-forced. Coat oven tray with cooking-oil spray.
2. Combine breadcrumbs, garlic, seasoning and herbs in medium bowl.
3. Coat chicken in yogurt, then breadcrumb mixture; place on oven tray. Bake, uncovered, about 30 minutes or until lightly browned and cooked through.

SERVES 2
per serving 4g total fat (1.3g saturated fat); 777kj (186 cal); 33g protein; 3.8g carbohydrate; 0.3g fibre
tip cook recipe just before serving.
serving suggestion serve with a tomato, cucumber and snow pea sprout salad drizzled with freshly squeezed lemon juice.

chicken, noodle and oyster-mushroom stir-fry

PREPARATION TIME 15 MINUTES COOKING TIME 15 MINUTES

You will need about 800g of broccoli for this recipe. Hokkien (or stir-fry) noodles are sold in cryovac packages in the refrigerated section of your supermarket.

500g hokkien noodles
500g chicken thigh fillets, chopped coarsely
1 clove garlic, crushed
200g broccoli florets
150g oyster mushrooms, halved
1 medium red onion (170g), sliced thinly
200g snow peas, halved
¼ cup (60ml) oyster sauce

1. Rinse noodles under hot water; drain. Transfer to large bowl; separate noodles with fork.
2. Stir-fry chicken in heated oiled wok, in batches, until browned all over and cooked through.
3. Stir-fry garlic, broccoli, mushrooms and onion in wok until onion just softens. Return chicken to wok with noodles, snow peas and sauce; stir-fry until vegetables are just tender.

SERVES 4
per serving 4.8g total fat (1g saturated fat); 2203kj (527 cal); 46.2g protein; 72.9g carbohydrate; 8g fibre
serving suggestion serve with a side dish of chopped fresh chilli or sambal oelek to add heat to the noodles.

chicken, kumara and pasta stir-fry

PREPARATION TIME 30 MINUTES (PLUS REFRIGERATION TIME) COOKING TIME 25 MINUTES

500g chicken breast fillets, sliced
⅓ cup shredded fresh basil
¼ cup (60ml) white wine vinegar
2 tablespoons lemon juice
1 teaspoon sugar
3 cloves garlic, crushed
1½ tablespoons olive oil
300g coloured fettuccine pasta
1 small kumara (250g), sliced
1 large onion (200g), sliced
150g snow peas, sliced

1. Combine chicken, ¼ cup of the basil, vinegar, juice, sugar, garlic and half the oil in large bowl. Cover; refrigerate several hours or overnight.
2. Drain chicken; reserve marinade. Cook pasta in large saucepan of boiling water, uncovered, until just tender; drain.
3. Meanwhile, boil, steam or microwave kumara until almost tender; drain.
4. Heat remaining oil in wok; stir-fry onion, over high heat until soft, remove. Add chicken, in batches, stir-fry until browned both sides.
5. Add kumara to wok; stir-fry, 3 minutes. Return onion to wok with reserved marinade, pasta and snow peas, cook, stirring, until marinade boils. Sprinkle with remaining basil.

SERVES 6
per serving 7.2g total fat (1.3g saturated fat); 1455kj (348 cal); 26.5g protein; 43.2g carbohydrate; 4.4g fibre
tip recipe best made just before serving.

spicy thai-style chicken

PREPARATION TIME 10 MINUTES COOKING TIME 20 MINUTES

500g lean minced chicken
3 cloves garlic, crushed
⅓ cup (80ml) sweet chilli sauce
1 tablespoon fish sauce
2 tablespoons salt-reduced soy sauce
4 green onions, chopped finely
2 tablespoons finely shredded fresh basil
500g baby buk choy, halved

1 Cook chicken in heated wok, stirring, until cooked through.
2 Add garlic and chilli sauce; cook, stirring, until mixture is browned. Stir in sauces, onion and basil.
3 Meanwhile, boil, steam or microwave buk choy until tender; drain.
4 Serve chicken immediately, with buk choy.

SERVES 4
per serving 10.7g total fat (3.1g saturated fat); 1037kj (248 cal); 26.7g protein; 11g carbohydrate; 2.3g fibre
tip cook recipe just before serving.

chinese-spiced chicken

PREPARATION TIME 20 MINUTES COOKING TIME 20 MINUTES

You will need a 20cm-square piece of clean, dry cotton muslin to make the bouquet garni – the classic French bag of dried spices often used to infuse stocks and sauces.

1 tablespoon peanut oil
6 green onions, chopped finely
2cm piece fresh ginger (10g), grated
1 clove garlic, crushed
2 tablespoons soy sauce
2 tablespoons dry sherry
1 teaspoon toasted sesame seeds
700g chicken breast fillets
375g fresh thin egg noodles

BOUQUET GARNI
2 star anise
1 cinnamon stick, crushed
1 teaspoon fennel seeds
3 whole cloves

1 Heat oil in small saucepan; cook onion, ginger and garlic, stirring, 1 minute. Add sauce, sherry and seeds; simmer, stirring, 1 minute. Remove pan from heat; reserve.
2 Make bouquet garni. Place bouquet garni and chicken in large saucepan of boiling water; return to a boil. Reduce heat, simmer, stirring occasionally, about 10 minutes or until chicken is cooked through. Cool chicken in poaching liquid 10 minutes. Remove chicken from pan then slice thinly. Discard bouquet garni.
3 Return poaching liquid in pan to a boil; cook noodles, uncovered, until just tender. Drain noodles, reserving 2 tablespoons of the poaching liquid; stir the liquid through noodles in large bowl. Divide noodles among serving bowls; top with chicken and onion mixture.

BOUQUET GARNI place ingredients in centre of 20cm muslin square; bring four corners together, tie together tightly with cotton kitchen string.

SERVES 4
per serving 10.1g total fat (2.1g saturated fat); 2098kj (502 cal); 49.4g protein; 49.8g carbohydrate; 2.4g fibre

honey sage chicken with fruity seasoning

PREPARATION TIME 30 MINUTES COOKING TIME 2 HOURS

1.6kg chicken

1 tablespoon low-salt soy sauce

1 tablespoon honey

FRUITY SEASONING

½ cup (100g) brown rice

¼ cup (45g) wild rice

¼ cup (40g) sultanas

¼ cup (35g) chopped dried apricots

¼ cup chopped fresh chives

1 tablespoon chopped fresh sage

1 clove garlic, crushed

1 egg white, beaten lightly

SAGE SAUCE

1 teaspoon cornflour

¼ cup (60ml) dry white wine

¾ cup (180ml) chicken stock

2 teaspoons chopped fresh sage

2 teaspoons worcestershire sauce

1. Make fruity seasoning.
2. Preheat oven to 180°C/160°C fan-forced.
3. Remove skin and fat from chicken. Fill chicken with fruity seasoning, secure opening with skewers. Tie legs together, tuck wings under, place chicken on wire rack in baking dish, brush evenly with some of the combined sauce and honey.
4. Bake, uncovered, about 1½ hours or until chicken is tender, brushing during first half of cooking with remaining honey mixture. Cover legs and wings with foil during cooking if chicken is browning too quickly.
5. Make sage sauce. Serve chicken with sauce.

FRUITY SEASONING cook brown rice in large saucepan of boiling water, uncovered, stirring to separate grains, 25 minutes or until just tender; drain. Cook wild rice in large saucepan of boiling water, uncovered, stirring to separate grains, 20 minutes or until just tender; drain. Combine rices with remaining ingredients; mix well.

SAGE SAUCE combine blended cornflour and wine with remaining ingredients in small saucepan; cook, stirring, until sauce boils and thickens.

SERVES 6

per serving 11.6g total fat (3.7g saturated fat); 1471kj 352(cal); 29.1g protein; 31.4g carbohydrate; 1.7g fibre

tip seasoning can be made a day ahead. Store, covered, in refrigerator.

barbecued chicken and lentil salad

PREPARATION TIME 30 MINUTES (PLUS REFRIGERATION TIME) COOKING TIME 30 MINUTES

640g chicken breast fillets
½ cup (125g) low-fat yogurt
1 teaspoon cracked black pepper
1 clove garlic, crushed
1 tablespoon chopped fresh basil
½ teaspoon ground turmeric
1 tablespoon hoisin sauce
cooking-oil spray
1 radicchio

LENTIL SALAD

1 medium red capsicum (200g)
1 medium yellow capsicum (200g)
1 cup (200g) brown lentils
1 litre (4 cups) water
1 clove garlic, flattened
⅓ cup (80ml) red wine vinegar
½ teaspoon sugar
2 teaspoons olive oil
350g baby curly endive

1. Combine chicken, yogurt, pepper, garlic, basil, turmeric and sauce in large bowl. Cover, refrigerate 1 hour.
2. Meanwhile, make lentil salad.
3. Remove chicken from marinade; discard marinade. Coat heated grill plate (or grill or barbecue) with cooking-oil spray; cook chicken, uncovered, on both sides until browned and tender. Slice chicken thinly.
4. Add chicken to lentil salad; toss gently to combine. Divide radicchio among serving plates, top with salad mixture.

LENTIL SALAD quarter capsicums, remove seeds and membranes, grill capsicums, skin-side up, until skin blisters and blackens. Peel skin, finely chop capsicums. Combine lentils, water and garlic in medium saucepan, bring to a boil. Reduce heat, simmer, uncovered, about 15 minutes or until lentils are just tender; drain, discard garlic. Place lentils and capsicums in bowl with combined vinegar, sugar and half the oil; toss gently to combine. Heat large frying pan, add half the remaining oil and half the endive; cook, stirring, until just wilted. Repeat with remaining oil and endive. Combine endive with lentil mixture.

SERVES 4
per serving 8.2g total fat (1.8g saturated fat); 668kj (399 cal); 55.5g protein; 25.5g carbohydrate; 11.1g fibre
tip lentil salad can be made a day ahead without endive. Store, covered, in refrigerator; add endive just before serving.

grilled chicken in lime chilli marinade

PREPARATION TIME 10 MINUTES (PLUS REFRIGERATION TIME) COOKING TIME 10 MINUTES

4 x 170g chicken breast fillets
cooking-oil spray
2 tablespoons finely chopped fresh coriander
1 lime, cut in wedges

LIME CHILLI MARINADE
⅓ cup (80ml) lime juice
1 clove garlic, crushed
2 teaspoons grated fresh ginger
1 tablespoon low-salt soy sauce
1 fresh red chilli, chopped finely
2 spring onions, chopped

1. Pound chicken with a mallet to an even thickness. Make lime chilli marinade.
2. Combine chicken and marinade in large bowl. Cover; refrigerate several hours or overnight.
3. Drain chicken; discard marinade. Coat heated grill pan (or grill or barbecue) with cooking-oil spray; cook on both sides until browned and tender.
4. Sprinkle with coriander, serve with lime wedges.

LIME CHILLI MARINADE combine ingredients in small bowl.

SERVES 4
per serving 4g total fat (1g saturated fat); 849kj (203 cal); 39.2g protein; 1g carbohydrate; 0.8g fibre
tip recipe can be prepared a day ahead. Store, covered, in refrigerator.

spicy grilled chicken

PREPARATION TIME 10 MINUTES (PLUS REFRIGERATION TIME) COOKING TIME 10 MINUTES

¼ cup (60ml) lemon juice
¼ cup (60ml) dry white wine
1 tablespoon honey
2 tablespoons finely chopped fresh coriander
1 tablespoon grated fresh ginger
2 fresh red thai chillies, chopped
2 cloves garlic, crushed
2 teaspoons ground turmeric
2 teaspoons cumin seeds
½ teaspoon ground cinnamon
4 x 170g chicken breast fillets
2 strips lemon rind, shredded finely
cooking-oil spray

1. Blend or process juice, wine, honey, coriander, ginger, chilli, garlic, turmeric, seeds and cinnamon until smooth.
2. Cut three slashes in each fillet. Combine chicken, rind and pureed mixture in large bowl. Cover; refrigerate several hours or overnight.
3. Drain chicken; reserve marinade. Coat heated grill plate (or grill or barbecue) with cooking-oil spray; cook chicken, uncovered, on both sides until tender, brushing with reserved marinade during cooking.

SERVES 4
per serving 4g total fat (1g saturated fat); 966kj (231 cal); 38.8g protein; 6.8g carbohydrate; 0.6g fibre
tip chicken can be prepared a day ahead. Store, covered, in refrigerator.

ginger chicken kebabs

PREPARATION TIME 15 MINUTES (PLUS REFRIGERATION TIME) COOKING TIME 15 MINUTES

Soak 6 bamboo skewers in cold water for at least an hour before use to prevent them scorching and splintering.

300g chicken breast fillets, chopped coarsely
1 tablespoon green ginger wine
1 tablespoon salt-reduced soy sauce
1 tablespoon lemon juice
1 teaspoon vegetable oil
2 teaspoons worcestershire sauce
2 teaspoons brown sugar
1 teaspoon dijon mustard
1 teaspoon grated fresh ginger

1. Combine chicken and remaining ingredients in large bowl. Cover; refrigerate several hours or overnight.
2. Preheat grill. Thread chicken onto skewers; reserve marinade. Cook under grill, brushing with marinade, until chicken is tender.
3. Serve kebabs sprinkled with sliced green onions, if desired.

SERVES 2
per serving 5.8g total fat (1.2g saturated fat); 924kj (221 cal); 34.7g protein; 5g carbohydrate; 0.2g fibre
tip chicken is best marinated overnight.

chicken and artichoke parcels

PREPARATION TIME 20 MINUTES COOKING TIME 25 MINUTES

¼ cup (60ml) dry white wine
½ cup (125ml) water
1 trimmed stick celery (75g), sliced thinly
1 small brown onion (80g), chopped finely
300g chicken breast fillets, chopped finely
1 tablespoon plain flour
½ cup (125ml) skim milk
400g can artichoke hearts in brine, drained, cut into quarters
2 tablespoons finely chopped fresh basil
8 sheets fillo pastry
cooking-oil spray

1. Preheat oven to 180°C/160°C fan-forced. Line oven tray with baking paper.
2. Place wine, the water, celery, onion and chicken in medium saucepan; bring to a boil. Reduce heat, simmer, about 5 minutes or until onion is soft and chicken is tender.
3. Add combined flour and milk, stirring until mixture boils and thickens. Remove from heat; stir in artichoke and basil.
4. Cut pastry sheets in half crossways; layer four halves together, brushing lightly with water between each layer. Repeat with remaining pastry sheets. Place one quarter of chicken mixture on one end of pastry; fold in sides. Roll to enclose filling. Repeat with remaining pastry and chicken mixture.
5. Place parcels on oven tray; coat with cooking-oil spray. Bake, uncovered, about 15 minutes or until pastry is browned lightly. Serve with mesclun salad, if desired.

MAKES 4
per parcel 4.1g total fat (0.8g saturated fat); 1041kj (249 cal); 24g protein; 25.8g carbohydrate; 3.7g fibre
tip parcels can be prepared a day ahead. Store, covered, in refrigerator. Uncooked parcels may be frozen.

poached chicken with tropical salsa

PREPARATION TIME 10 MINUTES (PLUS REFRIGERATION TIME) COOKING TIME 15 MINUTES

2 cups (500ml) chicken stock
4 x 170g chicken breast fillets

TROPICAL SALSA

½ small pawpaw (400g), chopped
½ medium avocado (125g), chopped
1 cup (170g) chopped watermelon
1 tablespoon lime juice
2 teaspoons angostura aromatic bitters
2 teaspoons shredded fresh mint

1 Bring stock to a boil in large saucepan, add chicken. Reduce heat, simmer, uncovered, about 10 minutes or until tender. Remove chicken from poaching liquid; pat dry with absorbent paper. Cover chicken; refrigerate until cold.
2 Make tropical salsa.
3 Slice cold chicken; top with salsa.

TROPICAL SALSA combine ingredients in small bowl.

SERVES 4
per serving 9.6g total fat (2.4g saturated fat); 1200kj (287 cal); 41.8g protein; 7.9g carbohydrate; 2.2g fibre

grilled tandoori chicken

PREPARATION TIME 10 MINUTES (PLUS REFRIGERATION TIME) COOKING TIME 15 MINUTES

2 x 200g chicken breast fillets
½ cup (125g) low-fat yogurt
1 tablespoon lemon juice
½ teaspoon finely grated fresh ginger
1 clove garlic, crushed
½ teaspoon caster sugar
½ teaspoon paprika
¼ teaspoon ground cumin
¼ teaspoon ground coriander
¼ teaspoon ground turmeric
pinch chilli powder

TOMATO, RED ONION AND CORIANDER SALSA

1 small tomato (130g), chopped finely
½ small red onion (50g), chopped finely
1 teaspoon sugar
1 tablespoon finely chopped fresh coriander

1 Combine chicken, yogurt, juice, ginger, garlic, sugar, paprika and spices in large bowl. Cover; refrigerate several hours or overnight.
2 Make tomato, red onion and coriander salsa.
3 Drain chicken; reserve marinade. Cook chicken on heated oiled grill pan (or grill or barbecue), brushing with reserved marinade, until browned both sides and tender. Slice chicken thickly.
4 Serve chicken with salsa, and steamed rice if desired.

TOMATO, RED ONION AND CORIANDER SALSA combine ingredients in small bowl.

SERVES 2
per serving 5.8g total fat (1.9g saturated fat); 1254kj (300 cal); 49.4g protein; 11.2g carbohydrate; 1.4g fibre
tip chicken is best marinated overnight. Store, covered, in refrigerator.

char-grilled chicken with mango salsa

PREPARATION TIME 10 MINUTES COOKING TIME 15 MINUTES

A 450g can of mango slices may be substituted for the fresh mango in this recipe.

4 x 170g chicken breast fillets
120g spinach, shredded finely
1 medium red onion (170g), chopped finely
1 medium mango (430g), chopped finely
1 tablespoon coarsely chopped fresh mint
¼ cup (20g) shaved parmesan cheese
¼ cup (60ml) sweet chilli sauce

1 Cook chicken on heated oiled gill plate (or grill or barbecue) until browned both sides and cooked through.
2 Meanwhile, combine spinach, onion, mango, mint, cheese and sauce in medium bowl; mix well.
3 Serve chicken topped with salsa.

SERVES 4
per serving 6.1g total fat (2.1g saturated fat); 1267kj (303 cal); 43.7g protein; 17.9g carbohydrate; 2.6g fibre

ginger, chicken and lime patties

PREPARATION TIME 20 MINUTES COOKING TIME 20 MINUTES

340g chicken breast fillets
1 tablespoon grated lime rind
1 tablespoon grated fresh ginger
2 teaspoons ground cumin
1 egg white
2 green onions, sliced
¼ cup (35g) plain flour

CHILLI SAUCE

2 medium red capsicums (400g)
1 medium brown onion (150g), chopped finely
4 fresh red thai chillies, chopped finely
415g can diced tomatoes
1 tablespoon brown sugar

1 Preheat oven to 180°C/160°C fan-forced.
2 Blend or process chicken until finely chopped. Add rind, ginger, cumin, egg and onion; process until mixture forms a paste. Using hands, shape mixture into eight patties, coat in flour; shake away excess flour.
3 Heat oiled large frying pan; cook patties about 2 minutes each side or until browned. Place patties on oven tray; bake, uncovered, about 15 minutes or until cooked through.
4 Make chilli sauce. Serve patties with sauce.

CHILLI SAUCE quarter capsicums, remove and discard seeds and membranes. Roast under grill or in very hot oven, skin-side up, until skin blisters and blackens. Cover capsicum pieces in plastic or paper for 5 minutes. Peel away skin; chop pieces finely. Heat oiled small saucepan; cook onion and chilli, stirring, about 2 minutes or until onion is soft. Stir in undrained tomato and sugar; simmer, uncovered, 5 minutes, stir in capsicum.

SERVES 4
per serving 2.5g total fat (0.5g saturated fat); 798kj (191 cal); 23.8g protein; 17.8g carbohydrate; 3.3g fibre

chicken with red pesto pasta

PREPARATION TIME 10 MINUTES COOKING TIME 25 MINUTES

We used sun-dried capsicum pesto for this recipe, but any bottled "red" pesto, such as tomato, could be used.

4 x 170g chicken breast fillets
¼ cup (75g) bottled red pesto
375g spaghetti
1 cup (70g) stale breadcrumbs
⅓ cup finely chopped fresh chives
2 teaspoons wholegrain mustard
½ cup (125ml) chicken stock

1. Coat chicken with half the pesto. Cook chicken on oiled grill plate (or grill or barbecue) until browned both sides and cooked through. Remove; cover to keep warm.
2. Meanwhile, cook spaghetti in large saucepan of boiling water, uncovered, until just tender; drain. Rinse under cold water; drain.
3. Heat oiled large pan; cook breadcrumbs, stirring, until browned. Stir in spaghetti with remaining pesto, chives, mustard and stock; cook, stirring, until hot.
4. Serve spaghetti with sliced chicken, and tomato wedges, if desired.

SERVES 4
per serving 13.3g total fat (3g saturated fat); 2746kj (657 cal); 54.7g protein; 78g carbohydrate; 6g fibre

chicken and mushroom pastry parcels

PREPARATION TIME 25 MINUTES COOKING TIME 35 MINUTES

510g chicken breast fillets, sliced thinly
100g mushrooms, chopped finely
1 small leek (200g), sliced thinly
½ cup (125ml) low-fat sour cream
1 tablespoon dijon mustard
½ cup (60g) finely grated low-fat cheddar cheese
2 teaspoons finely chopped fresh tarragon
8 sheets fillo pastry
cooking-oil spray

1. Preheat oven to 200°C/180°C fan-forced. Line oven tray with baking paper.
2. Heat oiled large frying pan; cook chicken, in batches, until lightly browned and cooked through.
3. Cook mushrooms in same pan, stirring, until lightly browned and tender. Add leek; cook, stirring, until leek is softened. Return chicken to pan with sour cream, mustard, cheese and tarragon; cook, stirring, until combined.
4. Cut pastry sheets in half crossways; layer four halves together, brushing with water between each layer. Repeat with remaining pastry sheets. Place ¼ of the chicken mixture on one short end of pastry; fold in sides, roll to enclose filling. Repeat with remaining chicken mixture and pastry.
5. Place parcels on oven tray; coat with cooking-oil spray. Bake, uncovered, 10 minutes or until pastry is browned lightly and chicken mixture is hot.

SERVES 4
per serving 14.7g total fat (7.2g saturated fat); 1601kj (383 cal); 39.4g protein; 22.8g carbohydrate; 2.4g fibre

chicken, lentil and spinach pasta

PREPARATION TIME 10 MINUTES COOKING TIME 25 MINUTES

2 teaspoons vegetable oil
1 small brown onion (80g), chopped finely
2 cloves garlic, crushed
150g minced chicken
½ cup (100g) red lentils
2¾ cups (680ml) chicken stock
2 tablespoons tomato paste
250g baby spinach leaves
375g shell pasta

1. Heat oil in medium frying pan; cook onion and garlic, stirring, until onion softens. Add chicken; cook, stirring, until chicken has changed in colour. Stir in lentils, stock and paste; simmer, uncovered, about 10 minutes or until lentils are tender and sauce thickened. Add spinach; stir until spinach is just wilted.
2. Meanwhile, cook pasta in large pan of boiling water, uncovered, until just tender; drain.
3. Combine pasta and chicken sauce in large bowl; to mix, toss well.

SERVES 4
per serving 7.8g total fat (1.8g saturated fat); 2090kj (500 cal); 27.8g protein; 79g carbohydrate; 10.8g fibre

steamed chicken breasts with lime

PREPARATION TIME 10 MINUTES COOKING TIME 20 MINUTES

This is a simple Asian dish that's not only low in fat, it's also quick to make. Sake is dry rice wine; it can be replaced with dry sherry or white wine if unavailable.

12 kaffir lime leaves, shredded finely
⅓ cup (80ml) lime juice
2 teaspoons grated fresh ginger
4 x 170g chicken breasts fillets
400g chinese broccoli, quartered

SOY AND GARLIC DIPPING SAUCE
2 tablespoons light soy sauce
2 tablespoons sake
2 tablespoons mild chilli sauce
1 teaspoon brown sugar
1 clove garlic, crushed
1 tablespoon coarsely chopped fresh coriander

1. Combine lime leaves, juice and ginger in small bowl.
2. Place each chicken breast on a large sheet of foil; drizzle with lime mixture. Fold foil over loosely to enclose chicken.
3. Place chicken in large bamboo steamer; steam chicken, covered, over wok of simmering water about 15 minutes or until chicken is cooked through.
4. Just before serving, add broccoli to chicken in steamer; steam, covered, until broccoli just wilts.
5. Make soy and garlic dipping sauce.
6. Serve chicken and broccoli with dipping sauce.

SOY AND GARLIC DIPPING SAUCE combine ingredients in small bowl.

SERVES 4
per serving 4.4g total fat (1.1g saturated fat); 1137kj (272 cal); 41.7g protein; 9.3g carbohydrate; 4.4g fibre
tip you can steam the chicken in a microwave oven, without the foil, if you prefer.
serving suggestion serve with steamed long-grain white rice.

chicken and crunchy noodle salad

PREPARATION TIME 5 MINUTES COOKING TIME 15 MINUTES

Crispy fried noodles are sold packaged (commonly a 100g packet) already deep-fried and ready to eat. They're sometimes labeled crunchy noodles and are available in two widths – thin and spaghetti-like, or wide and flat like fettuccine.

680g chicken breast fillets
500g baby buk choy, shredded coarsely
250g cherry tomatoes, halved
50g fresh shiitake mushrooms, sliced thinly
¼ cup firmly packed fresh coriander leaves
1 cup (80g) bean sprouts
3 green onions, sliced thinly
⅓ cup (80ml) light soy sauce
1 teaspoon sesame oil
2 tablespoons dry sherry
100g crispy fried noodles

1. Cook chicken, in batches, on heated oiled grill plate (or grill or barbecue) until browned both sides and cooked through. Stand 5 minutes; slice thinly.
2. Meanwhile, combine buk choy, tomato, mushrooms, coriander, sprouts and onion in large bowl.
3. Combine sauce, oil and sherry in screw-top jar; shake well.
4. Just before serving, add chicken and dressing to buk choy mixture with noodles; toss gently to combine.

SERVES 4
per serving 7.6g total fat (2.1g saturated fat); 1241kj (297 cal); 43.1g protein; 10.6g carbohydrate; 4.6g fibre

citrus chicken with chickpea salad

PREPARATION TIME 20 MINUTES COOKING TIME 15 MINUTES

4 x 170g chicken breast fillets, halved
1 tablespoon finely grated lemon rind
1 tablespoon finely grated lime rind
300g can chickpeas, rinsed, drained
1 medium red onion (170g), chopped finely
2 medium tomatoes (380g), chopped coarsely
1 tablespoon finely chopped fresh coriander leaves
1 medium avocado (250g), chopped coarsely
1 tablespoon lemon juice

1. Combine chicken, lemon rind and lime rind in medium bowl. Cover; refrigerate at least 3 hours or until required.
2. Place chickpeas, onion, tomato, coriander, avocado and juice in medium bowl; toss gently to combine.
3. Cook chicken mixture on heated oiled grill plate (or grill or barbecue) until chicken is browned both sides and cooked through. Spoon chickpea salad onto serving plates; top with warm chicken.

SERVES 4
per serving 14.9g total fat (3.3g saturated fat); 1467kj (351 cal); 43.7g protein; 10.1g carbohydrate; 4.7g fibre

oven-baked chicken schnitzel with spicy wedges

PREPARATION TIME 20 MINUTES COOKING TIME 40 MINUTES

1kg potatoes
1 egg white, beaten lightly
¼ teaspoon cayenne pepper
½ teaspoon sweet paprika
4 x 110g chicken thigh fillets
⅓ cup (50g) plain flour
2 egg whites, beaten lightly, extra
½ cup (35g) packaged breadcrumbs
½ cup (80g) corn flake crumbs
1 teaspoon garlic salt

1. Preheat oven to 220°C/200°C fan-forced. Oil shallow baking dish; oil oven tray.
2. Cut unpeeled potatoes into wedges. Combine potato, egg white, cayenne and paprika in large bowl. Place potato, in single layer, in baking dish; bake, uncovered, about 40 minutes or until browned lightly.
3. Meanwhile, trim fat from chicken. Using meat mallet, gently pound chicken between sheets of plastic wrap until 5mm thick. Toss chicken in flour; shake away excess. Dip chicken in small bowl containing extra egg white then toss in separate small bowl containing combined crumbs and salt. Place chicken on oven tray; bake, uncovered, about 20 minutes or until browned both sides and cooked through.
4. Serve chicken schnitzel with spicy wedges, and a green salad if desired.

SERVES 4
per serving 8.8g total fat (2.6g saturated fat); 1994kj (477 cal); 33g protein; 64.7g carbohydrate; 6.5g fibre
tip if you like, use stale breadcrumbs flavoured with grated lemon rind and finely chopped parsley in place of the corn flake crumbs.

vietnamese chicken salad

PREPARATION TIME 20 MINUTES COOKING TIME 5 MINUTES

You will need to purchase one large barbecued chicken weighing about 900g for this recipe, and one small wombok.

100g snow peas, trimmed
1 teaspoon sambal oelek
1 teaspoon sesame oil
⅓ cup (80ml) lime juice
⅓ cup (80ml) fish sauce
2 teaspoons sugar
4 cups (400g) shredded chicken
4 cups (320g) finely shredded wombok
4 garlic chives, chopped finely
1 medium red onion (170g), sliced thinly
½ cup coarsely chopped fresh mint
½ cup loosely packed fresh coriander leaves

1. Place snow peas in medium bowl. Cover with boiling water; drain immediately. Cover snow peas with cold water in same bowl; stand 2 minutes. Drain; slice thinly.
2. Place sambal, oil, juice, sauce and sugar in screw-top jar; shake well.
3. Place snow peas in large bowl with chicken, wombok, chives, onion, mint and dressing; toss gently to combine. Sprinkle coriander over salad.

SERVES 4
per serving 9.5g total fat (2.5g saturated fat); 1032kj (247 cal); 32.5g protein; 6.9g carbohydrate; 3.3g fibre

chicken, vegetable and noodle stir-fry

PREPARATION TIME 10 MINUTES COOKING TIME 10 MINUTES

500g fresh wide rice noodles
1 teaspoon sesame oil
500g chicken breast fillets, sliced thinly
250g oyster mushrooms, sliced thinly
¼ cup (60ml) oyster sauce
1 tablespoon fish sauce
1 tablespoon sugar
2 teaspoons sambal oelek
250g baby spinach leaves
¼ cup coarsely chopped fresh coriander

1 Rinse noodles in strainer under hot water. Separate noodles with fork; drain.

2 Meanwhile, heat oil in wok; stir-fry chicken, in batches, until browned all over and cooked through.

3 Stir-fry mushrooms in same wok until just tender. Return chicken to wok with noodles, sauces, sugar and sambal; stir-fry until heated through.

4 Remove from heat. Add baby spinach and coriander; toss gently to combine.

SERVES 4
per serving 5.5g total fat (0.9g saturated fat); 1843kj (441 cal); 37.4g protein; 59.2g carbohydrate; 5.9g fibre

chicken with buk choy and flat mushrooms

PREPARATION TIME 10 MINUTES (PLUS REFRIGERATION TIME) COOKING TIME 25 MINUTES

2 tablespoons honey
⅓ cup (80ml) soy sauce
2 tablespoons dry sherry
1 teaspoon five-spice powder
4cm piece fresh ginger (20g), grated
1 tablespoon peanut oil
4 x 170g chicken breast fillets
4 flat mushrooms (360g)
500g baby buk choy, quartered lengthways
1 cup (250ml) chicken stock
2 teaspoons cornflour
2 tablespoons water

1 Combine honey, soy sauce, sherry, five-spice, ginger and oil in small jug. Combine chicken and half of the honey mixture in medium bowl. Cover; refrigerate 10 minutes.

2 Meanwhile, cook mushrooms and buk choy, in batches, on heated oiled grill plate (or grill or barbecue) until just tender; cover to keep warm.

3 Cook drained chicken on same oiled grill plate (or grill or barbecue) until browned both sides and cooked through. Cover; stand 5 minutes. Slice thickly.

4 Meanwhile, combine remaining honey mixture in small saucepan with stock; bring to a boil. Stir in blended cornflour and water; cook, stirring, until sauce boils and thickens slightly.

5 Divide mushrooms and buk choy among serving plates; top with chicken, drizzle with sauce. Serve with steamed rice, if desired.

SERVES 4
per serving 9.3g total fat (2g saturated fat); 1430kj (342 cal); 45g protein; 17.1g carbohydrate; 4.2g fibre

chicken chilli stir-fry

PREPARATION TIME 10 MINUTES COOKING TIME 15 MINUTES

500g chicken breast fillets, sliced
3 fresh red thai chillies, sliced
1 clove garlic, crushed
300g snow peas
1 large red capsicum (350g), sliced
¼ cup (60ml) oyster sauce
2 tablespoons sliced fresh basil
1½ cups (120g) bean sprouts

1. Heat oiled wok; stir-fry chicken, in batches, until browned and tender.
2. Stir-fry chilli, garlic, snow peas and capsicum until vegetables are tender.
3. Return chicken to wok with remaining ingredients; stir-fry until hot.

SERVES 4
per serving 3.4g total fat (0.8g saturated fat); 878kj (210 cal); 33.3g protein; 10.8g carbohydrate; 3.8g fibre

nam jim chicken

PREPARATION TIME 20 MINUTES COOKING TIME 20 MINUTES

When removing coriander leaves from stalks, save the root part from one of the stalks for the nam jim sauce.

8 x 110g chicken thigh fillets
1 teaspoon ground cumin
1 teaspoon ground coriander
2 tablespoons grated palm sugar
1 cup loosely packed thai basil leaves
1 cup loosely packed fresh coriander leaves
3 cups (240g) bean sprouts

NAM JIM SAUCE
3 long green chillies, chopped coarsely
2 cloves garlic, quartered
10cm stick (20g) fresh lemon grass, chopped finely
3 green onions, chopped coarsely
1 coriander root, chopped coarsely
¼ cup (60ml) lime juice
1 tablespoon fish sauce
2 tablespoons grated palm sugar

1. Combine chicken, cumin, coriander and sugar in large bowl.
2. Cook chicken mixture in heated oiled large frying pan, in batches, until browned all over and cooked through.
3. Meanwhile, make nam jim sauce.
4. Serve chicken on combined herbs and sprouts; top with sauce.

NAM JIM SAUCE blend or process ingredients until smooth.

SERVES 4
per serving 16.1g total fat (4.9g saturated fat); 1576kj (377 cal); 43.8g protein; 14.7g carbohydrate; 2.9g fibre

herbed chicken kebabs with roasted pecans

PREPARATION TIME 35 MINUTES (PLUS REFRIGERATION TIME) COOKING TIME 15 MINUTES

Soak 12 bamboo skewers in water for at least 1 hour before use to prevent them scorching and splintering.

1kg chicken breast fillets, sliced thinly
½ cup finely chopped fresh chives
⅓ cup finely chopped fresh oregano
¼ cup finely chopped fresh marjoram
4 cloves garlic, crushed
1 tablespoon lemon pepper seasoning
2 tablespoons chicken stock
¼ cup (30g) coarsely chopped roasted pecans

1 Thread chicken onto skewers. Combine chives, oregano, marjoram, garlic, seasoning and stock in shallow baking dish; add chicken skewers, mix well. Cover; refrigerate at least 3 hours or until required.

2 Cook kebabs, in batches, on heated oiled grill plate (or grill or barbecue) until browned all over and cooked through. Serve with roasted pecans.

SERVES 6
per serving 7.5g total fat (1.3g saturated fat); 941kj (225 cal); 38.4g protein; 0.6g carbohydrate; 0.9g fibre

chicken and lentil cacciatore

PREPARATION TIME 15 MINUTES COOKING TIME 45 MINUTES

cooking-oil spray
8 chicken thigh cutlets (1.5kg)
1 medium onion (150g), chopped finely
1 clove garlic, crushed
2 x 400g cans crushed tomatoes
300g button mushrooms, sliced
1 tablespoon tomato paste
1 cup (250ml) chicken stock
½ teaspoon dried oregano
⅓ cup (65g) red lentils
½ cup (80g) seedless black olives
1 tablespoon drained capers
2 tablespoons coarsely chopped fresh flat-leaf parsley

1 Heat large saucepan, coat with cooking-oil spray; cook chicken, uncovered, turning occasionally until browned. Remove.

2 Cook onion and garlic in same pan, stirring, until onion is soft. Add undrained crushed tomatoes, mushrooms, paste, stock, oregano and lentils. Return chicken to pan, simmer, covered, about 30 minutes or until chicken is tender. Stir in olives, capers and parsley.

SERVES 6
per serving 13.6g total fat (4g saturated fat); 1392kj (333 cal); 39.1g protein; 13.9g carbohydrate; 5.1g fibre
tip recipe can be made a day ahead. Store, covered, in refrigerator.

herbed chicken kebabs with roasted pecans

light 'n' spicy crumbed chicken

light 'n' spicy crumbed chicken

PREPARATION TIME 20 MINUTES (PLUS REFRIGERATION TIME) COOKING TIME 15 MINUTES

12 x 75g chicken tenderloins
⅓ cup (50g) plain flour
2 egg whites, beaten lightly
⅓ cup (35g) packaged breadcrumbs
⅓ cup (35g) corn flake crumbs
2 teaspoons garlic salt
1 teaspoon lemon pepper

1. Preheat oven to 220°C/200°C fan-forced.
2. Toss chicken in flour; shake away excess flour. Coat chicken in egg, then in combined breadcrumbs, salt and pepper. Cover; refrigerate 15 minutes.
3. Place chicken on oven tray; bake, uncovered, about 15 minutes or until cooked through.

SERVES 4
per serving 5.7g total fat (1.5g saturated fat); 1534kj (367 cal); 55.8g protein; 22.2g carbohydrate; 1.1g fibre

chicken scaloppine with gremolata

PREPARATION TIME 30 MINUTES COOKING TIME 30 MINUTES

Gremolata is to osso buco what thousand island dressing is to prawn cocktail – you can't have one without the other. But this finely chopped blend of lemon rind, garlic and parsley is far too good to save for just the odd veal shank or two – and it's very well-suited to chicken.

2 large red capsicums (600g)
½ cup (125ml) dry white wine
½ cup (125ml) water
2 cups coarsely chopped fresh flat-leaf parsley
2 tablespoons coarsely grated lemon rind
2 tablespoons lemon juice
2 cloves garlic, quartered
8 x 170g chicken breast fillets
8 slices prosciutto (120g)

1. Quarter capsicums; remove seeds and membranes. Roast under grill or in very hot oven, skin-side up, until skin blisters and blackens. Cover capsicum pieces with plastic or paper 5 minutes; peel away skin. Blend or process capsicum, wine and the water until almost smooth; reserve.
2. Preheat oven to 180°C/160°C fan-forced. Oil large shallow baking dish.
3. Blend or process parsley, rind, juice and garlic until gremolata mixture is almost smooth.
4. Cut chicken in half horizontally almost all the way through; open out each fillet. Place between sheets of plastic wrap; pound gently with meat mallet until about 1cm thick. Divide gremolata among fillets; roll each fillet to enclose filling. Wrap each roll in prosciutto; secure with toothpicks.
5. Place chicken rolls in baking dish; bake, uncovered, about 30 minutes or until chicken is cooked through.
6. Place capsicum mixture in small saucepan; bring to a boil. Reduce heat, simmer, uncovered, about 3 minutes or until reduced by half. Add pan juices from chicken; return to a boil. Serve chicken on capsicum sauce.

SERVES 8
per serving 5g total fat (1.4g saturated fat); 961kj (230 cal); 42.7g protein; 0.5g carbohydrate; 1g fibre

chunky chicken and sugar snap pea stir-fry

PREPARATION TIME 10 MINUTES COOKING TIME 15 MINUTES

2 teaspoons peanut oil
1 medium onion (150g), chopped
1 medium red capsicum (200g), sliced thinly
100g sugar snap peas
500g chicken breast fillets, sliced thinly
2 teaspoons cornflour
⅔ cup (160ml) chicken stock
1 tablespoon low-salt soy sauce

1 Heat half of the oil in wok; stir-fry onion and capsicum, over high heat, until onion is just soft. Add peas; stir-fry 1 minute. Remove vegetables from wok.

2 Heat remaining oil in wok; stir-fry chicken, in batches, over high heat until browned lightly.

3 Return chicken and vegetables to wok with blended cornflour, stock and soy sauce; stir until mixture boils and thickens.

SERVES 4
per serving 5.5g total fat (1.3g saturated fat); 819kj (196 cal); 30.8g protein; 5.6g carbohydrate; 1.5g fibre
tip recipe best made just before serving.

chicken stir-fry with noodles

PREPARATION TIME 15 MINUTES COOKING TIME 10 MINUTES

250g fresh egg noodles
170g chicken breast fillet
5cm piece fresh ginger
2 teaspoons olive oil
1 clove garlic, crushed
1 teaspoon sambal oelek
½ teaspoon curry powder
1 medium red capsicum (200g), sliced thinly
1 bunch baby buk choy (500g), trimmed, halved
½ x 540g can whole baby corn, drained
3 green onions, chopped coarsely
½ teaspoon cornflour
¼ cup water (60ml)
1 tablespoon salt-reduced soy sauce

1 Place noodles in large heatproof bowl; cover with boiling water. Stand 3 minutes; drain.

2 Meanwhile, slice chicken thinly. Cut ginger into thin slices; cut slices into strips.

3 Heat oil in wok; stir-fry chicken, ginger, garlic, sambal oelek and curry powder until fragrant. Add capsicum, buk choy and corn; stir-fry about 3 minutes. Add noodles and onion; stir-fry until heated through.

4 Add blended cornflour, water and sauce; stir until mixture boils and thickens.

SERVES 2
per serving 8.8g total fat (1.4g saturated fat); 2224kj (532 cal); 37.2g protein; 74.5g carbohydrate; 10.2g fibre

thai basil chicken stir-fry

PREPARATION TIME 20 MINUTES (PLUS REFRIGERATION TIME) COOKING TIME 20 MINUTES

You will need to grate the rind from the lime before you juice it.

850g chicken breast fillets, sliced thinly
1 teaspoon sesame oil
½ cup (125ml) light soy sauce
¼ cup (75g) honey
¼ cup (60ml) lime juice
3 fresh red thai chillies, sliced thinly
2 teaspoons cornflour
2 tablespoons peanut oil
3 cloves garlic, crushed
2 large red onions (400g), sliced thinly
240g fresh baby corn
2 teaspoons finely grated lime rind
3 cups (240g) bean sprouts
2 cups loosely packed thai basil leaves
1 cup loosely packed fresh coriander leaves

1. Combine chicken, sesame oil, sauce, honey, juice, chilli and cornflour in large bowl. Cover; refrigerate 3 hours or overnight.
2. Drain chicken over medium bowl; reserve marinade.
3. Heat half of the peanut oil in wok; stir-fry chicken, in batches, until browned all over.
4. Heat remaining peanut oil in wok; stir-fry garlic, onion and corn until just tender. Return chicken to wok with reserved marinade and rind; stir-fry until sauce boils and chicken is cooked through.
5. Remove from heat. Add sprouts, basil and coriander; toss until combined.

SERVES 8
per serving 8.1g total fat (1.6g saturated fat); 1058kj (253 cal); 28.2g protein; 16.5g carbohydrate; 3.6g fibre
serving suggestion serve with steamed jasmine rice and wedges of fresh lime.

lemon chicken with fresh egg noodles

PREPARATION TIME 20 MINUTES (PLUS STANDING TIME) COOKING TIME 20 MINUTES

1kg chicken breast fillets
500g fresh asparagus
2 medium lemons (280g)
2 tablespoons vegetable oil
500g fresh egg noodles
4 cloves garlic, crushed
1 tablespoon grated fresh ginger
4 green onions, sliced thickly
1 cup (250ml) chicken stock
2 teaspoons fish sauce
¼ cup (60ml) lemon juice
10 fresh basil leaves, torn

1. Cut chicken into 3cm pieces. Cut asparagus diagonally into 3cm lengths. Halve lemons lengthways; slice thinly.
2. Heat half of the oil in wok; stir-fry chicken, in batches, until browned lightly. Add lemon; stir-fry about 2 minutes or until browned. Remove from wok; add to chicken.
3. Place noodles in large heatproof bowl; cover with boiling water. Stand until just tender; drain.
4. Meanwhile, heat remaining oil in wok; stir-fry garlic, ginger, asparagus and onion about 2 minutes or until vegetables are just soft.
5. Return chicken, noodles and lemon to wok with combined stock, sauce and juice; stir-fry, tossing, until hot. Remove from heat; stir in basil.

SERVES 8
per serving 8.5g total fat (1.5g saturated fat); 1526kj (365 cal); 36.1g protein; 34.4g carbohydrate; 3g fibre
tip chicken thigh fillets can be used in this recipe.
serving suggestion serve with stir-fried baby buk choy with ginger and garlic.

sesame chicken noodle salad

PREPARATION TIME 15 MINUTES COOKING TIME 20 MINUTES

680g chicken breast fillets, sliced
1 clove garlic, crushed
2 tablespoons sweet chilli sauce
½ teaspoon sesame oil
¼ cup (60ml) rice vinegar
2 tablespoons soy sauce
1 tablespoon lemon juice
1 green onion, sliced finely
2 teaspoons sugar
600g fresh egg noodles
1 medium yellow capsicum (200g)
1 large carrot (180g)
200g watercress, trimmed
1 tablespoon peanut oil
250g fresh asparagus, trimmed, halved
2 teaspoons toasted sesame seeds

1. Combine chicken, garlic and chilli sauce in large bowl.
2. Place sesame oil, vinegar, soy sauce, juice, onion and sugar in screw-top jar; shake well.
3. Cook noodles in large saucepan of boiling water, uncovered, until just tender; drain.
4. Discard seeds and membranes from capsicum, cut capsicum and carrot into long thin strips. Place noodles, capsicum, carrot and watercress in large serving bowl; toss gently to combine.
5. Heat peanut oil in wok; stir-fry chicken mixture, in batches, until browned and tender. Add asparagus to wok, stir-fry until just tender.
6. Add chicken and asparagus to noodle mixture, drizzle with dressing; toss gently to combine. Sprinkle with seeds.

SERVES 6
per serving 7.9g total fat (1.6g saturated fat); 1940kj (464 cal); 37.6g protein; 59.1g carbohydrate; 4.2g fibre

sweet soy chicken and noodles

PREPARATION TIME 15 MINUTES COOKING TIME 25 MINUTES

250g soba noodles
1 tablespoon peanut oil
600g chicken breast fillets, sliced
200g sugar snap peas
2 tablespoons sweet soy sauce
4 green onions, sliced thinly
6 red radishes (200g), sliced thinly
2 tablespoons finely chopped fresh coriander

1. Cook noodles in large saucepan of boiling water, uncovered, until just tender; drain. Rinse noodles under hot water; cover to keep warm.
2. Meanwhile, heat half the oil in wok; stir-fry chicken, in batches, until tender.
3. Heat remaining oil in wok; stir-fry peas until just tender. Return chicken to wok with sauce, onion and radish; cook, stirring, until hot.
4. Combine noodles and coriander in large bowl; top with chicken mixture.

SERVES 4
per serving 8.9g total fat (1.9g saturated fat); 1990kj (476 cal); 43.1g protein; 55.1g carbohydrate; 4g fibre

thai-style chicken and vegetable curry

PREPARATION TIME 15 MINUTES COOKING TIME 30 MINUTES

10cm stick (20g) fresh lemon grass, chopped finely
4 kaffir lime leaves, shredded
1 medium leek (350g), sliced thickly
2 tablespoons thai-style green curry paste
500g chicken tenderloins, halved
2 x 375ml cans evaporated low-fat milk
1 litre (4 cups) vegetable stock
2 tablespoons soy sauce
4 small zucchini (360g), chopped
300g green beans, halved
½ small wombok (200g), chopped
350g choy sum, chopped
200g baby spinach leaves
1½ teaspoons coconut essence
2 tablespoons lime juice
¼ cup coarsely chopped fresh coriander

1. Heat oiled large saucepan; cook lemon grass, lime leaves and leek, stirring, until leek is soft.
2. Add paste to pan; stir until fragrant. Add chicken; cook, stirring, until browned and tender.
3. Stir in milk, stock and sauce; simmer, uncovered, about 5 minutes or until thickened slightly. Add vegetables; simmer, uncovered, until vegetables are just tender. Stir in essence, juice and coriander.

SERVES 6
per serving 6g total fat (1.4g saturated fat); 1179kj (282 cal); 36.2g protein; 20.6g carbohydrate; 6.1g fibre

pan-fried turkey with garlic and thyme

PREPARATION TIME 10 MINUTES COOKING TIME 25 MINUTES

750g turkey breast fillets, halved
1 large brown onion (200g), sliced
4 cloves garlic, crushed
¼ cup (60ml) lemon juice
½ cup (125ml) evaporated low-fat milk
½ cup (125ml) chicken stock
1 tablespoon finely chopped fresh thyme
330g spinach, chopped coarsely
1 teaspoon cornflour
1 teaspoon water

1. Heat oiled large frying pan; cook turkey, in batches, until browned all over and tender.
2. Cook onion, garlic and juice in same pan, stirring, until onion is soft. Add milk, stock, thyme, spinach and blended cornflour and water; cook, stirring, until sauce boils and thickens slightly. Return turkey to pan with any juices; stir until hot.
3. Serve with mashed potato and steamed vegetables, if desired.

SERVES 6
per serving 4.5g total fat (1.1g saturated fat); 761kj (182 cal); 30.3g protein; 4.7g carbohydrate; 1.5g fibre

chicken and mixed pea stir-fry

PREPARATION TIME 15 MINUTES COOKING TIME 20 MINUTES

Char siu sauce is a Chinese barbecue sauce based on soy beans; it is available from most supermarkets.

1½ cups (300g) jasmine rice
1 tablespoon peanut oil
700g chicken breast fillets, sliced thinly
1 medium brown onion (150g), sliced thinly
1 fresh long red chilli, sliced thinly
1 clove garlic, crushed
150g sugar snap peas, trimmed
150g snow peas, trimmed
125g fresh baby corn, halved
2 tablespoons kecap manis
2 tablespoons char siu sauce
½ cup (125ml) chicken stock
1 tablespoon cornflour
2 tablespoons lime juice

1. Cook rice in large saucepan of boiling water, uncovered, until just tender; drain. Cover to keep warm.
2. Meanwhile, heat half of the oil in wok; stir-fry chicken, in batches, until browned and almost cooked through.
3. Heat remaining oil in wok; stir-fry onion, chilli and garlic until onion softens. Add peas and corn; stir-fry until vegetables are just tender. Return chicken to wok with sauces and stock; stir-fry about 2 minutes or until chicken is cooked through. Stir in blended cornflour and juice; stir-fry until sauce boils and thickens. Divide rice among serving plates; top with stir-fry.

SERVES 4
per serving 10.3g total fat (2.1g saturated fat); 2658kj (636 cal); 49.4g protein; 85.1g carbohydrate; 5.5g fibre

stir-fried turkey with lemon and chilli

PREPARATION TIME 10 MINUTES COOKING TIME 15 MINUTES

500g turkey breast fillets, sliced thinly
2 teaspoons finely grated lemon rind
2 fresh red thai chillies, chopped finely
2 teaspoons olive oil
2 cloves garlic, crushed
1 tablespoon finely chopped fresh lemon grass
1 large brown onion (200g), sliced thinly
600g fresh ramen noodles
300g baby buk choy, chopped
2 tablespoons black bean sauce
¼ cup (60ml) plum sauce
¾ cup (180ml) chicken stock

1. Combine turkey, rind and chilli in medium bowl.
2. Heat 1 teaspoon of the oil in wok; stir-fry turkey mixture, in batches, until browned and tender.
3. Heat remaining oil in wok; stir-fry garlic, lemon grass and onion until onion is soft. Add noodles and buk choy; stir-fry until buk choy is just wilted.
4. Return turkey to wok with sauces and stock; stir until sauce boils and thickens slightly.

SERVES 4
per serving 8.9g total fat (1.8g saturated fat); 2625kj (628 cal); 43.7g protein; 91.8g carbohydrate; 5.2g fibre

turkey and lemon risotto

PREPARATION TIME 10 MINUTES COOKING TIME 40 MINUTES

2 litres (8 cups) chicken stock
1 cup (250ml) dry white wine
½ cup (125ml) lemon juice
2 teaspoons low-fat dairy-free spread
1 medium brown onion (150g), chopped finely
2 cloves garlic, crushed
4 cups (800g) arborio rice
1½ cups (185g) frozen peas
650g turkey breast fillets
2 teaspoons finely grated lemon rind
2 teaspoons finely chopped fresh thyme
¼ cup (20g) finely grated parmesan cheese

1. Combine stock, wine and juice in large saucepan; bring to a boil. Reduce heat, simmer, uncovered.
2. Heat dairy-free spread in separate large saucepan; cook onion and garlic, stirring, until onion softens. Add rice; stir to coat in spread mixture. Stir in 1 cup of the hot stock mixture; cook, stirring, over low heat until liquid is absorbed. Continue adding stock mixture, in 1-cup batches, stirring until absorbed between each addition. Add peas; cook 5 minutes. Total cooking time should be about 35 minutes.
3. Meanwhile, cook turkey, in batches, in large oiled frying pan until browned both sides and cooked through; chop coarsely.
4. Gently stir turkey, rind, thyme and cheese into risotto.

SERVES 6
per serving 7.5g total fat (2.5g saturated fat); 2951kj (706 cal); 39.6g protein; 111.3g carbohydrate; 3.4g fibre
tip chicken breast fillets can be substituted for turkey fillets.
serving suggestion serve with a green salad and warmed loaf of Italian bread.

mains
beef and veal

mexican beef salad with fresh corn salsa

PREPARATION TIME 25 MINUTES COOKING TIME 20 MINUTES

Chipotle are what fresh jalapeño chillies are called after they've been dried and smoked. Having a deep, intensely smoky flavour rather than a searing heat, chipotles are dark brown, almost black in appearance; they are available from specialty spice stores and gourmet delicatessens. You will need four cobs of corn for this recipe.

4 dried chipotle chillies
⅓ cup (80ml) boiling water
1 medium red onion (150g), chopped coarsely
2 cups (500ml) water, extra
1 tablespoon ground cumin
1 cup (250ml) beef stock
300g piece beef eye fillet, cut into 3mm slices
2 tablespoons light sour cream
½ cup coarsely chopped fresh coriander

FRESH CORN SALSA
1 medium red onion (150g), chopped coarsely
4 cups (660g) fresh corn kernels
2 cloves garlic, crushed
⅓ cup (80ml) lime juice
3 long green chillies, sliced thinly
1 small avocado (200g), chopped coarsely

1. Soak chillies in the boiling water in small heatproof bowl for 10 minutes. When cool enough to handle, remove stalks; reserve chillies and liquid.
2. Meanwhile, make fresh corn salsa.
3. Cook onion in oiled large frying pan, stirring, until soft. Add the extra water, cumin, stock, chillies and reserved liquid; bring to a boil. Reduce heat, simmer, uncovered, 10 minutes. Using slotted spoon, remove solids from chilli poaching liquid; reserve.
4. Place beef, in single layer, in chilli poaching liquid; turn off heat. Turn beef over; using slotted spoon, remove beef from liquid after 30 seconds. Cover to keep warm.
5. Blend or process reserved solids with cream until almost smooth. Serve beef on salsa; top with chilli cream sauce and sprinkle with coriander.

FRESH CORN SALSA combine ingredients in medium bowl.

SERVES 4
per serving 14.5g total fat (4.2g saturated fat); 1555kj (372 cal); 27.8g protein; 31.3g carbohydrate; 9.7g fibre
tip the strained beef and chilli poaching liquid can be kept, covered, in the refrigerator or freezer, then used at a later date to impart its distinctive flavour to soups or sauces.
serving suggestion serve with warmed flour tortillas, if desired.

stir-fried mexican beef

PREPARATION TIME 15 MINUTES COOKING TIME 20 MINUTES

You can use rib eye (scotch fillet), rump, sirloin or topside in this recipe, if desired.

750g piece beef eye fillet, sliced thinly
35g packet taco seasoning mix
1 tablespoon peanut oil
1 large red onion (300g), sliced thinly
1 medium red capsicum (200g), sliced thinly
1 medium yellow capsicum (200g), sliced thinly
4 small tomatoes (520g), seeded, sliced
2 tablespoons fresh coriander leaves

1 Combine beef and seasoning in medium bowl. Heat half the oil in wok; stir-fry beef mixture and onion, in batches, until well browned.

2 Heat remaining oil in wok; stir-fry capsicums until just tender.

3 Return beef mixture to wok with tomato and coriander; stir-fry until hot.

SERVES 4
per serving 12.8g total fat (4.2g saturated fat); 1359kj (325 cal); 43.8g protein; 8.2g carbohydrate; 3.4g fibre

penne with chile con carne

PREPARATION TIME 8 MINUTES COOKING TIME 20 MINUTES

375g penne pasta
1 tablespoon peanut oil
1 large brown onion (200g), sliced thinly
2 cloves garlic, crushed
2 fresh small red thai chillies, chopped coarsely
1 teaspoon ground cumin
1 teaspoon ground coriander
350g yellow teardrop tomatoes, halved
500g thinly sliced roast beef
420g can kidney beans, drained, rinsed
600ml bottled tomato pasta sauce
⅓ cup loosely packed fresh coriander leaves

1 Cook pasta in large saucepan of boiling water, uncovered, until just tender; drain.

2 Meanwhile, heat oil in another large saucepan; cook onion, garlic, chilli and ground spices, stirring, until onion softens. Add tomato; cook, stirring, until tomato is just soft. Add beef, beans and sauce; bring to a boil. Reduce heat, simmer, uncovered, until sauce thickens slightly.

3 Place pasta in pan with chile con carne; toss gently over heat until combined and hot. Stir in fresh coriander.

SERVES 4
per serving 13.1g total fat (3.9g saturated fat); 2989kj (715 cal); 51g protein; 97g carbohydrate; 14.9g fibre

beef with red wine sauce and polenta

PREPARATION TIME 5 MINUTES COOKING TIME 25 MINUTES

4 x 150g beef eye fillet steaks
¾ cup (180ml) dry red wine
⅓ cup (80ml) redcurrant jelly
1 litre (4 cups) chicken stock
1½ cups (250g) polenta
½ cup (40g) finely grated parmesan cheese

1 Heat oiled large pan; cook beef until browned both sides and cooked as desired. Remove beef from pan; cover to keep warm.

2 Add wine and jelly to same pan; cook, stirring, until sauce thickens slightly. Cover to keep warm.

3 Meanwhile, bring stock to boil in large pan, add polenta; simmer, stirring, about 5 minutes or until polenta thickens, stir in cheese.

4 Serve beef with red wine sauce and polenta.

SERVES 4
per serving 12g total fat (5.6g saturated fat); 2140kj (512 cal); 44.5g protein; 48.5g carbohydrate; 1.8g fibre

spiced-rubbed beef fillet with chickpea and preserved lemon salad

PREPARATION TIME 20 MINUTES (PLUS REFRIGERATION TIME) COOKING TIME 15 MINUTES

Kalonji, also known as nigella, are black, teardrop-shaped seeds used extensively in Indian cooking to impart a sharp, almost nutty flavour.

1 teaspoon coriander seeds
1 teaspoon kalonji seeds
1 teaspoon dried chilli flakes
1 teaspoon sea salt
1 clove garlic, crushed
600g piece beef eye fillet, trimmed
6 large egg tomatoes (540g), peeled
425g can chickpeas, rinsed, drained
2 tablespoons finely chopped preserved lemon rind
⅔ cup loosely packed fresh flat-leaf parsley leaves
⅔ cup loosely packed fresh coriander leaves
1 tablespoon lemon juice

1 Using mortar and pestle, crush seeds, chilli, salt and garlic into coarse paste; rub paste onto beef. Cover; refrigerate 20 minutes.

2 Meanwhile, quarter tomatoes; discard seeds and pulp. Chop tomato flesh finely. Place in medium bowl with chickpeas, rind, herbs and juice; toss gently to combine.

3 Cook beef on oiled heated grill plate (or grill or barbecue) until browned all over and cooked as desired. Cover; stand 10 minutes, then slice thinly. Serve beef on salad.

SERVES 4
per serving 8g total fat (2.9g saturated fat); 1162kj (278 cal); 38.4g protein; 12.8g carbohydrate; 6.2g fibre

seasoned beef fillet

PREPARATION TIME 15 MINUTES COOKING TIME 35 MINUTES

1 medium brown onion (150g), chopped finely
2 tablespoons finely chopped walnuts
½ cup (35g) stale breadcrumbs
½ teaspoon finely grated orange rind
1 tablespoon dry red wine
¼ cup (60g) wholegrain mustard
2 tablespoons chopped fresh chives
500g piece beef eye fillet
½ cup (125ml) orange juice

1. Heat oiled small saucepan; cook onion, stirring, until soft. Place onion in small bowl with nuts, breadcrumbs, rind, wine, 2 tablespoons of the mustard and chives; mix well. [Can be made ahead to this stage. Cover, refrigerate until required.]
2. Preheat oven to 220°C/200°C fan-forced.
3. Cut deep pocket in side of beef, place seasoning in pocket; secure with kitchen string. Heat oiled flameproof baking dish; brown beef all over. Bake beef, uncovered, about 25 minutes or until cooked as desired. Remove beef from dish, cover; rest 5 minutes. Slice thickly.
4. Heat same dish, stir in remaining mustard and juice; cook, stirring, until mixture boils. Serve sauce with beef.

SERVES 4
per serving 9.2g total fat (2.5g saturated fat); 1049kj (251 cal); 30.3g protein; 10.6g carbohydrate; 1.9g fibre

beef fillet with gremolata and semi-dried tomato polenta

PREPARATION TIME 15 MINUTES (PLUS REFRIGERATION TIME) COOKING TIME 25 MINUTES

1½ cups (375ml) water
1½ cups (375ml) vegetable stock
¾ cup (120g) polenta
⅓ cup (75g) semi-dried tomatoes, chopped coarsely
2 tablespoons finely grated parmesan cheese
500g piece beef eye fillet

GREMOLATA
½ cup coarsely chopped fresh flat-leaf parsley
1 clove garlic, crushed
1 tablespoon finely grated lemon rind
¼ cup (60ml) lemon juice

1. Oil 23cm-square cake pan.
2. Combine the water and stock in large saucepan; bring to a boil. Gradually add polenta to liquid, stirring constantly. Reduce heat, cook, stirring constantly, about 10 minutes or until polenta thickens. Stir in tomato and cheese; spread into pan. Cover; refrigerate about 1 hour or until firm.
3. Meanwhile, make gremolata.
4. Cook beef in heated oiled large frying pan until browned all over and cooked as desired. Cover; stand 10 minutes. Slice thickly.
5. Meanwhile, turn polenta onto board; cut into four squares, cut each square diagonally into two triangles. Cook polenta triangles in same pan, in batches, until browned lightly both sides.
6. Divide polenta among serving plates; top with beef then gremolata.

GREMOLATA combine ingredients in small bowl.

SERVES 4
per serving 8.9g total fat (3.4g saturated fat); 1400kj (335 cal); 34g protein; 28.3g carbohydrate; 4.2g fibre

steaks with capsicum salsa

PREPARATION TIME 15 MINUTES COOKING TIME 10 MINUTES

1 small red capsicum (150g), chopped finely
1 small green capsicum (150g), chopped finely
1 medium red onion (170g), chopped finely
1 large tomato (250g), seeded, chopped finely
1 tablespoon finely chopped fresh coriander
¼ cup (60ml) oil-free french dressing
2 cloves garlic, crushed
1 teaspoon ground cumin
4 x 150g beef eye fillet steaks

1. Combine capsicums, onion, tomato, coriander, dressing, garlic and cumin in medium bowl; mix well.
2. Cook beef on heated oiled grill plate (or grill or barbecue) until browned both sides and cooked as desired.
3. Serve beef with capsicum salsa.

SERVES 4
per serving 6.5g total fat (2.7g saturated fat); 915kj (219 cal); 34.5g protein; 4.9g carbohydrate; 2.2g fibre

beef and beer casserole

PREPARATION TIME 10 MINUTES COOKING TIME 1 HOUR

400g piece lean rump steak
1½ tablespoons plain flour
2 teaspoons olive oil
1 medium leek (350g), sliced thickly
1 small red capsicum (150g), chopped coarsely
100g button mushrooms
1 medium tomato (190g), peeled, chopped finely
1 cup (250ml) beer
½ cup (125ml) water
2 teaspoons tomato paste
1 tablespoon finely chopped fresh flat-leaf parsley
2 teaspoons finely chopped fresh oregano

1. Trim all visible fat from steak; cut steak into cubes, toss in flour. Cook steak in large heated oiled saucepan until browned all over. Remove from pan.
2. Cook leek, capsicum and mushrooms in same pan, stirring, about 5 minutes or until leek is soft.
3. Add steak to pan with tomato, beer, the water and paste; bring to a boil. Reduce heat, simmer, covered, for 40 minutes. Remove lid, simmer, further 10 minutes or until sauce has thickened slightly and meat is tender.
4. Just before serving, stir in herbs. Serve with soft polenta or steamed baby potatoes, if desired.

SERVES 2
per serving 10.6g total fat (2.9g saturated fat); 1747kj (418 cal); 53.8g protein; 17.5g carbohydrate; 6.4g fibre
tip casserole can be made a day ahead. Store, covered, in refrigerator.

moroccan beef salad with couscous

PREPARATION TIME 10 MINUTES COOKING TIME 1 HOUR

1 cup (250ml) vegetable stock
1½ cups (300g) couscous
500g piece beef rump steak
½ cup (75g) dried apricots, sliced
½ cup (80g) sultanas
1 medium red onion (170g), sliced thinly
¼ cup finely chopped fresh mint
2 tablespoons finely chopped fresh dill
1 tablespoon pine nuts
2 teaspoons cumin seeds
¾ cup (180ml) oil-free french dressing

1. Bring stock to a boil in large saucepan; remove from heat. Stir in couscous; stand, covered, about 5 minutes or until stock is absorbed.
2. Meanwhile, cook beef on heated oiled grill plate (or grill or barbecue) until browned both sides and cooked as desired; slice beef thinly.
3. Fluff couscous with fork, add apricots, sultanas, onion and herbs; mix gently.
4. Dry-fry pine nuts and cumin in small frying pan, stirring, over low heat until seeds are just fragrant and pine nuts are toasted. Combine nut mixture with dressing in small bowl; drizzle over beef and couscous.

SERVES 4
per serving 6.7g total fat (1.7g saturated fat); 2378kj (569 cal); 42.2g protein; 83.3g carbohydrate; 4.4g fibre

pepper steak with scalloped potatoes

PREPARATION TIME 15 MINUTES COOKING TIME 55 MINUTES

2 medium brown onions (300g), sliced thinly
2 cloves garlic, crushed
5 medium potatoes (1kg), sliced thinly
½ cup (120g) light sour cream
½ cup (125ml) chicken stock
1 cup (125g) coarsely grated low-fat cheddar cheese
6 x 100g beef eye fillet steaks
2 teaspoons cracked black pepper
1 clove garlic, crushed, extra
1 tablespoon cornflour
1 cup (250ml) beef stock

1. Preheat oven to 180°C/160°C fan-forced.
2. Cook onion and garlic in heated oiled large frying pan until onion softens.
3. Layer onion mixture with potato slices in shallow 2.5 litre (10-cup) baking dish, finishing with potato layer. Pour combined sour cream and stock over potato mixture; sprinkle with cheese.
4. Bake potato mixture, covered, 45 minutes. Uncover; bake about 10 minutes or until scalloped potatoes are tender and browned lightly on top.
5. Meanwhile, coat beef all over with pepper; cook, in batches, in heated oiled large frying pan until cooked as desired. Cover beef to keep warm.
6. Cook extra garlic in same pan, stirring, until fragrant. Add blended cornflour and stock, stirring over heat until sauce mixture boils and thickens slightly. Drizzle steaks with sauce; serve with scalloped potatoes.

SERVES 6
per serving 10.1g total fat (5.5g saturated fat); 1417kj (339 cal); 34.6g protein; 26.4g carbohydrate; 4.1g fibre

beef in red wine

PREPARATION TIME 15 MINUTES COOKING TIME 1 HOURS 15 MINUTES

350g piece beef blade steak
2 medium brown onions (300g), chopped finely
1 clove garlic, crushed
100g mushrooms, sliced thickly
415ml can tomato puree
2 teaspoons worcestershire sauce
½ cup dry red wine (125ml)
1 trimmed stick celery (75g), chopped coarsely
2 medium carrots (240g), chopped coarsely
2 tablespoons fresh flat-leaf parsley leaves

1. Trim all visible fat from steak; cut steak into cubes. Cook steak in heated large saucepan until browned all over.
2. Add onion to pan with garlic and mushrooms; cook, stirring, about 2 minutes or until onion is soft. Stir in puree, sauce and wine; bring to a boil. Reduce heat, simmer, covered, about 45 minutes.
3. Add celery and carrot to pan; cook, covered, further 15 minutes or until vegetables are tender. Serve sprinkled with parsley.

SERVES 2
per serving 9.4g total fat (3.7g saturated fat); 1697kj (406 cal); 45.2g protein; 24g carbohydrate; 11.3g fibre
tip recipe can be made a day ahead. Store, covered, in refrigerator.
serving suggestion serve with couscous, if desired.

beef and pear with garlic mustard sauce

PREPARATION TIME 10 MINUTES (PLUS STANDING TIME) COOKING TIME 25 MINUTES

1 medium pear (230g), quartered
¾ cup (180ml) water
½ cup (125ml) orange juice
350g piece scotch fillet steak
½ teaspoon olive oil
2 cloves garlic, crushed
2 teaspoons wholegrain mustard
2 teaspoons cornflour
1 tablespoon brandy
1 clove garlic, crushed, extra

1. Place pear, the water and juice in small saucepan; bring to a boil. Remove pan from heat; cool pear in liquid.
2. Preheat oven to 180°C/160°C fan-forced.
3. Trim all visible fat from steak. Heat oil in medium saucepan; cook fillet until browned all over. Place fillet in baking dish; roast, covered, about 20 minutes or until tender. Cover; stand 5 minutes. Slice thickly
4. Meanwhile, drain pear, reserving 1¼ cups liquid. Add garlic and mustard to same small pan; cook 1 minute. Stir in blended cornflour and reserved liquid; stir over heat until mixture boils and thickens.
5. Stir in brandy and extra garlic. Serve sliced beef with pear and sauce. Serve with wilted spinach and steamed asparagus, if desired.

SERVES 2
per serving 8.9g total fat (3.4g saturated fat); 1425kj (341 cal); 38.8g protein; 21.8g carbohydrate; 3.7g fibre
tip cook recipe just before serving.

fettuccine bolognese

PREPARATION TIME 5 MINUTES COOKING TIME 25 MINUTES

1 small brown onion (80g), chopped finely
2 cloves garlic, crushed
1 small carrot (70g), chopped finely
1 trimmed stick celery (75g), chopped finely
400g lean minced beef
2 cups (500ml) bottled tomato pasta sauce
½ cup (125ml) beef stock
375g fettuccine pasta

1 Cook onion and garlic in heated large frying pan, stirring, until onion softens. Add carrot and celery; cook, stirring, until vegetables are just tender.

2 Add beef to pan; cook, stirring, until changed in colour. Add sauce and stock; bring to a boil. Reduce heat, simmer, uncovered, about 15 minutes or until mixture thickens slightly.

3 Meanwhile, cook pasta in large saucepan of boiling water, uncovered, until just tender; drain. Serve pasta topped with bolognese sauce.

SERVES 4
per serving 9.2g total fat (3.3g saturated fat); 2316kj (554 cal); 34g protein; 83g carbohydrate; 8.9g fibre
tip the flavour of the bolognese will improve if it is made a day ahead; reheat just before serving.

meatballs in rosemary paprika sauce

PREPARATION TIME 15 MINUTES COOKING TIME 45 MINUTES

250g lean minced beef
½ cup (35g) stale breadcrumbs
1 tablespoon finely chopped fresh parsley
1 tablespoon finely chopped fresh chives
1 egg white
1 teaspoon worcestershire sauce
1 teaspoon vegetable oil
250g tagliatelle pasta

ROSEMARY PAPRIKA SAUCE

410g can crushed tomatoes
1 cup (250ml) water
2 tablespoons dry red wine
1 medium brown onion (150g), chopped finely
½ teaspoon worcestershire sauce
1 teaspoon paprika
3 sprigs rosemary

1 Combine mince, breadcrumbs, parsley, chives, egg white and sauce in large bowl. Shape mixture into small meatballs.

2 Heat oil in medium saucepan; cook meatballs until well browned all over and cooked through. Drain on absorbent paper.

3 Make rosemary paprika sauce.

4 Meanwhile, cook pasta in large saucepan of boiling water, uncovered, until just tender; drain.

5 Add meatballs to rosemary paprika sauce; stir until heated through. Serve with pasta, and a crisp green leaf salad, if desired.

ROSEMARY PAPRIKA SAUCE place undrained tomatoes with remaining ingredients in medium saucepan; bring to a boil. Reduce heat, simmer, uncovered, for about 20 minutes or until thickened slightly. Remove and discard rosemary sprigs.

SERVES 2
per serving 13.4g total fat (4.3g saturated fat); 3198kj (765 cal); 46.3g protein; 109.3g carbohydrate; 10.5g fibre
tip recipe can be made a day ahead and refrigerated, covered, or frozen. Cook pasta close to serving.

teriyaki beef skewers

PREPARATION TIME 20 MINUTES (PLUS REFRIGERATION TIME) COOKING TIME 10 MINUTES

Soak 12 bamboo skewers in water for at least 1 hour before use to prevent them scorching and splintering.

2 large red onions (600g)
500g piece beef rump steak, sliced thinly
¼ cup (60ml) teriyaki sauce
1 tablespoon tomato paste
1 clove garlic, crushed
1 teaspoon brown sugar
2 green onions, sliced finely

1 Cut red onions in half; cut each half into 6 wedges. Thread onion wedges and beef onto skewers.
2 Combine sauce, paste, garlic and sugar in small bowl; brush sauce mixture over skewers. Cover; refrigerate at least 3 hours or until required.
3 Cook skewers on heated oiled grill plate (or grill or barbecue) until brown and cooked as desired. Serve skewers sprinkled with green onion, and steamed rice, if desired.

SERVES 4
per serving 3.4g total fat (1.4g saturated fat); 815kj (195 cal); 32.5g protein; 8g carbohydrate; 2.5g fibre

beef and onion kebabs

PREPARATION TIME 20 MINUTES (PLUS REFRIGERATION TIME) COOKING TIME 10 MINUTES

Soak 6 bamboo skewers in water for at least 1 hour before using to prevent them scorching and splintering.

350g piece lean rump steak
9 baby onions (225g), halved

MARINADE
¼ cup (60ml) honey
¼ cup (60ml) lemon juice
2 teaspoons grated fresh ginger
2 teaspoons worcestershire sauce
¼ cup (60ml) tomato sauce
1 tablespoon finely chopped fresh oregano

1 Trim all visible fat from steak; chop steak into bite-size pieces. Thread steak and onion onto skewers.
2 Make marinade.
3 Place kebabs in shallow dish; add marinade. Cover; refrigerate overnight.
4 Cook kebabs on heated grill pan (or grill or barbecue), brushing with marinade, until tender. Serve with a bitter leaf salad, if desired.

MARINADE combine ingredients in bowl; mix well.

SERVES 2
per serving 4.8g total fat (1.9g saturated fat); 1751kj (419 cal); 43.4g protein; 51.2g carbohydrate; 2.3g fibre

teriyaki beef skewers

artichoke and eggplant veal rolls

artichoke and eggplant veal rolls

PREPARATION TIME 20 MINUTES COOKING TIME 30 MINUTES

400g can artichokes, drained
3 green onions, chopped coarsely
1 clove garlic, quartered
1 medium eggplant (300g), sliced thinly
8 x 90g veal steaks
1 large brown onion (200g), chopped coarsely
2 medium red capsicums (400g), chopped coarsely
4 trimmed sticks celery (300g), chopped coarsely
4 small tomatoes (520g), seeded, chopped coarsely
½ cup (125ml) brandy
½ cup (125ml) beef stock
2 tablespoons tomato paste

1. Blend or process artichokes, onion and garlic until mixture forms a paste.
2. Cook eggplant in heated large oiled frying pan, in batches, until browned both sides.
3. Place veal pieces on board; spread each with artichoke mixture then top with eggplant. Roll veal to enclose filling; secure each roll with toothpick or kitchen string.
4. Cook veal, in batches, in same pan until cooked as desired. Cover veal rolls to keep warm.
5. Cook onion in same pan, stirring, until softened. Add capsicum, celery, tomato and brandy; cook, stirring, until vegetables are tender and pan liquid reduces by half. Add stock and tomato paste; cook, stirring, until mixture boils and thickens slightly.
6. Cut each veal roll into thirds. Place four of the thirds on each serving plate; top with vegetable sauce.

SERVES 6
per serving 2.8g total fat (0.6g saturated fat); 986kj (236 cal); 32.3g protein; 9.1g carbohydrate; 5.9g fibre

peppered veal medallions

PREPARATION TIME 10 MINUTES (PLUS REFRIGERATION TIME) COOKING TIME 10 MINUTES

4 x 80g veal medallions
2 tablespoons drained canned green peppercorns, chopped finely
¼ cup (60ml) brandy
½ cup (125ml) water
1 teaspoon cornflour
2 tablespoons light sour cream

1. Trim all visible fat from veal. Combine veal, peppercorns and brandy in medium bowl. Cover; refrigerate for several hours or overnight.
2. Drain veal; reserve marinade. Cook veal in heated large saucepan until tender. Remove from pan; keep warm.
3. Combine reserved marinade and blended cornflour and water in same pan; bring to a boil. Remove from heat, stir in cream. Return to heat, simmer, 5 minutes or until sauce thickens. Pour over veal just before serving. Serve with steamed baby beans, if desired.

SERVES 2
per serving 6.5g total fat (3.4g saturated fat); 1162kj (278 cal); 36.4g protein; 2.2g carbohydrate; 0g fibre

beef donburi

PREPARATION TIME 15 MINUTES COOKING TIME 10 MINUTES

Donburi refers to a certain size of rice bowl, usually with a lid, and also the meat or poultry/rice combination which is served in it. Koshihikari rice is grown from Japanese seed; substitute medium-grain white rice, if desired.

1 cup (200g) koshihikari rice
500g piece beef rump steak, sliced thinly
1 clove garlic, crushed
1 teaspoon grated fresh ginger
½ cup (125ml) light soy sauce
½ cup (125ml) mirin
1 tablespoon peanut oil
6 green onions, sliced thinly

1. Cook rice in large saucepan of boiling water, uncovered, until just tender; drain.
2. Meanwhile, combine beef, garlic and ginger in medium bowl with half of the sauce and half of the mirin.
3. Cook beef mixture in heated oiled large frying pan, in batches, stirring, until browned all over. Return beef to pan with remaining sauce and mirin; bring to a boil.
4. Serve beef mixture over rice in large soup or rice bowls; sprinkle with onion.

SERVES 4
per serving 8.1g total fat (2.3g saturated fat); 1609kj (385 cal); 34.6g protein; 41.2g carbohydrate; 0.9g fibre
tip you can use thinly sliced chicken breast fillets rather than beef in this recipe; if you do, thinly slice a large brown onion and add it to the chicken mixture before cooking.
serving suggestion serve with vegetable tempura.

hokkien noodle stir-fry

PREPARATION TIME 15 MINUTES COOKING TIME 15 MINUTES

500g hokkien noodles
1 tablespoon peanut oil
1 teaspoon sesame oil
500g piece beef eye fillet, sliced thinly
1 medium brown onion (150g), sliced thickly
1 clove garlic, crushed
2 teaspoons grated fresh ginger
1 medium red capsicum (200g), sliced thinly
1 medium green capsicum (200g), sliced thinly
2 tablespoons lemon juice
2 tablespoons sweet chilli sauce
1 tablespoon toasted sesame seeds
1 tablespoon finely chopped fresh coriander
1 tablespoon chopped fresh mint

1. Rinse noodles under hot water; drain. Transfer to large bowl; separate noodles with fork.
2. Heat both oils in wok; stir-fry beef, in batches, until browned all over.
3. Stir-fry onion, garlic and ginger in wok until onion softens. Add capsicums; stir-fry until just tender.
4. Return beef to wok with noodles, juice and sauce; stir-fry until hot. Stir in seeds and herbs.

SERVES 4
per serving 14.2g total fat (3.7g saturated fat); 2454kj (587 cal); 72.2g protein; 41.2g carbohydrate; 4.2g fibre
tip place beef in the freezer about 1 hour before using to make it easier to slice.

thai beef salad

PREPARATION TIME 10 MINUTES (PLUS REFRIGERATION TIME) COOKING TIME 10 MINUTES

500g piece beef rump steak
¼ cup (60ml) lime juice
2 tablespoons shredded fresh mint leaves
150g baby spinach leaves
2 lebanese cucumbers (260g), seeded, sliced
1 tablespoon white wine vinegar
2 tablespoons fish sauce
1 tablespoon brown sugar

1 Combine beef with juice and mint in medium bowl. Cover; refrigerate at least 3 hours or until required.

2 Cook beef in heated olied large frying pan until cooked as desired. Cover beef, rest 5 minutes. Cut into thin slices.

3 Place beef in large bowl with spinach, cucumber and combined vinegar, sauce and sugar; toss gently to combine.

SERVES 4
per serving 3.5g total fat (1.4g saturated fat); 761kj (182 cal); 31.3g protein; 5.4g carbohydrate; 2g fibre

satay beef and stir-fried vegetables with rice

PREPARATION TIME 20 MINUTES COOKING TIME 20 MINUTES

1 litre (4 cups) water
1 cup (200g) basmati rice
1 teaspoon peanut oil
500g piece lean beef topside, sliced thinly
1 large brown onion (200g), sliced thinly
1 clove garlic, crushed
2cm piece fresh ginger (10g), grated finely
2 fresh red thai chillies, chopped finely
1 medium red capsicum (200g), chopped coarsely
1 medium green capsicum (200g), chopped coarsely
100g button mushrooms, halved
225g can bamboo shoots, drained
1 teaspoon curry powder
2 teaspoons cornflour
½ cup (125ml) chicken stock
¼ cup (70g) light smooth peanut butter
2 tablespoons oyster sauce
1 tablespoon coarsely chopped roasted unsalted peanuts

1 Bring the water to a boil in large saucepan; stir in rice. Boil, uncovered, about 15 minutes or until rice is just tender. Drain, rinse under hot water; drain rice again, cover to keep warm.

2 Meanwhile, heat oil in wok; stir-fry beef, in batches, until browned all over.

3 Reheat meat juices in wok, add onion and garlic; stir-fry until onion softens. Add ginger, chilli, capsicums, mushrooms, bamboo shoots and curry powder; stir-fry until vegetables are just tender.

4 Pour blended cornflour and stock into wok; stir to combine with vegetable mixture. Return beef to wok with peanut butter and oyster sauce; bring to a boil. Boil, stirring, until sauce thickens slightly, and beef is cooked as desired. Sprinkle with peanuts; serve with rice.

SERVES 4
per serving 14.1g total fat (2.2g saturated fat); 2103kj (503 cal); 37.8g protein; 55.6g carbohydrate; 3.7g fibre
tip you can use sliced lamb fillets or sliced chicken thigh fillets instead of the beef, if you prefer.

fettuccine veal goulash

PREPARATION TIME 15 MINUTES COOKING TIME 15 MINUTES

400g piece veal fillet
2 teaspoons olive oil
1 medium brown onion (150g), sliced finely
2 cloves garlic, crushed
1 teaspoon sweet paprika
1½ cups (375ml) beef stock
2 tablespoons sour cream
1 tablespoon lemon juice
1 tablespoon wholegrain mustard
375g fettuccine pasta
250g spinach, trimmed, shredded coarsely
1 tablespoon fresh dill tips

1 Cook veal in large heated frying pan, turning, until browned and cooked as desired. Cover; stand 5 minutes. Cut into thin slices, keep warm.
2 Heat oil in same pan; cook onion, garlic and paprika, stirring, until onion softens. Add stock; bring to a boil. Reduce heat, simmer, uncovered, 5 minutes. Add sour cream, juice and mustard; cook, stirring, 1 minute.
3 Meanwhile, cook pasta in large saucepan of boiling water, uncovered, until just tender; drain.
4 Place veal, goulash mixture and pasta in large bowl with spinach and dill; toss gently to combine.

SERVES 4
per serving 9.1g total fat (3.5g saturated fat); 2111kj (505 cal); 35.6g protein; 68.6g carbohydrate; 6.2g fibre
tip change the dill to tarragon and add a teaspoon of worcestershire sauce to make this dish similar to a traditional stroganoff in flavour.

veal cutlets with warm tomato-caper salsa

PREPARATION TIME 10 MINUTES (PLUS REFRIGERATION TIME) COOKING TIME 25 MINUTES

4 x 200g medium veal cutlets
2 cloves garlic, crushed
1 tablespoon finely grated lemon rind
1 clove garlic, crushed, extra
1 tablespoon finely grated lemon rind, extra
2 medium zucchini (240g), chopped coarsely
3 large tomatoes (750g), chopped coarsely
¼ cup (60ml) chicken stock
2 tablespoons tomato paste
2 tablespoons chopped fresh oregano
2 tablespoons drained baby capers

1 Combine veal with garlic and rind in large bowl. Cover; refrigerate at least 3 hours or until required.
2 Cook extra garlic and extra rind in oiled large frying pan, stirring, until fragrant. Add zucchini, tomato, stock and paste; simmer, uncovered, until vegetables are tender and salsa is thickened.
3 Cook veal on heated oiled grill plate (or grill or barbecue) until browned and cooked as desired.
4 Meanwhile, stir oregano and capers into salsa until hot. Serve veal with tomato-caper salsa.

SERVES 4
per serving 4.3g total fat (1.2g saturated fat); 915kj (219 cal); 37.5g protein; 6.4g carbohydrate; 4.1g fibre

pasta with veal and baby beans

PREPARATION TIME 10 MINUTES COOKING TIME 20 MINUTES

250g instant curly lasagne sheets
1 tablespoon olive oil
500g veal leg steaks, sliced thinly
1 medium (170g) red onion, sliced thinly
300g button mushrooms, halved
6 slices (90g) prosciutto
250g frozen whole baby beans, thawed
1 tablespoon finely chopped fresh sage leaves
¼ cup (60ml) balsamic vinegar
¾ cup (180ml) chicken stock

1. Break pasta into 5cm squares. Cook pasta in large saucepan of boiling water, uncovered, until just tender; drain. Cover pasta to keep warm.
2. Meanwhile, heat half the oil in large frying pan; cook veal and onion, in batches, until browned.
3. Heat remaining oil in same pan; cook mushrooms, stirring, until tender. Return veal mixture to pan with prosciutto, beans, sage, vinegar and stock; stir until hot.
4. Serve pasta topped with veal mixture.

SERVES 4
per serving 7.5g total fat (1.5g saturated fat); 1835kj (439 cal); 42.2g protein; 49g carbohydrate; 7.4g fibre

mustard veal with polenta and spinach puree

PREPARATION TIME 15 MINUTES COOKING TIME 20 MINUTES

4 x 150g veal chops
⅓ cup (95g) wholegrain mustard
2 tablespoons coarsely chopped fresh oregano
2 cloves garlic, crushed
4 large egg tomatoes (360g), halved
2 cups (500ml) water
1 teaspoon salt
1 cup (170g) polenta
¾ cup (180ml) skim milk
¼ cup (20g) finely grated parmesan cheese
2kg spinach, trimmed
2 cloves garlic, crushed, extra
2 anchovy fillets, drained
2 tablespoons lemon juice
¼ cup (60ml) beef stock

1. Combine veal, mustard, oregano and garlic in medium bowl.
2. Cook veal mixture and tomato, in batches, on heated oiled grill plate (or grill or barbecue) until veal is browned and cooked as desired and tomato is browned and tender.
3. Meanwhile, bring combined water and salt to a boil in medium saucepan. Stir in polenta; cook, stirring, about 10 minutes or until polenta thickens. Add milk; cook, stirring, about 5 minutes or until polenta thickens. Stir in cheese.
4. Boil, steam or microwave spinach until just wilted; squeeze out excess liquid with hands. Blend or process spinach with remaining ingredients until pureed.
5. Serve veal chops with tomato, polenta and pureed spinach.

SERVES 4
per serving 5.8g total fat (1.7g saturated fat); 1496kj (358 cal); 38g protein; 37.2g carbohydrate; 10.5g fibre
tip fresh rosemary or thyme can be substituted for the oregano.
serving suggestion top steaks with fresh sage leaves, and serve with a radicchio or rocket salad dressed in balsamic vinegar.

veal with marsala sauce

PREPARATION TIME 15 MINUTES (PLUS REFRIGERATION TIME) COOKING TIME 15 MINUTES

4 x 75g veal steaks
¼ cup (60ml) marsala
1 tablespoon lemon juice
½ teaspoon olive oil
1 large carrot (180g)
1 large zucchini (150g)
1 teaspoon cornflour
¾ cup water (180ml)
1 clove garlic, crushed
3 teaspoons plum jam
3 green onions, sliced thinly

1. Trim all visible fat from veal; pound veal thinly. Combine veal with marsala and juice in large bowl. Cover; refrigerate several hours or overnight.
2. Drain veal; reserve marinade. Heat oil in medium saucepan; cook veal until tender. Remove from pan.
3. Cut carrot and zucchini into 10cm lengths. Cut each piece into thin strips; cut strips into matchstick-size pieces. Boil, steam or microwave until vegetables are tender; keep warm.
4. Place blended cornflour and reserved marinade in small saucepan with the water, garlic and jam; cook, stirring, over heat until mixture boils and thickens.
5. Serve veal with sauce and topped with vegetables and onion.

SERVES 2
per serving 4g total fat (0.9g saturated fat); 1141kj (273 cal); 35.9g protein; 14.7g carbohydrate; 2.8g fibre
serving suggestion serve veal on a bed of potato mash.

veal and fettuccine in sage mustard sauce

PREPARATION TIME 10 MINUTES COOKING TIME 15 MINUTES

500g fettuccine pasta
4 x 160g veal steaks
2 cloves garlic, crushed
2 tablespoons wholegrain mustard
¾ cup (180ml) dry white wine
1 cup (250ml) chicken stock
2 teaspoons finely shredded fresh sage
300g snow peas, sliced thinly

1. Cook pasta in large saucepan of boiling water, uncovered, until tender; drain.
2. Meanwhle, cook veal, in batches, in large oiled frying pan until browned and cooked as desired. Cover to keep warm.
3. Cook garlic and mustard in same pan, stirring, 1 minute. Add wine and stock; bring to a boil. Reduce heat, simmer, uncovered, about 5 minutes or until liquid reduces by half. Stir in sage.
4. Meanwhile, boil, steam or microwave snow peas until just tender; drain.
5. Cut veal pieces in half on the diagonal. Combine pasta and snow peas; divide among serving plates. Top with veal; drizzle with sauce.

SERVES 4
per serving 4.9g total fat (1.2g saturated fat); 2801kj (670 cal); 54.6g protein; 92.5g carbohydrate; 8.5g fibre
serving suggestion sprinkle pasta with tiny whole fresh sage leaves.

veal pizzaiola

PREPARATION TIME 10 MINUTES COOKING TIME 20 MINUTES

4 x 125g lean veal steaks
1½ tablespoons plain flour
2 teaspoons olive oil
1 clove garlic, crushed
2 tablespoons dry white wine
1 tablespoon chopped fresh oregano
½ cup (125ml) beef stock
3 cups (750ml) bottled pasta sauce
1 tablespoon chopped fresh flat-leaf parsley
⅔ cup (100g) seedless black olives

1 Toss veal in flour; shake away any excess. Heat oil in large frying pan; cook veal, stirring, over high heat until browned on both sides and tender. Remove from pan.

2 Add garlic to same pan, then wine and oregano; simmer, uncovered, until reduced by half. Add stock and sauce, simmer, uncovered, about 10 minutes or until sauce thickens slightly.

3 Return veal to pan with parsley and olives; stir until hot.

SERVES 4
per serving 6.6g total fat (1.3g saturated fat); 1342kj (321 cal); 33.4g protein; 31g carbohydrate; 4.9g fibre

veal with potato pea mash

PREPARATION TIME 10 MINUTES COOKING TIME 20 MINUTES

450g veal steaks
⅓ cup (50g) plain flour
1 egg white, beaten lightly
2 tablespoons skim milk
1 cup (160g) corn flake crumbs
1 teaspoon finely grated lemon rind
2 tablespoons finely chopped fresh flat-leaf parsley
cooking-oil spray
4 medium potatoes (800g)
¼ cup (60ml) buttermilk
¾ cup (180ml) chicken stock
2 cups (250g) frozen peas
1 lemon, cut into 8 wedges

1 Preheat oven to 240°C/220°C fan-forced. Oil oven tray.

2 Cut each steak in half. Toss veal in flour; shake away any excess. Coat veal in combined egg white and milk, then in combined crumbs, rind and parsley.

3 Place veal in single layer on oven tray; coat lightly with cooking-oil spray. Bake, uncovered, about 5 minutes or until cooked through. Cover; stand 5 minutes. Slice thickly.

4 Meanwhile, boil, steam or microwave potatoes until soft; drain. Mash potatoes with buttermilk in medium bowl; cover to keep warm.

5 Place stock in medium saucepan; bring to a boil. Add peas; cook, uncovered, until stock reduces by half. Blend or process pea mixture until almost pureed.

6 Gently swirl pea mixture into potato mash to give marbled effect. Divide potato and pea mash among plates; top with veal. Serve with lemon.

SERVES 4
per serving 5.6g total fat (1.4g saturated fat); 2123kj (508 cal); 40.1g protein; 71.6g carbohydrate; 9.2g fibre
tip veal can be crumbed several hours ahead. Store, covered, in refrigerator.
serving suggestion serve with a contrasting coloured vegetable such as boiled or steamed carrots, corn on the cob, or oven-roasted tomatoes.

veal cutlets with tomato basil sauce

PREPARATION TIME 10 MINUTES COOKING TIME 25 MINUTES

2 x 150g veal cutlets
2 teaspoons olive oil
4 tomatoes (760g), peeled, chopped finely
½ cup water (125ml)
1 fresh small red chilli, chopped finely
1 clove garlic, crushed
2 teaspoons sugar
1½ tablespoons balsamic vinegar
1 tablespoon torn fresh basil leaves

1 Trim all visible fat from veal. Heat oil in medium saucepan; cook veal until browned on both sides and tender. Remove from pan; keep warm.

2 Add tomatoes, the water, chilli, garlic and sugar to pan; cook, stirring, over heat about 10 minutes or until tomatoes are soft and sauce has thickened. Add vinegar and basil; cook, stirring, 2 minutes.

3 Serve veal with tomato basil sauce.

SERVES 2
per serving 7.8g total fat (1.5g saturated fat); 982kj (235 cal); 29.5g protein; 10.4g carbohydrate; 4.5g fibre
tip sauce can be made a day ahead; store, covered, in refrigerator. Cook veal just before serving.
serving suggestion serve with roasted kipfler potates and steamed baby beans.

roast veal rack with herb stuffing

PREPARATION TIME 20 MINUTES COOKING TIME 35 MINUTES

1 small brown onion (80g), chopped finely
1 clove garlic, crushed
½ trimmed celery stalk (40g), chopped finely
¾ cup (45g) stale breadcrumbs
1 tablespoon dijon mustard
1 teaspoon finely chopped fresh thyme
1 tablespoon finely chopped fresh flat-leaf parsley
1 teaspoon finely grated lemon rind
2 teaspoons sea salt
2 teaspoons cracked black pepper
800g veal rack (4 cutlets), trimmed
1 medium brown onion (150g), chopped coarsely
1½ cups (375ml) beef stock
2 teaspoons olive oil
2 teaspoons balsamic vinegar
½ cup (125ml) beef stock, extra

1 Preheat oven to 220°C/200°C fan-forced.

2 Cook finely chopped onion, garlic and celery in heated oiled small frying pan, stirring, until vegetables soften. Add breadcrumbs; cook until breadcrumbs brown lightly. Remove from heat; stir in mustard, herbs, rind, half of the salt and half of the pepper. Cool 10 minutes.

3 Using sharp knife, make a tunnel through veal rack, close to the bone; fill with herb mixture.

4 Add coarsely chopped onion and stock to large flameproof baking dish. Place veal in dish; drizzle with oil, sprinkle with remaining salt and pepper. Roast, uncovered, about 30 minutes or until cooked as desired. Remove veal from dish, cover; stand 10 minutes.

5 Stir vinegar and extra stock into veal juices in dish; bring to a boil. Strain into medium jug; serve with veal along with steamed green beans, if desired.

SERVES 4
per serving 6.9g total fat (1.7g saturated fat); 1091kj (261 cal); 38.5g protein; 10.7g carbohydrate; 1.7g fibre

lemon and rosemary veal cutlets

PREPARATION TIME 20 MINUTES (PLUS REFRIGERATION TIME) COOKING TIME 25 MINUTES

1 tablespoon finely chopped fresh rosemary
2 tablespoons finely grated lemon rind
2 tablespoons olive oil
4 x 200g veal chops, trimmed
1kg kipfler potatoes
2 tablespoons lemon juice
1 clove garlic, crushed
8 red radishes (280g), sliced thinly
4 green onions, sliced thinly

1. Combine rosemary, rind and oil in small jug; stand 10 minutes. Combine half of the marinade and veal in medium bowl. Cover; refrigerate 3 hours or overnight. Reserve remaining marinade.
2. Boil, steam or microwave unpeeled potatoes until just tender; drain. Quarter potatoes lengthways.
3. Stir juice and garlic into reserved marinade.
4. Cook veal mixture in heated oiled large frying pan until browned and cooked as desired.
5. Place potato, radish and onion in large bowl; toss gently to combine. Serve veal on salad; drizzle with reserved marinade.

SERVES 4
per serving 11.6g total fat (1.8g saturated fat); 1672kj (400 cal); 37.5g protein; 34.9g carbohydrate; 6.1g fibre

barbecued veal chops with polenta

PREPARATION TIME 20 MINUTES (PLUS REFRIGERATION TIME) COOKING TIME 1 HOUR

3 cups (750ml) water
½ cup (125ml) milk
1½ cups (255g) polenta
1 teaspoon sea salt
1 teaspoon cracked black pepper
6 large tomatoes (1.5kg), quartered
1 tablespoon balsamic vinegar
6 x 165g veal loin chops
150g baby spinach leaves

RED WINE SAUCE
20g butter
1 small brown onion (80g), chopped finely
1 clove garlic, crushed
1 tablespoon plain flour
1½ cups (375ml) beef stock
½ cup (125ml) dry red wine
1 tablespoon brown sugar
1 tablespoon tomato paste

1. Preheat oven to 220°C/200°C fan-forced. Oil 19cm x 29cm slice pan.
2. Heat the water and milk in large saucepan (do not boil). Add polenta; cook, stirring, about 5 minutes or until liquid is absorbed and polenta thickens. Stir in salt and pepper. Spoon polenta into pan; press firmly to ensure even thickness. When cool, cover; refrigerate about 2 hours or until firm.
3. Meanwhile, combine tomato and vinegar in baking dish; roast, uncovered, about 35 minutes or until soft. Cover; keep warm.
4. Make red wine sauce.
5. Turn polenta onto board; trim edges. Cut into six squares; cut each square in half diagonally. Cook polenta on heated oiled grill plate (or grill or barbecue) until browned both sides and heated through. Cover; keep warm.
6. Cook veal on heated oiled grill plate (or grill or barbecue) until browned and cooked as desired. Serve veal with tomato, polenta and spinach, drizzled with red wine sauce.

RED WINE SAUCE melt butter in medium saucepan; cook onion and garlic, stirring, until onion is soft. Stir in flour; cook, stirring, until mixture bubbles. Add stock, wine, sugar and paste; cook, stirring, about 5 minutes or until mixture thickens. Strain into small jug.

SERVES 6
per serving 6.5g total fat (3g saturated fat); 1526kj (365 cal); 32.5g protein; 39.6g carbohydrate; 5.2g fibre
serving suggestion serve with a simply dressed green leaf salad.

mains

pork

risotto cakes with basil sauce and pancetta

PREPARATION TIME 15 MINUTES COOKING TIME 35 MINUTES

½ cup (125ml) dry white wine
1 medium brown onion (150g), chopped finely
1 clove garlic, crushed
1 cup (200g) arborio rice
3 cups (750ml) chicken stock
2 tablespoons finely chopped fresh parsley
2 tablespoons finely chopped fresh chives
2 tablespoons finely grated parmesan cheese
1 egg white, beaten lightly
4 slices pancetta (60g)
1 teaspoon cornflour
1 teaspoon water
¾ cup (180ml) low-fat evaporated milk
1 tablespoon finely chopped fresh basil

1. Heat 2 tablespoons of the wine in large saucepan, add onion and garlic; cook, stirring, about 2 minutes or until onion softens. Add rice and remaining wine; cook, stirring, about 3 minutes or until wine is reduced by half. Stir in stock, bring to a boil. Reduce heat, simmer, covered, 15 minutes, stirring midway through cooking. Remove from heat, stir in parsley, chives and cheese; cool. Stir in egg white. Using hands, shape risotto mixture into four patties. [Can be made ahead to this stage. Cover; refrigerate until required.]
2. Preheat oven to 220°C/200°C fan-forced.
3. Place pancetta on oven tray; bake, uncovered, about 5 minutes or until crisp; drain on absorbent paper. Break pancetta into pieces.
4. Reduce oven to 180°C/160°C fan-forced.
5. Cook risotto cakes in heated oiled large frying pan until browned both sides. Place cakes on oven tray; bake, uncovered, about 10 minutes or until hot.
6. Meanwhile, blend cornflour with water in small saucepan; add milk, stir over heat until mixture boils and thickens slightly. Stir in basil.
7. Drizzle sauce over risotto cakes; top with pancetta.

SERVES 4
per serving 5.2g total fat (2.6g saturated fat); 1338kj (320 cal); 14.9g protein; 48.2g carbohydrate; 1.9g fibre

pork, pine nut and cointreau risotto

PREPARATION TIME 10 MINUTES (PLUS STANDING TIME) COOKING TIME 35 MINUTES

500g pork fillets
1 tablespoon teriyaki marinade
1 teaspoon finely grated orange rind
3 cloves garlic, crushed
1 large brown onion (200g), chopped finely
2 cups (400g) arborio rice
1.25 litres (5 cups) chicken stock
½ cup (125ml) dry white wine
2 tablespoons cointreau
150g baby spinach leaves
2 tablespoons pine nuts, toasted
2 tablespoons coarsely chopped fresh lemon thyme

1 Preheat oven to 220°C/200°C fan-forced.
2 Place pork on rack in baking dish; brush with combined marinade and rind. Bake, uncovered, 20 minutes. Cover; stand 5 minutes. Slice thinly.
3 Meanwhile, cook garlic and onion in heated oiled large saucepan, stirring, until onion softens. Add rice, stock, wine and cointreau, bring to a boil. Reduce heat, simmer, covered, 15 minutes, stirring midway through cooking. Remove from heat, stand, covered, 10 minutes. Gently stir in spinach, pine nuts, thyme and pork.

SERVES 4
per serving 10g total fat (2.1g saturated fat); 2738kj (655 cal); 40.4g protein; 88.9g carbohydrate; 4.7g fibre

pork rissoles on potato rösti with leek puree

PREPARATION TIME 30 MINUTES COOKING TIME 45 MINUTES

1kg lean pork mince
2 cloves garlic, crushed
1 medium brown onion (150g), chopped finely
½ cup coarsely chopped fresh mint
1 egg white, beaten lightly
1 cup (70g) stale breadcrumbs
5 medium potatoes (1kg)
¼ cup (35g) plain flour
1 egg white, beaten lightly, extra
2 large leeks (1kg), chopped coarsely
2 tablespoons skim milk

1 Preheat oven to 220°C/200°C fan-forced. Oil oven trays.
2 Combine pork, garlic, onion, mint, egg white and breadcrumbs in large bowl. Using hands, shape pork mixture into 18 patties; place on oven tray. Cover; refrigerate 30 minutes.
3 Meanwhile, peel and coarsely grate potatoes; using hand, squeeze out excess liquid. Combine potato, flour and extra egg white in large bowl. Using hands, shape potato mixture into 12 patties. Place potato rösti, in single layer, on oven trays; bake, uncovered, turning once, about 30 minutes or until rösti are browned both sides.
4 Cook leek in heated oiled large heavy-based saucepan, stirring, until softened. Blend or process leek with milk until mixture forms a thick puree.
5 Meanwhile, cook pork rissoles in heated oiled large frying pan, in batches, until browned both sides and cooked through.
6 Stack three rissoles and two rösti on each serving plate; top with leek puree.

SERVES 6
per serving 3.7g total fat (1g saturated fat); 1538kj (368 cal); 47g protein; 35.3g carbohydrate; 6.3g fibre
tip brown onions can be substituted for leeks, if preferred.

pork with port and mushroom sauce

PREPARATION TIME 10 MINUTES COOKING TIME 15 MINUTES

4 x 100g pork medallions

PORT AND MUSHROOM SAUCE

2 teaspoons monounsaturated or polyunsaturated margarine
100g swiss brown mushrooms
½ cup (125ml) beef stock
½ cup (125ml) water
1 teaspoon worcestershire sauce
2 tablespoons port

1 Trim all visible fat from pork. Cook pork in heated large frying pan about 3 minutes each side or until cooked as desired.

2 Meanwhile, make port and mushroom sauce.

3 Serve pork with port and mushroom sauce.

PORT AND MUSHROOM SAUCE melt margarine in heated small saucepan, add mushrooms; cook, stirring, until browned. Add remaining ingredients; bring to a boil. Reduce heat, simmer, uncovered, about 5 minutes or until liquid is reduced by half and sauce has thickened slightly.

SERVES 2
per serving 6.8g total fat (1.7g saturated fat); 1212kj (290 cal); 47.8g protein; 4.2g carbohydrate; 1.3g fibre
serving suggestion serve with kumara mash and baby rocket leaves.

pork rice-paper rolls

PREPARATION TIME 30 MINUTES COOKING TIME 10 MINUTES

When soaked in hot water, vietnamese rice-paper sheets (banh trang) make pliable wrappers for a host of fillings. You will need a small wombok for this recipe.

350g pork mince
1 clove garlic, crushed
1 teaspoon grated fresh ginger
1 teaspoon five-spice powder
350g finely shredded wombok
4 green onions, sliced thinly
1 tablespoon soy sauce
¼ cup (60ml) oyster sauce
¼ cup tightly packed, coarsely chopped fresh coriander leaves
12 x 22cm rice paper sheets
¼ cup (60ml) sweet chilli sauce
2 tablespoons lime juice

1 Cook pork, garlic, ginger and spice in large frying pan, stirring, until pork is changed in colour and cooked through.

2 Add wombok, onion, sauces and 2 tablespoons of the coriander to pan; cook, stirring, until wombok is just wilted.

3 Place one sheet of rice paper in medium bowl of warm water until softened slightly; lift sheet carefully from water, place on board, pat dry with absorbent paper. Place a twelfth of the filling mixture in centre of sheet; fold in sides, roll top to bottom to enclose filling. Repeat with remaining rice paper sheets and filling.

4 Place rolls in single layer in large steamer set over large saucepan of simmering water; steam, covered, 5 minutes or until just heated through.

5 Combine remaining coriander, chilli sauce and juice in small bowl. Serve rolls with dipping sauce.

SERVES 4
per serving 6.8g total fat (2.4g saturated fat); 915kj (219 cal); 21g protein; 17.5g carbohydrate; 2.1g fibre
tip rolls can be prepared a day ahead. Store, covered, in refrigerator.

butterflied pork steaks with pear and apple salsa

PREPARATION TIME 15 MINUTES COOKING TIME 10 MINUTES

1 tablespoon water
2 tablespoons lemon juice
2 teaspoons sugar
1 medium green apple (150g), diced into 1cm pieces
1 medium red apple (150g), diced into 1cm pieces
1 small pear (180g), peeled, diced into 1cm pieces
1 long green chilli, chopped finely
1 tablespoon finely chopped fresh mint
8 x 100g butterflied pork steaks, trimmed

1. Combine the water, juice and sugar in medium bowl, stirring, until sugar dissolves. Add apples, pear, chilli and mint; toss gently to combine.
2. Cook pork on heated oiled grill plate (or grill or barbecue) until browned and cooked as desired.
3. Serve pork with pear and apple salsa.

SERVES 4
per serving 2.1g total fat (0.6g saturated fat); 1145kj (274 cal); 49.2g protein; 14.1g carbohydrate; 2.2g fibre

roast pork with rosemary

PREPARATION TIME 20 MINUTES (PLUS COOLING TIME) COOKING TIME 50 MINUTES

1 teaspoon olive oil
2 cloves garlic, crushed
1 tablespoon chopped fresh rosemary
1 large onion (200g), chopped
150g button mushrooms, sliced
500g spinach, trimmed, chopped coarsely
4 x 200g lean pork fillets

SAUCE

1 teaspoon cornflour
½ cup (125ml) chicken stock
½ teaspoon balsamic vinegar
½ teaspoon chopped fresh rosemary

1. Heat oil in saucepan; cook garlic, rosemary, onion and mushrooms, stirring, until onion is soft. Add spinach; cook, stirring, until spinach is just wilted. Cool.
2. Preheat oven to 200°C/180°C fan-forced.
3. Cut a pocket in each fillet, fill with spinach mixture. Tie fillets at 1.5cm intervals. Cook pork in same pan until browned all over.
4. Place pork on wire rack in baking dish. Bake, uncovered, about 40 minutes or until cooked through; reserve juices for sauce.
5. Make sauce. Serve pork with sauce.

   SAUCE combine blended cornflour, reserved pan juices and stock, vinegar and rosemary in small pan; cook, stirring, until it boils and thickens slightly.

SERVES 4
per serving 5.1g total fat (1.4g saturated fat); 874kj (209 cal); 36.8g protein; 3.7g carbohydrate; 3.5g fibre
tip filling can be prepared several hours ahead. Store, covered, in refrigerator.

marmalade-glazed pork cutlets

PREPARATION TIME 5 MINUTES COOKING TIME 20 MINUTES

½ cup (125ml) dry red wine
⅓ cup (115g) orange marmalade
1 clove garlic, crushed
⅓ cup (80ml) fresh orange juice
1 tablespoon olive oil
4 x 235g pork cutlets

1 Combine wine, marmalade, garlic and juice in small saucepan; bring to a boil. Remove from heat.

2 Heat oil in large frying pan; cook pork until browned and cooked as desired, brushing occasionally with marmalade glaze.

SERVES 4
per serving 11.7g total fat (3.3g saturated fat); 1530kj (366 cal); 40.3g protein; 20.5g carbohydrate; 0.4g fibre
serving suggestion serve with steamed rice and stir-fried baby buk choy.

italian pork steaks with baked capsicum salad

PREPARATION TIME 20 MINUTES COOKING TIME 1 HOUR 10 MINUTES

4 x 150g lean pork butterfly steaks
½ teaspoon cracked black pepper
½ teaspoon dried oregano
cooking-oil spray
1 teaspoon cornflour
1 cup (250ml) chicken stock
2 teaspoons red wine vinegar

BAKED CAPSICUM SALAD

2 medium yellow capsicums (400g)
cooking-oil spray
2 large egg tomatoes (180g), halved
90g button mushrooms, sliced
4 cloves garlic, crushed
¼ teaspoon dried oregano
2 teaspoons olive oil
16 seedless black olives (80g)
2 tablespoons grated parmesan cheese

1 Preheat oven to 200°C/180°C fan-forced. Coat oven tray with cooking-oil spray. Make baked capsicum salad.

2 Sprinkle pork with pepper and oregano. Coat heated large frying pan with cooking-oil spray; cook pork until tender. Remove from pan.

3 Add blended cornflour and stock to same pan; cook, stirring, until mixture boils and thickens. Add vinegar. Return pork to pan, stir until hot.

4 Serve with baked capsicum salad.

BAKED CAPSICUM SALAD cut capsicums in half, remove seeds and membranes, place capsicums on oven tray. Fill capsicums with tomatoes, mushrooms and garlic. Sprinkle with oregano and oil. Bake, uncovered, 40 minutes. Add olives, sprinkle with cheese, bake further 15 minutes or until capsicums are tender.

SERVES 4
per serving 6.4g total fat (1.8g saturated fat); 1108kj (265 cal); 41.4g protein; 10g carbohydrate; 2.7g fibre
tip recipe can be made a day ahead. Store, covered, in refrigerator.

pork with pear and apple sauce

PREPARATION TIME 20 MINUTES (PLUS REFRIGERATION TIME) COOKING TIME 50 MINUTES

4 x 150g lean pork butterfly steaks
2 tablespoons low-salt soy sauce
1 tablespoon lemon juice
1 tablespoon honey
1 clove garlic, crushed
3 teaspoons chopped fresh thyme

PEAR AND APPLE SAUCE

10g butter
1 medium pear (180g), quartered
1 large apple (200g), quartered
8 small spring onions (80g), halved
2 teaspoons sugar
1 teaspoon cornflour
½ cup (125ml) chicken stock
¼ cup (60ml) water

1. Combine pork, sauce, juice, honey, garlic and thyme in large bowl. Cover; refrigerate several hours or overnight.
2. Drain pork; reserve ¼ cup of the marinade. Cook pork in heated frying pan until browned and cooked as desired.
3. Make pear and apple sauce. Serve pork with sauce.

PEAR AND APPLE SAUCE heat butter in saucepan, add fruit, onions and sugar; cook, stirring, about 5 minutes or until fruit is browned lightly. Add reserved marinade to pan with blended cornflour, stock and the water, bring to a boil. Reduce heat, simmer, covered, stirring occasionally, about 5 minutes or until fruit is tender.

SERVES 4
per serving 3.8g total fat (1.9g saturated fat); 1108kj (265 cal); 38.2g protein; 19.5g carbohydrate; 2.3g fibre
tip sauce can be made a day ahead. Store, covered, in refrigerator.

chilli pork and bean feast

PREPARATION TIME 10 MINUTES COOKING TIME 40 MINUTES

600g pork butterfly steaks
1 teaspoon vegetable oil
1 clove garlic, crushed
1 medium brown onion (150g), chopped finely
1 cup water (250ml)
410g can tomatoes
1 tablespoon tomato paste
½ teaspoon chilli powder
½ teaspoon ground cumin
½ teaspoon ground coriander
310g can red kidney beans, rinsed, drained
1 medium green capsicum (200g), chopped finely

1. Trim all visible fat from pork (you should have 300g trimmed meat). Blend or process pork until minced.
2. Heat oil in medium saucepan, add garlic and onion; cook, stirring, until onion is soft. Add pork; cook, stirring, until pork is browned all over.
3. Stir in the water, undrained crushed tomatoes, paste, chilli, cumin and coriander; bring to a boil. Reduce heat, simmer, uncovered, 30 minutes. Add beans and capsicum; stir until heated through. Serve with crisp lebanese bread wedges, if desired.

SERVES 2
per serving 6.5g total fat (1.3g saturated fat); 2132kj (510 cal); 84.2g protein; 26.9g carbohydrate; 11.4g fibre
tip recipe can be made up to 2 days ahead. Store, covered, in refrigerator.

rosemary pork with orange sauce

PREPARATION TIME 10 MINUTES COOKING TIME 30 MINUTES

You will need 2 oranges for this recipe.

300g pork fillets
2 teaspoons olive oil
1 tablespoon grand marnier
½ cup (125ml) chicken stock
1 teaspoon cornflour
1 tablespoon water
½ cup (125ml) orange juice
2 sprigs fresh rosemary

1. Preheat oven to 180°C/160°C fan-forced.
2. Trim all visible fat from pork. Heat oil in medium saucepan; cook pork until browned all over. Place pork on rack in flameproof baking dish.
3. Add liqueur and stock to same pan; bring to a boil. Pour into baking dish. Bake, covered, about 20 minutes or until pork is tender. Remove pork from rack; keep warm.
4. Pour combined blended cornflour and water with juice into baking dish; cook, stirring, over heat until mixture boils and thickens. Stir in rosemary.
5. Serve pork with sauce and, if desired, steamed green and yellow zucchini and torn witlof.

SERVES 2
per serving 8.4g total fat (2g saturated fat); 1175kj (281 cal); 34g protein; 11.3g carbohydrate; 0.2g fibre

pork loin with couscous and apples

PREPARATION TIME 35 MINUTES COOKING TIME 1 HOUR

1 cup (200g) couscous
1 cup (250ml) boiling water
⅓ cup (55g) seeded prunes, chopped finely
1 tablespoon roasted pine nuts
2 tablespoons coarsely chopped fresh coriander
¼ cup coarsely chopped fresh flat-leaf parsley
500g rindless boneless pork loin
2½ cups (625ml) alcoholic apple cider
2 medium apples (300g), peeled, cored, sliced thickly
1 large red onion (300g), cut into thick wedges
2 tablespoons brown sugar

1. Preheat oven to 200°C/180°C fan-forced.
2. Combine couscous with the water in medium heatproof bowl, cover; stand about 5 minutes or until water is absorbed, fluffing with fork occasionally. Using fork, toss prunes, nuts, coriander and parsley into couscous.
3. Trim any excess fat from pork. Place pork on board, upside-down; slice through thickest part of pork horizontally, without cutting through to the other side. Open pork out to form one large piece; press 1 cup of the couscous mixture against loin along width of pork. Roll pork to enclose stuffing; secure with kitchen string at 2cm intervals.
4. Place rolled pork on rack in large shallow flameproof baking dish; pour 2 cups of the cider over pork. Roast, uncovered, about 50 minutes or until cooked through. Remove pork from baking dish; cover to keep warm.
5. Place remaining couscous mixture in small ovenproof dish; bake, covered, about 10 minutes or until heated through.
6. Meanwhile, heat pan juices in baking dish on top of stove; add remaining cider, apple, onion and sugar. Cook, stirring, until apple is just tender. Serve sliced pork with apple mixture and couscous.

SERVES 4
per serving 7.3g total fat (1.8g saturated fat); 2128kj (509 cal); 29g protein; 72g carbohydrate; 4g fibre

rosemary pork with orange sauce

mulled-wine pork with stone fruits

mulled-wine pork with stone fruits

PREPARATION TIME 15 MINUTES COOKING TIME 15 MINUTES

"Mulled" wine has been heated and spiced, and is a favourite winter drink in cold climates. Here, we've used the best of the summer's stone-fruit crop to prove that mulled wine can be consumed any time of year.

2 cups (500ml) water
1 cup (250ml) dry white wine
½ cup (110g) sugar
2 cinnamon sticks
5 cloves
¼ cup (60ml) brandy
2 medium peaches (300g), stoned, quartered
4 medium plums (450g), stoned, quartered
2 medium nectarines (340g), stoned, quartered
4 medium apricots (200g), stoned, quartered
800g pork fillets, trimmed
1 fresh long red chilli, sliced thinly
1 long green chilli, sliced thinly

1. Combine the water, wine and sugar in heated large frying pan, stirring constantly, without boiling, until sugar dissolves. Bring to a boil; add cinnamon, cloves, brandy and fruit. Reduce heat, simmer, uncovered, about 5 minutes or until fruit is just tender. Using slotted spoon, transfer fruit to large bowl; cover to keep warm.
2. Return poaching liquid to a boil; add pork. Reduce heat, simmer, covered, about 10 minutes or until pork is cooked as desired. Cool pork in poaching liquid 10 minutes then slice thickly. Discard poaching liquid.
3. Combine chillies with fruit; divide fruit and any fruit juices among serving plates, top with pork.

SERVES 4
per serving 4.9g total fat (1.6g saturated fat); 2073kj (496 cal); 46.3g protein; 47.8g carbohydrate; 5.7g fibre

pork loin with water chestnut and mushroom filling

PREPARATION TIME 30 MINUTES (PLUS COOLING TIME) COOKING TIME 1 HOUR 10 MINUTES

1 small brown onion (80g)
1 fresh red thai chilli, chopped finely
100g canned water chestnuts, sliced thinly
100g fresh shiitake mushrooms, sliced thinly
1 tablespoon finely chopped fresh lemon thyme
1.3kg boneless pork loin
15 baby spinach leaves

1. Slice onion into thin rings. Heat oiled large saucepan; cook onion, chilli, chestnuts, mushrooms and thyme, stirring, until chestnuts are browned lightly and onion is soft. Cool for 10 minutes.
2. Discard rind and fat from pork. Place pork, cut-side up, on board. Make a horizontal cut through the centre of the meaty eye to create a flap; do not cut all the way through. Open out flap, cover pork with spinach, top with water chestnut filling. Roll pork tightly from a long side; tie with kitchen string at 2cm intervals to make an even shape. [Can be made ahead to this stage. Cover; refrigerate until required.]
3. Preheat oven to 220°C/200°C fan-forced. Cook pork in heated oiled large flameproof dish over heat until browned all over. Transfer dish to oven; bake, uncovered, about 1 hour or until tender.

SERVES 6
per serving 9.6g total fat (3.7g saturated fat); 1204kj (288 cal); 46.1g protein; 4.1g carbohydrate; 1.2g fibre

peanut pork schnitzels

PREPARATION TIME 10 MINUTES COOKING TIME 5 MINUTES

2 tablespoons peanut butter
2 tablespoons low-fat yogurt
2 teaspoons lemon juice
1 clove garlic, crushed
2 teaspoons honey
1 teaspoon ground cumin
6 x 165g pork leg schnitzels

1. Combine peanut butter, yogurt, juice, garlic, honey and cumin in small bowl. Brush pork with peanut butter mixture.
2. Cook pork on heated oiled grill plate (or grill or barbecue) until browned and cooked as desired.

SERVES 6
per serving 5.2g total fat (1.1g saturated fat); 552kj (132 cal); 17.8g protein; 3.3g carbohydrate; 1g fibre

orange pork medallions with roast vegetables

PREPARATION TIME 20 MINUTES (PLUS REFRIGERATION TIME) COOKING TIME 40 MINUTES

4 x 180g pork loin medallion steaks
1 tablespoon finely grated fresh ginger
¼ cup (60ml) grand marnier
2 medium oranges (360g)
8 kipfler potatoes (300g)
cooking-oil spray
1 medium kumara (400g)
2 medium leeks (700g)

1. Combine pork, ginger and 1 tablespoon of the liqueur in large bowl. Cover; refrigerate at least 3 hours or until required.
2. Peel oranges; cut each orange into four thick slices. Combine orange slices and remaining liqueur in medium bowl. Cover; refrigerate at least 3 hours or until required.
3. Preheat oven to 220°C/200°C fan-forced. Oil baking dish.
4. Cut potatoes in half lengthways. Place in baking dish; coat with cooking-oil spray. Roast, uncovered, 10 minutes. Cut kumara in half crossways; cut each half into eight wedges, coat with cooking-oil spray. Add kumara to baking dish; bake, uncovered, 20 minutes. Cut leeks in half lengthways; cut each half crossways into four equal pieces. Add leek to baking dish; bake, uncovered, about 10 minutes or until all vegetables are browned and tender.
5. Meanwhile, cook pork on heated oiled grill plate (or grill or barbecue) about 5 minutes each side or until browned and cooked through. Remove; cover to keep warm.
6. Drain orange over medium bowl; reserve liqueur. Cook orange slices, in batches, on same grill plate for 2 minutes each side or until tender.
7. Serve pork with orange slices and roasted vegetables; drizzle reserved liqueur over orange slices.

SERVES 4
per serving 5.9g total fat (1.4g saturated fat); 1902kj (445 cal); 48.2g protein; 40g carbohydrate; 7.4g fibre

pork with tomato relish

PREPARATION TIME 10 MINUTES COOKING TIME 25 MINUTES

1 medium brown onion (150g), chopped finely
8 medium egg tomatoes (600g), halved
1 teaspoon ground cardamom
¼ cup (50g) brown sugar
¼ cup (60ml) balsamic vinegar
¼ cup (60ml) water
4 x 180g pork cutlets

1. Cook onion in heated oiled large saucepan, stirring, until soft. Add tomato, cardamom and sugar; cook, stirring, until sugar dissolves. Add vinegar and water, bring to a boil. Reduce heat, simmer, uncovered, about 20 minutes or until mixture thickens.
2. Meanwhile, cook pork on heated oiled grill plate (or grill or barbecue) until browned and cooked as desired.
3. Serve pork with tomato relish, and pasta, if desired.

SERVES 4
per serving 5.6g total fat (2.1g saturated fat); 1028kj (246 cal); 32.4g protein; 16.3g carbohydrate; 2.2g fibre

pork with ratatouille and potatoes

PREPARATION TIME 10 MINUTES COOKING TIME 25 MINUTES

1kg tiny new potatoes, halved
1 medium brown onion (150g), chopped coarsely
2 cloves garlic, crushed
4 baby eggplants (240g), chopped coarsely
2 medium green zucchini (240g), chopped coarsely
400g can tomatoes
2 tablespoons finely shredded fresh basil
4 x 150g pork steaks

1. Preheat oven to 240°C/200°C fan-forced. Oil large baking dish.
2. Place potatoes in baking dish; roast, uncovered, about 25 minutes or until browned and crisp.
3. Meanwhile, cook onion and garlic in heated large frying pan, stirring, until onion softens. Add eggplant and zucchini; cook, stirring, until vegetables are just tender.
4. Stir in undrained crushed tomatoes; bring to a boil. Reduce heat, simmer, uncovered, about 5 minutes or until vegetables are tender and sauce thickens. Stir in basil.
5. Cook pork, in batches, in heated medium frying pan until browned and cooked as desired. Slice pork thickly.
6. Serve pork with potatoes and ratatouille.

SERVES 4
per serving 2.8g total fat (0.6g saturated fat); 1513kj (362 cal); 42.6g protein; 39.8g carbohydrate; 8.9g fibre
tip ratatouille can be made a day ahead; store, covered, in refrigerator.
serving suggestion serve with a green salad.

japanese fried noodles

PREPARATION TIME 10 MINUTES COOKING TIME 15 MINUTES

250g dried wheat noodles
2 tablespoons peanut oil
500g pork fillets, sliced thinly
1 large brown onion (200g), sliced thinly
1 medium red capsicum (200g), sliced thinly
1 medium green capsicum (200g), sliced thinly
2 cups (140g) coarsely shredded wombok
¼ cup (60ml) tonkatsu sauce
¼ cup (60ml) sukiyaki sauce

1. Cook noodles in large saucepan of boiling water, uncovered, until just tender; drain. Rinse under cold water; drain well.
2. Meanwhile, heat half of the oil in wok; stir-fry pork, in batches, until browned all over.
3. Heat remaining oil in wok; stir-fry onion until soft. Add capsicums; stir-fry until just tender.
4. Return pork to wok with noodles, wombok and sauces; stir-fry until wombok just wilts.

SERVES 4
per serving 12.9g total fat (2.8g saturated fat); 2036kj (487 cal); 37.6g protein; 54.7g carbohydrate; 4.1g fibre
tip you can use soba, fresh hokkien or rice noodles in this dish.

hoisin pork kebabs with pancakes

PREPARATION TIME 10 MINUTES (PLUS REFRIGERATION AND STANDING TIME) COOKING TIME 20 MINUTES

Soak 12 bamboo skewers in water for at least 1 hour before use to prevent them scorching and splintering.

750g pork fillets, sliced thinly
½ cup (125ml) hoisin sauce
2 tablespoons plum sauce
2 cloves garlic, crushed
1½ cups (225g) plain flour
1½ teaspoons sugar
¾ cup (180ml) boiling water
2 green onions
1 small green cucumber (130g)

1. Combine pork, sauces and garlic in large bowl. Cover; refrigerate at least 3 hours or until required.
2. Combine flour and sugar in large bowl, add water; stir quickly with wooden spoon until ingredients cling together. Knead dough on floured surface about 10 minutes or until smooth. Wrap dough in plastic; stand 30 minutes. Divide dough into 16 pieces; roll each piece into a 16cm round. Heat small frying pan; dry-fry 1 pancake until browned lightly both sides. Repeat with remaining dough. Keep cooked pancakes covered to prevent drying out. [Can be made ahead to this stage. Separate pancakes with plastic wrap, seal in plastic bag; refrigerate until required.]
3. Thread pork onto skewers. Cook pork kebabs, in batches, on heated oiled grill plate (or grill or barbecue) until browned all over and cooked as desired. [if it's necessary to reheat pancakes, remove plastic wrap, wrap in foil, bake in 180°C/160°C fan-forced oven about 10 minutes or until hot.]
4. Meanwhile, finely slice onions diagonally. Halve cucumber lengthways; discard seeds, slice cucumber finely lengthways. Serve kebabs with warm pancakes, onion, cucumber and extra plum sauce, if desired.

SERVES 4
per serving 7g total fat (1.9g saturated fat); 2103kj (503 cal); 48.1g protein; 61.2g carbohydrate; 6.3g fibre

spicy chinese pork spare ribs

PREPARATION TIME 10 MINUTES (PLUS REFRIGERATION TIME) COOKING TIME 40 MINUTES

2kg lean american-style pork spare ribs
1 tablespoon honey
2 tablespoons sweet sherry
1 tablespoon teriyaki sauce
½ teaspoon five spice powder
2 cloves garlic, crushed
2 teaspoons grated fresh ginger
1 teaspoon sesame oil
¼ cup (60ml) low-salt soy sauce
1 teaspoon sambal oelek
2 tablespoons chopped fresh coriander leaves
1 teaspoon sichuan pepper

1. Cut ribs into serving pieces (about 3 bones per serving). Combine ribs with remaining ingredients in large bowl. Cover; refrigerate several hours or overnight.
2. Preheat oven to 200°C/180°C fan-forced.
3. Drain ribs; reserve marinade. Place ribs in single layer on wire racks in baking dishes. Bake, uncovered, about 40 minutes or until tender, brushing with reserved marinade during cooking.

SERVES 4
per serving 4.8g total fat (1.3g saturated fat); 1229kj (294 cal); 52.1g protein; 7.7g carbohydrate; 0.2g fibre
tip recipe can be prepared up to 2 days ahead. Store, covered, in refrigerator.

stir-fried pork and noodles

PREPARATION TIME 30 MINUTES COOKING TIME 10 MINUTES

Because the cooking time is so brief in a stir-fry, it's best to use a cut of meat that doesn't need to be slow-cooked in order to be tender; we recommend you use thinly sliced pork fillet or rump in this recipe.

250g fresh egg noodles
2 teaspoons peanut oil
1 clove garlic, crushed
1½ teaspoons five-spice powder
500g pork fillets, sliced thinly
2 small red capsicums (300g), sliced diagonally
2 tablespoons oyster sauce
1 tablespoon soy sauce
1 teaspoon sesame oil
2 teaspoons cornflour
1⅓ cups (330ml) chicken stock
5 green onions, sliced thinly
600g wombok, finely shredded

1. Place noodles in large heatproof bowl, cover with boiling water; stand 3 minutes, using a fork to separate the noodles. Drain into a colander or large strainer.
2. Place half of the peanut oil in a heated wok; stir-fry garlic and five-spice briefly, until just fragrant. Add pork, in batches, to wok; stir-fry over high heat until browned and almost cooked through.
3. Heat remaining peanut oil in wok; stir-fry capsicum for 1 minute. Return pork to wok with sauces, sesame oil and blended cornflour and chicken stock; stir-fry over high heat, tossing, until pork mixture just starts to boil and thickens slightly. Add noodles, onion and wombok to wok; stir-fry over high heat, tossing to combine, until heated through.

SERVES 4
per serving 7.6g total fat (1.9g saturated fat); 1618kj (387 cal); 37.5g protein; 41.1g carbohydrate; 3.9g fibre

satay pork and noodle stir-fry

PREPARATION TIME 10 MINUTES COOKING TIME 25 MINUTES

500g fresh egg noodles
1 tablespoon vegetable oil
500g pork fillets, sliced thinly
2 cloves garlic, crushed
8 green onions, sliced thinly
¾ cup (180ml) beef stock
⅓ cup (85g) crunchy peanut butter
¼ cup (60ml) sweet chilli sauce
2 teaspoons lemon juice
400g packet fresh asian-style stir-fry vegetables

1 Place noodles in large heatproof bowl, cover with boiling water, stand until just tender; drain.
2 Heat half the oil in wok; stir-fry pork, in batches, until browned.
3 Heat remaining oil in wok; stir-fry garlic and onion until soft. Add stock, peanut butter, sauce and juice, simmer, uncovered, 1 minute.
4 Return pork to wok with vegetables and noodles, cook, stirring, until hot.

SERVES 6
per serving 13.5g total fat (2.5g saturated fat); 1944kj (465 cal); 31.9g protein; 53.5g carbohydrate; 7.5g fibre

gingered pork with stir-fried vegetables

PREPARATION TIME 15 MINUTES (PLUS REFRIGERATION TIME) COOKING TIME 40 MINUTES

500g lean pork fillets
¼ cup (60ml) low-salt soy sauce
2 tablespoons dry red wine
1 tablespoon golden syrup
1 tablespoon brown sugar
2 cloves garlic, crushed
1 tablespoon grated fresh ginger
2 teaspoons peanut oil
1 medium onion (150g), chopped coarsely
1 small carrot (70g), sliced finely
1 medium zucchini (120g), sliced
2 teaspoons cornflour
150g snow peas, halved
1¼ cups (100g) bean sprouts

1 Combine pork, sauce, wine, golden syrup, sugar, garlic and ginger in large bowl. Cover; refrigerate several hours or overnight, turning occasionally.
2 Preheat oven to 180°C/160°C fan-forced.
3 Drain pork; reserve marinade. Cook pork in heated frying pan until browned all over. Transfer pork to wire rack in baking dish; bake, uncovered, about 30 minutes or until tender. Slice diagonally.
4 Heat oil in wok; stir-fry onion, carrot and zucchini over high heat until tender.
5 Blend cornflour with reserved marinade and enough water to make 1 cup (250ml) liquid. Add to wok with snow peas and sprouts, stir until sauce boils and thickens slightly.
6 Serve pork with stir-fried vegetables.

SERVES 4
per serving 5.4g total fat (1.4g saturated fat); 1007kj (241 cal); 31.2g protein; 15.1g carbohydrate; 3.2g fibre

chilli pork noodles

PREPARATION TIME 10 MINUTES COOKING TIME 10 MINUTES

Udon, wide Japanese noodles made from wheat flour, are available fresh or dried from Asian supermarkets. You can substitute any dried flat wheat noodle, but check the manufacturer's instructions regarding their preparation.

500g udon noodles
1 tablespoon peanut oil
2 tablespoons finely chopped garlic chives
3 cloves garlic, crushed
3 fresh red thai chillies, chopped finely
500g pork mince
¼ cup (60ml) light soy sauce
½ cup (125ml) chicken stock
1 cup (80g) bean sprouts
4 green onions, sliced thinly

1 Cook noodles in large saucepan of boiling water, uncovered, until just tender; drain.
2 Meanwhile, heat oil in wok; stir-fry chives, garlic and chilli until fragrant. Add pork; stir-fry until cooked through. Add sauce and stock; stir-fry until hot.
3 Serve pork mixture on noodles; top with sprouts and onion.

SERVES 4
per serving 14.5g total fat (4.2g saturated fat); 1981kj (474 cal); 32g protein; 52.9g carbohydrate; 2.5g fibre
tip dried udon are available in different thicknesses, so the cooking time will vary depending on the size.
serving suggestion serve with asian greens in oyster sauce.

pork and black bean stir-fry

PREPARATION TIME 25 MINUTES (PLUS REFRIGERATION TIME) COOKING TIME 15 MINUTES

750g pork fillets, sliced thinly
1 fresh red thai chilli, chopped finely
1 clove garlic, crushed
¾ cup (180ml) chicken stock
⅓ cup (80ml) black bean sauce
1 tablespoon oyster sauce
1 teaspoon sesame oil
1 tablespoon peanut oil
1 large brown onion (200g), sliced thinly
2 small carrots (140g), sliced thinly
2 baby buk choy (300g), trimmed, quartered lengthways
425g can baby corn, drained

1 Combine pork, chilli, garlic, stock, sauces and sesame oil in large bowl. Cover; refrigerate 3 hours or overnight.
2 Drain pork; reserve marinade. Heat half of the peanut oil in wok; stir-fry pork, in batches, until browned all over.
3 Heat remaining peanut oil in same wok; stir-fry onion and carrot until onion just softens. Add buk choy; stir-fry until just tender.
4 Return pork to wok with corn; stir-fry until pork is cooked through. Add reserved marinade; bring to a boil. Toss gently to combine.

SERVES 4
per serving 11.2g total fat (2.7g saturated fat); 1379kj (330 cal); 45.4g protein; 11.6g carbohydrate; 5.3g fibre
tip you can vary the vegetables if you like, but remember to stir-fry those that take longer to cook, such as onion, carrot, celery and cauliflower before faster-cooking vegetables such as mushrooms, capsicum, broccoli or snow peas. Add the softest vegetables, or those that need the least amount of cooking, such as cabbage, asian greens, fresh herbs, green onion or bean sprouts, last.
serving suggestion serve with steamed jasmine rice.

curried pork stir-fry with wild rice

PREPARATION TIME 15 MINUTES COOKING TIME 15 MINUTES

2 cups (400g) basmati rice
½ cup (90g) wild rice
800g pork fillets, sliced thinly
2 teaspoons vegetable oil
2 cloves garlic, crushed
1 teaspoon grated fresh ginger
1 teaspoon ground coriander
1 teaspoon ground cumin
1 teaspoon ground turmeric
2 teaspoons garam masala
500g brussels sprouts, halved
300g patty-pan squash, quartered
1 medium leek (350g), sliced thinly
¼ cup (60ml) lemon juice
¼ cup (60ml) water
200g low-fat yogurt
1 tablespoon finely chopped fresh mint
1 tablespoon finely chopped fresh coriander
½ cup (140g) low-fat yogurt, extra

1. Cook rices, in separate medium saucepans of boiling water, until each is just tender (wild rice will take longer to cook than basmati); drain. Combine rices in large bowl; cover to keep warm.
2. Meanwhile, stir-fry pork in heated wok, in batches, until browned all over.
3. Heat oil in wok; stir-fry garlic, ginger and spices until fragrant. Add sprouts, squash, leek, juice and the water; stir-fry until vegetables are just tender.
4. Return pork to wok with yogurt and fresh herbs; stir-fry until combined.
5. Serve pork stir-fry with rice; drizzle with extra yogurt.

SERVES 6
per serving 6.5g total fat (2g saturated fat); 2220kj (531 cal); 42.5g protein; 73.5g carbohydrate; 5.8g fibre

fried rice

PREPARATION TIME 10 MINUTES COOKING TIME 10 MINUTES

Also known as "clever rice", doondara rice is a white, long-grain, Australian-grown rice that can be found at your local supermarket. You will need to cook about 1½ cups of rice for this recipe.

2 teaspoons peanut oil
1 medium brown onion (150g), chopped coarsely
2 cloves garlic, crushed
2 teaspoons grated fresh ginger
300g lean pork mince
1 untrimmed stick celery (150g), sliced thickly
1 small red capsicum (150g), chopped coarsely
1 large zucchini (150g), chopped coarsely
4 cups (600g) cooked doongara rice
¾ cup (90g) frozen peas, thawed
¼ cup (60ml) soy sauce
2 green onions, sliced thinly

1. Heat oil in wok; stir-fry brown onion, garlic and ginger until onion has just softened. Add pork; stir-fry until brown and cooked through.
2. Add celery, capsicum and zucchini to wok; stir-fry until just tender. Add rice, peas and sauce; stir-fry until hot. Toss green onion through fried rice just before serving.

SERVES 4

per serving 9.1g total fat (2.5g saturated fat); 1551kj (371 cal); 23.4g protein; 48.1g carbohydrate; 4.2g fibre

tip cold rice, cooked the day before you intend to prepare the recipe, is best for this dish; the individual grains remain separate from one another and won't get mushy when reheated in the wok. Spread the cooked rice on a tray and allow to cool before covering and refrigerating overnight.

serving suggestion top each serving with a just-fried egg garnished with freshly chopped red chilli. Spoon a little kecap manis over the egg and rice.

mains
lamb

lamb with harissa carrot puree

PREPARATION TIME 10 MINUTES (PLUS STANDING TIME) COOKING TIME 25 MINUTES

While harissa, that exquisitely piquant blend of chilli, garlic, caraway and other spices, can be bought at nearly every supermarket these days, here we've made a delicious low-fat version without oil.

1 medium red capsicum (200g)
8 large carrots (1.5kg), chopped coarsely
40g low-fat dairy-free spread
2 fresh red thai chillies, chopped coarsely
1 clove garlic, crushed
1 tablespoon ground cumin
1 tablespoon ground coriander
1 teaspoon caraway seeds
1 cup (250ml) buttermilk
1 tablespoon coarsely chopped fresh flat-leaf parsley
12 lamb fillets (960g)
2 teaspoons ground cumin, extra
2 teaspoons ground coriander, extra

1. Quarter capsicum; remove and discard seeds and membrane. Roast, under grill or in very hot oven, skin-side up, until skin blisters and blackens. Cover capsicum pieces in plastic or paper 5 minutes; peel away and discard skin. Chop capsicum coarsely.
2. Boil, steam or microwave carrot until tender. Drain; keep warm.
3. Heat dairy-free spread in small heavy-based saucepan; cook chilli, garlic, cumin, coriander and caraway, stirring, until chilli softens and harissa is fragrant. Stir in buttermilk. Blend or process chilli-spice mixture with capsicum, carrot and parsley, in batches, until mixture forms a smooth puree.
4. Coat lamb, all over, with combined extra spices. Cook lamb, in batches, on heated oiled grill plate (or grill or barbecue) until browned all over and cooked as desired. Serve with harissa carrot puree.

SERVES 6
per serving 9.6g total fat (3.6g saturated fat); 1274kj (305 cal); 39.1g protein; 15g carbohydrate; 6.7g fibre
serving suggestion serve with a bowl of low-fat yogurt flavoured with chilli and mint.

lamb and fetta rissoles

PREPARATION TIME 10 MINUTES COOKING TIME 15 MINUTES

400g lamb mince
1 small brown onion (80g), chopped finely
1 clove garlic, crushed
⅓ cup (40g) seeded black olives, chopped
60g low-fat fetta cheese, crumbled
½ cup (35g) stale breadcrumbs
1 egg white

1 Combine all ingredients in bowl; mix well. Shape mixture into eight rissoles.
2 Heat oiled large frying pan; cook rissoles until browned both sides and cooked through.

SERVES 4
per serving 9.5g total fat (4.6g saturated fat); 963kj (230 cal); 26.7g protein; 9.3g carbohydrate; 0.9g fibre

warm pasta and lamb salad

PREPARATION TIME 15 MINUTES (PLUS REFRIGERATION TIME) COOKING TIME 35 MINUTES

500g lean lamb fillets, sliced
2 teaspoons olive oil
3 teaspoons sugar
⅓ cup (80ml) lemon juice
1 tablespoon dry red wine
1 tablespoon sweet chilli sauce
1 clove garlic, crushed
2 tablespoons chopped fresh rosemary
4 medium egg tomatoes (300g), quartered
500g spiral pasta
cooking-oil spray
½ cup (125ml) beef stock
2 tablespoons chopped fresh flat-leaf parsley
500g spinach, trimmed, chopped coarsely

1 Combine lamb, oil, 1 teaspoon of the sugar, juice, wine, sauce, garlic and rosemary in bowl. Cover; refrigerate 3 hours or overnight.
2 Preheat oven to 180°C/160°C fan-forced.
3 Drain lamb; reserve marinade. Place tomatoes in single layer on oven tray, sprinkle with remaining sugar; bake, uncovered, 20 minutes.
4 Meanwhile cook pasta in large saucepan of boiling water, uncovered, until just tender; drain.
5 Coat large frying pan with cooking-oil spray; cook lamb, in batches, until browned and tender. Return lamb to pan, add reserved marinade, stock and parsley, stir until mixture boils.
6 Place tomatoes, pasta and lamb in large serving bowl with spinach; toss gently to combine.

SERVES 6
per serving 6.6g total fat (1.8g saturated fat); 1864kj (445 cal); 30.9g protein; 63.2g carbohydrate; 4.4g fibre
tip recipe best made close to serving.

lamb cutlets with potato and parsnip mash

PREPARATION TIME 15 MINUTES (PLUS REFRIGERATION TIME) COOKING TIME 20 MINUTES

18 french-trimmed lamb cutlets (1.4kg)
4 cloves garlic, crushed
2 teaspoons grated fresh ginger
¼ cup coarsely chopped fresh mint
⅓ cup (80ml) balsamic vinegar
2 large potatoes (600g), chopped coarsely
5 medium parsnips (625g), chopped coarsely
½ cup (125ml) buttermilk
1½ cups (375ml) vegetable stock

1. Combine lamb, garlic, ginger, mint and half of the vinegar in large bowl. Cover; refrigerate 3 hours or overnight.
2. Boil, steam or microwave potato and parsnip until tender; drain. Mash potato and parsnip in large bowl with buttermilk until smooth.
3. Meanwhile, heat large oiled frying pan; cook lamb, in batches, until browned both sides and cooked as desired. Cover to keep warm.
4. Add remaining vinegar and stock to same pan; bring to a boil. Reduce heat, simmer, uncovered, until sauce reduces by two-thirds. Serve lamb with mash; drizzle with strained sauce.

SERVES 6
per serving 11.9g total fat (5.7g saturated fat); 1374kj (328 cal); 32g protein; 22g carbohydrate; 4.4g fibre
serving suggestion serve with sliced ripe tomatoes drizzled with balsamic vinegar.

lamb hot pot with couscous

PREPARATION TIME 15 MINUTES (PLUS STANDING TIME) COOKING TIME 45 MINUTES

600g lamb leg chops
1 tablespoon plain flour
2 teaspoons olive oil
1 medium brown onion (150g), cut into thin wedges
1 teaspoon ground cinnamon
1 teaspoon ground turmeric
1 cup (250ml) water
½ cup (125ml) beef stock
100g prunes, pitted
2 tablespoons finely chopped fresh coriander

COUSCOUS
1 cup (250ml) boiling water
1 cup (200g) couscous

1. Trim all visible fat from lamb. Cut lamb into cubes; toss in flour.
2. Heat oil in large saucepan; cook onion until soft. Add lamb; cook until lamb is browned all over. Stir in cinnamon and turmeric; cook 1 minute.
3. Stir in the water, stock and prunes; bring to a boil. Reduce heat, simmer, covered, for about 30 minutes or until lamb is tender.
4. Make couscous. Serve lamb with couscous, sprinkled with coriander.

COUSCOUS pour the water over couscous in medium bowl; stand for 5 minutes or until liquid is absorbed, fluffing with fork occasionally to separate grains.

SERVES 2
per serving 18.9g total fat (7.3g saturated fat); 3613kj (863 cal); 65g protein; 107g carbohydrate; 6.2g fibre
tips hot pot can be made a day ahead; store, covered, in the refrigerator. Couscous is best made close to serving time.

lamb and apricot tagine with citrus couscous

PREPARATION TIME 20 MINUTES (PLUS STANDING TIME) COOKING TIME 1 HOUR

A tagine is a Moroccan slow-cooked meat or vegetable stew that is traditionally served with warm couscous.

1⅔ cups (250g) dried apricots
¾ cup (180ml) orange juice
½ cup (125ml) boiling water
2 tablespoons olive oil
900g lamb steaks, chopped coarsely
2 medium red capsicums (400g), chopped coarsely
1 large brown onion (200g), chopped coarsely
2 medium kumara (800g), chopped coarsely
3 cloves garlic, crushed
1 teaspoon ground cinnamon
2 teaspoons ground cumin
2 teaspoons ground coriander
1 cup (250ml) dry red wine
1 litre (4 cups) chicken stock
2 tablespoons honey
1 cup loosely packed fresh coriander leaves
200g low-fat yogurt

CITRUS COUSCOUS

1 litre (4 cups) water
4 cups (800g) couscous
1 tablespoon finely grated orange rind
2 teaspoons finely grated lemon rind
2 teaspoons finely grated lime rind

1. Combine apricots, juice and the water in small bowl. Cover; allow to stand 45 minutes.
2. Meanwhile, heat half of the oil in large saucepan; cook lamb, in batches, until browned all over.
3. Heat remaining oil in same pan; cook capsicum, onion, kumara, garlic and ground spices, stirring, until onion softens and mixture is fragrant. Add wine; bring to a boil. Reduce heat, simmer, uncovered, about 5 minutes or until liquid reduces by half.
4. Return lamb to pan with undrained apricots, stock and honey; bring to a boil. Reduce heat, simmer, covered, about 50 minutes or until lamb is tender. Remove from heat; stir in fresh coriander.
5. Make citrus couscous.
6. Serve lamb on citrus couscous; drizzle with yogurt.

CITRUS COUSCOUS bring the water to a boil in medium saucepan; stir in couscous and rinds. Remove from heat; stand, covered, about 5 minutes or until liquid is absorbed, fluffing with fork occasionally to separate grains.

SERVES 8
per serving 12.8g total fat (4.3g saturated fat); 3279kj (783 cal); 44.8g protein; 115.8g carbohydrate; 6.8g fibre

moroccan lamb shanks with polenta and white beans

PREPARATION TIME 25 MINUTES (PLUS STANDING TIME) COOKING TIME 2 HOURS

1½ cups (300g) dried haricot beans
12 french-trimmed lamb shanks (approximately 2.6kg)
¼ cup (35g) plain flour
1 tablespoon olive oil
2 medium red onions (340g), chopped finely
2 cloves garlic, crushed
2 teaspoons ground cumin
½ teaspoon ground cardamom
½ teaspoon ground ginger
2 teaspoons finely grated lemon rind
⅓ cup (80ml) lemon juice
2 x 400g cans crushed tomatoes
2½ cups (625ml) beef stock
¼ cup (70g) tomato paste
3 cups (750ml) water
3 cups (750ml) milk
2 cups (340g) polenta
2 teaspoons finely grated lemon rind, extra
¼ cup finely chopped fresh flat-leaf parsley
¼ cup finely chopped fresh coriander

1. Cover beans with cold water in large bowl. Soak overnight; drain.
2. Coat lamb in flour; shake off excess. Heat oil in large saucepan; cook lamb, in batches, until browned all over. Add onion and garlic; cook, stirring, until onion is soft. Add spices; cook, stirring, about 2 minutes or until fragrant.
3. Stir in beans, rind, juice, undrained tomatoes, stock and paste; bring to a boil. Reduce heat, simmer, covered, 40 minutes. Uncover; simmer about 50 minutes or until both lamb and beans are tender.
4. Heat the water and milk in large saucepan (do not boil). Gradually add polenta; cook, stirring, about 5 minutes or until liquid is absorbed and polenta softens.
5. Serve lamb mixture on polenta, sprinkled with combined extra rind, parsley and coriander.

SERVES 6
per serving 17.8g total fat (7.4g saturated fat); 3861kj (922 cal); 111.8g protein; 78.4g carbohydrate; 14.4g fibre

lamb chermoulla with chickpea salad

PREPARATION TIME 15 MINUTES COOKING TIME 15 MINUTES

Chermoulla is a Moroccan mixture of fresh and ground spices including coriander, cumin and paprika. It can be used as a marinade for chicken, meat and fish.

300g green beans, trimmed
2 teaspoons cracked black pepper
2 teaspoons ground cumin
2 teaspoons ground coriander
1 teaspoon hot paprika
2 tablespoons coarsely chopped fresh flat-leaf parsley
2 tablespoons coarsely chopped fresh coriander
2 tablespoons coarsely chopped fresh mint
1 tablespoon coarsely grated lemon rind
¼ cup (60ml) water
1 medium red onion (170g), chopped finely
8 lamb fillets (700g)
400g can brown lentils, rinsed, drained
300g can chickpeas, rinsed, drained
⅓ cup coarsely chopped fresh flat-leaf parsley, extra
2 cloves garlic, crushed
2 tablespoons lemon juice

1 Cut beans into 3cm lengths; boil, steam or microwave beans until just tender. Refresh under cold water; drain.

2 Blend or process pepper, spices, herbs, rind, the water and half of the onion until mixture forms a paste.

3 Combine lamb and chermoulla paste in large bowl.

4 Cook lamb mixture, in batches, on heated oiled grill plate (or grill or barbecue) until browned and cooked as desired. Cover; stand 5 minutes before slicing thickly.

5 Combine beans, lentils, chickpeas, extra parsley, garlic and juice with remaining onion in large bowl; toss gently to combine. Serve chickpea salad with lamb.

SERVES 4

per serving 8.5g total fat (3.1g saturated fat); 1553kj (371 cal); 50.5g protein; 22.2g carbohydrate; 9.7g fibre

tip the salad can be assembled several hours ahead; add juice just before serving.

linguine with lamb, asparagus and gremolata

PREPARATION TIME 20 MINUTES COOKING TIME 15 MINUTES

375g linguine pasta
375g lamb fillets
500g fresh asparagus, trimmed, chopped coarsely
⅓ cup finely grated lemon rind
4 cloves garlic, crushed
1 cup coarsely chopped fresh flat-leaf parsley
½ cup (125ml) lemon juice
8 green onions, sliced thinly
1 tablespoon olive oil

1. Cook pasta in large saucepan of boiling water until just tender; drain. Place in large bowl; cover to keep warm.
2. Meanwhile, cook lamb on heated oiled grill plate (or grill or barbecue) until browned all over and cooked as desired. Cover; stand 5 minutes, slice thinly.
3. Boil, steam or microwave asparagus until just tender; drain.
4. Combine remaining ingredients in small bowl; pour over pasta. Add lamb and asparagus; toss gently to combine.

SERVES 6
per serving 6.4g total fat (1.6g saturated fat); 1448kj (346 cal); 23.9g protein; 46.3g carbohydrate; 3.9g fibre
tip recipe is good served warm or at room temperature. If not serving immediately, do not toss the ingredients together or the pasta witll absorb the dressing.

moroccan lamb with couscous

PREPARATION TIME 15 MINUTES (PLUS REFRIGERATION TIME) COOKING TIME 15 MINUTES

Yogurt is used in both the marinade and as the sauce for the lamb in this recipe.

700g lamb fillets
1 tablespoon ground cumin
1 tablespoon ground coriander
1 teaspoon ground cinnamon
¾ cup (210g) low-fat yogurt
1½ cups (300g) couscous
1½ cups (375ml) boiling water
1 teaspoon peanut oil
⅓ cup (50g) dried currants
2 teaspoons finely grated lemon rind
2 teaspoons lemon juice
¼ cup coarsely chopped fresh coriander

1. Combine lamb, spices and ⅓ cup of the yogurt in medium bowl. Cover; refrigerate 3 hours or overnight.
2. Cook lamb mixture on heated oiled grill plate (or grill or barbecue) until browned and cooked as desired. Cover; stand 5 minutes, slice thinly.
3. Meanwhile, combine couscous, the water and oil in large heatproof bowl. Cover; stand 5 minutes or until liquid is absorbed, fluffing with fork occasionally to separate grains. Stir in currants, rind, juice and fresh coriander; toss with fork to combine.
4. Serve lamb with couscous; drizzle with remaining yogurt.

SERVES 4
per serving 8.1g total fat (3.2g saturated fat); 2349kj (561 cal); 51.5g protein; 68.8g carbohydrate; 1.7g fibre
tip substitute some finely chopped preserved lemon rind for the lemon juice and rind in the couscous.
serving suggestion serve with harissa, the fiery North African condiment.

linguine with lamb, asparagus and gremolata

pepper-grilled lamb with roasted root vegetables

pepper-grilled lamb fillets with roasted root vegetables

PREPARATION TIME 30 MINUTES (PLUS STANDING TIME) COOKING TIME 1 HOUR

All manner of baby vegetables are available at better greengrocers and some supermarkets. You could also serve baby cauliflower, baby turnips and baby pumpkin with the lamb in this recipe.

1kg baby beetroots, trimmed
6 small parsnips (360g), quartered
500g baby new potatoes, halved
400g baby carrots, trimmed
8 baby onions (200g), halved
4 cloves garlic, peeled
¼ cup (60ml) orange juice
¼ cup (90g) honey
1 tablespoon wholegrain mustard
960g lamb fillets
1½ tablespoons cracked black pepper

1. Preheat oven to 200°C/180°C fan-forced. Oil large baking dish.
2. Boil, steam or microwave unpeeled beetroot until tender; drain. When cool enough to handle, peel beetroot.
3. Combine beetroot in baking dish with parsnip, potato, carrot, onion and garlic. Pour combined juice, honey and mustard over vegetables; roast, uncovered, stirring occasionally, about 45 minutes or until vegetables are browned and tender.
4. Meanwhile, coat lamb all over with pepper. Cook lamb on heated oiled grill plate (or grill or barbecue) until browned all over and cooked as desired. Cover; stand 10 minutes. Slice thickly.
5. Serve vegetables topped with lamb.

SERVES 8
per serving 4.8g total fat (1.9g saturated fat); 1305kj (312 cal); 31.7g protein; 35g carbohydrate; 7.9g fibre

marinated lamb backstraps with lentil and rocket salad

PREPARATION TIME 15 MINUTES (PLUS REFRIGERATION TIME) COOKING TIME 15 MINUTES

Puy lentils are from the region of the same name in France. Very small and particularly fast cooking, they have a delicate, almost nut-like flavour.

4 x 200g lamb backstraps, trimmed
⅓ cup (80ml) balsamic vinegar
4 cloves garlic, crushed
¼ cup finely chopped fresh thyme
1 cup (200g) puy lentils
6 large egg tomatoes (540g), chopped finely
100g baby rocket leaves
1 tablespoon finely grated lemon rind
2 tablespoons lemon juice

1. Combine lamb, vinegar, garlic and half of the thyme in large bowl. Cover; refrigerate 3 hours or overnight.
2. Cook lentils in medium saucepan of boiling water, uncovered, until tender; drain.
3. Meanwhile, cook drained lamb on heated oiled grill plate (or grill or barbecue) until browned both sides and cooked as desired. Cover lamb; stand 5 minutes, slice thickly.
4. Place lentils in large bowl with tomato, rocket, rind, juice and remaining thyme; toss gently to combine. Divide salad among serving plates; top with lamb.

SERVES 4
per serving 8.6g total fat (3.4g saturated fat); 1700kj (406 cal); 58g protein; 23.3g carbohydrate; 9.7g fibre

black and white sesame crusted lamb

PREPARATION TIME 10 MINUTES COOKING TIME 15 MINUTES

2 cloves garlic, crushed
1 tablespoon lemon juice
1 tablespoon finely chopped fresh parsley
2 teaspoons dijon mustard
500g piece lamb eye of loin
1 tablespoon white sesame seeds
1 tablespoon black sesame seeds

1 Preheat oven to 240°C/220°C fan-forced.

2 Combine garlic, juice, parsley and mustard in small bowl. Place lamb on wire rack over baking dish; brush garlic mixture all over lamb, sprinkle with combined seeds.

3 Bake lamb, uncovered, about 15 minutes or until lamb is browned all over and cooked as desired. Cover; rest 5 minutes. Slice just before serving.

SERVES 4
per serving 8.6g total fat (3g saturated fat); 581kj (139 cal); 14.7g protein; 0.4g carbohydrate; 0.9g fibre

herb-crusted lamb with braised vegetables

PREPARATION TIME 20 MINUTES COOKING TIME 1 HOUR 10 MINUTES

¼ cup (50g) pearl barley
4 x 200g lamb eyes of loin
⅓ cup coarsely chopped fresh flat-leaf parsley
2 tablespoons chopped fresh coriander
1 tablespoon chopped fresh thyme
1 tablespoon cajun seasoning
1 teaspoon vegetable oil
1 medium red onion (170g), sliced
1 small fennel bulb (425g), sliced
2 medium parsnips (250g), chopped coarsely
1 bunch baby carrots (20)
1 medium red capsicum (200g), chopped coarsely
½ cup (125ml) beef stock
¼ cup (60ml) dry white wine
1 tablespoon balsamic vinegar
1 bunch (300g) baby buk choy, chopped coarsely

1 Cook barley in large saucepan of boiling water, uncovered, about 30 minutes or until tender; drain.

2 Preheat oven to 200°C/180°C fan-forced. Line oven tray with baking paper.

3 Combine lamb, herbs and seasoning in large bowl. Place lamb on oven tray; bake, uncovered, about 15 minutes or until lamb is browned and cooked as desired. Keep warm.

4 Heat oil in saucepan; cook onion and fennel, stirring, until onion is soft. Add parsnips, carrots, capsicum, stock, wine and vinegar; simmer, covered, about 15 minutes or until vegetables are tender. Add barley and buk choy; cook, stirring, until buk choy is just wilted.

5 Serve lamb sliced with braised vegetables.

SERVES 4
per serving 10.9g total fat (4.4g saturated fat); 1488kj (356 cal); 28.4g protein; 32.9g carbohydrate; 13.8g fibre
tip barley can be cooked a day ahead. Store, covered, in refrigerator.

lamb kofta with chilli and yogurt sauce

PREPARATION TIME 20 MINUTES COOKING TIME 10 MINUTES

You will need 18 bamboo skewers for this recipe; soak them in water for at least an hour before use to help prevent them from splintering or scorching.

1kg lean lamb mince
1 large brown onion (200g), chopped finely
1 clove garlic, crushed
1 tablespoon ground cumin
2 teaspoons ground turmeric
2 teaspoons ground allspice
1 tablespoon finely chopped fresh mint
2 tablespoons finely chopped fresh flat-leaf parsley
1 egg, beaten lightly
6 pocket pitta, quartered

YOGURT SAUCE

200g low-fat yogurt
1 clove garlic, crushed
1 tablespoon finely chopped fresh flat-leaf parsley

CHILLI TOMATO SAUCE

¼ cup (60ml) tomato sauce
¼ cup (60ml) chilli sauce

1. Using hands, combine lamb, onion, garlic, spices, herbs and egg in large bowl; shape mixture into 18 balls. Mould balls around skewers to form sausage shapes.
2. Cook kofta, in batches, on heated oiled grill plate (or grill or barbecue) until browned all over and cooked through.
3. Meanwhile, make yogurt sauce. Make chilli tomato sauce.
4. Serve kofta with pitta, yogurt sauce and chilli tomato sauce.

YOGURT SAUCE combine ingredients in small bowl.

CHILLI TOMATO SAUCE combine ingredients in small bowl.

SERVES 6
per serving 14.3g total fat (5.8g saturated fat); 2125kj (507 cal); 44.7g protein; 49.2g carbohydrate; 3.7g fibre

pasta and herb salad with lamb fillets

PREPARATION TIME 5 MINUTES (PLUS REFRIGERATION TIME) COOKING TIME 15 MINUTES

This salad can be served warm or cold. You can substitute your favourite pasta for the farfalle.

375g farfalle pasta
400g lamb fillets
2 cloves garlic, crushed
1 tablespoon wholegrain mustard
250g yellow teardrop tomatoes, halved
1 medium red onion (170g), sliced thinly
50g baby rocket leaves
¼ cup finely shredded fresh basil
1 tablespoon fresh thyme leaves
¼ cup (60ml) balsamic vinegar

1. Cook pasta in large saucepan of boiling water, uncovered, until just tender; drain.
2. Rub lamb all over with combined garlic and mustard; cook on heated oiled grill plate (or grill or barbecue) until browned both sides and cooked as desired. Stand 5 minutes; slice thinly.
3. Place pasta and lamb in large bowl with tomato, onion, rocket, basil, thyme and vinegar; toss gently to combine.

SERVES 4
per serving 4.9g total fat (1.8g saturated fat); 1931kj (461 cal); 33.9g protein; 68.3g carbohydrate; 5.3g fibre
serving suggestion serve with a loaf of fresh crusty bread.

penne with lamb and roasted capsicum

PREPARATION TIME 10 MINUTES COOKING TIME 15 MINUTES

3 large red capsicums (1kg)
500g lamb fillets
2 tablespoons olive oil
2 teaspoons ground cumin
2 x 415g cans tomato puree
½ cup (60g) drained semi-dried tomatoes, chopped coarsely
375g penne pasta
¼ cup finely shredded fresh basil

1. Quarter capsicums, remove seeds and membranes. Place capsicum on oven tray, skin-side up; roast under heated grill or in very hot oven until skin blisters and blackens. Cover capsicum pieces with plastic or paper for 5 minutes; peel away skin. Slice capsicum pieces thinly.
2. Combine lamb, oil and cumin in medium bowl. Cook lamb, in batches, in large heated oiled frying pan (or grill or barbecue) until browned all over and cooked as desired. Stand 5 minutes; cut into thin slices.
3. Add puree, tomato and capsicum to heated pan; bring to a boil. Reduce heat, simmer, uncovered, about 5 minutes or until sauce thickens slightly.
4. Meanwhile, cook pasta in large saucepan of boiling water, uncovered, until just tender; drain.
5. Place lamb, sauce and pasta in large bowl with basil; toss gently to combine.

SERVES 4
per serving 15.9g total fat (3.6g saturated fat); 2884kj (689 cal); 45.9g protein; 88.4g carbohydrate; 11.7g fibre

korean-style barbecued cutlets

PREPARATION TIME 15 MINUTES COOKING TIME 5 MINUTES

This recipe is an adaptation of the famous Korean barbecued dish bulgogi, where strips of beef are coated in a spicy mixture and barbecued over glowing coals. Today, a variety of meats – including chicken, pork and lamb – are cooked in this manner.

16 lamb cutlets (1kg), trimmed
½ cup (125ml) light soy sauce
1 cup (250ml) mirin
2 green onions, sliced thinly
2 cloves garlic, crushed
1 tablespoon grated fresh ginger
1 tablespoon brown sugar
1 tablespoon cracked black pepper
1 tablespoon plain flour

1 Combine cutlets with remaining ingredients in large bowl.

2 Drain cutlets; reserve marinade. Cook cutlets on heated oiled grill plate (or grill or barbecue) until browned both sides and cooked as desired; brushing occasionally with reserved marinade during cooking.

SERVES 4
per serving 8.8g total fat (3.9g saturated fat); 1002kj (239 cal); 30.3g protein; 7g carbohydrate; 1g fibre
tip cutlets can be marinated a day ahead; store, covered, in refrigerator. Traditionally, bulgogi beef was marinated overnight to intensify the flavour.
serving suggestion serve with steamed jasmine rice and asian greens, like buk choy, snake beans or snow peas.

lamb fillets in herb vinaigrette

PREPARATION TIME 10 MINUTES (PLUS STANDING TIME) COOKING TIME 10 MINUTES

300g lamb fillets
2 teaspoons cracked black peppercorns

HERB VINAIGRETTE
2 teaspoons vegetable oil
1½ tablespoons tarragon vinegar
1 tablespoon water
2 teaspoons sugar
1 teaspoon drained canned green peppercorns
½ teaspoon wholegrain mustard
2 green onions, chopped finely
2 teaspoons finely chopped fresh flat-leaf parsley
1 teaspoon fresh thyme leaves

1 Trim all visible fat from fillets. Press peppercorns onto fillets.

2 Cook lamb in heated medium saucepan until tender. Cover; stand 5 minutes, slice thickly.

3 Make herb vinaigrette.

4 Place lamb and vinaigrette in large bowl; toss gently to combine. Serve with thickly sliced egg tomatoes, if desired.

HERB VINAIGRETTE combine ingredients in medium bowl.

SERVES 2
per serving 10.1g total fat (2.7g saturated fat); 1033kj (247 cal); 33.3g protein; 5.1g carbohydrate; 0.8g fibre
tip recipe can be prepared 3 hours ahead. Store, covered, in refrigerator.

lamb satay

PREPARATION TIME 30 MINUTES COOKING TIME 20 MINUTES

Soak 12 small bamboo skewers in cold water for at least an hour to prevent them from splintering or scorching.

500g lean lamb fillets
3 cloves garlic, crushed
2 teaspoons fish sauce
2 tablespoons sweet chilli sauce
2 teaspoons grated fresh ginger
¼ cup (60ml) lime juice
2 tablespoons low-salt crunchy peanut butter
1 teaspoon ground cumin
1 teaspoon ground turmeric
cooking-oil spray

SAUCE

¼ cup (60ml) white vinegar
2 tablespoons sugar or powdered artificial sweetener
1 tablespoon sweet chilli sauce
1 tablespoon coarsley chopped roasted unsalted peanuts
1 tablespoon coarsley chopped fresh coriander

1. Cut fillets in half lengthways, then cut into thin strips. Combine lamb, garlic, sauces, ginger, juice, peanut butter and spices in bowl. Cover; refrigerate 1 hour.
2. Thread lamb onto skewers. Coat heated grill pan (or grill or barbecue) with cooking-oil spray; cook skewers until lamb is tender.
3. Make sauce.
4. Serve skewers with sauce.

SAUCE place vinegar and sugar in small saucepan; cook, stirring, over heat until sugar is dissolved. Boil, uncovered, 2 minutes. Stir in sauce, peanuts and coriander.

SERVES 4
per serving 13.7g total fat (3.5g saturated fat); 1174kj (280 cal); 32.2g protein; 6.1g carbohydrate; 2.8g fibre
tip recipe can be prepared a day ahead. Store, covered, in refrigerator.

thai lamb salad

PREPARATION TIME 20 MINUTES (PLUS STANDING TIME) COOKING TIME 10 MINUTES

100g bean thread noodles
500g lamb fillets, trimmed
1 medium red onion (170g), sliced thinly
3 green onions, sliced thinly
1 cup (80g) bean sprouts
1 cup loosely packed fresh coriander leaves
1 cup loosely packed fresh mint leaves
1 cup loosely packed vietnamese mint leaves
1 lebanese cucumber (130g), seeded, sliced thinly
2 fresh red thai chillies, sliced thinly
200g cherry tomatoes, halved
2 cloves garlic, crushed
1 tablespoon finely chopped fresh lemon grass
⅓ cup (80ml) lime juice
1 tablespoon fish sauce
1 tablespoon soy sauce

1. Place noodles in medium heatproof bowl; cover with boiling water. Stand until just tender; drain. Rinse noodles under cold water; drain well.
2. Cook lamb on heated oiled grill plate (or grill or barbecue) until browned and cooked as desired. Stand 5 minutes; slice thinly.
3. Meanwhile, combine onions, sprouts, herbs, cucumber, chilli and tomato in large bowl. Add lamb and combined remaining ingredients; toss gently to combine. Serve salad with noodles.

SERVES 4
per serving 5.2g total fat (2.1g saturated fat); 943kj (225 cal); 31.5g protein; 11.9g carbohydrate; 5.4g fibre

mains
vegetarian

mushroom and spinach risotto

PREPARATION TIME 10 MINUTES COOKING TIME 25 MINUTES

Arborio, a short-grained, pearly rice variety, is ideal for this recipe because it absorbs the stock while remaining chewy in the centre of the grain.

10g butter
1 medium brown onion (150g), chopped coarsely
1 clove garlic, crushed
2 cups (400g) arborio rice
1 cup (250ml) dry white wine
2 cups (500ml) vegetable stock
1½ cups (375ml) water
150g button mushrooms, sliced thickly
500g spinach, trimmed, chopped coarsely
¼ cup coarsely chopped fresh flat-leaf parsley
¾ cup (60g) coarsely grated parmesan cheese

1. Place butter, onion and garlic in a large microwave-safe bowl; cook on high (100%) 2 minutes or until onion softens. Add rice, stir; cook, covered, on high (100%) 1 minute. Add wine, stock and the water, stir; cook, covered, on high (100%) 15 minutes, stirring occasionally.
2. Add mushrooms, stir; cook, covered, on high (100%) 5 minutes, or until most of the liquid is absorbed.
3. Transfer risotto mixture to large serving bowl; stir through spinach, parsley and cheese.

SERVES 4
per serving 8.3g total fat (4.8g saturated fat); 2169kj (519 cal); 17.4g protein; 82.5g carbohydrate; 4.3g fibre
tip you can substitute medium-grain white rice for the arborio rice.
serving suggestion serve with a rocket salad drizzled with balsamic dressing and shaved parmesan.

artichoke risotto

PREPARATION TIME 10 MINUTES COOKING TIME 25 MINUTES

While the short-grained arborio is traditionally used in a risotto, we chose to use the longer-grained doongara rice here because it has both a lower GI rating and is more amendable to being cooked with the liquids added all at once.

2 teaspoons olive oil
1 medium brown onion (150g), chopped finely
3 cloves garlic, crushed
6 green onions, sliced thinly
2 cups (400g) doongara rice
¾ cup (180ml) dry white wine
1½ cups (375ml) vegetable stock
3 cups (750ml) water
400g can artichoke hearts, drained, sliced thinly
½ cup (40g) finely grated parmesan cheese

1 Heat oil in large saucepan; cook brown onion, garlic and half of the green onion, stirring, until brown onion softens. Add rice, wine, stock and the water; bring to a boil. Reduce heat, simmer, covered, 15 minutes, stirring occasionally.

2 Stir in artichokes, cheese and remaining green onion; cook, stirring, about 5 minutes or until artichokes are heated through.

SERVES 6
per serving 4.5g total fat (1.8g saturated fat); 1338kj (320 cal); 9.2g protein; 55.3g carbohydrate; 2.6g fibre
serving suggestion serve with a salad of grape tomatoes, sliced fennel and a few fresh basil leaves.

mixed mushroom risotto

PREPARATION TIME 10 MINUTES COOKING TIME 45 MINUTES

3 cups (750ml) vegetable stock
2 cups (500ml) water
1 tablespoon olive oil
200g swiss brown mushrooms, quartered
150g oyster mushrooms, halved
200g button mushrooms, halved
2 cloves garlic, crushed
1 medium brown onion (150g), chopped coarsely
2 cups (400g) arborio rice
1 tablespoon finely chopped fresh tarragon
⅓ cup (80g) sour cream
1 tablespoon wholegrain mustard

1 Bring stock and the water to a boil in large saucepan. Reduce heat, simmer, uncovered, while cooking mushrooms.

2 Heat half of the oil in large saucepan; cook mushrooms, in batches, until just tender.

3 Heat remaining oil in same pan; cook garlic and onion, stirring, until onion softens. Add rice to pan; stir over medium heat until slightly changed in colour. Stir in 1-cup batches of the hot stock mixture; cook, over medium heat, stirring, until liquid is absorbed after each addition.

4 Add mushrooms and tarragon to risotto when last cup of stock mixture has been added and is almost absorbed. Total cooking time for rice should be about 35 minutes or until rice is just tender.

5 Serve risotto topped with combined sour cream and mustard.

SERVES 4
per serving 14.3g total fat (6.4g saturated fat); 2203kj (527 cal); 14.7g protein; 84.5g carbohydrate; 5.8g fibre

leek and asparagus risotto

PREPARATION TIME 15 MINUTES COOKING TIME 45 MINUTES

1½ cups (375ml) dry white wine
1.5 litres (6 cups) vegetable stock
2 teaspoons low-fat dairy-free spread
2 medium leeks (700g), sliced thinly
2 cloves garlic, crushed
3 cups (600g) arborio rice
500g fresh asparagus, trimmed, chopped coarsely
⅓ cup (25g) finely grated parmesan cheese

1 Combine wine and stock in large saucepan; bring to a boil. Reduce heat, simmer, covered, to keep hot.

2 Meanwhile, heat dairy-free spread in large saucepan; cook leek and garlic, stirring, until leek softens. Add rice; stir to coat in leek mixture. Stir in 1 cup of the hot stock mixture; cook, stirring, over low heat until liquid is absorbed. Continue adding stock mixture, in 1-cup batches, stirring, until liquid is absorbed after each addition. Total cooking time should be about 30 minutes or until rice is just tender.

3 Add asparagus; cook, stirring, until asparagus is just tender. Just before serving, stir in cheese.

SERVES 8
per serving 2.9g total fat (1.2g saturated fat); 1480kj (354 cal); 10.4g protein; 63.3g carbohydrate; 2.8g fibre
serving suggestion serve sprinkled with freshly ground black pepper and finely chopped fresh basil leaves.

vegetable risotto

PREPARATION TIME 10 MINUTES (PLUS STANDING TIME) COOKING TIME 45 MINUTES

1 small eggplant (230g), chopped finely
2 teaspoons olive oil
1 small brown onion (80g), chopped finely
1 clove garlic, crushed
¾ cup brown rice (150g)
¾ cup vegetable stock (80ml)
2 cups water (500ml)
2 medium zucchini (240g)
2 medium tomatoes (380g), peeled, chopped finely
125g mushrooms, sliced thinly
¼ cup (20g) coarsely grated parmesan cheese
1 tablespoon fresh oregano leaves

1 Place eggplant in colander; sprinkle with salt. Stand for 30 minutes; rinse well under cold water. Pat dry with absorbent paper.

2 Heat oil in large saucepan; cook onion and garlic until soft. Add rice, stock and the water; bring to boil. Simmer, covered, for about 30 minutes or until rice is tender and almost all the liquid is absorbed.

3 Using a vegetable peeler, cut zucchini into ribbons.

4 Stir eggplant, zucchini, tomato and mushroom into rice; cook for about 3 minutes or until vegetables are softened. Stir in half the cheese and oregano; serve risotto sprinkled with remaining cheese.

SERVES 2
per serving 10.8g total fat (3.2g saturated fat); 1835kj (439 cal); 16.8g protein; 68g carbohydrate; 10.4g fibre

lentil, vegetable and brown rice pilaf

PREPARATION TIME 10 MINUTES COOKING TIME 40 MINUTES

1 trimmed stick celery (75g), coarsely chopped
1 medium carrot (120g), chopped
1 medium onion (150g), chopped
1 teaspoon ground cumin
2 teaspoons mild curry powder
1 teaspoon celery salt
1 cup (200g) brown lentils
½ cup (100g) brown rice
1 litre (4 cups) water
1 teaspoon grated fresh ginger
2 tablespoons chopped fresh flat-leaf parsley

1. Place celery, carrot, onion, cumin, curry powder, salt, lentils, rice, the water and ginger in medium saucepan; bring to a boil. Reduce heat, simmer, covered, about 40 minutes or until rice is tender and water absorbed.
2. Serve sprinkled with parsley.

SERVES 4
per serving 1.7g total fat (0.3g saturated fat); 995kj (238 cal); 41.5g protein; 14.9g carbohydrate; 9.4g fibre

spicy split pea risotto

PREPARATION TIME 10 MINUTES (PLUS STANDING TIME) COOKING TIME 1 HOUR 40 MINUTES

1 cup (200g) yellow split peas
2 tablespoons olive oil
1 large brown onion (150g), chopped finely
2 cloves garlic, crushed
1 teaspoon ground ginger
1 teaspoon garam masala
1 teaspoon ground cumin
½ teaspoon ground turmeric
pinch chilli powder
3 medium tomatoes (570g), peeled, chopped finely
1 large potato (300g), chopped finely
½ cup (100g) long-grain brown rice
2¼ cups (560ml) vegetable stock
2 tablespoons lemon juice
¼ cup finely chopped fresh coriander

1. Place peas in medium bowl, cover with cold water; cover with plastic wrap. Stand overnight; drain peas.
2. Heat oil in large saucepan; cook onion, garlic and spices, stirring, until onion is soft. Add tomato, potato and rice; cook, stirring, 2 minutes.
3. Add stock and juice to pan; simmer, covered, 30 minutes.
4. Add peas to pan; simmer, covered, 1 hour or until peas are tender and most of the liquid is absorbed.
5. Just before serving, stir in coriander.

SERVES 4
per serving 11.5g total fat (1.8g saturated fat); 1685kj (403 cal); 18.3g protein; 55g carbohydrate; 9.1g fibre
tips split peas must be prepared a day ahead. Keep, covered, at room temperature. Add 300g poached flaked smoked fish just before serving, if desired.

nasi goreng

PREPARATION TIME 10 MINUTES COOKING TIME 15 MINUTES

You will need to cook about 1¼ cups (250g) long-grain white rice for this recipe.

1 tablespoon peanut oil
1 medium brown onion (150g), chopped coarsely
2 cloves garlic, crushed
1 fresh red thai chilli, sliced thinly
250g firm tofu, chopped finely
3 cups cooked long-grain white rice
⅓ cup (80ml) light soy sauce
2 green onions, sliced thinly
4 eggs

1. Heat oil in wok; stir-fry brown onion, garlic and chilli until onion softens.
2. Add tofu; stir-fry until tofu browns lightly.
3. Add rice, sauce and green onion; stir-fry until hot and well combined.
4. Meanwhile, heat oiled medium frying pan; cook eggs, in batches, on both sides, until just cooked.
5. Divide nasi goreng among serving plates; top each with a fried egg.

SERVES 4
per serving 14.6g total fat (3.1g saturated fat); 1446kj (346 cal); 18.7g protein; 34.7g carbohydrate; 2.5g fibre
tips rice can be made a day ahead; store, covered, in refrigerator. The egg yolks should still be runny so they drizzle over the rice.

vegetable fried rice

PREPARATION TIME 15 MINUTES COOKING TIME 15 MINUTES

You will need to cook about ⅓ cup (65g) long-grain white rice for this recipe.

1 clove garlic, crushed
1 teaspoon finely grated fresh ginger
2 tablespoons water
1 medium carrot (120g), chopped finely
½ small red capsicum (75g), chopped finely
2 small zucchini (180g), chopped finely
1 cup cooked long-grain white rice
2 tablespoons salt-reduced soy sauce
3 green onions, chopped finely
2 tablespoons finely chopped fresh coriander

1. Combine garlic, ginger and the water in wok; cook over heat until ginger is soft. Add carrot, capsicum and zucchini; cook for 5 minutes.
2. Stir in remaining ingredients; stir over heat until heated through.

SERVES 2
per serving 0.6g total fat (0g saturated fat); 685kj (164 cal); 5.6g protein; 33.2g carbohydrate; 4.4g fibre
tip recipe can be made 3 hours ahead. Store, covered, in refrigerator.

mushroom and asparagus salad

PREPARATION TIME 15 MINUTES COOKING TIME 20 MINUTES

Swiss brown mushrooms, also known as cremini or roman mushrooms, are similar in appearance to button mushrooms, but are a slightly darker brown in colour. The large variety are often known as portobello mushrooms.

400g swiss brown mushrooms
200g fresh shiitake mushrooms
500g green asparagus, trimmed
500g white asparagus, trimmed
2 teaspoons finely grated lemon rind
¼ cup (60ml) lemon juice
2 tablespoons olive oil
1 clove garlic, crushed
1 cup loosely packed fresh flat-leaf parsley leaves
2 tablespoons toasted pine nuts

1. Cook mushrooms and asparagus, in batches, on heated oiled grill plate (or grill or barbecue) until browned and just tender.
2. Meanwhile, place rind, juice, oil and garlic in screw-top jar; shake well.
3. Place grilled vegetables in large bowl with parsley, nuts and dressing; toss gently to combine.

SERVES 4
per serving 14.8g total fat (1.6g saturated fat); 915kj (219 cal); 10.4g protein; 11.1g carbohydrate; 7.6g fibre

black bean, rice and vegetable pilaf

PREPARATION TIME 10 MINUTES COOKING TIME 55 MINUTES

½ cup (100g) black turtle beans
1 large red onion (300g)
30g butter
1 teaspoon cumin seeds
1 teaspoon coriander seeds
1 cinnamon stick
6 cardamom pods
3 cloves
1 teaspoon ground turmeric
1 teaspoon garam masala
1 medium carrot (120g), sliced thinly
1½ cups (300g) long-grain white rice
1½ cups (375ml) vegetable stock
1½ cups (375ml) water
1 medium green capsicum (200g), chopped finely

1. Cook beans in medium saucepan of boiling water, uncovered, 40 minutes or until tender; drain.
2. Cut onion into eight wedges. Heat butter in large saucepan; cook onion and spices, stirring, about 1 minute or until fragrant. Add carrot and rice, stir until combined.
3. Add stock and the water to pan; simmer, covered, 8 minutes. Add beans and capsicum; simmer, covered, 2 minutes or until rice is tender and liquid absorbed.

SERVES 4
per serving 7.5g total fat (4.4g saturated fat); 1760kj (421 cal); 13.5g protein; 74.1g carbohydrate; 8g fibre

pasta salad with roasted vegetables and chilli cream sauce

PREPARATION TIME 25 MINUTES COOKING TIME 30 MINUTES

Pappardelle is a long, flat, fairly wide pasta sometimes scalloped along its long sides. It can be used layered like lasagne or, as here, tossed with vegetables and a rich creamy sauce.

2 medium red capsicums (400g)
2 medium yellow capsicums (400g)
375g pappardelle pasta
6 baby eggplants (360g), sliced thickly
2 flat mushrooms (160g)
180g haloumi cheese, sliced thinly
1 cup loosely packed fresh basil leaves

CHILLI CREAM SAUCE

10 large egg tomatoes (900g), halved
2 cloves garlic, crushed
4 fresh small red thai chillies, sliced thinly
2 tablespoons cream

1 Preheat oven to 240°C/220°C fan-forced. Make chilli cream sauce.

2 Meanwhile, quarter capsicums; discard seeds and membranes. Roast under grill or in very hot oven, skin-side up, until skin blisters and blackens. Cover capsicum pieces with plastic or paper for 5 minutes; peel away skin. Slice capsicum thickly.

3 Cook pasta in large saucepan of boiling water, uncovered, until tender; drain.

4 Meanwhile, cook eggplant, mushrooms and cheese, in batches, on heated oiled grill plate (or grill or barbecue) until browned and just tender. Slice mushrooms thickly; chop cheese coarsely.

5 Place vegetables, pasta and cheese in large bowl with sauce and basil; toss gently to combine. Sprinkle with extra fresh basil leaves, if desired.

CHILLI CREAM SAUCE line two oven trays with baking paper. Place tomato, cut-side up, in single layer, on oven trays; roast, uncovered, 20 minutes or until softened. Blend or process half of the tomato with garlic, chilli and cream until pureed. Chop remaining tomato coarsely; stir into sauce.

SERVES 4
per serving 13.3g total fat (7.6g saturated fat); 2324kj (556 cal); 27.3g protein; 80.6g carbohydrate; 12.4g fibre

warm pasta salad with mustard mayonnaise

PREPARATION TIME 15 MINUTES COOKING TIME 25 MINUTES

We used bow tie (farfalle) for this recipe but any short pasta may be used in its place.

½ cup (30g) dehydrated sun-dried tomatoes
250g short pasta
⅔ cup (160ml) low-fat mayonnaise
2 tablespoons wholegrain mustard
1 tablespoon lemon juice
2 cloves garlic, crushed
2 tablespoons hot water
200g baby rocket leaves
2 small red onions (200g), sliced finely
¼ cup (40g) seeded black olives, sliced coarsely

1. Place tomato in small heatproof bowl, cover with boiling water, stand about 15 minutes or until softened; drain. Slice tomato thinly.
2. Meanwhile, cook pasta in large saucepan of boiling water, uncovered, until just tender; drain. Cover to keep warm.
3. Combine mayonnaise, mustard, juice, garlic and water in small bowl.
4. Place tomato, pasta, mustard mayonnaise, rocket, onion and olives in large serving bowl; toss gently to combine.

SERVES 4
per serving 8.9g total fat (2g saturated fat); 1722kj (412 cal); 22.3g protein; 59.4g carbohydrate; 6.5g fibre

roasted red capsicum tarts

PREPARATION TIME 25 MINUTES COOKING TIME 25 MINUTES

2 medium red capsicums (400g)
2 large brown onions (400g), sliced thinly
¼ cup (60ml) balsamic vinegar
¼ cup (50g) brown sugar
4 sheets fillo pastry
cooking-oil spray
2 tablespoons finely chopped fresh basil
⅓ cup (25g) finely grated parmesan cheese

1. Preheat oven to 220°C/200°C fan-forced. Oil four 12cm-round loose-base quiche dishes.
2. Quarter capsicums, remove and discard seeds and membranes. Roast under grill or in very hot oven, skin-side up, until skin blisters and blackens. Cover capsicum pieces in plastic or paper for 5 minutes; peel away skin. Slice capsicum into thin strips.
3. Heat small saucepan; cook onion and vinegar, stirring, about 3 minutes or until onion softens. Stir in sugar; cook, stirring, about 5 minutes or until sugar dissolves and mixture thickens.
4. Cut pastry to make sixteen 14cm-squares. Place one pastry square in one quiche dish, coat with cooking-oil spray; top with another pastry square, placing corners just to the right of previous square's corners. Repeat layering, using four pastry squares in each quiche dish. Place dishes on oven tray; bake, uncovered, about 5 minutes or until pastry is crisp.
5. Spoon onion mixture into pastry cases, top with capsicum, sprinkle with basil and cheese. Bake, uncovered, about 5 minutes or until hot.

SERVES 4
per serving 3.9g total fat (1.5g saturated fat); 765kj (183 cal); 6.9g protein; 30.1g carbohydrate; 2.7g fibre

lentil patties with yogurt mint sauce

PREPARATION TIME 20 MINUTES (PLUS COOLING TIME) COOKING TIME 30 MINUTES

½ cup (100g) red lentils
½ trimmed stick celery (35g), chopped finely
1 small carrot (70g), chopped finely
2 cups (500ml) water
½ teaspoon ground coriander
½ teaspoon ground cumin
1 cup (70g) stale breadcrumbs
2 tablespoons plain flour
1 egg white, beaten lightly
1 cup (70g) stale breadcrumbs, extra
1 tablespoon finely chopped fresh flat-leaf parsley
1 tablespoon vegetable oil

YOGURT MINT SAUCE

½ cup (125g) low-fat yogurt
1 tablespoon finely chopped fresh mint
1 small clove garlic, crushed
1 teaspoon lemon juice

1. Place lentils, celery, carrot, the water, coriander and cumin in large saucepan; bring to a boil. Reduce hat, simmer, covered, about 20 minutes or until mixture is thickened; cool.
2. Stir breadcrumbs into lentil mixture; shape mixture into four patties. Toss in flour; dip in egg white, then combined extra breadcrumbs and parsley.
3. Heat oil in large frying pan; cook patties until well browned on both sides. Drain on absorbent paper.
4. Meanwhile, make yogurt mint sauce. Serve patties with sauce and a green leaf salad, if desired.

YOGURT MINT SAUCE combine all ingredients in bowl; mix well.

SERVES 2
per serving 14.1g total fat (2.5g saturated fat); 2349kj (562 cal); 28.4g protein; 80.3g carbohydrate; 12g fibre
tip patties can be prepared a day ahead. Store uncooked, covered, in refrigerator or freezer. Cook just before serving.

lentil patties with yogurt mint sauce

vegetable moussaka

vegetable moussaka

PREPARATION TIME 10 MINUTES (PLUS COOLING TIME) COOKING TIME 50 MINUTES

1 large eggplant (500g), sliced thickly
2 large tomatoes (500g), chopped finely
1 teaspoon sugar
2 teaspoons monounsaturated or polyunsaturated margarine
1 tablespoon plain flour
1 cup (250ml) skim milk
2 tablespoons finely grated parmesan cheese
2 tablespoons finely chopped fresh basil

1. Preheat oven to 200°C/180°C fan-forced.
2. Place eggplant in single layer on oven tray; bake, uncovered, 15 minutes. Turn, bake further 15 minutes or until browned lightly; cool for 10 minutes.
3. Combine tomato and sugar in small saucepan; cook, stirring occasionally, about 30 minutes or until tomato is soft and liquid almost evaporated.
4. Meanwhile, melt margarine in small saucepan, add flour; cook, stirring, for 1 minute. Gradually add milk; cook, stirring, over medium heat until sauce boils and thickens. Stir in half the cheese and half the basil. Stir remaining basil through tomato mixture.
5. Reduce oven to 180°C/160°C fan-forced.
6. Spread one-third of tomato mixture, eggplant and cheese sauce in two ovenproof dishes (2-cup capacity); repeat with two more layers. Sprinkle with remaining cheese; bake, uncovered, 15 minutes or until browned lightly.

SERVES 2
per serving 6.6g total fat (2.1g saturated fat); 844kj (202 cal); 13g protein; 21.9g carbohydrate; 7.3g fibre
tip moussaka can be prepared 3 hours ahead. Store, covered, in refrigerator.

hot vegetable and tofu salad

PREPARATION TIME 15 MINUTES COOKING TIME 10 MINUTES

1 medium red onion (170g)
3cm piece fresh ginger (15g)
2 teaspoons vegetable oil
250g packet firm tofu, chopped coarsely
1 small carrot (70g), sliced thinly
1 small red capsicum (150g), sliced thinly
100g broccoli, chopped coarsely
100g snow peas
1 trimmed stick celery (75g), sliced thinly
½ cup vegetable stock (125ml)
2 tablespoons hoisin sauce
1 tablespoon salt-reduced soy sauce

1. Cut onion in half; cut halves into thin wedges. Cut ginger into thin slices; cut slices into thin strips.
2. Heat oil in wok; cook onion, ginger and tofu until onion is soft and tofu lightly browned.
3. Stir in remaining ingredients; bring to a boil. Simmer, uncovered, for about 5 minutes or until vegetables are tender.

SERVES 2
per serving 14.1g total fat (1.9g saturated fat); 1246kj (298 cal); 23.5g protein; 18.7g carbohydrate; 9.4g fibre

pasta with roasted mushrooms and tomato

PREPARATION TIME 15 MINUTES COOKING TIME 20 MINUTES

200g field mushrooms
200g button mushrooms
200g swiss brown mushrooms
250g cherry tomatoes
½ cup (125ml) vegetable stock
2 teaspoons garlic salt
375g fettuccine pasta
¼ cup torn fresh basil leaves
¼ cup (20g) coarsely grated parmesan cheese

1 Preheat oven to 220°C/200°C fan-forced.

2 Cut field mushrooms into quarters. Combine all mushrooms, tomatoes and stock in baking dish; sprinkle with salt. Bake, uncovered, about 20 minutes or until mushrooms are tender and tomatoes softened.

3 Meanwhile, cook pasta in large saucepan of boiling water, uncovered, until just tender; drain.

4 Add mushroom mixture to pasta; toss gently to combine. Sprinkle with basil and cheese.

SERVES 4
per serving 3.3g total fat (1.3g saturated fat); 1626kj (389 cal); 18.5g protein; 69.8g carbohydrate; 9.5g fibre

silver beet, mushroom and capsicum frittata

PREPARATION TIME 15 MINUTES COOKING TIME 45 MINUTES

500g silver beet, trimmed, chopped coarsely
1 tablespoon low-fat dairy-free spread
1 medium brown onion (150g), chopped finely
2 cloves garlic, crushed
1 medium red capsicum (200g), chopped finely
2 trimmed sticks celery (150g), chopped finely
100g button mushrooms, sliced thinly
2 large carrots (360g), grated coarsely
¼ cup (40g) polenta
¼ cup coarsely chopped fresh basil
3 eggs, beaten lightly
3 egg whites, beaten lightly
⅓ cup (80ml) no-fat milk

1 Preheat oven to 180°C/160°c fan-forced. Line 20cm x 30cm lamington pan with baking paper.

2 Boil, steam or microwave silver beet; drain on absorbent paper.

3 Melt spread in large deep frying pan; cook onion and garlic, stirring, until onion softens. Add capsicum, celery and mushrooms; cook, stirring, until vegetables just soften.

4 Stir silver beet, carrot, polenta and basil into vegetable mixture. Remove from heat; cool 5 minutes.

5 Add eggs, whites and milk to cooled vegetable mixture; stir to combine. Spread frittata mixture into pan; bake, uncovered, about 35 minutes or until lightly browned and firm to the touch.

SERVES 4
per serving 6.8g total fat (1.6g saturated fat); 782kj (187 cal); 13.8g protein; 17.8g carbohydrate; 7.4g fibre
tip this frittata is just as good eaten at room temperature as it is hot from the oven.
serving suggestion serve with mixed tomato salad made from grape, cherry and teardrop tomatoes.

herbed ricotta ravioli in tomato broth

PREPARATION TIME 20 MINUTES (PLUS REFRIGERATION TIME) COOKING TIME 10 MINUTES

⅓ cup (30g) finely grated parmesan cheese
⅔ cup (130g) low-fat ricotta cheese
1 tablespoon finely chopped fresh basil
2 tablespoons finely chopped fresh chives
24 wonton wrappers
16 medium egg tomatoes (1.2kg)
2 green onions, sliced thinly

1. Combine cheeses and herbs in small bowl. Place one rounded teaspoon of cheese mixture in centre of each of 12 wonton wrappers; brush around edge with a little water. Top each with a remaining wrapper, press around edges firmly to seal. Place ravioli on tray, cover; refrigerate 20 minutes.
2. Meanwhile, bring large saucepan of water to a boil. Place cored tomatoes in pan; return to a boil. Cook, uncovered, 2 minutes. Strain tomatoes over large bowl; reserve cooking liquid.
3. Blend or process tomatoes, in batches, until smooth; push through a food mill (mouli) or sieve into small saucepan; bring to a boil. Reduce heat, simmer broth, uncovered, 5 minutes.
4. Meanwhile, cook ravioli in large saucepan of reserved cooking liquid, uncovered, about 4 minutes or until ravioli float to the surface; discard cooking liquid. Divide tomato broth and ravioli among serving bowls; sprinkle with onion.

SERVES 4
per serving 6.3g total fat (3.6g saturated fat); 874kj (209 cal); 12.2g protein; 25.4g carbohydrate; 4.6g fibre

risoni with cherry tomatoes, squash and spinach

PREPARATION TIME 30 MINUTES COOKING TIME 30 MINUTES

You can use any other grain-sized pasta (such as orzo or puntalette) if the risoni is not readily available.

500g cherry tomatoes, halved
500g patty-pan squash, quartered
8 cloves garlic, quartered
¼ cup firmly packed fresh oregano
¼ cup (60ml) olive oil
⅓ cup (50g) pine nuts
1kg risoni pasta
3 fresh red thai chillies, chopped finely
250g baby spinach, trimmed
½ cup firmly packed, coarsely chopped fresh basil

1. Preheat oven to 180°C/160°C fan-forced.
2. Combine tomato, squash, garlic, half of the oregano and 1 tablespoon of the oil in large shallow baking dish. Roast, uncovered, 20 minutes. Add pine nuts to vegetable mixture; roast, uncovered, about 10 minutes or until tomato is tender and nuts are browned.
3. Meanwhile, cook pasta in large saucepan of boiling water, uncovered, until just tender; drain. Cover to keep warm.
4. Heat remaining oil in large saucepan; cook chilli, stirring, 1 minute. Stir in pasta, spinach, basil and remaining oregano; toss gently until combined. Stir in tomato mixture; serve immediately.

SERVES 8
per serving 13g total fat (1.5g saturated fat); 2332kj (558 cal); 17.5g protein; 91.4g carbohydrate; 10.1g fibre
serving suggestion serve with warmed crusty bread rolls, such as rosette.

bean and potato bake

PREPARATION TIME 10 MINUTES COOKING TIME 25 MINUTES

4 small potatoes (480g), sliced thinly
2 green onions, sliced thinly
½ x 220g can mexican chilli beans
½ cup (125ml) skim milk
¼ cup (20g) grated parmesan cheese

1 Preheat oven to 180°C/160°C fan-forced. Oil two 1 cup (250ml) ovenproof dishes.

2 Layer potato, onion and beans in dishes. Pour milk over vegetables; sprinkle with cheese. Bake, uncovered, about 25 minutes or until vegetables are soft.

SERVES 2
per serving 4.4g total fat (2.4g saturated fat); 1120kj (268 cal); 16.3g protein; 40.8g carbohydrate; 7.5g fibre

vegetarian pizza

PREPARATION TIME 20 MINUTES (PLUS STANDING TIME) COOKING TIME 25 MINUTES

7g sachet dried yeast
½ teaspoon sugar
½ cup (125ml) warm water
1½ cups (225g) plain flour
1 teaspoon vegetable oil
¼ cup (65g) tomato paste
½ cup (100g) canned drained red kidney beans
1 small red onion (100g), sliced thinly
1 small zucchini (90g), sliced thinly
1 small red capsicum (150g), sliced thinly
4 baby mushrooms, sliced thinly
¼ cup (25g) grated light mozzarella cheese
1 tablespoon grated parmesan cheese
1 tablespoon fresh basil leaves

1 Place yeast with sugar in large bowl; stir in the water. Cover; stand in warm place for about 10 minutes or until mixture is frothy.

2 Sift flour into large bowl; stir in yeast mixture and oil. Mix to a firm dough. Turn dough onto floured surface; knead for about 5 minutes or until dough is smooth and elastic.

3 Return dough to bowl; cover. Stand in warm place about 45 minutes or until doubled in size. Turn dough onto lightly floured surface; knead until smooth.

4 Preheat oven to 200°C/180°C fan-forced.

5 Roll dough large enough to line 20cm pizza tray. Spread dough with paste; top with kidney beans, onion, zucchini, capsicum, mushrooms and cheses. Bake, uncovered, about 25 minutes or until crust is crisp. Serve pizza with basil leaves sprinkled on top.

SERVES 2
per serving 7.9g total fat (2.7g saturated fat); 2353kj (563 cal); 25.5g protein; 95.9g carbohydrate; 11.5g fibre
tip pizza can be prepared 3 hours ahead; store uncooked, covered, in refrigerator. Cook just before serving.

tempeh sang choy bow

PREPARATION TIME 10 MINUTES COOKING TIME 5 MINUTES

Tempeh is a meat alternative made from fermented soy beans.

1 tablespoon vegetable oil
2 cloves garlic, crushed
1 medium carrot (120g), grated coarsely
100g mushrooms, chopped coarsely
227g canned bamboo shoots, drained, sliced thinly
4 green onions, chopped finely
300g tempeh, chopped finely
2 tablespoons hoisin sauce
2 tablespoons light soy sauce
8 iceberg lettuce leaves

1 Heat oil in large wok; stir-fry garlic, carrot, mushrooms and bamboo shoots about 2 minutes or until vegetables just soften.
2 Add onion and tempeh to wok; stir-fry until tempeh is hot. Add sauces; stir to combine.
3 To serve, divide tempeh mixture among lettuce leaves.

SERVES 4
per serving 10.5g total fat (1.4g saturated fat); 736kj (176 cal); 12.1g protein; 8.4g carbohydrate; 6.4g fibre
tip add some crispy fried noodles to tempeh mixture.
serving suggestion serve with bowls of chilli and soy sauce, to be added to taste.

roast baby vegetable pizza

PREPARATION TIME 15 MINUTES COOKING TIME 40 MINUTES

3 small zucchini (160g), sliced thinly
4 baby eggplants (240g), sliced thinly
10 cherry tomatoes, halved
1 baby fennel (130g), sliced thinly
100g button mushrooms, sliced thinly
⅔ cup (190g) bottled tomato pasta sauce
¼ cup coarsely chopped fresh basil
4 wholemeal pocket pitta
⅓ cup (40g) coarsely grated low-fat cheddar cheese

1 Preheat oven to 220°C/200°C fan-forced. Oil shallow medium baking dish.
2 Place zucchini, eggplant and tomato in baking dish; roast, uncovered, 20 minutes.
3 Add fennel, mushrooms and all but 2 tablespoons of the pasta sauce to dish; roast, covered, further 10 minutes. Stir in basil.
4 Divide reserved pasta sauce among pitta; top each with equal amounts of the vegetable mixture and cheese. Place on oven tray; cook, uncovered, about 10 minutes or until cheese melts and pizzas are heated through.

SERVES 4
per serving 3g total fat (0.8g saturated fat); 1124kj (269 cal); 13.5g protein; 46.5g carbohydrate; 9.5g fibre

pasta with tomatoes, artichokes and olives

PREPARATION TIME 15 MINUTES COOKING TIME 20 MINUTES

2 teaspoons olive oil
1 medium brown onion (150g), chopped finely
2 cloves garlic, crushed
¼ cup (60ml) dry white wine
2 x 425g cans tomatoes
2 tablespoons tomato paste
½ teaspoon sugar
½ cup (80g) seeded black olives
390g can artichoke hearts, drained, quartered
2 tablespoons finely sliced fresh basil leaves
375g spiral pasta
⅓ cup (25g) shaved parmesan cheese

1 Heat oil in large pan; cook onion and garlic, stirring, until onion softens. Add wine, undrained crushed tomatoes, paste and sugar; simmer, uncovered, about 15 minutes or until sauce is thickened. Add olives, artichokes and basil; stir until hot.

2 Meanwhile, cook pasta in large saucepan of boiling water, uncovered, until just tender; drain.

3 Combine pasta with half the sauce in large bowl; toss gently to combine. Serve pasta topped with remaining sauce and cheese.

SERVES 4
per serving 6.3g total fat (1.9g saturated fat); 1935kj (463 cal); 16.9g protein; 80.7g carbohydrate; 10.5g fibre

ricotta and spinach stuffed pasta shells

PREPARATION TIME 20 MINUTES COOKING TIME 1 HOUR 5 MINUTES

Large pasta shells, called conchiglioni in Italian, are available from gourmet delicatessens; you can use 16 cannelloni shells instead.

32 large pasta shells (280g)
500g spinach, trimmed
250g low-fat ricotta cheese
500g low-fat cottage cheese
600ml bottled tomato pasta sauce
1 cup (250ml) vegetable stock
1 tablespoon finely grated parmesan cheese

1 Cook pasta in large saucepan of boiling water, uncovered, 3 minutes; drain. Cool slightly.

2 Preheat oven to 180°C/160°C fan-forced. Oil shallow 2-litre (8 cup) ovenproof dish.

3 Boil, steam or microwave spinach until just wilted; drain. Chop spinach finely; squeeze out excess liquid.

4 Combine spinach in large bowl with cheeses; spoon spinach mixture into pasta shells.

5 Combine sauce and stock in ovenproof dish. Place pasta shells in dish; sprinkle with parmesan. Bake, covered, about 1 hour or until pasta is tender.

SERVES 4
per serving 10g total fat (5.3g saturated fat); 2278kj (545 cal); 41.9g protein; 71.3g carbohydrate; 8.6g fibre
serving suggestion serve with a loaf of ciabatta and a fresh green salad drizzled with a balsamic vinegar dressing.

gnocchi with caramelised pumpkin and sage sauce

PREPARATION TIME 15 MINUTES COOKING TIME 45 MINUTES

500g pumpkin
¼ cup (60ml) vegetable stock
1 large (500g) leek, sliced thinly
1 tablespoon brown sugar
1½ cups (375ml) water
2 teaspoons finely chopped fresh sage leaves
½ cup (125ml) low-fat evaporated milk
1kg fresh potato gnocchi

1. Preheat oven to 220°C/200°C fan-forced. Oil baking dish.
2. Chop pumpkin into 1cm cubes; place in baking dish. Bake, uncovered, about 30 minutes or until pumpkin is tender.
3. Bring stock to boil in large saucepan; cook leek, stirring, until leek softens. Add pumpkin and sugar; cook, stirring, about 10 minutes or until pumpkin caramelises. Stir in water, sage and milk; blend or process pumpkin mixture, in batches, until smooth. Return pumpkin sauce to same pan; stir over heat until hot.
4. Meanwhile, cook gnocchi in large saucepan of boiling water, uncovered, until just tender; drain. Toss hot gnocchi through hot pumpkin sauce.

SERVES 4
per serving 3.7g total fat (1.8g saturated fat); 1923kj (460 cal); 16.8g protein; 88.9g carbohydrate; 9g fibre

herbed ratatouille with pasta

PREPARATION TIME 10 MINUTES COOKING TIME 20 MINUTES

1 teaspoon olive oil
1 clove garlic, crushed
1 medium brown onion (150g), chopped coarsely
1 medium eggplant (300g), chopped coarsely
3 medium zucchini (360g), chopped coarsely
1 medium green capsicum (200g), chopped coarsely
2 medium tomatoes (380g), chopped coarsely
1 tablespoon dry red wine
⅓ cup water (80ml)
1 tablespoon tomato paste
2 tablespoons coarsely chopped fresh basil
300g short pasta

1. Heat oil in large saucepan; cook garlic and onion until soft. Stir in eggplant; cook until eggplant is soft. Remove from pan; drain on absorbent paper.
2. Cook zucchini and capsicum separately, following same method as eggplant.
3. Return vegetables to pan with tomato, wine, the water and paste; cook 5 minutes or until mixture is heated through. Just before serving, stir through basil.
4. Cook pasta in large saucepan of boiling water, uncovered, until just tender; drain. Serve with ratatouille.

SERVES 2
per serving 5.2g total fat (0.6g saturated fat); 2684kj (642 cal); 24.4g protein; 120.3g carbohydrate; 17.5g fibre
tip ratatouille can be made a day ahead. Store, covered, in refrigerator.

eggplant, tomato and leek lasagne

PREPARATION TIME 25 MINUTES (PLUS STANDING TIME) COOKING TIME 1 HOUR 30 MINUTES

3 medium eggplants (900g)
coarse cooking salt
1 large brown onion (200g), chopped finely
4 cloves garlic, crushed
3 large tomatoes (750g), chopped coarsely
2 tablespoons tomato paste
¼ cup shredded fresh basil leaves
1 tablespoon low-fat margarine
2 medium leeks (700g), chopped finely
2 tablespoons sugar
4 x 16cm x 30cm (200g) fresh lasagne sheets
1 cup (125g) grated low-fat cheddar cheese

1. Cut eggplants lengthways into 1cm slices; place slices in colander, sprinkle with salt, stand 30 minutes. Rinse eggplant under cold water; drain on absorbent paper.
2. Cook eggplant slices, in batches, in heated oiled large frying pan until softened and browned both sides.
3. Cook onion and half the garlic in same pan, stirring, until onion softens. Stir in tomato, paste and basil; simmer, uncovered, about 20 minutes or until thickened slightly. Blend or process tomato mixture until just combined.
4. Preheat oven to 200°C/180°C fan-forced. Oil deep 19-cm square (10-cup) ovenproof dish.
5. Heat margarine in same pan; cook leek and remaining garlic, stirring, until leek is soft. Add sugar; cook, stirring, about 5 minutes or until leek is browned lightly. Cut one lasagne sheet to cover base of ovenproof dish; place in position. Top with ¼ of the eggplant, ¼ of the leek mixture, ¼ of the tomato mixture and ¼ of the cheese. Repeat layers three times, ending with cheese. Bake, uncovered, 50 minutes.

SERVES 6

per serving 4g total fat (1.3g saturated fat); 1041kj (249 cal); 15.4g protein; 38.1g carbohydrate; 8.3g fibre

tip this recipe can be made ahead. Store, covered, in refrigerator. Before serving, reheat at 180°C/160°C fan-forced about 50 minutes or until heated through.

potato lentil patties

PREPARATION TIME 20 MINUTES COOKING TIME 40 MINUTES

1kg pontiac potatoes
½ cup (100g) red lentils
2 teaspoons olive oil
1 small brown onion (80g), chopped finely
1 clove garlic, crushed
1 egg, beaten lightly
2 tablespoons finely chopped fresh chives
1 tablespoon finely shredded fresh basil leaves
⅓ cup (25g) finely grated parmesan cheese
½ cup (125ml) sweet chilli sauce

1. Boil, steam or microwave potatoes until soft; drain, mash.
2. Meanwhile, place lentils in large saucepan of boiling water; simmer, uncovered, about 8 minutes or until tender. Drain, rinse under cold water; drain.
3. Heat oil in small frying pan; cook onion and garlic, stirring, until onion is soft.
4. Combine potato, lentils, onion mixture, egg and herbs in large bowl; mix well. Using hands, shape mixture into 12 patties; refrigerate until firm.
5. Preheat oven to 200°C/180°C fan-forced. Line oven tray with baking paper.
6. Place patties on oven tray; sprinkle with cheese. Bake, uncovered, about 30 minutes or until browned. Serve with chilli sauce, and salad, if desired.

SERVES 4
per serving 6.2g total fat (2.1g saturated fat); 1145kj (274 cal); 10.3g protein; 43.2g carbohydrate; 4.2g fibre
tip patties can be prepared ahead. Store uncooked, covered, in refrigerator. Just before serving, cook in oven.

pasta with fetta and red capsicum dressing

PREPARATION TIME 15 MINUTES COOKING TIME 15 MINUTES

We used rigatoni in this recipe, but any short, macaroni-type pasta can be used in its place.

375g pasta
2 medium tomatoes (380g), seeded, sliced thinly
1 small red onion (100g), sliced thinly
¼ cup fresh flat-leaf parsley leaves
90g low-fat fetta cheese

RED CAPSICUM DRESSING

1 small red capsicum (150g)
1 clove garlic, crushed
1 teaspoon coarsely chopped fresh thyme
1 tablespoon red wine vinegar
1 tablespoon lemon juice
⅓ cup (80ml) vegetable stock

1. Cook pasta in large saucepan of boiling water, uncovered, until just tender; drain.
2. Meanwhile, make red capsicum dressing.
3. Place hot pasta and dressing in large bowl with tomato, onion and parsley; toss gently to combine. Sprinkle with crumbled cheese.

RED CAPSICUM DRESSING quarter capsicum, remove and discard seeds and membranes. Roast under grill or in very hot oven, skin-side up, until skin blisters and blackens. Cover capsicum pieces in plastic or paper for 5 minutes. Peel away skin; chop capsicum roughly. Blend or process capsicum with remaining ingredients until smooth. Sieve dressing into small bowl.

SERVES 4
per serving 4.6g total fat (2.3g saturated fat); 1680kj (402 cal); 18.3g protein; 70g carbohydrate; 6.7g fibre

pasta with fresh tomato sauce

PREPARATION TIME 15 MINUTES COOKING TIME 5 MINUTES

375g fresh lasagne sheets, sliced thickly
1 tablespoon extra virgin olive oil
6 medium tomatoes (900g), peeled, seeded, chopped coarsely
¼ cup coarsely chopped fresh basil
2 cloves garlic, crushed
2 teaspoons red wine vinegar
1 fresh red thai chilli, chopped finely
80g low-fat fetta cheese, crumbled

1. Cook pasta in large saucepan of boiling water, uncovered, until just tender; drain. Sprinkle half of the oil over pasta; toss gently to combine.
2. Combine tomato, basil, garlic, remaining oil, vinegar and chilli in bowl.
3. Divide pasta among serving plates, spoon tomato mixture over pasta; sprinkle with cheese.

SERVES 4
per serving 8.7g total fat (2.7g saturated fat); 1827kj (437 cal); 17.8g protein; 69.9g carbohydrate; 7.4g fibre
tips to peel tomatoes, slice a cross in the bottom of tomato. Place tomatoes in large bowl of boiling water for 1 minute; drain. Rinse under cold water; peel. Fresh lasagne sheets, available loose by weight from good delis or in cryovac packages from supermarkets, take virtually no time at all to cook.

lentil cottage pie

PREPARATION TIME 10 MINUTES COOKING TIME 45 MINUTES (PLUS STANDING TIME)

800g medium new potatoes, quartered
2 tablespoons low-fat dairy-free spread
1 medium brown onion (150g), chopped finely
1 clove garlic, crushed
415g can crushed tomatoes
1 cup (250ml) vegetable stock
1 cup (250ml) water
2 tablespoons tomato paste
⅓ cup (80ml) dry red wine
⅔ cup (130g) red lentils
1 medium carrot (120g), chopped finely
½ cup (60g) frozen peas, thawed
2 tablespoons worcestershire sauce
⅓ cup coarsely chopped fresh flat-leaf parsley

1. Preheat oven to 220°C/200°C fan-forced.
2. Boil, steam or microwave potato until tender; drain. Mash in large bowl with half of the spread.
3. Melt remaining spread in medium deep frying pan; cook onion and garlic, stirring, until onion softens. Add undrained tomatoes, stock, the water, paste, wine, lentils and carrot; bring to a boil. Reduce heat, simmer, uncovered, 15 minutes, stirring occasionally. Add peas, sauce and parsley; cook, uncovered, 5 minutes.
4. Spoon lentil mixture into shallow 1-litre (4 cup) ovenproof dish. Spread potato mash on top. Bake, uncovered, 20 minutes. Stand pie 10 minutes before serving.

SERVES 4
per serving 5.3g total fat (0.9g saturated fat); 1250kj (299 cal); 15.5g protein; 43.9g carbohydrate; 11.2g fibre
tip if you're not concerned with keeping the fat content of this dish low, stir ½ cup finely grated parmesan cheese into the potato mash before baking the cottage pie.
serving suggestion serve with a simple green salad, if desired.

chilli beans with spicy tortilla crisps

PREPARATION TIME 20 MINUTES COOKING TIME 1 HOUR 15 MINUTES

1 tablespoon olive oil
2 medium brown onions (300g), chopped finely
1 teaspoon bottled crushed garlic
1 medium red capsicum (200g), chopped finely
420g can red kidney beans, rinsed, drained
400g can borlotti beans, rinsed, drained
2 x 425g cans tomatoes
2 teaspoons bottled chopped red chilli
½ cup (125ml) vegetable stock
1 tablespoon tomato paste
2 tablespoons finely chopped fresh coriander
2 x 18cm flour tortillas
cooking-oil spray
½ teaspoon mexican chilli powder
½ medium avocado (125g), chopped finely

1 Preheat oven to 240°C/220°C fan-forced.
2 Heat oil in large frying pan; cook onion and garlic until onion is soft. Add capsicum, beans, undrained crushed tomatoes, chilli, stock and paste; simmer, uncovered, about 30 minutes or until thickened. Stir in coriander.
3 Meanwhile, cut tortillas into wedges; place on oven trays. Coat with cooking-oil spray, sprinkle with chilli powder; bake, uncovered, about 8 minutes or until browned and crisp.
4 Serve chilli beans with tortilla crisps and avocado.

SERVES 4
per serving 13g total fat (2.3g saturated fat); 1471kj (352 cal); 15.7g protein; 44.7g carbohydrate; 11.9g fibre

mixed mushroom ragout with soft polenta

PREPARATION TIME 20 MINUTES COOKING TIME 50 MINUTES

2 tablespoons low-fat dairy-free spread
2 large brown onions (400g), chopped coarsely
3 cloves garlic, crushed
¼ cup (35g) plain flour
400g button mushrooms
400g swiss brown mushrooms, quartered
400g flat mushrooms, sliced thickly
2 tablespoons tomato paste
⅔ cup (160ml) dry red wine
1.25 litres (5 cups) water
1 litre (4 cups) vegetable stock
2 teaspoons finely chopped fresh thyme
2 cups (340g) polenta
1 cup (250ml) skim milk
¼ cup (20g) finely grated parmesan cheese

1. Heat dairy-free spread in large saucepan; cook onion and garlic, stirring, until onion softens. Add flour; cook, stirring, until mixture bubbles. Add mushrooms; cook, stirring, until mushrooms are just tender.
2. Add tomato paste and wine to mushroom mixture; bring to a boil. Reduce heat, simmer, uncovered, until liquid reduces by half. Add 2 cups of the water and half of the stock; return to a boil. Reduce heat, simmer, uncovered, 30 minutes. Stir in thyme.
3. Meanwhile, combine the remaining water and remaining stock in another large saucepan; bring to a boil. Add polenta; cook, stirring, until polenta boils and thickens. Add milk and cheese; cook, stirring, until cheese has melted.
4. Serve mushroom ragout on polenta.

SERVES 8
per serving 4.7g total fat (1.3g saturated fat); 1145kj (274 cal); 14g protein; 39.9g carbohydrate; 6.2g fibre
serving suggestion top with sprigs of fresh thyme.

mediterranean-style capsicum rolls

PREPARATION TIME 20 MINUTES COOKING TIME 10 MINUTES

6 medium yellow capsicums (1.2kg)
1 medium brown onion (150g), chopped finely
1 clove garlic, crushed
250g asparagus, trimmed, chopped finely
⅓ cup (40g) seeded black olives, chopped coarsely
¼ cup (50g) crumbled low-fat fetta cheese
2 tablespoons pepitas, toasted, chopped finely
½ cup (125ml) oil-free french dressing

1. Halve capsicums, remove and discard seeds and membranes. Roast under grill or in very hot oven, skin-side up, until skin blisters and blackens. Cover capsicum halves in plastic or paper for 5 minutes; peel away skin.
2. Meanwhile, heat oiled medium pan; cook onion and garlic until onion softens. Add asparagus and olives; cook, stirring, until asparagus is tender. Transfer asparagus mixture to large bowl; stir in cheese and pepitas.
3. Divide asparagus mixture among capsicum halves, roll capsicum around filling. Place rolls seam-side down on serving plates; drizzle with dressing. Serve with baby spinach leaves, if desired.

SERVES 4
per serving 5.3g total fat (1.6g saturated fat); 723kj (173 cal); 10.3g protein; 20.8g carbohydrate; 4.8g fibre

stuffed capsicums with lentils

PREPARATION TIME 15 MINUTES COOKING TIME 30 MINUTES

1 tablespoon olive oil
1 small brown onion (80g), chopped finely
1 clove garlic, crushed
1 small carrot (70g), chopped finely
1 small green zucchini (90g), chopped finely
¼ cup (60ml) water
¼ cup (50g) red lentils
¼ cup (55g) risoni
1 tablespoon tomato paste
1 cup (250ml) vegetable stock
12 baby red capsicums (540g)
2 tablespoons finely grated parmesan cheese

1. Preheat oven to 220°C/200°C fan-forced. Line oven tray with baking paper.
2. Heat oil in large saucepan; cook onion and garlic, stirring, until onion softens. Add carrot and zucchini; cook, stirring, until vegetables are tender. Stir in the water, lentils, risoni, paste and stock; bring to a boil. Reduce heat, simmer, uncovered, about 10 minutes or until lentils are tender.
3. Meanwhile, carefully cut tops off capsicums; discard tops. Discard seeds and membranes, leaving capsicums intact. Place capsicums on oven tray; roast, uncovered, about 15 minutes or until just softened.
4. Preheat grill. Divide lentil mixture among capsicums; sprinkle with cheese. Place under grill until cheese melts.

SERVES 4
per serving 6.7g total fat (1.5g saturated fat); 765kj (183 cal); 9.2g protein; 21.8g carbohydrate; 5g fibre

soft polenta with braised vegetables

PREPARATION TIME 15 MINUTES COOKING TIME 15 MINUTES

2½ cups (625ml) water
1 cup (170g) polenta
½ cup (40g) finely grated parmesan cheese
1 tablespoon olive oil
1 medium brown onion (150g), sliced thinly
1 clove garlic, crushed
200g button mushrooms, halved
2 medium green zucchini (240g), sliced thickly
8 yellow patty-pan squash (100g), quartered
600ml bottled tomato pasta sauce
¾ cup (180ml) vegetable stock

1 Bring the water to a boil in medium saucepan. Sprinkle polenta gradually into water, stirring constantly. Cover, reduce heat to low; cook, stirring occasionally, about 10 minutes or until polenta thickens. Add cheese, stir until melted.

2 Meanwhile, heat oil in medium saucepan; cook onion and garlic, stirring, until onion softens. Add mushrooms; cook, stirring, 3 minutes. Add zucchini and squash; cook, stirring, 2 minutes. Add sauce and stock; bring to a boil. Reduce heat, simmer, covered, about 8 minutes or until vegetables are just tender.

3 Serve polenta with braised vegetables.

SERVES 4
per serving 10.5g total fat (3.1g saturated fat); 1471kj (352 cal); 13.9g protein; 50.7g carbohydrate; 7.7g fibre
tip braised vegetables can be prepared in advance. Refrigerate, covered, and reheat just before serving.
serving suggestion serve with a tossed green salad and crusty Italian bread, such as ciabatta.

rice-and-fetta-filled roasted capsicums

PREPARATION TIME 15 MINUTES COOKING TIME 30 MINUTES

2 large red capsicums (700g)
2 teaspoons olive oil
1 small brown onion (80g), chopped finely
2 cloves garlic, crushed
¾ cup (150g) medium-grain white rice
1 cup (250ml) vegetable stock
1 cup (250ml) water
1 tablespoon lemon juice
300g spinach, chopped coarsely
2 tablespoons coarsely chopped fresh mint
1 tablespoon pine nuts, toasted
1 tablespoon dried currants
50g fetta cheese, crumbled

1 Preheat oven to 220°C/200°C fan-forced.

2 Halve and seed capsicums; place in large baking dish. Roast, uncovered, 15 minutes.

3 Meanwhile, heat oil in medium saucepan; cook onion and garlic, stirring, until onion softens. Add rice, stock, the water and juice; bring to a boil. Reduce heat, simmer, covered, stirring occasionally, about 15 minutes or until rice is just tender. Add spinach, mint, nuts and currants; stir until well combined.

4 Spoon rice mixture into capsicum halves; sprinkle tops with cheese. Roast, uncovered, about 15 minutes or until cheese browns lightly.

SERVES 4
per serving 8.7g total fat (2.6g saturated fat); 1129kj (270 cal); 9.8g protein; 37.9g carbohydrate; 3.9g fibre

spicy roasted pumpkin couscous

PREPARATION TIME 10 MINUTES COOKING TIME 20 MINUTES

1 tablespoon olive oil
2 cloves garlic, crushed
1 large red onion (200g), sliced thickly
500g pumpkin, peeled, chopped coarsely
3 teaspoons ground cumin
2 teaspoons ground coriander
1 cup (200g) couscous
1 cup (250ml) boiling water
20g butter
2 tablespoons coarsely chopped fresh flat-leaf parsley

1. Preheat oven to 220°C/200°C fan-forced.
2. Heat oil in medium flameproof baking dish; cook garlic, onion and pumpkin, stirring, over heat, until vegetables are browned lightly. Add spices; cook, stirring, about 2 minutes or until fragrant.
3. Roast pumpkim mixture, uncovered, about 15 minutes or until pumpkin is just tender.
4. Meanwhile, combine couscous with the water and butter in large heatproof bowl; cover, stand about 5 minutes or until water is absorbed, fluffing with fork occasionally to separate grains.
5. Add pumpkin mixture to couscous; stir in parsley.

SERVES 4
per serving 9.5g total fat (3.7g saturated fat); 1308kj (313 cal); 9.5g protein; 47.2g carbohydrate; 2.8g fibre

creamy mushroom pasta

PREPARATION TIME 15 MINUTES COOKING TIME 15 MINUTES

Skim milk keeps the fat count down but the creamy taste intact. You can use any kind of short pasta you like – penne, rigatoni – in place of the shells.

375g shell pasta
¼ cup (60ml) vegetable stock
1 clove garlic, crushed
500g button mushrooms, sliced thickly
1 cup (125g) frozen peas
4 green onions, sliced thinly
1 litre (4 cups) skim milk
1½ tablespoons cornflour
2 tablespoons water
¼ cup coarsely chopped fresh flat-leaf parsley
1 tablespoon wholegrain mustard
½ cup (40g) finely grated parmesan cheese
2 tablespoons finely chopped fresh chives

1. Cook pasta in large saucepan of boiling water, uncovered, until just tender; drain, keep warm.
2. Bring stock to a boil in same cleaned saucepan; cook garlic and mushrooms, stirring, until mushrooms soften and liquid evaporates. Stir in peas and half of the onion; cook, stirring, until onion softens.
3. Add milk and blended cornflour and water; cook, stirring, over low heat until sauce boils and thickens slightly.
4. Remove sauce from heat; stir in pasta, remaining onion, parsley, mustard and cheese. Serve sprinkled with chives.

SERVES 4
per serving 6.7g total fat (1.5g saturated fat); 765kj (183 cal); 9.2g protein; 21.8g carbohydrate; 5g fibre
tips swiss brown, flat or oyster mushrooms could be used instead of button. Toss pasta through sauce just before serving – it will soak up all the sauce if tossed too early.
serving suggestion serve with crusty sourdough bread.

vegetable and cottage cheese terrine

PREPARATION TIME **40 MINUTES** (PLUS REFRIGERATION TIME)

Buy zucchini just large enough to make 13cm-long strips once trimmed and sliced.

2½ cups (500g) cottage cheese
1 small yellow zucchini (90g), grated coarsely
4 green onions, chopped finely
1 tablespoon finely shredded fresh basil
1 tablespoon finely chopped fresh oregano
1 teaspoon finely chopped fresh thyme
1 clove garlic, crushed
1 teaspoon lemon juice
1 large green zucchini (150g)
1 large yellow zucchini (150g)
20g baby spinach leaves, shredded coarsely
2 teaspoons olive oil

CAPSICUM AND TOMATO SAUCE

2 medium tomatoes (380g), chopped finely
1 small yellow capsicum (150g), chopped finely
2 green onions, chopped finely
1 tablespoon finely shredded fresh basil
1 clove garlic, crushed
2 teaspoons olive oil
2 teaspoons lemon juice

1. Drain cheese in muslin-lined strainer or colander set over large bowl. Cover then weight cheese with an upright saucer topped with a heavy can. Drain overnight in refrigerator; discard liquid.
2. Line base and two long sides of 8cm x 25cm bar pan with baking paper or plastic wrap, extending paper 5cm above sides of pan.
3. Combine drained cheese in medium bowl with grated zucchini, onion, herbs, garlic and juice.
4. Discard ends of both large zucchini; using vegetable peeler, slice into thin strips (discard outer strips of both zucchini).
5. Overlap alternate-coloured zucchini strips in pan, starting from centre of base and extending over both long sides. Cover both short sides of pan with alternate-coloured zucchini strips, ensuring slices overlap to cover corners and extend over both short sides.
6. Spread half of the cheese mixture into zucchini-lined pan; cover with spinach, carefully spread remaining cheese mixture over spinach. Fold zucchini strips at short sides over filling then repeat with strips over long sides to completely enclose filling (mixture will be slightly higher than pan). Cover terrine tightly with foil; refrigerate 1 hour.
7. Meanwhile, make capsicum and tomato sauce.
8. Turn terrine onto serving plate; drizzle with oil. Using fine serrated knife, cut terrine crossways into thick slices; serve with sauce.

CAPSICUM AND TOMATO SAUCE combine ingredients in small bowl.

SERVES 4

per serving 12.3g total fat (5.4g saturated fat); 966kj (231 cal); 21.9g protein; 8.2g carbohydrate; 3.5g fibre

tip do not add any salt to the cottage-cheese mixture as this will cause the filling to become too wet.

serving suggestion serve with a salad of baby rocket and baby spinach leaves.

vegetable and cottage cheese terrine

mushroom, tomato and zucchini skewers with white bean puree

mushroom, tomato and zucchini skewers with white bean puree

PREPARATION TIME 15 MINUTES COOKING TIME 15 MINUTES

You will need 12 small bamboo skewers for this recipe; soak skewers in cold water for at least 1 hour to prevent them from splintering or scorching.

1 large red onion (300g)
200g button mushrooms
250g cherry tomatoes
2 large zucchini (300g), chopped coarsely
2 tablespoons balsamic vinegar
2 tablespoons olive oil

WHITE BEAN PUREE

2 x 400g cans white beans, rinsed, drained
1 cup (250ml) vegetable stock
1 clove garlic, quartered
1 tablespoon lemon juice
1 tablespoon olive oil

1. Make white bean puree.
2. Cut onion through the middle into 12 wedges.
3. Thread onion, mushrooms, tomatoes and zucchini alternately, onto skewers. Place skewers on large tray; drizzle with combined vinegar and oil.
4. Cook skewers on heated oiled grill plate (or grill or barbecue) until browned all over and tender.
5. Serve skewers on white bean puree.

WHITE BEAN PUREE combine beans and stock in large saucepan; bring to a boil. Reduce heat, simmer, uncovered, about 10 minutes or until liquid is absorbed. Blend or process bean mixture with garlic, juice and oil until smooth.

SERVES 4
per serving 15g total fat (2.2g saturated fat); 1233kj (295 cal); 16.1g protein; 25.5g carbohydrate; 13.9g fibre

stir-fried hokkien mee

PREPARATION TIME 15 MINUTES COOKING TIME 10 MINUTES

600g hokkien noodles
2 tablespoons vegetable oil
2 cloves garlic, crushed
2 teaspoons grated fresh ginger
3 kaffir lime leaves, chopped finely
1 large red capsicum (350g), sliced thinly
500g baby buk choy, chopped coarsely
6 green onions, chopped coarsely
1 cup (80g) bean sprouts
1 teaspoon cornflour
⅓ cup (80ml) kecap manis
2 tablespoons sweet chilli sauce
1 teaspoon sesame oil
1 tablespoon water

1. Place noodles in large heatproof bowl; cover with boiling water, separate with fork, drain.
2. Meanwhile, heat vegetable oil in wok; stir-fry garlic, ginger, lime leaves, capsicum and buk choy until vegetables are almost tender.
3. Add onion, sprouts and noodles; stir to combine. Blend cornflour with kecap manis, sauce, sesame oil and the water, add to wok; stir-fry until mixture boils and thickens slightly.

SERVES 4
per serving 12.6g total fat (1.7g saturated fat); 2567kj (614 cal); 18.2g protein; 105.8g carbohydrate; 6.6g fibre

chickpeas with kumara and tomato

PREPARATION TIME 10 MINUTES COOKING TIME 25 MINUTES

1 tablespoon ghee
2 medium brown onions (300g), chopped finely
2 cloves garlic, crushed
2 teaspoons ground cumin
2 teaspoons ground coriander
¼ teaspoon cardamom seeds
1 teaspoon chilli powder
1 large kumara (500g), chopped coarsely
2 cups (500ml) vegetable stock
1 tablespoon tomato paste
300g can chickpeas, rinsed, drained
4 medium tomatoes (760g), peeled, seeded, chopped
⅓ cup (65g) red lentils, rinsed
2 tablespoons finely chopped fresh coriander

1. Heat ghee in large saucepan; cook onion and garlic, stirring, until onion softens. Add spices; stir over heat until fragrant.
2. Add kumara, stock, paste, chickpeas, tomato and lentils; simmer, covered, about 15 minutes or until lentils are soft. Stir in coriander.

SERVES 4
per serving 6.5g total fat (3.3g saturated fat); 1049kj (251 cal); 13.2g protein; 34.9g carbohydrate; 9.9g fibre
serving suggestions serve with low-fat yogurt, extra coriander and couscous.

stir-fried vegetables with rice noodles

PREPARATION TIME 15 MINUTES COOKING TIME 10 MINUTES

250g dried rice noodles
1 tablespoon peanut oil
1 teaspoon sesame oil
1 large brown onion (200g), sliced thickly
1 clove garlic, crushed
¼ cup (60ml) soy sauce
⅓ cup (80ml) sweet chilli sauce
2 teaspoons cornflour
½ cup (125ml) water
2 teaspoons grated fresh ginger
1 tablespoon sweet sherry
1 medium red capsicum (200g), chopped coarsely
180g broccoli florets
150g snow peas, halved lengthways
425g can baby corn cobs, drained, halved lengthways

1 Place noodles in medium heatproof bowl, cover with boiling water, stand until tender; drain.

2 Meanwhile, heat oils in wok; stir-fry onion and garlic until onion softens. Add combined sauces, blended cornflour and water, ginger and sherry; stir until sauce boils and slightly thickens.

3 Add capsicum, broccoli, snow peas and corn; stir-fry until vegetables are just tender.

4 Serve noodles with stir-fried vegetables.

SERVES 4
per serving 7.1g total fat (1.1g saturated fat); 1442kj (345 cal); 10.3g protein; 57.9g carbohydrate; 7.1g fibre

vegetarian pizzas with pepita pesto

PREPARATION TIME 50 MINUTES (PLUS STANDING TIME) COOKING TIME 25 MINUTES

½ cup (75g) pepitas
¼ cup firmly packed fresh basil leaves
¼ cup firmly packed fresh flat-leaf parsley sprigs
1 clove garlic, crushed
¼ cup (60ml) tomato puree
cooking-oil spray
1 small (300g) kumara
150g button mushrooms, sliced
½ cup (60g) grated low-fat cheddar cheese
½ cup (50g) grated low-fat mozzarella cheese
½ cup (40g) grated parmesan cheese

PIZZA DOUGH

2 teaspoons (7g) dried yeast
1 teaspoon sugar
¼ cup (60ml) warm water
1½ cups (240g) wholemeal plain flour
½ teaspoon salt
⅓ cup (80ml) warm low-fat milk
2 teaspoons olive oil

1 Make pizza dough.

2 Dry-fry pepitas in frying pan, stirring, over low heat about 5 minutes or until pepitas have popped; cool.

3 Process pepitas, herbs and garlic until combined. While motor is operating, gradually add puree.

4 Preheat oven to 200°C/180°C fan-forced. Coat oven trays with cooking-oil spray.

5 Using a vegetable peeler, cut kumara into ribbons. Divide pizza dough into four portions. Roll each portion on floured surface to 15cm round, place on oven trays.

6 Divide pepita pesto among pizzas, top with kumara and mushrooms, sprinkle with combined cheeses. Bake, uncovered, about 20 minutes or until browned and crisp.

PIZZA DOUGH combine yeast and sugar in small bowl, stir in water, cover; stand in warm place about 10 minutes or until mixture is frothy. Sift flour and salt into large bowl, stir in yeast mixture, milk and oil, mix to a firm dough. Turn dough onto floured surface, knead about 5 minutes or until dough is smooth and elastic. Place dough in bowl coated with cooking-oil spray; cover, stand in warm place about 30 minutes or until doubled in size.

SERVES 4
per serving 20.2g total fat (6.2g saturated fat); 2115kj (506 cal); 29.1g protein; 51.7g carbohydrate; 11.7g fibre
tip recipe best made just before serving.

spicy bean casserole

PREPARATION TIME 10 MINUTES (PLUS STANDING TIME) COOKING TIME 1 HOUR

½ cup (100g) dried red kidney beans
½ cup (100g) dried chick peas
2 teaspoons monounsaturated or polyunsaturated margarine
1 medium red onion (170g), sliced thinly
1 medium carrot (120g), chopped coarsely
1 small red capsicum (150g), chopped finely
1 clove garlic, crushed
1 fresh small red chilli, chopped finely
1 teaspoon ground cumin
½ teaspoon ground cinnamon
½ teaspoon ground nutmeg
410g can tomatoes
½ cup (125ml) vegetable stock
2 teaspoons tomato paste
½ cup (100g) canned corn kernels, drained
2 teaspoons finely chopped fresh flat-leaf parsley

1 Cover beans and chick peas with water in small bowl. Soak overnight; drain.
2 Heat margarine in large saucepan; cook onion, carrot, capsicum, garlic and chilli until onion is soft.
3 Stir in cumin, cinnamon and nutmeg; cook for 1 minute. Stir in beans and chick peas, undrained crushed tomatoes, stock and paste; bring to a boil. Reduce heat, simmer, covered, for about 45 minutes, stirring occasionally, or until beans and chick peas are tender.
4 Stir in corn; simmer further 5 minutes. Just before serving, sprinkle with chopped parsley.

SERVES 2
per serving 8.5g total fat (1.3g saturated fat); 1789kj (428 cal); 26.5g protein; 60.2g carbohydrate; 24.9g fibre
tip recipe can be made a day ahead. Store, covered, in refrigerator.

tofu and spinach stir-fry

PREPARATION TIME 10 MINUTES (PLUS REFRIGERATION TIME) COOKING TIME 15 MINUTES

350g firm tofu
½ cup (120ml) hoisin sauce
1 tablespoon soy sauce
1 teaspoon finely grated fresh ginger
2 cloves garlic, crushed
2 teaspoons peanut oil
1 large brown onion (200g), sliced
1 medium red capsicum (200g), sliced thinly
200g snow peas
350g spinach, shredded
420g fresh egg noodles

1. Drain tofu; cut into 2cm cubes. Combine tofu, sauces, ginger and garlic in medium bowl. Cover; refrigerate at least 3 hours or until required.
2. Heat oil in wok; stir-fry onion and capsicum until soft. Add peas; stir-fry until hot. Add tofu mixture and spinach; stir-fry until hot.
3. Meanwhile, place noodles in large heatproof bowl, cover with boiling water, stand until just tender; drain.
4. Place noodles in bowls, top with tofu and vegetable mixture.

SERVES 4
per serving 10.8g total fat (1.6g saturated fat); 2040kj (488 cal); 25.3g protein; 71.4g carbohydrate; 9g fibre

masoor dhal with vegetables

PREPARATION TIME 15 MINUTES COOKING TIME 20 MINUTES

Masoor dhal is the Indian name of the common red lentil found in your local supermarket. Feel free to substitute any of your favourite vegetables if you prefer them to the ones suggested in this recipe.

1 tablespoon peanut oil
2 medium brown onions (300g), sliced thinly
2 medium carrots (240g), chopped coarsely
2 tablespoons hot curry paste
3 cups (750ml) water
2 cups (200g) cauliflower florets
3 baby eggplants (180g), chopped coarsely
2 medium zucchini (240g), chopped coarsely
¾ cup (150g) red lentils
100g green beans, halved
2 tablespoons coarsely chopped fresh coriander

1. Heat oil in large saucepan; cook onion and carrot, stirring, until onion softens. Add curry paste; cook, stirring, until fragrant.
2. Add the water and cauliflower; bring to a boil. Add eggplant, zucchini and lentils; return to a boil. Reduce heat, simmer, uncovered, about 15 minutes or until lentils are tender.
3. Add beans; cook, stirring, until beans are tender. Stir in coriander.

SERVES 4
per serving 9.4g total fat (1.3g saturated fat); 966kj (231 cal); 13.8g protein; 23.8g carbohydrate; 12g fibre
tip this recipe can be made as a lentil vegetable soup with the addition of more water or, even better, vegetable stock.
serving suggestion serve with pappadums, puffed in a microwave oven, and steamed white rice.

cabbage, zucchini and capsicum stir-fry

PREPARATION TIME 15 MINUTES COOKING TIME 10 MINUTES

375g thin egg noodles
1 tablespoon peanut oil
1 medium red onion (170g), sliced
2 medium zucchini (240g), sliced
1 large red capsicum (350g), sliced
½ medium wombok (300g), chopped
½ teaspoon dried crushed chillies
1 tablespoon low-salt soy sauce
½ cup (125ml) vegetable stock
2 tablespoons brown malt vinegar
½ teaspoon brown sugar
1 cup (80g) bean sprouts
⅓ cup coarsely chopped fresh coriander

1. Cook noodles in large saucepan of boiling water, uncovered, until just tender; drain.
2. Heat oil in wok; stir-fry onion, zucchini, capsicum and wombok until onion is soft. Add chillies, sauce, stock, vinegar and sugar; cook, stirring, until mixture boils. Remove from heat; stir in sprouts and coriander.
3. Serve vegetable stir-fry with noodles.

SERVES 4
per serving 6.1g total fat (1.1g saturated fat); 1400kj (335 cal); 13.4g protein; 55.4g carbohydrate; 5.7g fibre

ginger tofu and vegetable stir-fry

PREPARATION TIME 15 MINUTES COOKING TIME 10 MINUTES

3 chinese dried mushrooms
1 medium carrot (120g)
1 medium yellow capsicum (200g)
375g packet firm tofu, drained
2 teaspoons peanut oil
1 teaspoon sesame oil
2 teaspoons finely grated fresh ginger
2 cloves garlic, crushed
1 cup (80g) bean sprouts
250g baby buk choy, shredded
⅓ cup (60g) drained water chestnuts, sliced
2 tablespoons hoisin sauce
2 teaspoons cornflour
1 tablespoon water
6 lettuce leaves

1. Place mushrooms in heatproof bowl, cover with boiling water, stand 20 minutes; drain. Discard liquid and stems; slice caps.
2. Cut carrot and capsicum into long thin strips. Cut tofu into 1cm cubes.
3. Heat oils in wok; stir-fry ginger and garlic about 1 minute. Add carrot and capsicum, stir-fry until vegetables are just tender.
4. Add mushrooms, sprouts, buk choy, chestnuts, sauce and blended cornflour and water; cook, stirring, until sauce boils and thickens. Stir in tofu.
5. Serve tofu and vegetable stir-fry in trimmed lettuce leaves.

SERVES 6
per serving 7g total fat (1g saturated fat); 539kj (129 cal); 9.7g protein; 7g carbohydrate; 4.2g fibre

curried vegetables

PREPARATION TIME 15 MINUTES COOKING TIME 25 MINUTES

¼ cup (60ml) water
1 teaspoon ground cumin
1 teaspoon ground coriander
1 teaspoon garam masala
1 teaspoon curry powder
1 medium brown onion (150g), chopped finely
410g can tomatoes
1¾ cups (430ml) water, extra
4 baby potatoes (400g), quartered
2 medium carrots (240g), chopped finely
300g cauliflower, chopped finely
60g sugar snap peas
375g broccoli, chopped finely
4 small yellow squash (200g), halved

1. Heat the water in large saucepan; stir in spices and onion. Simmer until mixture is reduced by half.
2. Add undrained crushed tomatoes, the extra water, potato, carrot and cauliflower; bring to a boil. Reduce heat, simmer, covered, about 10 minutes or until potato is just soft.
3. Add peas, broccoli and squash; simmer, covered, further 5 minutes or until liquid is reduced slightly and vegetables are soft.

SERVES 2
per serving 1.9g total fat (0g saturated fat); 1304kj (312 cal); 23.4g protein; 48.5g carbohydrate; 23g fibre
tip curry can be made a day ahead. Store, covered, in refrigerator.

tofu stir-fry

PREPARATION TIME 20 MINUTES (PLUS STANDING TIME) COOKING TIME 30 MINUTES

400g fresh firm tofu
400g fresh egg noodles
1 tablespoon sesame oil
2 cloves garlic, crushed
2 fresh red thai chillies, sliced thinly
1 small red onion (100g), cut into wedges
1 medium red capsicum (200g), chopped coarsely
150g green beans, halved
200g swiss brown mushrooms, halved
4 green onions, sliced thinly
2 tablespoons soy sauce
2 tablespoons hoisin sauce
1 tablespoon brown sugar

1. Preheat oven to 220°C/200°C fan-forced. Line oven tray with baking paper.
2. Press tofu between two chopping boards or trays, place weight on top; elevate boards slightly to allow tofu liquid to drain away. Stand 20 minutes. Cut tofu into 2cm cubes; place on oven tray. Bake, uncovered, 25 minutes or until browned lightly.
3. Meanwhile, place noodles in large heatproof bowl, cover with boiling water; stand until just tender, separating noodles carefully with a fork. Drain; cover to keep warm.
4. Heat oil in wok; stir-fry garlic, chilli and red onion until onion softens. Add capsicum; stir-fry 2 minutes. Add beans and mushrooms; stir-fry until vegetables are just tender. Add tofu with green onion, sauces and sugar; stir-fry until sauce thickens slightly. Serve stir-fry tossed with noodles.

SERVES 4
per serving 13g total fat (1.9g saturated fat); 2002kj (479 cal); 26.1g protein; 63.6g carbohydrate; 7.2g fibre
tip some Asian supermarkets sell tofu already fried and cut into squares; while this will contain more fat than our oven-browned tofu, it will shorten preparation time.

stir-fried mushrooms, beans and buk choy

PREPARATION TIME 10 MINUTES COOKING TIME 10 MINUTES

1 teaspoon sesame oil
1 tablespoon vegetable oil
500g baby buk choy, quartered
1 small wombok (400g), shredded coarsely
450g broccoli, chopped finely
100g fresh shiitake mushrooms
150g oyster mushrooms
310g can red kidney beans, rinsed, drained
⅓ cup (80ml) hoisin sauce
¼ cup (60ml) lime juice
¼ cup (60ml) orange juice

1. Heat oils in wok; stir-fry buk choy and wombok until just wilted.
2. Add broccoli, mushrooms, beans, sauce and juices; cook, covered, about 3 minutes or until broccoli is tender.

SERVES 4
per serving 8g total fat (1g saturated fat); 920kj (220 cal); 13.3g protein; 23.2g carbohydrate; 15.4g fibre
tip add 16 shelled cooked prawns to wok just before serving, if desired.

snow pea and asian-green stir-fry

PREPARATION TIME 10 MINUTES (PLUS STANDING TIME) COOKING TIME 10 MINUTES

375g dried rice noodles
1 tablespoon peanut oil
1 medium brown onion (150g), sliced thinly
1 clove garlic, crushed
2 teaspoons grated fresh ginger
4 baby buk choy (600g), trimmed, halved lengthways
250g choy sum, trimmed
250g chinese broccoli, chopped coarsely
200g snow peas, halved
2 tablespoons light soy sauce
¼ cup (60ml) hoisin sauce
¼ cup (60ml) plum sauce
¼ cup (60ml) vegetable stock
2 teaspoons sesame oil
1 tablespoon toasted white sesame seeds

1. Place noodles in medium heatproof bowl, cover with boiling water, stand until just tender; drain.
2. Heat peanut oil in wok; stir-fry onion, garlic and ginger until onion softens.
3. Add buk choy, choy sum, broccoli and snow peas with combined sauces, stock and sesame oil; stir-fry until greens are just tender.
4. Serve stir-fry on noodles; sprinkle with seeds.

SERVES 4
per serving 11.3g total fat (1.5g saturated fat); 2031kj (486 cal); 13.2g protein; 82.3g carbohydrate; 10.3g fibre
tips add tofu to the stir-fry if you want to boost the protein content. You can substitute your favourite noodles for the rice noodles, if preferred. You can also vary the asian greens according to what's available at the greengrocer.
serving suggestion sprinkle with chopped fresh red chilli for spicy noodles.

vegetarian spring rolls with sweet and sour sauce

PREPARATION TIME 20 MINUTES COOKING TIME 25 MINUTES

1 teaspoon vegetable oil
1 clove garlic, crushed
50g fresh shiitake mushrooms, sliced thinly
2 green onions, sliced thinly
¼ medium red capsicum (50g), sliced thinly
2 cups (160g) shredded wombok
2 teaspoons soy sauce
6 spring roll wrappers
1 egg white, beaten lightly

SWEET AND SOUR SAUCE

½ cup (125ml) pineapple juice
2 tablespoons white vinegar
1 tablespoon tomato sauce
2 teaspoons brown sugar
1 teaspoon cornflour
1 teaspoon water

1. Preheat oven to 200°C/180°C fan-forced. Line oven tray with baking paper.
2. Heat oil and garlic in large saucepan; cook mushrooms for 2 minutes. Add onion, capsicum and wombok; cook, covered, until wombok is wilted. Stir in sauce.
3. Divide mixture among wrappers; fold sides in, roll up. Brush rolls lightly with egg white. Place rolls on oven tray; bake, uncovered, about 25 minutes or until lightly browned.
4. Make sauce. Serve spring rolls with sauce.

SWEET AND SOUR SAUCE combine juice, vinegar, sauce and sugar in medium saucepan. Blend cornflour and the water; add to pan. Stir over heat until sauce boils and thickens slightly.

MAKES 6
per roll 1.1g total fat (0.2g saturated fat); 276kj (66 cal); 2.3g protein; 11.6g carbohydrate; 1.1g fibre
tip rolls can be prepared 3 hours ahead. Store uncooked, covered, in refrigerator. Bake just before serving.

chickpea, pumpkin and eggplant curry

PREPARATION TIME 20 MINUTES COOKING TIME 40 MINUTES

1 tablespoon vegetable oil
1 medium brown onion (150g), chopped coarsely
2 cloves garlic, crushed
4 baby eggplants (200g), chopped coarsely
¼ cup (75g) medium curry paste
½ cup (600g) butternut pumpkin, peeled, chopped coarsely
½ cauliflower (500g), chopped
1½ cups (375ml) vegetable stock
425g can crushed tomatoes
400g can chickpeas, rinsed, drained
1 cup (280g) yogurt
½ cup finely shredded fresh mint

1. Heat oil in large saucepan; cook onion, garlic and eggplant, stirring, until just tender. Add curry paste; cook, stirring, until fragrant.
2. Add pumpkin, cauliflower, stock and undrained tomatoes; bring to a boil. Reduce heat, simmer, covered, 20 minutes. Add chickpeas; simmer, covered, 10 minutes or until vegetables are tender.
3. Meanwhile, combine yogurt and mint in small bowl.
4. Serve curry with yogurt mixture.

SERVES 4
per serving 15.7g total fat (3.5g saturated fat); 1379kj (330 cal); 16.5g protein; 30.1g carbohydrate; 11.7g fibre

vegetable and tofu stir-fry

PREPARATION TIME 15 MINUTES COOKING TIME 25 MINUTES

We used vermicelli-style rice noodles in this recipe.

250g thin dried rice noodles
2 tablespoons peanut oil
2 cloves garlic, crushed
1 tablespoon grated fresh ginger
150g fried tofu
2 medium carrots (240g), sliced thinly
1 medium red capsicum (200g), sliced thinly
250g chinese broccoli, chopped coarsely
1 tablespoon cornflour
1 tablespoon brown sugar
⅓ cup (80ml) hoisin sauce
⅓ cup (80ml) light soy sauce
2 tablespoons mirin

1. Place noodles in medium heatproof bowl; cover with boiling water. Stand until just tender; drain.
2. Heat oil in wok; stir-fry garlic, ginger, tofu, carrot, capsicum and broccoli until vegetables are just tender.
3. Add blended cornflour, sugar, sauces and mirin; stir-fry until mixture boils and thickens. Add noodles; stir-fry until hot.

SERVES 4
per serving 12.9g total fat (2g saturated fat); 1664kj (398 cal); 12.6g protein; 56.5g carbohydrate; 6.2g fibre
tip mirin is a sweetened rice wine used in Japanese cooking. It is sometimes referred to simply as rice wine, but should not be confused with sake, the Japanese rice wine made for drinking. You can substitute sweet white wine or sherry for mirin.
serving suggestion serve gow gees or spring rolls as a starter to this stir-fry.

chilli tofu and noodle salad

PREPARATION TIME 15 MINUTES (PLUS REFRIGERATION TIME)

¼ cup (60ml) lime juice
2 tablespoons sweet chilli sauce
2 teaspoons kecap manis
300g firm tofu, chopped coarsely
1 large carrot (180g)
1 lebanese cucumber (130g)
4 green onions
5cm piece fresh ginger (25g)
250g bean thread noodles
½ cup (75g) roasted unsalted cashew nuts
2 tablespoons coarsely chopped fresh coriander
2 tablespoons coarsely chopped fresh mint
2 tablespoons coarsely chopped fresh thai basil
1 fresh red thai chilli, sliced thinly

1. Combine juice, sauce and kecap manis in screw-topped jar; shake well.
2. Place tofu and half of the dressing in large bowl. Cover; refrigerate 1 hour.
3. Meanwhile, using vegetable peeler or sharp knife, cut carrot, cucumber, onion and ginger into long, thin strips.
4. Place noodles in medium heatproof bowl; cover with boiling water. Stand until just tender; drain.
5. Combine noodles and vegetables with tofu mixture. Add nuts, herbs, chilli and remaining dressing; toss gently to combine.

SERVES 4
per serving 15.4g total fat (2.4g saturated fat); 1806kj (432 cal); 17.4g protein; 55.1g carbohydrate; 5.9g fibre
tip kecap manis, an Indonesian thick soy sauce which has sugar and spices added, can be found at Asian food stores and some supermarkets.

hoisin vegetable stir-fry

PREPARATION TIME 15 MINUTES COOKING TIME 10 MINUTES

You will need half a small wombok for this recipe.

500g fresh rice noodles
1½ tablespoons peanut oil
2 eggs, beaten lightly
2 teaspoons sesame oil
1 medium carrot (120g), sliced thinly
1 small red capsicum (150g), sliced thinly
1 cup (80g) bean sprouts
3 cups (210g) shredded wombok
4 green onions, sliced thinly
¼ cup (60ml) hoisin sauce
1 tablespoon light soy sauce
2 teaspoons sambal oelek

1. Rinse noodles under hot water; drain. Transfer to large bowl; separate noodles with fork.
2. Brush heated wok with a little of the peanut oil. Add egg; swirl to cover base of wok. Cook, covered, about 3 minutes or until cooked through. Roll omelette tightly; slice thinly.
3. Heat sesame oil in wok; stir-fry carrot until just tender. Add capsicum, sprouts, wombok and onion; stir-fry until just tender. Remove vegetables; keep warm.
4. Heat remaining peanut oil in wok; stir-fry noodles, sauces and sambal until sauce thickens and noodles are heated through. Return vegetables to wok; stir-fry until hot.
5. Serve stir-fry topped with omelette.

SERVES 4
per serving 13.7g total fat (2.5g saturated fat); 1722kj (412 cal); 10.5g protein; 61.2g carbohydrate; 5.5g fibre
tip you could substitute dried noodles for fresh noodles, if you prefer. Dried noodles should be soaked in boiling water to soften them before use.
serving suggestion serve with grilled or barbecued chicken or seafood.

singapore noodles

PREPARATION TIME 10 MINUTES COOKING TIME 20 MINUTES

250g rice vermicelli
4 eggs, beaten lightly
2 teaspoons vegetable oil
1 medium brown onion (150g), chopped coarsely
2 cloves garlic, crushed
2 teaspoons grated fresh ginger
150g baby buk choy, chopped coarsely
200g snow peas, halved
1 small red capsicum (150g), sliced thickly
2 tablespoons soy sauce
2 tablespoons hoisin sauce
2 tablespoons sweet chilli sauce
1 cup loosely packed fresh coriander leaves
3 cups (240g) bean sprouts

1. Place noodles in large heatproof bowl, cover with boiling water, stand until just tender; drain. Using scissors, cut noodles into 10cm lengths.
2. Heat lightly oiled wok. Add half of the egg, swirling wok to form thin omelette. Remove omelette from wok; roll, cut into thin slices. Repeat with remaining egg.
3. Heat oil in wok; stir-fry onion until soft. Add garlic and ginger; stir-fry 1 minute. Add buk choy, snow peas, capsicum and sauces; stir-fry until vegetables are just tender.
4. Add noodles and omelette strips with coriander and sprouts; toss gently to combine.

SERVES 4
per serving 8.9g total fat (1.9g saturated fat); 1526kj (365 cal); 16.5g protein; 53.7g carbohydrate; 6.2g fibre
serving suggestion serve with a platter of cucumber spears, quartered hard-boiled eggs, tomato wedges and sliced pawpaw to make this meal authentically Singaporean.

spinach and pumpkin curry

PREPARATION TIME 15 MINUTES COOKING TIME 25 MINUTES

1kg pumpkin, peeled
1 tablespoon ghee
2 medium brown onions (300g), sliced thinly
2 cloves garlic, crushed
1 teaspoon grated fresh ginger
2 green thai chillies, sliced
1 teaspoon ground coriander
1 teaspoon ground cumin
1 teaspoon black mustard seeds
½ teaspoon ground turmeric
1½ cups (375ml) vegetable stock
150g spinach, chopped coarsely
⅓ cup loosely packed fresh coriander leaves
1 tablespoon flaked almonds, toasted

1. Cut pumpkin into 3cm pieces.
2. Heat ghee in large saucepan; cook onion, stirring, until browned. Add garlic, ginger, chilli and spices; stir over heat until fragrant.
3. Add pumpkin and stock to pan; simmer, covered, about 15 minutes or until pumpkin is tender. Add spinach and coriander; stir, tossing, until spinach has just wilted.
4. Just before serving, sprinkle with nuts. Serve with steamed rice, if desired.

SERVES 4
per serving 7.1g total fat (3.8g saturated fat); 669kj (160 cal); 7.5g protein; 16.8g carbohydrate; 4.6g fibre

desserts

vanilla bean ice-cream with espresso sauce

PREPARATION TIME 10 MINUTES (PLUS FREEZING TIME) COOKING TIME 15 MINUTES (PLUS STANDING TIME)

1 vanilla bean
1 cup (250ml) light evaporated milk
⅓ cup (80ml) light cream
2 egg yolks
½ cup (110g) caster sugar
½ cup (125ml) boiling water
1 tablespoon ground espresso coffee beans

1. Split vanilla bean lengthways; scrape seeds into small saucepan. Add vanilla bean, evaporated milk and cream; bring to a boil. Remove pan from heat, cover; stand 20 minutes. Discard vanilla bean.
2. Meanwhile, using electric mixer, beat egg yolks and sugar in small bowl until thick and creamy; gradually stir in vanilla mixture.
3. Return mixture to same pan; cook, stirring, over low heat, about 15 minutes or until mixture thickens slightly (do not allow to boil).
4. Strain ice-cream mixture into 20cm x 30cm lamington pan, cover surface with foil; cool to room temperature. Freeze until almost set.
5. Place ice-cream in large bowl; chop coarsely. Using electric mixer, beat ice-cream until smooth. Pour into 14cm x 21cm loaf pan, cover; freeze until ice-cream is firm.
6. Just before serving, combine the water and coffee in coffee plunger; stand 2 minutes before plunging. Cool 5 minutes before serving over ice-cream.

SERVES 4
per serving 6.9g total fat (3.7g saturated fat); 945kj (226 cal); 7.2g protein; 35.5g carbohydrate; 0g fibre

vanilla bean ice-cream with espresso sauce

melon granita trio

melon granita trio

PREPARATION TIME 45 MINUTES (PLUS FREEZING TIME) COOKING TIME 10 MINUTES

You will need a small rockmelon (1.3kg), a small honeydew melon (1.3kg), and a small watermelon (1.5kg) for this recipe.

3 cups (750ml) water

1½ cups (330g) sugar

800g seeded, peeled, coarsely chopped rockmelon

800g seeded, peeled, coarsely chopped honeydew melon

800g seeded, peeled, coarsely chopped watermelon

1. Combine the water and sugar in medium saucepan. Stir over heat, without boiling, until sugar dissolves; bring to a boil. Reduce heat, simmer, uncovered, without stirring, about 2 minutes or until syrup thickens slightly.
2. Blend or process rockmelon until almost smooth; push through sieve into shallow metal cake pan. Combine with a third of the sugar syrup. Repeat process with honeydew and half of the remaining syrup in separate metal cake pan, then with watermelon and remaining syrup in another cake pan.
3. Cover each pan with foil; freeze about 3 hours or until granita mixtures are just set.
4. Keeping granita mixtures separate, scrape into bowls, then beat each with electric mixer until smooth. Return each to their respective pans, cover with foil; freeze overnight or until each granita sets firmly.
5. Serve granita, layered in alternate scoops, in individual glasses.

SERVES 8
per serving 0.4g total fat (0g saturated fat); 877kj (210 cal); 1g protein; 52.2g carbohydrate; 1.8g fibre
serving suggestion serve scoops of granitas on top of fresh seasonal fruit salad.

fruit with creamy chocolate dip

PREPARATION TIME 15 MINUTES (PLUS REFRIGERATION TIME)

Tia maria is a coffee-flavoured liqueur; you can use kahlua as a substitute.

250g cottage cheese
200ml low-fat vanilla yogurt
2 teaspoons cocoa powder
½ cup (100g) firmly packed brown sugar
2 tablespoons tia maria
250g strawberries
2 large bananas (460g)
2 large red apples (400g)

1 Blend or process cheese, yogurt, cocoa, sugar and liqueur until smooth. Spoon mixture into serving bowl. Cover; refrigerate 30 minutes.

2 Just before serving, cut strawberries in half; slice bananas and apples into bite-size pieces. Serve fruit with dip.

SERVES 4
per serving 6.5g total fat (4g saturated fat); 1568kj (375 cal); 15.3g protein; 63.4g carbohydrate; 4.3g fibre

banana and carob chip ice-cream

PREPARATION TIME 15 MINUTES (PLUS FREEZING TIME)

You will need 3 medium (600g) overripe bananas for this recipe

1 cup (250ml) low-fat evaporated milk
1 cup mashed bananas
½ cup (125ml) low-fat yogurt
¼ cup (60ml) low-fat milk
¼ cup (60ml) maple-flavoured syrup
2 teaspoons vanilla essence
⅓ cup (50g) carob buttons, coarsely chopped

1 Pour evaporated milk into loaf pan. Cover with foil; freeze until just firm.

2 Process frozen evaporated milk, banana, yogurt, milk, syrup and essence until thick and creamy. Pour mixture into 15cm x 25cm loaf pan. Cover with foil; freeze until just firm.

3 Repeat processing; stir in carob. Cover; freeze until firm.

SERVES 4
per serving 2.8g total fat (2.1g saturated fat); 1004kj (240 cal); 9.2g protein; 45.6g carbohydrate; 1.4g fibre
tip ice-cream can be made a week ahead. Store, covered, in freezer.

raspberries and watermelon with hazelnut syrup

PREPARATION TIME 15 MINUTES COOKING TIME 5 MINUTES

Use fresh or frozen raspberries in this recipe.

1.5kg watermelon
150g raspberries
¼ cup shredded fresh mint leaves
½ cup (125ml) lemon juice
2 tablespoons raw sugar
⅓ cup (40g) coarsely chopped roasted hazelnuts

1 Discard watermelon rind; chop watermelon into large pieces. Combine watermelon, raspberries and mint in large heatproof bowl.

2 Combine juice, sugar and nuts in small pan; stir, over low heat, until sugar is dissolved. Bring to boil. Pour hot syrup over watermelon mixture.

SERVES 4
per serving 7g total fat (0.3g saturated fat); 729kj (174 cal); 3.1g protein; 24.1g carbohydrate; 5g fibre

pear and rhubarb crumble

PREPARATION TIME 20 MINUTES COOKING TIME 25 MINUTES

2¾ cups (300g) chopped fresh rhubarb
2 tablespoons caster sugar
½ cup (125ml) water
¼ cup (60ml) orange juice
8 medium pears (1.4kg), peeled, chopped
¾ cup (120g) chopped raisins

CRUMBLE TOPPING

1 cup (30g) corn flakes
½ cup (55g) natural muesli
25g butter, melted
2 tablespoons honey

1 Preheat oven to 180°C/160°C fan-forced.

2 Combine rhubarb, sugar, water, juice and pears in saucepan; bring to a boil. Reduce heat, simmer, uncovered, until pears are just tender. Stir in raisins.

3 Meanwhile, make crumble topping.

4 Spoon rhubarb mixture into 1.5 litre (6-cup) ovenproof dish; sprinkle with crumble topping. Bake, uncovered, about 15 minutes or until browned.

CRUMBLE TOPPING combine corn flakes and muesli in medium bowl, add butter and honey; mix well.

SERVES 8
per serving 3.6g total fat (1.9g saturated fat); 936kj (224 cal); 2.4g protein; 46.9g carbohydrate; 5.3g fibre

lemon sorbet

PREPARATION TIME 15 MINUTES (PLUS STANDING AND FREEZING TIME) COOKING TIME 10 MINUTES

You will need four medium-sized lemons for this recipe.

1 cup (220g) caster sugar
¼ cup finely grated lemon rind
2½ cups (625ml) water
¾ cup (180ml) lemon juice
1 egg white

1. Stir the sugar, rind and the water in small saucepan over heat, without boiling, until sugar dissolves; bring to a boil. Boil, uncovered, without stirring, about 5 minutes or until syrup thickens slightly. Strain into medium heatproof jug; cool to room temperature. Stir in juice.
2. Pour sorbet mixture into 14cm x 21cm loaf pan. Cover with foil; freeze for about 3 hours or until almost set.
3. Blend or process mixture with egg white until smooth; pour into same pan. Cover with foil; freeze 3 hours or overnight.

SERVES 4
per serving 0.1g total fat (0g saturated fat); 956kj (228 cal); 1.2g protein; 56.5g carbohydrate; 0.4g fibre
tip you can also freeze the sorbet-egg white mixture in an ice-cream machine following the manufacturer's instructions.

watermelon sorbet

PREPARATION TIME 15 MINUTES (PLUS STANDING AND FREEZING TIME) COOKING TIME 10 MINUTES

You will need a 1.2kg piece of watermelon for this recipe.

½ cup (110g) caster sugar
½ cup (125ml) water
850g coarsely chopped seedless watermelon
1 egg white

1. Stir sugar and the water in small saucepan over heat, without boiling, until sugar dissolves; bring to a boil. Boil, uncovered, without stirring, about 5 minutes or until syrup thickens slightly. Transfer to large heatproof jug; cool to room temperature.
2. Meanwhile, blend or process watermelon until smooth; strain through fine sieve into cooled sugar syrup. Stir to combine.
3. Pour sorbet mixture into 14cm x 21cm loaf pan, cover with foil; freeze about 3 hours or until almost set.
4. Blend or process mixture with egg white until smooth; pour into same pan. Cover with foil; freeze 3 hours or overnight.

SERVES 4
per serving 0.4g total fat (0g saturated fat); 659kj (157 cal); 1.5g protein; 38g carbohydrate; 1.3g fibre
tip you can also freeze the sorbet-egg white mixture in an ice-cream machine following the manufacturer's instructions.

mango, apple and passionfruit sorbet

PREPARATION TIME 15 MINUTES (PLUS FREEZING TIME) COOKING TIME 15 MINUTES (PLUS COOLING TIME)

You will need about 6 passionfruit for this recipe.

½ cup (110g) caster sugar

2 cups (500ml) apple juice

½ cup (125ml) water

425g can sliced mango in light syrup, drained

½ cup (125ml) passionfruit pulp

4 egg whites

1. Stir sugar, juice and the water in medium saucepan over heat, without boiling, until sugar dissolves; bring to a boil. Simmer, uncovered, without stirring, about 12 minutes or until syrup thickens slightly (syrup must not change colour); cool.
2. Blend or process mango until smooth. Stir mango and passionfruit into sugar syrup; pour into 20 x 30cm lamington pan. Cover with foil; freeze until just firm.
3. Beat sorbet mixture in small bowl with electric mixer until thick and fluffy; return to pan. Cover with foil; freeze until just firm.
4. Repeat beating process in large bowl; add egg whites, one at a time, beating until fluffy. Pour mixture into same pan. Cover with foil; freeze until firm.

SERVES 4

per serving 0.2g total fat (0g saturated fat); 1033kj (247 cal); 56.6g protein; 5.5g carbohydrate; 5.4g fibre

honey buttermilk ice-cream with fresh fruit salsa

PREPARATION TIME 30 MINUTES (PLUS FREEZING TIME) COOKING TIME 15 MINUTES

Buttermilk is a tangy dairy product made in a similar way to yogurt. It has a fat content of 1.8g per 100ml. We used low-fat evaporated milk with a fat count of 1.6g per 100ml.

2 teaspoons gelatine
¼ cup (60ml) water
1½ cups (375ml) low-fat evaporated milk
½ cup (175g) honey
1½ cups (375ml) buttermilk

FRUIT SALSA

1 small pineapple (800g), chopped coarsely
1 large mango (600g), chopped coarsely
3 medium kiwi fruit (255g), chopped coarsely
250g strawberries, chopped coarsely

1. Sprinkle gelatine over the water in small heatproof jug; stand jug in pan of simmering water. Stir until gelatine dissolves; cool.
2. Meanwhile, place evaporated milk in medium saucepan; bring to a boil. Remove from heat; stir in gelatine mixture and honey. Transfer to medium bowl; cool.
3. Beat buttermilk in small bowl with electric mixer until buttermilk is frothy.
4. Beat evaporated milk mixture with electric mixer until light and frothy. With motor operating, gradually pour in buttermilk; beat until combined.
5. Pour into 2-litre (8 cup) metal container. Cover with foil; freeze 3 hours or until just set.
6. Beat ice-cream with electric mixer until smooth. Cover with foil; freeze overnight or until set.
7. Just before serving, make fruit salsa. Serve ice-cream with fruit salsa.

FRUIT SALSA combine fruit in medium bowl.

SERVES 6 (APPROXIMATELY 2 LITRES ICE-CREAM)
per serving 3g total fat (1.8g saturated fat); 1196kj (286 cal); 11.5g protein; 53.8g carbohydrate; 4.6g fibre
tip you can also freeze the ice-cream mixture in an ice-cream machine following the manufacturer's instructions.

sparkling lime granita

PREPARATION TIME 10 MINUTES COOKING TIME 10 MINUTES (PLUS FREEZING TIME)

You will need about 6 large limes for this recipe; grate rind before squeezing juice. We used a sparkling pinot noir chardonnay for this recipe, but any sparkling white wine may be used.

½ cup (110g) caster sugar
½ cup (125ml) fresh lime juice
¼ cup (60ml) water
2 cups (500ml) sparkling white wine
2 tablespoons finely grated lime rind
1 egg white, beaten lightly

1. Stir sugar, juice and the water in small saucepan, over low heat until sugar dissolves; bring to a boil. Simmer, uncovered, 5 minutes. Stir in wine and rind. Pour mixture into loaf pan. Cover with foil; freeze until just firm.
2. Chop mixture, place in large bowl of electric mixer; beat in egg white until combined. Pour mixture into same pan. Cover; freeze until firm.

SERVES 4
per serving 0.07g total fat (0g saturated fat); 830kj (198 cal); 1.4g protein; 29.3g carbohydrate; 0.3g fibre
tip recipe can be prepared ahead to end of step 1 and frozen, covered, up to 2 days.

coffee granita with walnut crisps

PREPARATION TIME 25 MINUTES (PLUS FREEZING TIME) COOKING TIME 10 MINUTES

2 cups (500ml) boiling water
¼ cup (30g) ground espresso coffee beans
⅓ cup (75g) caster sugar
10g butter
1 tablespoon honey
1 tablespoon plain flour
1 tablespoon icing sugar
2 tablespoons finely chopped roasted walnuts

1. Combine the water and coffee in small coffee plunger; stand 5 minutes before plunging. Pour into medium jug, add caster sugar; stir until sugar dissolves. Pour coffee mixture into 20cm x 30cm lamington pan. Cover with foil; freeze about 3 hours or until almost set.
2. Using fork, scrape granita from bottom and sides of pan, mixing frozen with unfrozen mixture. Cover; return to freezer. Repeat process every hour for about 4 hours or until large ice crystals form and granita has a dry, shard-like appearance.
3. Meanwhile, melt butter with honey in small saucepan over low heat; stir in flour, icing sugar and nuts. Place walnut crisp mixture into small bowl. Cover; refrigerate 1 hour.
4. Preheat oven to 220°C/200°C fan-forced. Line oven trays with baking paper.
5. Drop level teaspoons of the crisp mixture on oven trays about 10cm apart; bake, uncovered, about 3 minutes or until crisps are browned lightly. Remove from oven; cool 1 minute. Using spatula, lift crisps carefully and place over rolling pin to cool. Serve granita with walnut crisps.

SERVES 4
per serving 5.2g total fat (1.6g saturated fat); 715kj (170 cal); 2g protein; 30.3g carbohydrate; 1.6g fibre

apricot strudel

PREPARATION TIME 20 MINUTES COOKING TIME 20 MINUTES

825g can apricot slices in natural syrup, drained
2 tablespoons brown sugar
1 teaspoon ground cinnamon
¾ cup (120g) sultanas
¼ cup (35g) roasted hazelnuts, chopped finely
6 sheets fillo pastry
1 tablespoon no-fat milk
1 tablespoon icing sugar

1. Preheat oven to 200°C/180°C fan-forced. Grease oven tray.
2. Combine apricots, brown sugar, cinnamon, sultanas and nuts in medium bowl.
3. Stack fillo sheets, brushing each lightly with milk as you layer. Spread apricot filling over fillo, leaving 5cm space at edge of both short sides and 2cm at edge of one long side. Fold short sides over; starting from filled long-side edge, roll strudel to enclose filling. Place, seam-side down, on tray.
4. Brush strudel with remaining milk. Bake, uncovered, about 25 minutes or until lightly browned. Dust strudel with icing sugar before serving, warm or cold, with ice-cream, if desired.

SERVES 6
per serving 3.5g total fat (0.2g saturated fat); 801kj (191 cal); 3.7g protein; 36.6g carbohydrate; 3.5g fibre

apple and pear strudel

PREPARATION TIME 10 MINUTES COOKING TIME 15 MINUTES (PLUS COOLING TIME)

1 medium apple (150g)
1 medium pear (230g)
1 tablespoon caster sugar
½ teaspoon finely grated lemon rind
¼ teaspoon ground cinnamon
2 tablespoons water
3 sheets fillo pastry

CUSTARD SAUCE

3 teaspoons custard powder
3 teaspoons caster sugar
¾ cup (180ml) skim milk

1. Preheat oven to 220°C/200°C fan-forced. Line oven tray with baking paper.
2. Peel apple and pear; cut each into quarters, and each quarter into three wedges. Place fruit in large saucepan with sugar, rind, cinnamon and the water; cook until fruit is soft. Cool.
3. Layer pastry sheets together; fold in half. Spoon fruit mixture along centre of pastry. Fold in ends; fold sides over fruit.
4. Place strudel, with folded edge underneath, onto oven tray; bake, uncovered, about 15 minutes or until well browned.
5. Make custard sauce. Serve strudel with sauce.

CUSTARD SAUCE combine custard powder and sugar in medium saucepan; gradually pour in milk, stirring over heat until sauce boils and thickens.

SERVES 2
per serving 0.8g total fat (0.2g saturated fat); 1041kj (249 cal); 5.9g protein; 55.6g carbohydrate; 3.9g fibre
tip strudel can be prepared a day ahead; store uncooked, covered, in refrigerator. Bake just before serving.

grilled nashi with rosewater syrup

PREPARATION TIME 10 MINUTES COOKING TIME 20 MINUTES

2 cups (500ml) water

¾ cup (165g) caster sugar

2½ teaspoons rosewater

4 medium nashi (1kg), halved

1 tablespoon honey

1 tablespoon brown sugar

1. Stir water, caster sugar and rosewater in medium saucepan over heat, without boiling, until sugar dissolves. Add nashi; simmer, uncovered, about 10 minutes or until nashi are tender.
2. Drain nashi over large heatproof bowl; reserve syrup, cover to keep warm.
3. Preheat grill. Place nashi on oven tray, drizzle with honey, sprinkle with brown sugar. Place under grill until sugar dissolves.
4. Serve nashi warm or cold with reserved warm rosewater syrup.

SERVES 4

per serving 0.2g total fat (0g saturated fat); 1237kj (295 cal); 0.9g protein; 75.2g carbohydrate; 4.7g fibre

chocolate and ice-cream fillo sandwiches

PREPARATION TIME 15 MINUTES COOKING TIME 10 MINUTES

4 sheets fillo pastry

cooking-oil spray

1 egg white, beaten lightly

1 tablespoon shelled pistachios, chopped finely

2 teaspoons caster sugar

¼ teaspoon ground cinnamon

400g low-fat vanilla ice-cream

½ cup (125ml) diet chocolate topping

1. Preheat oven to 220°C/200°C fan-forced.
2. Stack fillo sheets together, coating between each layer with cooking-oil spray. Cut fillo stack in half lengthways, then cut each half into quarters crossways; you will have eight rectangular fillo stacks in all.
3. Place all stacks on oven trays. Brush four stacks with egg white, sprinkle with nuts, then combined sugar and cinnamon. Bake stacks, uncovered, about 5 minutes or until golden brown and crisp.
4. Just before serving, place one of the plain stacks on each plate, top with scoops of ice-cream, drizzle with topping; sandwich with remaining stacks.

SERVES 4

per serving 5.8g total fat (2.3g saturated fat); 1171kj (280 cal); 7.6g protein; 51.2g carbohydrate; 0.5g fibre

rhubarb and strawberry sponge pudding

PREPARATION TIME 20 MINUTES COOKING TIME 50 MINUTES

Rhubarb has an intensely tart flavour which makes it a natural dessert and pie filling when sweetened and combined with other fruit. You will need about 10 stems of rhubarb for this recipe.

5 cups (700g) coarsely chopped, trimmed rhubarb
2 tablespoons sugar
2 tablespoons orange juice
500g strawberries, hulled, sliced thinly
280g packet sponge cake mix

1 Preheat oven to 180°C/160°C fan-forced.
2 Cook rhubarb, sugar and juice in large saucepan, stirring, over low heat, until sugar dissolves. Cook, uncovered, further 10 minutes or until rhubarb is tender. Stir in strawberries.
3 Divide rhubarb mixture among eight 1-cup (250ml) ovenproof dishes; bake, uncovered, 5 minutes.
4 Meanwhile, prepare sponge according to packet instructions; spoon evenly among rhubarb dishes. Bake, uncovered, further 30 minutes.

SERVES 8
per serving 0.5g total fat (0.1g saturated fat); 703kj (168 cal); 5g protein; 35.7g carbohydrate; 4.9g fibre
serving suggestion serve with low-fat custard or thickened light cream.

banana pudding with espresso syrup

PREPARATION TIME 15 MINUTES COOKING TIME 50 MINUTES

2 eggs
1 cup (200g) firmly packed brown sugar
2 cups mashed banana
½ cup (140g) low-fat yogurt
40g butter, melted
2 teaspoons vanilla essence
2 cups (300g) self-raising flour
1½ teaspoons ground cinnamon
1 teaspoon bicarbonate of soda

ESPRESSO SYRUP
¾ cup (165g) sugar
1 tablespoon dry instant coffee granules
¾ cup (180ml) water

1 Preheat oven to 180°C/160°C fan-forced. Grease deep 20cm-round cake pan; line base with baking paper.
2 Beat eggs in small bowl with electric mixer until thick and creamy. Add sugar; continue beating 5 minutes. Fold in banana, yogurt, butter and essence, then sifted flour, cinnamon and soda; pour mixture into pan.
3 Bake, uncovered, about 50 minutes. Stand cake in pan 5 minutes. Turn onto wire rack over tray; remove paper.
4 Make espresso syrup; drizzle half of the hot syrup over hot cake. Serve immediately with remaining hot syrup.

ESPRESSO SYRUP stir sugar, coffee and the water in small saucepan, over heat, without boiling, until sugar dissolves. Bring to a boil; transfer to heatproof jug.

SERVES 8
per serving 4.7g total fat (2.8g saturated fat); 1659kj (396 cal); 6g protein; 84g carbohydrate; 3.1g fibre
serving suggestion serve hot pudding with low-fat vanilla ice-cream.

citrus rice pudding

PREPARATION TIME 15 MINUTES (PLUS STANDING TIME) COOKING TIME 1 HOUR 10 MINUTES

Also labelled "clever rice", doongara rice is a white long-grain rice grown in Australia that can be found at your local supermarket. You will need to cook about ½ cup of rice for this recipe.

2 cups (500ml) no-fat milk
1 vanilla bean, halved lengthways
1 teaspoon finely grated lemon rind
1 teaspoon finely grated lime rind
2 teaspoons finely grated orange rind
2 eggs
1 egg white
½ cup (110g) caster sugar
1½ cups (225g) cooked doongara rice
½ cup (125ml) low-fat cream

1. Preheat oven to 160°C/140°C fan-forced. Grease shallow oval 1.5-litre (6 cup) ovenproof dish.
2. Combine milk, vanilla bean and rinds in medium saucepan; bring to a boil. Remove from heat; stand, covered, 5 minutes.
3. Meanwhile, whisk eggs, egg white and sugar in medium bowl. Gradually whisk hot milk mixture into egg mixture; discard vanilla bean.
4. Spread rice into dish; pour egg mixture carefully over rice. Place dish in large baking dish; add enough boiling water to baking dish to come halfway up side of pudding dish.
5. Bake, uncovered, about 1 hour or until set. Serve warm with cream.

SERVES 8
per serving 4.8g total fat (2.7g saturated fat); 973kj (232 cal); 7.1g protein; 40.4g carbohydrate; 0.3g fibre

apple bread pudding

PREPARATION TIME 20 MINUTES COOKING TIME 1 HOUR 10 MINUTES (PLUS STANDING TIME)

2 medium apples (300g)
2 tablespoons brown sugar
1 tablespoon water
2½ cups (625ml) no-fat milk
1 vanilla bean, halved lengthways
4 slices thick fruit bread
3 eggs
½ teaspoon ground cinnamon
¼ teaspoon ground nutmeg

1. Peel, core and quarter apples; cut each quarter into 3mm slices. Stir brown sugar and the water in medium frying pan over low heat, add apples; simmer, uncovered, about 5 minutes or until tender, stirring occasionally.
2. Preheat oven to 160°C/140°C fan-forced. Grease deep 1.5-litre (6 cup) ovenproof dish.
3. Combine milk and vanilla bean in medium saucepan; bring to a boil. Remove from heat; stand, covered, 5 minutes. Discard vanilla bean.
4. Meanwhile, cut bread slices into quarters. Arrange bread and apple in alternate layers in dish.
5. Whisk eggs, cinnamon and nutmeg in medium bowl. Gradually whisk hot milk mixture into egg mixture. Pour egg mixture carefully over bread and apple. Place dish in large baking dish; add enough boiling water to baking dish to come halfway up side of pudding dish.
6. Bake, uncovered, about 1 hour or until set. Serve with low-fat ice-cream or cream, if desired.

SERVES 6
per serving 3.4g total fat (1g saturated fat); 714kj (171 cal); 9.5g protein; 25.5g carbohydrate; 1.6g fibre

mocha self-saucing pudding

PREPARATION TIME 10 MINUTES COOKING TIME 45 MINUTES

Originally the name of a Middle-Eastern seaport from which premium arabic coffee was exported, the word mocha has evolved to describe the serendipitous combination of coffee and chocolate.

1 cup (150g) self-raising flour
⅓ cup (35g) cocoa powder
¾ cup (165g) caster sugar
2½ teaspoons instant coffee granules
½ cup (125ml) skim milk
1 tablespoon vegetable oil
½ cup (100g) firmly packed brown sugar
1¼ cups (310ml) boiling water
1 tablespoon icing sugar

1. Preheat oven to 160°C/140°C fan-forced.
2. Sift flour, 2 tablespoons of the cocoa, sugar and 2 teaspoons of the coffee granules into 1.25-litre (5-cup) ovenproof dish; gradually stir in milk and oil.
3. Sift brown sugar, remaining cocoa and remaining coffee evenly over flour mixture; gently pour the water over pudding mixture.
4. Bake, uncovered, about 45 minutes. Serve dusted with sifted icing sugar.

SERVES 4
per serving 6.3g total fat (1.4g saturated fat); 1958kj (468 cal); 7g protein; 98.5g carbohydrate; 2.2g fibre
tip this recipe is best served hot as the pudding will quickly absorb the sauce.

rich chocolate self-saucing pudding

PREPARATION TIME 15 MINUTES COOKING TIME 40 MINUTES

cooking-oil spray
1 cup (150g) self-raising flour
¾ cup (165g) caster sugar
2 tablespoons cocoa powder
½ cup (125ml) skim milk
1 teaspoon vanilla essence
30g monounsaturated or polyunsaturated margarine, melted
½ cup (100g) firmly packed brown sugar
2 tablespoons cocoa powder, extra
1⅓ cups (330ml) hot water

1. Preheat oven to 180°C/160°C fan-forced. Coat six ¾-cup (180ml) dishes with cooking-oil spray.
2. Sift flour, caster sugar and cocoa into large bowl. Add combined milk, essence and margarine; stir until smooth.
3. Divide mixture among dishes; sift combined brown sugar and extra cocoa evenly over top. Carefully pour the hot water over each pudding. Bake, uncovered, about 40 minutes or until puddings are firm.
4. Serve dusted with sifted cocoa powder, if desired.

SERVES 6
per serving 4.9g total fat (1.3g saturated fat); 1288kj (308 cal); 4.2g protein; 63.5g carbohydrate; 1.2g fibre
tip recipe best cooked just before serving.

grilled figs with cinnamon-scented ricotta

PREPARATION TIME 10 MINUTES COOKING TIME 5 MINUTES

9 large figs (720g), halved
¼ cup (60ml) lime juice
¼ cup (50g) firmly packed brown sugar
1 cup (200g) low-fat ricotta cheese
½ teaspoon ground cinnamon
1 tablespoon caster sugar

1 Preheat grill. Place figs, cut-side up, on large oven tray; brush with combined juice and brown sugar. Place under grill until figs are browned lightly.
2 Meanwhile, combine cheese, cinnamon and caster sugar in small bowl. Serve ricotta mixture with figs.

SERVES 6
per serving 3.3g total fat (1.9g saturated fat); 555kj (133 cal); 5.3g protein; 21g carbohydrate; 3g fibre
serving suggestion serve with a glass of chilled sauternes.

peach galette

PREPARATION TIME 10 MINUTES COOKING TIME 15 MINUTES

A galette is a French flaky pastry tart that can be either savoury or sweet, and makes a popular summer dessert. Any of the season's stone fruits, such as plums or nectarines, can be substituted for the peaches.

1 sheet ready-rolled puff pastry with canola, thawed
3 medium peaches (450g)
1 tablespoon brown sugar
1 tablespoon plum jam, warmed, strained

1 Preheat oven to 220°C/200°C fan-forced. Grease oven tray; place pastry sheet on tray.
2 Place unpeeled peaches in large heatproof bowl; cover with boiling water. Stand about 1 minute or until skins can be slipped off peaches easily. Slice peaches thinly; discard seeds.
3 Arrange peach slices on pastry, leaving 2cm border around edge; fold over edges of pastry. Sprinkle sugar evenly over peach galette.
4 Bake, uncovered, about 15 minutes or until pastry is browned lightly. Brush hot galette with jam.

SERVES 6
per serving 6.4g total fat (0.5g saturated fat); 597kj (143 cal); 2.2g protein; 19.1g carbohydrate; 1.3g fibre
serving suggestion serve dusted with icing sugar.

apple and plum strudel with vanilla yogurt

PREPARATION TIME 45 MINUTES COOKING TIME 45 MINUTES (PLUS COOLING TIME)

cooking-oil spray
2 large apples (400g), peeled, cored
825g can whole dark plums, drained
2 teaspoons grated lemon rind
⅓ cup (65g) firmly packed brown sugar
¼ cup (60ml) maple-flavoured syrup
¼ cup (60ml) water
1 cinnamon stick
½ cup (60g) almond meal
6 sheets fillo pastry

VANILLA YOGURT

⅓ cup (80ml) low-fat milk
¾ cup (180ml) low-fat yogurt
2 teaspoons vanilla essence
¼ cup (40g) icing sugar

1. Preheat oven to 180°C/160°C fan-forced. Coat oven tray with cooking-oil spray. Cut each apple into 12 pieces. Halve plums; discard stones.
2. Cook apples, rind, sugar, syrup, water and cinnamon in large saucepan, stirring over low heat, without boiling, until sugar is dissolved; bring to a boil. Simmer, uncovered, about 10 minutes or until apples are just tender, stirring occasionally.
3. Drain apples, discard cinnamon and syrup; cool. Combine apples, plums and nuts in medium bowl.
4. Layer pastry sheets together, coating every second sheet with cooking-oil spray. Spoon apple mixture along long edge of pastry, leaving 8cm border at each end. Roll up strudel, tucking in ends while rolling, coat lightly with cooking-oil spray. Place strudel on oven tray; bake, uncovered, 30 minutes or until browned.
5. Make vanilla yogurt.
6. Dust strudel with sifted icing sugar; sprinkle with candied lemon rind, if desired. Serve with vanilla yogurt.

VANILLA YOGURT combine ingredients in small bowl.

SERVES 6
per serving 6.4g total fat (0.6g saturated fat); 1257kj (300 cal); 6.3g protein; 55.3g carbohydrate; 3.3g fibre
tip strudel and vanilla yogurt can be prepared a day ahead. Store, covered separately, in refrigerator.

blueberry and fillo pastry stacks

PREPARATION TIME 15 MINUTES COOKING TIME 10 MINUTES

4 sheets fillo pastry

cooking-oil spray

125g packaged light cream cheese

½ cup (125ml) light cream

2 teaspoons finely grated orange rind

2 tablespoons icing sugar

BLUEBERRY SAUCE

300g blueberries

¼ cup (55g) caster sugar

2 tablespoons orange juice

1 teaspoon cornflour

1. Preheat oven to 200°C/180°C fan-forced. Grease oven trays.
2. Coat one fillo sheet with oil; layer with another fillo sheet. Halve fillo stack lengthways; cut each half into thirds to form six fillo squares. Repeat process with remaining fillo sheets. Place 12 fillo squares onto trays; coat with oil. Bake, uncovered, about 5 minutes or until browned lightly; cool 10 minutes.
3. Meanwhile, make blueberry sauce.
4. Beat cheese, cream, rind and half of the sugar in small bowl with electric mixer until smooth.
5. Place one fillo square on each serving plate; spoon half of the cheese mixture and half of the blueberry sauce over squares. Repeat layering process, finishing with fillo squares; dust with remaining sifted sugar.

BLUEBERRY SAUCE cook blueberries, sugar and half of the juice in small saucepan, stirring, until sugar dissolves. Stir in blended cornflour and remaining juice; cook, stirring, until mixture boils and thickens slightly. Remove from heat; cool 10 minutes.

SERVES 4

per serving 14.9g total fat (9.2g saturated fat); 1336kj (319 cal); 7.4g protein; 40.2g carbohydrate; 1.8g fibre

mini éclairs with vanilla cream

PREPARATION TIME 15 MINUTES COOKING TIME 30 MINUTES (PLUS COOLING TIME)

1 teaspoon monounsaturated or polyunsaturated margarine
½ cup (125ml) water
⅓ cup (50g) self-raising flour
2 egg whites
1 tablespoon icing sugar

VANILLA CREAM
200g low-fat vanilla yogurt
1 teaspoon gelatine
2 teaspoons water

1 Make vanilla cream.

2 Preheat oven to 220°C/200°C fan-forced.

3 Place margarine and the water in medium saucepan; bring to a boil. Add sifted flour all at once, stirring vigorously for about 30 seconds or until smooth. Transfer mixture to small bowl of electric mixer; cool for 5 minutes. Gradually add egg whites, beating well between each addition. Mixture will separate, but will come together with further beating.

4 Spoon mixture into piping bag fitted with 1cm piping tube. Pipe 12 x 5cm thick lengths of mixture onto oven tray. Bake, uncovered, 10 minutes.

5 Reduce oven temperature to 180°C/160°C fan-forced; bake, uncovered, further 15 minutes or until well browned. Cool.

6 When éclairs are cold, cut in half. Scoop out any uncooked mixture; discard. Fill éclairs with vanilla cream; dust with a little sifted icing sugar. Serve with mixed berries, if desired.

VANILLA CREAM allow yogurt to come to room temperature. Sprinkle gelatine over the water in cup. Stand in small saucepan of simmering water. Stir until dissolved; cool. Combine yogurt and gelatine mixture in medium bowl; refrigerate until set.

MAKES 12
per serving 0.6g total fat (0.2g saturated fat); 168kj (40 cal); 2.1g protein; 6.6g carbohydrate; 0.2g fibre
tip unfilled éclairs can be made ahead and frozen until required. Eclairs are best assembled just before serving.

mini éclairs with vanilla cream

fig and orange pinwheels

fig and orange pinwheels

PREPARATION TIME 15 MINUTES (PLUS STANDING TIME) COOKING TIME 20 MINUTES (PLUS COOLING TIME)

These pinwheels may be drizzled with a simple orange icing if desired, but remember, it will add extra kilojoules.

1¾ cups (250g) dried figs, chopped finely
¼ cup (60ml) orange juice
3 cups (450g) self-raising flour
20g monounsaturated or polyunsaturated margarine
1 tablespoon grated orange rind
1 cup (250ml) skim milk
¼ cup (60ml) water, approximately

1 Combine figs and juice in large bowl; stand for several hours or overnight.

2 Preheat oven to 220°C/200°C fan-forced. Grease deep round 23cm cake pan; line base with baking paper.

3 Sift flour into large bowl; rub in margarine. Stir in rind and milk with enough of the water to mix to a firm dough; knead on floured surface until smooth. Roll dough to 20cm x 40cm rectangle. Sprinkle fig mixture evenly over dough. Roll up dough from long side; cut into 12 slices.

4 Place slices in pan; bake, uncovered, about 20 minutes or until cooked through. Stand for 5 minutes before turning onto wire rack to cool.

MAKES 12
per pinwheel 1.8g total fat (0.3g saturated fat); 814kj (194 cal); 5.3g protein; 39.3g carbohydrate; 4.5g fibre
tip recipe can be made 3 hours ahead. Store in an airtight container, or freeze.

fresh figs in honey and fennel syrup with muscat granita

PREPARATION TIME 15 MINUTES COOKING TIME 10 MINUTES (PLUS COOLING AND FREEZING TIME)

Muscat is a sweet, aromatic dessert wine, possessing an almost musty flavour. It is made from the fully matured muscatel grape. Tokay, sweet riesling or gewürztraminer can be substituted for the muscat in the granita; drink what remains of the wine with this dessert.

½ cup (110g) caster sugar

1 teaspoon black peppercorns

1 teaspoon finely grated lemon rind

1 tablespoon lemon juice

1 cup (250ml) water

½ cup (125ml) muscat

1 tablespoon fennel seeds

½ cup (125ml) water, extra

¼ cup (90g) honey

8 large fresh figs (640g)

1. Combine sugar, peppercorns, rind, juice, the water and muscat in small saucepan; bring to a boil. Cool 10 minutes; strain into 14cm x 21cm loaf pan. Cover with foil; freeze about 4 hours or until firm, scraping granita from bottom and sides of pan with fork every hour.
2. Dry-fry fennel seeds in small saucepan until fragrant. Add the extra water and honey; bring to a boil. Reduce heat, simmer, uncovered, without stirring, about 5 minutes or until mixture thickens slightly. Strain through sieve into small jug; discard seeds. Cool syrup 10 minutes.
3. Cut figs lengthways into five slices; divide among serving plates, drizzle with syrup, top with granita.

SERVES 4

per serving 0.4g total fat (0g saturated fat); 1052kj (251 cal); 2g protein; 56.6g carbohydrate; 3.3g fibre

lime and lemon grass mangoes

PREPARATION TIME 10 MINUTES COOKING TIME 20 MINUTES

2 cups (440g) sugar

2 cups (500ml) water

1 tablespoon finely grated lime rind

¼ cup (60ml) lime juice

10cm piece (20g) fresh lemon grass, sliced finely

2 kaffir lime leaves, sliced finely

4 large mangoes (2.4kg)

1. Stir sugar, water, rind, juice, lemon grass and lime leaves in medium saucepan, over low heat, until sugar dissolves; bring to a boil. Reduce heat, simmer, uncovered, about 15 minutes or until syrup has thickened slightly.
2. Meanwhile, cut through mango lengthways, on each side of seed, to give two cheeks; peel away skin.
3. Place mango cheeks in large heatproof bowl; pour syrup over mango, serve warm or cold.

SERVES 4
per serving 0.9g total fat (0g saturated fat); 2780kj (664 cal); 4.4g protein; 163.8g carbohydrate; 6.5g fibre

poached pears in asian-spiced syrup

PREPARATION TIME 5 MINUTES COOKING TIME 40 MINUTES

6 medium pears (1.2kg)

2 cups (440g) sugar

1 litre (4 cups) water

1 vanilla bean

2 cinnamon sticks

2 star anise

2 cardamom pods, bruised

1. Peel pears, leaving stems intact.
2. Stir sugar and the water in large saucepan over heat, without boiling, until sugar dissolves. Split vanilla bean in half lengthways; scrape seeds directly into sugar syrup.
3. Add pears to syrup with cinnamon, star anise and cardamom; bring to a boil. Reduce heat, simmer, covered, about 20 minutes or until pears are just tender, turning occasionally. Remove from heat; cool in syrup.
4. Remove pears from syrup. Strain syrup over medium jug; discard solids and all but 2 cups of the syrup.
5. Bring reserved syrup to a boil in small saucepan. Reduce heat, simmer, uncovered, about 15 minutes or until syrup reduces by half. Remove from heat; cool.
6. Divide pears among serving bowls; drizzle with syrup.

SERVES 6
per serving 0.2g total fat (0g saturated fat); 1515kj (362 cal); 0.5g protein; 93.7g carbohydrate; 3.7g fibre
serving suggestion serve with whipped light cream or low-fat fruit yogurt.

chocolate ricotta tart

PREPARATION TIME 15 MINUTES (PLUS REFRIGERATION TIME) COOKING TIME 35 MINUTES

¼ cup (35g) white self-raising flour
¼ cup (40g) wholemeal self-raising flour
2 tablespoons caster sugar
2 teaspoons cocoa powder
30g low-fat dairy-free spread
2 teaspoons water
1 egg yolk

RICOTTA FILLING

150g low-fat ricotta cheese
1 egg
1 egg yolk
¼ cup (70g) low-fat yogurt
¼ cup (55g) caster sugar
2 teaspoons white plain flour
2 tablespoons dark choc bits
2 teaspoons coffee-flavoured liqueur

1. Grease 18cm round loose-based flan tin.
2. Process flours, sugar, sifted cocoa and spread until crumbly; add the water and egg yolk, process until ingredients just cling together. Knead dough gently on floured surface until smooth. Cover; refrigerate 30 minutes.
3. Preheat oven to 200°C/180°C fan-forced.
4. Press dough into flan tin; cover with enough baking paper to extend 5cm over edge, fill with dried beans or rice. Place tin on oven tray; bake 10 minutes. Remove beans and paper; bake further 5 minutes or until pastry is lightly browned. Cool.
5. Meanwhile, make ricotta filling.
6. Reduce oven temperature to 180°C/160°C fan-forced.
7. Pour filling into tin; bake, uncovered, about 20 minutes. Cool; refrigerate until firm.

RICOTTA FILLING beat ricotta, egg, egg yolk, yogurt, sugar and flour in medium bowl with electric mixer until smooth. Stir in choc bits and liqueur.

SERVES 8
per serving 6.1g total fat (2.5g saturated fat); 581kj (139 cal); 4.9g protein; 16.2g carbohydrate; 0.7g fibre

mango lime syrup cake

PREPARATION TIME 20 MINUTES COOKING TIME 20 MINUTES

30g butter, melted

2 tablespoons brown sugar

1 large mango (600g), sliced thinly

2 eggs

⅓ cup (75g) caster sugar

½ cup (75g) wheaten cornflour

1 tablespoon custard powder

½ teaspoon cream of tartar

¼ teaspoon bicarbonate of soda

LIME SYRUP

¾ cup (165g) caster sugar

⅓ cup (80ml) lime juice

⅓ cup (80ml) water

2 teaspoons finely grated lime rind

1. Preheat oven to 200°C/180°C fan-forced. Grease deep 22cm-round cake pan.
2. Pour butter over base of pan; sift brown sugar evenly over butter, top with mango slices.
3. Beat eggs and sugar in small bowl with electric mixer about 5 minutes or until thick and creamy.
4. Sift dry ingredients three times onto baking paper; fold into egg mixture. Pour sponge mixture into pan; bake, uncovered, about 20 minutes.
5. Meanwhile, make lime syrup.
6. Turn cake onto wire rack set over tray; pour half of the lime syrup over hot cake. Serve cake with remaining syrup.

LIME SYRUP stir sugar, juice and the water in small saucepan over heat, without boiling, until sugar dissolves; bring to a boil. Boil, uncovered, without stirring, about 5 minutes or until syrup thickens slightly. Cool 10 minutes; stir in rind.

SERVES 8

per serving 4.5g total fat (2.4g saturated fat); 1021kj (244 cal); 2.3g protein; 49.7g carbohydrate; 0.9g fibre

tip you can make lime syrup a day ahead. Store, covered, in refrigerator.

ginger and almond biscotti ice-cream sandwiches

PREPARATION TIME 25 MINUTES (PLUS STANDING AND REFRIGERATION TIME) COOKING TIME 45 MINUTES

3 egg whites
½ cup (110g) caster sugar
1 teaspoon vanilla extract
¾ cup (110g) plain flour
¼ cup (30g) almond meal
2 tablespoons finely chopped crystallised ginger
¼ cup (40g) toasted blanched almonds
⅔ cup (160ml) low-fat ice-cream

1. Preheat oven to 180°C/160°C fan-forced. Grease 8cm x 25cm bar cake pan; line base and long sides with baking paper, extending paper 5cm over sides of pan.
2. Beat egg whites in small bowl with electric mixer until soft peaks form. With motor operating, gradually add sugar, beating, until sugar dissolves. Beat in extract then fold in flour, almond meal, ginger and nuts.
3. Spread mixture into pan; bake, uncovered, about 25 minutes or until firm. Cool to room temperature in pan. Cover; refrigerate 2 hours.
4. Preheat oven to 160°C/140°C fan-forced. Line oven tray with baking paper.
5. Trim short ends of loaf; cut loaf crossways into four equal pieces. Trim all brown sides from pieces; slice each piece horizontally into four pieces. Place on tray; bake, uncovered, about 20 minutes or until biscotti are crisp and browned lightly. Cool on tray.
6. Sandwich biscotti with ice-cream.

MAKES 8
per sandwich 7.2g total fat (1.1g saturated fat); 825kj (197 cal); 6.1g protein; 27.7g carbohydrate; 1.3g fibre
tip biscotti can be made up to a week ahead. Store in an airtight container.

strawberry almond tart

PREPARATION TIME 40 MINUTES (PLUS REFRIGERATION TIME) COOKING TIME 20 MINUTES

1¼ cups (185g) self-raising flour
⅓ cup (40g) almond meal
2 tablespoons caster sugar
30g butter or margarine
½ cup (125ml) low-fat sour cream
cooking-oil spray
500g strawberries, halved
2 tablespoons apricot jam, warmed, sieved

FILLING

¾ cup (150g) low-fat ricotta cheese
200g carton low-fat vanilla fromage frais
2 tablespoons icing sugar
½ teaspoon grated orange rind

1 Process flour, nuts, sugar and butter until mixture resembles breadcrumbs. Add cream, process until ingredients just come together. Press dough into a ball, knead gently on floured surface until smooth. Cover; refrigerate 30 minutes.

2 Coat 24cm round loose-base flan tin with cooking-oil spray. Roll pastry between sheets of baking paper until large enough to line flan tin. Lift pastry into tin, ease into side, trim edge. Prick base with fork; refrigerate 30 minutes.

3 Preheat oven to 200°C/180°C fan-forced.

4 Cover pastry with baking paper, fill with dried beans or rice; place on oven tray. Bake 10 minutes. Remove paper and beans carefully from pastry case; bake further 10 minutes or until browned. Cool.

5 Meanwhile, make filling.

6 Spread filling into pastry case, top with strawberries, brush with jam.

FILLING combine ingredients in small bowl.

SERVES 8

per serving 14g total fat (5.9g saturated fat); 1201kj (287 cal); 8.3g protein; 32.5g carbohydrate; 2.8g fibre

tip recipe can be made a day ahead. Store, covered, in refrigerator.

grilled bananas with malibu syrup

PREPARATION TIME 10 MINUTES COOKING TIME 5 MINUTES

Malibu is the brand name of a rum-based coconut liqueur

4 large ripe bananas (920g)
⅓ cup (80ml) maple syrup
2 tablespoons malibu
¼ cup (15g) shredded coconut, toasted

1 Split bananas lengthways. Combine maple syrup and liqueur; brush about a quarter of the mixture over the cut-sides of bananas.

2 Cook bananas, cut-side down, on heated oiled grill plate (or grill or barbecue) until lightly browned and heated through.

3 Serve bananas while hot, drizzled with warmed remaining syrup and toasted coconut.

SERVES 4
per serving 2.7g total fat (2.2g saturated fat); 1104kj (264 cal); 2.9g protein; 54.3g carbohydrate; 3.9g fibre
serving suggestion serve with whipped cream and small glasses of espresso.

petite pecan pies

PREPARATION TIME 15 MINUTES COOKING TIME 20 MINUTES

8 x 8cm-square fresh wonton wrappers
2 tablespoons pecans
1 egg white, beaten lightly
1 tablespoon light corn syrup
2 tablespoons brown sugar
1 teaspoon low-fat margarine, melted

1 Preheat oven to 160°C/140°C fan-forced. Grease four holes of 12-hole ⅓-cup (80ml) muffin pan.

2 Place one wrapper in each muffin hole; top with another wrapper, ensuring corners do not cover those of first wrapper. Bake, uncovered, 5 minutes or until crisp and browned lightly; cool.

3 Slice pecans into thirds lengthways, combine with remaining ingredients in small bowl; pour into wonton cases. Bake, uncovered, further 15 minutes or until set; cool in pans.

SERVES 4
per serving 3.6g total fat (0.3g saturated fat); 472kj (113 cal); 2.4g protein; 18.1g carbohydrate; 0.7g fibre
tip recipe can be made 2 days ahead. Store in airtight container.

apple and date meringue pie

PREPARATION TIME 30 MINUTES (PLUS COOLING TIME) COOKING TIME 30 MINUTES (PLUS COOLING TIME)

cooking-oil spray
30g butter
2 tablespoons caster sugar
1½ cups (225g) self-raising flour
2 tablespoons custard powder
⅓ cup (80ml) low-fat evaporated milk, approximately

FILLING

4 large apples (800g), peeled, chopped
1 cup (250ml) apple juice
½ teaspoon ground cinnamon
1 tablespoon caster sugar
10 seedless fresh dates (230g), chopped coarsely
1 tablespoon cornflour
1 tablespoon water

MERINGUE

3 egg whites
⅔ cup (150g) caster sugar

1 Coat 24cm round loose-base flan tin with cooking-oil spray.
2 Process butter, sugar, flour and custard powder until combined. Add enough milk to make ingredients just come together. Knead on floured surface until smooth, wrap in plastic, refrigerate 30 minutes.
3 Preheat oven to 200°C/180°C fan-forced.
4 Roll dough on floured surface until large enough to line flan tin. Lift pastry into tin, ease into side, trim edge. Cover pastry with baking paper, fill with dried beans or rice, place on oven tray. Bake 10 minutes. Remove paper and beans carefully from pastry case; bake further 5 minutes or until browned. Cool.
5 Reduce oven temperature to 180°C/160°C fan-forced.
6 Make filling. Make meringue.
7 Spoon filling into pastry case, top with meringue. Bake, uncovered, about 5 minutes or until lightly browned.

FILLING combine apples, juice, cinnamon and sugar in large saucepan; bring to a boil. Reduce heat, simmer, uncovered, until apples are just tender. Add dates, cook, stirring, 1 minute. Add blended cornflour and water, stir until mixture boils and thickens; cool.

MERINGUE beat egg whites in small bowl with electric mixer until soft peaks form; gradually add sugar, beating until dissolved between additions.

SERVES 8
per serving 4.1g total fat (2.3g saturated fat); 1383kj (331 cal); 5.4g protein; 69.4g carbohydrate; 3.8g fibre
tip pastry case can be made a day ahead; store in airtight container until required. Assemble pie just before serving.

chocolate brownies

PREPARATION TIME 15 MINUTES COOKING TIME 25 MINUTES

2 eggs
⅓ cup (75g) firmly packed brown sugar
2 teaspoons instant coffee granules
2 tablespoons cocoa powder
1 tablespoon water
1 tablespoon olive oil
40g low-fat dairy-free spread, melted
¼ cup (40g) wholemeal self-raising flour
¼ cup (45g) dark chocolate choc bits
1 teaspoon cocoa powder, extra
2 teaspoons icing sugar

1 Preheat oven to 180°C/160°C fan-forced. Grease deep 19cm-square pan; line base with baking paper.
2 Beat eggs and sugar in small bowl with electric mixer until thick and creamy. Transfer to medium bowl.
3 Meanwhile, blend coffee and cocoa with the water and oil in small bowl until smooth. Stir in spread. Fold cocoa mixture into egg mixture; fold in flour and choc bits. Pour mixture into pan.
4 Bake, uncovered, about 25 minutes or until brownie is firm to the touch. Stand 30 minutes; turn onto wire rack. Cut into 16 squares.
5 Serve brownies dusted with sifted combined extra cocoa and icing sugar, and low-fat ice-cream, if desired.

MAKES 16
per brownie 3.8g total fat (1.1g saturated fat); 303kj (72 cal); 1.5g protein; 8.5g carbohydrate; 0.4g fibre

poached pear, date and orange compote

PREPARATION TIME 40 MINUTES (PLUS COOLING AND REFRIGERATION TIME) COOKING TIME 20 MINUTES

4 medium firm pears (720g)

3 medium oranges (540g)

⅓ cup (75g) caster sugar

2 cups (500ml) apple juice

½ cup (125ml) orange juice

1 cup (250ml) water

1 cinnamon stick

12 fresh dates (250g), seeded, halved

2 tablespoons cointreau

SPICED CREAM

⅓ cup (65g) low-fat ricotta cheese, sieved

½ cup (125ml) low-fat sour cream

1 tablespoon honey

½ teaspoon ground cinnamon

1. Peel pears. Using a zester, cut grooves into pears at an angle.
2. Using vegetable peeler, peel rind thinly from one orange; cut rind into strips. Peel remaining oranges, discard seeds and pith, cut all oranges between membranes into segments.
3. Stir sugar, juices, the water and cinnamon in large saucepan over heat, without boiling, until sugar is dissolved. Add pears and rind, simmer, covered, about 15 minutes or until pears are just tender.
4. Place pears in large heatproof bowl, pour hot syrup over pears. Add orange segments, dates and liqueur; cool. Cover; refrigerate 3 hours or overnight.
5. Just before serving, make spiced cream.

SPICED CREAM combine ingredients in small bowl.

SERVES 8

per serving 4.1g total fat (2.6g saturated fat); 934kj (223 cal); 2.5g protein; 43.6g carbohydrate; 3.8g fibre

tip compote and spiced cream can be made a day ahead. Store, covered separately, in refrigerator.

custard tarts with low-fat sweet pastry

PREPARATION TIME 20 MINUTES (PLUS REFRIGERATION TIME) COOKING TIME 20 MINUTES (PLUS COOLING TIME)

1 cup (150g) plain flour
2 tablespoons icing sugar
1 tablespoon custard powder
20g monounsaturated or polyunsaturated margarine
¼ cup cold water (60ml), approximately
250g small strawberries, halved
75g blueberries
2 tablespoons diet apricot jam, sieved
2 teaspoons boiling water

CUSTARD FILLING

2 teaspoons gelatine
2 tablespoons water
1 tablespoon caster sugar
1½ tablespoons custard powder
1 cup (250ml) skim milk
1 teaspoon vanilla essence

1. Place flour, sugar, custard powder and margarine in large bowl of food processor; process until combined. With motor operating, add enough of the water until mixture just begins to form a ball. Knead dough on lightly floured surface until smooth. Cover; refrigerate for 30 minutes.
2. Preheat oven to 180°C/160°C fan-forced.
3. Divide dough into four portions; roll out dough until 5mm thick. Place into four deep 10cm fluted flan tins. Line each pastry case with a piece of baking paper, filled with dried beans or rice; place on oven tray. Bake about 10 minutes. Remove paper and beans; bake further 10 minutes or until lightly browned. Cool in tins.
4. Meanwhile, make custard filling.
5. Remove pastry cases from tins; fill with custard filling. Refrigerate until custard is set.
6. Arrange berries on tarts; brush with combined jam and the boiling water.

CUSTARD FILLING sprinkle gelatine over the water in cup; stand in small saucepan of simmering water. Stir until dissolved. Combine sugar with custard powder in small saucepan; gradually stir in milk. Stir over heat until mixture boils and thickens. Stir in essence and gelatine mixture.

MAKES 4
per tart 4.1g total fat (0.7g saturated fat); 1096kj (262 cal); 8.8g protein; 47.4g carbohydrate; 3.2g fibre
tip tarts can be made a day ahead. Store, covered, in refrigerator.

fresh figs and dates in saffron syrup

PREPARATION TIME 25 MINUTES (PLUS COOLING TIME) COOKING TIME 30 MINUTES

cooking-oil spray

½ cup (110g) caster sugar

¾ cup (180ml) water

1 cup (250ml) dry white wine

5cm piece orange rind

pinch saffron threads

1 cinnamon stick

12 medium fresh figs (600g), halved

8 seedless fresh dates

CRISP BISCUITS

30g soft butter or margarine

¼ cup (55g) caster sugar

1 egg white

2½ tablespoons plain flour

1. Preheat oven to 220°C/200°C fan-forced. Coat oven trays with cooking-oil spray; make crisp biscuits.
2. Stir sugar, the water and wine in medium saucepan over heat, without boiling, until sugar is dissolved. Add rind, saffron and cinnamon, simmer 15 minutes, strain; discard cinnamon, rind and threads.
3. Add figs to saffron syrup, boil, uncovered, about 3 minutes or until syrup is thickened slightly. Remove from heat, add dates, cover; cool. Serve with crisp biscuits.

CRISP BISCUITS beat butter, sugar and egg white in small bowl with electric mixer on low speed until smooth and changed in colour; stir in sifted flour. Spoon mixture into piping bag fitted with 5mm plain tube. Pipe 8cm lengths onto oven trays; make biscuits slightly wider at both ends. Allow six biscuits per tray. Tap tray on bench to make biscuits spread slightly. Bake, uncovered, about 5 minutes or until edges are browned. Lift onto wire racks to cool.

SERVES 4

per serving 7.5g total fat (4.2g saturated fat); 1708kj (408 cal); 4.4g protein; 73.1g carbohydrate; 6.1g fibre

tip recipe can be made a day ahead. Store fruits in saffron syrup, covered, in refrigerator; crisp biscuits, in airtight container.

caramelised oranges with ice-cream

PREPARATION TIME 10 MINUTES COOKING TIME 10 MINUTES

Navel or jaffa (spanish) oranges are ideal for this recipe because they have very few seeds.

4 large oranges (1.2kg)

2 tablespoons brown sugar

2 tablespoons grand marnier

200g low-fat vanilla ice-cream

1 Peel oranges, removing as much white pith as possible; cut crossways into thick slices.
2 Preheat grill. Place orange, in single layer, on oven tray. Sprinkle with sugar; drizzle with liqueur. Place under grill, cooking orange on both sides until just caramelised.
3 Divide ice-cream and orange among serving dishes; drizzle with pan juices.

SERVES 4
per serving 3.5g total fat (2.1g saturated fat); 834kj (199 cal); 4.9g protein; 35.4g carbohydrate; 4.3g fibre
serving suggestion sprinkle with finely chopped mint or purple basil.
tip cointreau or triple sec can be substituted for grand marnier.

stone-fruit jelly

PREPARATION TIME 15 MINUTES (PLUS REFRIGERATION TIME) COOKING TIME 10 MINUTES

We used a sparkling white wine having a sweet, fruity flavour for this recipe.

½ cup (110g) caster sugar

3 cups (750ml) sparkling white wine

2 tablespoons gelatine

½ cup (125ml) water

2 tablespoons lemon juice

1 large nectarine (170g), sliced thinly

2 medium apricots (100g), sliced thinly

1 medium peach (150g), sliced thinly

150g raspberries

1 Combine sugar and 1 cup of the wine in small saucepan; bring to a boil. Reduce heat, simmer, uncovered, 5 minutes. Transfer to large heatproof bowl.
2 Meanwhile, sprinkle gelatine over the water in small heatproof jug. Stand jug in small saucepan of simmering water; stir until gelatine dissolves.
3 Whisk gelatine mixture and juice into warm wine mixture. Stir in remaining wine.
4 Divide fruit among four 1¼-cup (310ml) serving glasses; pour wine mixture over fruit. Cover; refrigerate about 3 hours or until set.

SERVES 4
per serving 0.3g total fat (0g saturated fat); 1248kj (298 cal); 7.3g protein; 38.6g carbohydrate; 3.9g fibre

pineapple crunch

PREPARATION TIME 10 MINUTES COOKING TIME 20 MINUTES

We used just right breakfast cereal in this recipe but you can use any flake and dried fruit cereal, even a muesli or granola-like product.

850g can crushed pineapple, drained
2 small nashis (360g), chopped coarsely
1 tablespoon malibu liqueur
3 cups (150g) just right
2 tablespoons pepitas
2 tablespoons sunflower seeds
⅓ cup (95g) low-fat yogurt
2 tablespoons honey

1. Preheat oven to 180°C/160°C fan-forced. Grease four 1-cup (250ml) ovenproof dishes; place on oven tray.
2. Combine pineapple, nashi and malibu in medium bowl; divide among prepared dishes.
3. Using one hand, crumble cereal in same bowl; stir in seeds, yogurt and honey. Divide mixture among prepared dishes.
4. Bake, uncovered, about 20 minutes or until browned lightly.

SERVES 4
per serving 7.8g total fat (1.4g saturated fat); 1443kj (345 cal); 8.1g protein; 60g carbohydrate; 7.9g fibre
tip you can substitute chopped, drained canned peaches or apricots for the pineapple in this recipe.
serving suggestion serve topped with low-fat yogurt or low-fat ice-cream and a dollop of fresh passionfruit pulp or drizzle of honey.

chocolate fudge cake

PREPARATION TIME 20 MINUTES COOKING TIME 40 MINUTES

85g dark chocolate, chopped finely
½ cup (50g) cocoa powder
1 cup (200g) firmly packed brown sugar
½ cup (125ml) boiling water
2 egg yolks
¼ cup (30g) almond meal
⅓ cup (50g) wholemeal plain flour
4 egg whites

1. Preheat oven to 180°C/160°C fan-forced. Line base and side of deep 20cm-round cake pan.
2. Combine chocolate, cocoa and sugar with the water in large bowl; stir until smooth. Add egg yolks; whisk to combine. Fold in almond meal and flour.
3. Beat egg whites in small bowl with electric mixer until firm peaks form. Gently fold egg white into chocolate mixture, in two batches; pour into pan.
4. Bake, uncovered, about 40 minutes. Stand in pan 5 minutes. Turn onto wire rack to cool.

SERVES 8
per serving 7.3g total fat (2.9g saturated fat); 956kj (228 cal); 5.7g protein; 36.4g carbohydrate; 1.4g fibre
serving suggestion serve warm with fresh strawberries, dusted with icing sugar.

chocolate fudge cake

fig-topped cheesecake

fig-topped cheesecake

PREPARATION TIME 25 MINUTES (PLUS REFRIGERATION TIME)

"Nice" biscuits make a perfect base for this yummy cheesecake.

11 plain sweet biscuits (135g)
2 teaspoons gelatine
2 tablespoons water
200g low-fat yogurt
250g light cream cheese, softened
¼ cup (90g) honey
1 teaspoon ground cardamom
2 fresh figs (120g), cut into wedges

1. Grease deep 19cm-square cake pan; line base and sides with baking paper, extending 5cm above two opposing sides of pan.
2. Place biscuits in pan; trim to cover base in a single layer.
3. Sprinkle gelatine over the water in small heatproof jug; place jug in small pan of simmering water, stir until gelatine dissolves. Cool 5 minutes.
4. Beat yogurt and cream cheese in small bowl with electric mixer until smooth. Stir in honey and cardamom then gelatine mixture; pour into pan. Cover; refrigerate about 4 hours or until set. Serve topped with fig.

SERVES 16
per serving 4.3g total fat (2.2g saturated fat); 398kj (95 cal); 3.1g protein; 11.4g carbohydrate; 0.4g fibre

lime cheesecake

PREPARATION TIME 30 MINUTES (PLUS REFRIGERATION TIME) COOKING TIME 10 MINUTES

80g plain biscuits
40g low-fat dairy-free spread, melted
2 teaspoons gelatine
1 tablespoon water
⅓ cup (80ml) lime juice
⅔ cup (150g) sugar
½ cup (100g) low-fat ricotta cheese
100g packaged low-fat cream cheese
2 teaspoons finely grated lime rind
3 egg whites

1. Grease 18cm springform pan; line base with baking paper.
2. Blend or process biscuits and dairy-free spread until mixture resembles fine breadcrumbs. Using one hand, press biscuit mixture evenly over base of prepared pan. Refrigerate until firm.
3. Sprinkle gelatine over the water in heatproof jug; stand jug in medium saucepan of simmering water. Stir until gelatine dissolves; reserve mixture.
4. Combine juice and sugar in small saucepan. Stir over heat, without boiling, until sugar dissolves; bring to a boil. Reduce heat, simmer 1 minute.
5. Meanwhile, beat cheeses and rind in medium bowl with electric mixer until mixture is smooth.
6. Beat egg whites in small bowl with electric mixer until soft peaks form; with motor operating, gradually add hot sugar syrup. Whisk slightly warm gelatine mixture and egg white mixture into cheese mixture; pour mixture into pan. Cover; refrigerate about 2 hours or until set.

SERVES 8
per serving 7.4g total fat (3.6g saturated fat); 726kj (173 cal); 5.1g protein; 22.6g carbohydrate; 0.2g fibre
serving suggestion just before serving, pipe whipped light cream on cheesecake and decorate with thin lime wedges.

orange and raspberry jellies

PREPARATION TIME 35 MINUTES (PLUS REFRIGERATION TIME)

½ cup (125ml) water

¼ cup (55g) caster sugar

1 cup (250ml) orange juice

2 tablespoons cointreau or grand marnier

2 tablespoons gelatine

¼ cup (60ml) water, extra

RASPBERRY JELLY

¾ cup (180ml) water

⅓ cup (75g) caster sugar

1½ cups (185g) raspberries

2 tablespoons bacardi rum

200g carton low-fat vanilla fromage frais

1. Line two 3-cup (750ml) dishes with plastic wrap. Combine water and sugar in small pan, stir over heat, without boiling, until sugar is dissolved. Remove from heat, stir in juice and liqueur.
2. Sprinkle gelatine over extra water in cup, stand in small pan of simmering water, stir until dissolved; cool 5 minutes.
3. Add half the gelatine mixture to the orange mixture, pour into one of the dishes; refrigerate until set.
4. Make raspberry jelly.

RASPBERRY JELLY stir water and sugar in small saucepan over heat, without boiling, until sugar is dissolved; remove from heat. Process raspberries and sugar syrup until smooth, push mixture through a fine sieve into a medium bowl. Add rum, raspberry mixture and remaining gelatine mixture, pour into prepared dish; refrigerate until set.

SERVES 4

per serving 0.5g total fat (0.1g saturated fat); 1216kj (290 cal); 10.6g protein; 51.3g carbohydrate; 2.7g fibre

tip store, covered, in refrigerator.

serving suggestion serve jellies with fromage frais.

tropical fruit salad

PREPARATION TIME 20 MINUTES (PLUS STANDING AND REFRIGERATION TIME) COOKING TIME 15 MINUTES

You will need three passionfruit for this recipe.

⅓ cup (135g) grated palm sugar
2 cups (500ml) water
2cm piece fresh ginger (10g), chopped finely
2 star anise
2 tablespoons lime juice
¼ cup coarsely chopped fresh mint
2 large mangoes (1.2kg), diced into 2cm pieces
1 small honeydew melon (900g), diced into 2cm pieces
1 small pineapple (800g), chopped coarsely
2 medium oranges (480g), segmented
¼ cup (60ml) passionfruit pulp
12 fresh lychees (300g), halved

1. Stir sugar and the water in small saucepan over heat, without boiling, until sugar dissolves; bring to a boil. Boil, uncovered, without stirring, 5 minutes. Add ginger and star anise; simmer, uncovered, about 5 minutes or until syrup thickens slightly. Discard star anise; cool to room temperature. Stir in juice and mint.
2. Place prepared fruit in large bowl with syrup; toss gently to combine. Refrigerate until cold.

SERVES 6
per serving 0.8g total fat (0g saturated fat); 1196kj (286 cal); 4.5g protein; 65.5g carbohydrate; 8g fibre

tropical fruit skewers with coconut dressing

PREPARATION TIME 30 MINUTES COOKING TIME 5 MINUTES

You will need eight long bamboo skewers; soak in water for at least an hour before use to prevent scorching and splintering.

2 medium bananas (400g)
½ medium pineapple (625g)
2 large starfruit (320g)
1 large mango (600g), chopped coarsely

COCONUT DRESSING

⅓ cup (80ml) coconut-flavoured liqueur
¼ cup (60ml) light coconut milk
1 tablespoon grated palm sugar
1cm piece fresh ginger (5g), grated

1 Make coconut dressing.
2 Cut each unpeeled banana into eight pieces. Cut unpeeled pineapple into eight slices; cut slices in half. Cut each starfruit into eight slices.
3 Thread fruit onto skewers, alternating varieties. Cook skewers on heated grill plate (or grill or barbecue), brushing with a little of the dressing, until browned lightly.
4 Serve skewers drizzled with remaining dressing.

COCONUT DRESSING place ingredients in screw-top jar; shake well.

SERVES 4
per serving 1.5g total fat (0g saturated fat); 1027kj (245 cal); 3.5g protein; 47.4g carbohydrate; 6g fibre
tip we used malibu for the dressing, but you can use any coconut-flavoured liqueur.

black forest parfaits

PREPARATION TIME 30 MINUTES (PLUS REFRIGERATION TIME)

We used flyte chocolate bars for this recipe, which are low-fat, bite-sized milk chocolate bars with a light whipped chocolate centre. Jam rollettes are miniature swiss rolls.

2 x 85g packets cherry jelly crystals
6 jam rollettes (150g), chopped coarsely
¼ cup (60ml) sweet sherry
425g can stoneless black cherries, drained
1½ cups (375ml) low-fat vanilla custard
3 x 20g low-fat chocolate bars, sliced thinly

1 Make jelly according to directions on packet; place in large jug. Refrigerate about 1 hour or until jelly is almost set.
2 Meanwhile, combine rollettes and sherry in small bowl. Reserve half of the rollette mixture; cover until required.
3 Divide remaining rollette mixture among six 1⅓-cup (330ml) serving glasses. Pour half of the jelly mixture evenly over rollette mixture in glasses; sprinkle with half of the cherries. Refrigerate 5 minutes.
4 Continue layering with reserved rollette mixture, then all of the custard, the remaining jelly and, finally, the remaining cherries. Cover parfaits; refrigerate overnight.
5 Serve parfaits sprinkled evenly with chocolate.

SERVES 6
per serving 3.5g total fat (1.3g saturated fat); 1334kj (319 cal); 32.6g protein; 65.4g carbohydrate; 1.2g fibre
serving suggestion serve topped with whipped light cream.

pear oatmeal cake

PREPARATION TIME 15 MINUTES (PLUS STANDING TIME) COOKING TIME 1 HOUR

2 x 425g cans pear halves in syrup
1 cup (90g) rolled oats
½ cup (125g) low-fat dairy-free spread
½ teaspoon vanilla essence
¾ cup (150g) firmly packed brown sugar
2 eggs
¾ cup (110g) white self-raising flour
¾ cup (120g) wholemeal self-raising flour
½ teaspoon bicarbonate of soda
2 teaspoons ground ginger

1. Preheat oven to 200°C/180°C fan-forced. Grease deep 23cm-square cake pan; line base and sides with baking paper.
2. Drain pears over small saucepan. Heat syrup with oats, remove from heat; stand 20 minutes.
3. Meanwhile, beat spread, vanilla and sugar in small bowl with electric mixer until combined. Beat in eggs, one at a time, until combined.
4. Add oat mixture and combined sifted remaining ingredients; stir until well combined. Pour mixture into pan; place pears on top, cut-side down.
5. Bake, uncovered, about 55 minutes. Serve warm.

SERVES 16
per serving 4.4g total fat (0.8g saturated fat); 655kj (156 cal); 3.1g protein; 26.5g carbohydrate; 2.1g fibre

tiramisu

PREPARATION TIME 20 MINUTES (PLUS REFRIGERATION TIME) COOKING TIME 25 MINUTES

3 eggs
½ cup (110g) caster sugar
¼ cup (40g) wholemeal self-raising flour
¼ cup (35g) white self-raising flour
¼ cup (35g) cornflour
1 teaspoon gelatine
1 tablespoon cold water
1½ cups (300g) low-fat ricotta cheese
¼ cup (60ml) no-fat milk
¼ cup (55g) caster sugar, extra
2 tablespoons instant coffee granules
2 tablespoons boiling water
⅓ cup (80ml) no-fat milk, extra
½ cup (125ml) coffee-flavoured liqueur
10g dark chocolate, grated finely

1 Preheat oven to 180°C/160°C fan-forced. Grease 22cm springform tin; line base with baking paper.
2 Beat eggs in small bowl with electric mixer until thick and creamy. Gradually add sugar, beating until sugar dissolves. Fold triple-sifted flours into egg mixture until just combined. Spread into springform tin.
3 Bake, uncovered, about 25 minutes. Turn onto wire rack to cool.
4 Meanwhile, sprinkle gelatine over the cold water in small heatproof jug; place jug in small pan of simmering water, stir until gelatine dissolves. Cool, 5 minutes.
5 Blend or process cheese, milk and extra sugar until smooth. With motor operating, add gelatine mixture; process until combined. Dissolve coffee in the boiling water in small bowl; add extra milk and liqueur.
6 Cut cake in half horizontally. Return one cake half to same springform tin, brush half of the coffee mixture over cake; top with half of the ricotta mixture. Repeat with remaining cake half, coffee mixture and ricotta mixture. Cover; refrigerate for at least 3 hours.
7 Just before serving, sprinkle tiramisu with grated chocolate.

SERVES 12
per serving 3.9g total fat (2g saturated fat); 780kj (186 cal); 6g protein; 28.2g carbohydrate; 0.9g fibre

plum and cinnamon cake

PREPARATION TIME 15 MINUTES COOKING TIME 25 MINUTES

½ cup (125g) low-fat dairy-free spread
1 teaspoon vanilla essence
½ cup (100g) firmly packed brown sugar
3 eggs, separated
½ cup (75g) white self-raising flour
½ cup (80g) wholemeal self-raising flour
1 teaspoon ground cinnamon
4 whole canned plums in syrup, drained, halved, seeded

1 Preheat oven to 180°C/160°C fan-forced. Grease 20cm ring pan; line base and sides with baking paper.

2 Beat spread, essence, sugar and egg yolks in small bowl with electric mixer until light and fluffy. Transfer mixture to medium bowl; stir in flours and cinnamon.

3 Beat egg whites in clean small bowl with electric mixer until soft peaks form; gently fold whites into cake batter. Spread batter into ring pan; place plums on top, cut-side down.

4 Bake, uncovered, about 30 minutes. Stand 10 minutes; turn onto wire rack, turn top-side up to cool. Serve dusted with icing sugar, if desired.

SERVES 12
per serving 5.8g total fat (1.1g saturated fat); 1118kj (267 cal); 3.7g protein; 51g carbohydrate; 4.2g fibre
tip you'll probably have to open an 810g can of whole plums in syrup to get the required amount for this recipe. You can serve the remaining plums alongside this cake, or you can freeze them (in syrup) until you wish to use them for another recipe.

strawberry and rhubarb muffins

PREPARATION TIME 15 MINUTES COOKING TIME 20 MINUTES

You will need about 4 large trimmed rhubarb stems for this recipe.

125g strawberries, sliced thinly
3 cups (450g) wholemeal self-raising flour
½ cup (100g) firmly packed brown sugar
1 teaspoon ground cinnamon
1 teaspoon vanilla essence
60g low-fat dairy-free spread, melted
¾ cup (180ml) no-fat soy milk
2 eggs, beaten lightly
2 cups (250g) finely chopped rhubarb
¼ cup (60g) apple sauce

1. Preheat oven to 200°C/180°C fan-forced. Grease 12-hole (⅓ cup/80ml) muffin pan. Reserve 12 slices of strawberry.
2. Combine flour, sugar and cinnamon in large bowl. Add essence, spread, milk and eggs; mix to combine. Gently stir in remaining strawberries, rhubarb and apple sauce.
3. Divide mixture among holes of muffin pan; top each with a reserved strawberry slice. Bake, uncovered, about 20 minutes. Serve warm or at room temperature.

MAKES 12
per muffin 3.7g total fat (0.7g saturated fat); 819kj (196 cal); 6.7g protein; 33.8g carbohydrate; 5.2g fibre

apricot upside-down cakes

PREPARATION TIME 20 MINUTES COOKING TIME 20 MINUTES

1 tablespoon brown sugar
12 canned apricot halves in syrup, drained
2 eggs
¾ cup (150g) firmly packed brown sugar, extra
¾ cup (90g) almond meal
1 teaspoon vanilla essence
⅓ cup (50g) wholemeal self-raising flour
½ cup (125ml) no-fat milk
¼ cup (80g) light apricot conserve, warmed

1. Preheat oven to 180°C/160°C fan-forced. Grease 12-hole (⅓ cup/80ml) muffin pan.
2. Sprinkle sugar equally into holes of prepared pan; place one apricot half, cut-side down, into each hole.
3. Beat eggs and extra sugar in medium bowl with electric mixer until light and fluffy. Stir in almond meal, essence, flour and milk. Divide mixture among holes of pan.
4. Bake, uncovered, about 20 minutes. Stand 5 minutes; turn onto wire rack, brush conserve over hot cakes. Serve cakes warm or at room temperature.

MAKES 12 CAKES
per cake 5.1g total fat (0.6g saturated fat); 555kj (133 cal); 3.6g protein; 18.9g carbohydrate; 1.4g fibre
tip you'll probably have to open a 415g can of apricot halves to get the required amount for this recipe. Serve the remaining apricot halves with the cakes.

moist orange cake

PREPARATION TIME 15 MINUTES COOKING TIME 20 MINUTES (PLUS STANDING TIME)

4 large oranges (1.2kg)
60g low-fat dairy-free spread
1 cup (220g) caster sugar
2 eggs
⅓ cup (40g) almond meal
1 cup (160g) wholemeal self-raising flour
2 tablespoons no-fat soy milk

1. Preheat oven to 160°C/140°C fan-forced. Grease shallow 23cm-round cake pan; line base with baking paper.
2. Finely grate ½ teaspoon of rind from one orange; slice 1 tablespoon of thin strips of rind from same orange. Reserve rinds. Squeeze the peeled orange; reserve ⅔ cup (160ml) juice. Peel remaining three oranges; separate into segments. Reserve segments.
3. Beat spread, ⅓ cup of the sugar and the finely grated rind in small bowl with electric mixer until pale and creamy. Add eggs; beat until combined. Add almond meal, flour, milk and 1 tablespoon of the reserved juice; stir to combine. Spread batter into pan. Bake, uncovered, about 20 minutes.
4. Meanwhile, combine remaining juice and remaining sugar in small saucepan over heat, without boiling, until sugar dissolves; bring to a boil. Add reserved rind strips; reduce heat, simmer, uncovered, about 3 minutes or until syrup thickens slightly.
5. Remove cake from oven. Stand 5 minutes; turn onto wire rack. Using skewer, pierce cake several times; brush with ¼ cup of the hot syrup.
6. Serve cake sliced, with reserved orange segments and remaining syrup.

SERVES 12
per serving 5g total fat (0.7g saturated fat); 792kj (189 cal); 4.2g protein; 32.5g carbohydrate; 3.2g fibre

pear and ginger cake

PREPARATION TIME 15 MINUTES COOKING TIME 45 MINUTES (PLUS STANDING TIME)

You need 8 even-sized pear halves for this recipe; arrange them on cake mixture before baking in such a way that each serving will include a whole pear half. This cake is best served warm.

1 cup (150g) self-raising flour
½ cup (75g) plain flour
1 tablespoon ground ginger
¼ teaspoon bicarbonate of soda
⅓ cup (120g) treacle
60g low-fat dairy-free spread
⅔ cup (150g) firmly packed brown sugar
1 egg, beaten lightly
¼ cup (60ml) milk
825g can pear halves, drained
¼ cup (80g) apricot jam

1. Preheat oven to 180°C/160°C fan-forced. Grease 20cm x 30cm lamington pan; line base with baking paper.
2. Sift flours with ginger and soda into large bowl.
3. Combine treacle, dairy-free spread and sugar in small saucepan; stir over heat, without boiling, until sugar dissolves. Cool 5 minutes.
4. Pour treacle mixture into flour mixture; stir until combined. Stir in egg and milk. Pour into pan; top with pear, cut-side down, arranged to make eight equal-sized servings.
5. Bake, uncovered, about 40 minutes; stand cake in pan 10 minutes. Turn onto wire rack; remove baking paper. Turn cake top-side up to cool.
6. Warm jam in small saucepan over low heat. Strain jam through sieve; brush warm cake with warm jam.

SERVES 8
per serving 4.2g total fat (0.9g saturated fat); 1225kj (293 cal); 4.5g protein; 60.7g carbohydrate; 2.4g fibre
serving suggestion serve with low-fat custard.

raspberry yogurt cake

PREPARATION TIME 30 MINUTES COOKING TIME 1 HOUR 5 MINUTES

½ cup (125g) low-fat dairy-free spread
¾ cup (165g) firmly packed brown sugar
2 eggs
1¼ cups (200g) wholemeal self-raising flour
½ cup (140g) low-fat yogurt
100g frozen raspberries

CREAM CHEESE FROSTING

80g light cream cheese, softened
⅓ cup (55g) icing sugar
1 teaspoon lemon juice

1. Preheat oven to 180°C/160°C fan-forced. Grease 14cm x 21cm loaf pan; line base and two long sides with baking paper, extending paper 5cm above edges of pan.
2. Beat spread and sugar in medium bowl with electric mixer until light and fluffy. Add eggs, one at a time, beating until just combined.
3. Transfer mixture to medium bowl; stir in flour, yogurt and raspberries. Spread mixture into loaf pan.
4. Bake, uncovered, about 1 hour 5 minutes. Stand 10 minutes, turn onto wire rack; turn top-side up to cool.
5. Make cream cheese frosting.
6. Place cake on serving plate; using spatula, spread cake top with frosting.

CREAM CHEESE FROSTING whisk cheese, sugar and lemon juice in small bowl until smooth.

SERVES 12
per serving 6.5g total fat (1.7g saturated fat); 802kj (192 cal); 4.5g protein; 29.6g carbohydrate; 2.3g fibre

berry mousse

PREPARATION TIME 10 MINUTES (PLUS REFRIGERATION TIME)

2 teaspoons gelatine
2 tablespoons water
2 egg whites
⅓ cup (75g) caster sugar
2 x 200g cartons low-fat berry-flavoured yogurt
150g fresh mixed berries

1. Sprinkle gelatine over the water in small heatproof jug; place jug in small pan of simmering water, stir until gelatine dissolves. Cool.
2. Meanwhile, beat egg whites in small bowl with electric mixer until soft peaks form. Gradually add sugar, beating until sugar dissolves.
3. Place yogurt in medium bowl; stir in gelatine mixture, fold in egg white mixture.
4. Spoon mousse mixture into serving bowl. Cover; refrigerate about 2 hours or until set. Top mousse with berries to serve.

SERVES 4
per serving 0.2g total fat (0.1g saturated fat); 707kj (169 cal); 9g protein; 32.8g carbohydrate; 0.9g fibre

peach and buttermilk cake

PREPARATION TIME 15 MINUTES COOKING TIME 45 MINUTES

2 cups (320g) wholemeal self-raising flour
¾ cup (150g) firmly packed brown sugar
2 teaspoons ground cinnamon
1 teaspoon ground ginger
1 egg, beaten lightly
1 egg white, beaten lightly
1 tablespoon monounsaturated or polyunsaturated oil
1 cup (250ml) buttermilk
415g can sliced peaches in natural juice, drained

1. Preheat oven to 180°C/160°C fan-forced. Grease 20cm sandwich pan; line base with baking paper.
2. Beat flour, sugar, spices, egg, egg white, oil and buttermilk in large bowl of electric mixer until combined.
3. Spread three-quarters of the mixture into pan, top with peaches; spread with remaining mixture.
4. Bake, uncovered, about 45 minutes or until browned lightly and cooked through. Stand cake for 5 minutes before turning out of pan. Serve cake warm, dusted lightly with sifted icing sugar, if desired.

SERVES 8
per serving 4.4g total fat (0.9g saturated fat); 1081kj (258 cal); 7.7g protein; 47.3g carbohydrate; 4.9g fibre

chocolate mousse

PREPARATION TIME 10 MINUTES (PLUS REFRIGERATION TIME)

The word mousse is a French description for froth or foam, a look usually achieved by lots of kilojoule-laden whipped cream. Here, we've used low-fat frûche for equally delicious results, but without the excess fat and energy.

1 tablespoon instant coffee granules
1 tablespoon cocoa powder
2 teaspoons hot water
160g dark chocolate, melted
3 cups (800g) french vanilla low-fat frûche
50g dark chocolate, extra, grated

1. Dissolve coffee and cocoa in the water in medium bowl. Stir in melted chocolate and frûche; beat with electric mixer on medium speed about 3 minutes or until mixture is smooth.
2. Divide mixture evenly among eight ½-cup (125ml) serving glasses. Cover; refrigerate overnight.
3. Serve mousse sprinkled with grated chocolate.

SERVES 8
per serving 8g total fat (4.7g saturated fat); 961kj (230 cal); 10.1g protein; 28.2g carbohydrate; 0.7g fibre
tip frûche is a commercial dessert having less than 0.5g fat per 100g; substitute fromage frais or a low-fat vanilla yogurt if you cannot find it but be aware that the fat count will rise slightly if frûche isn't used.
serving suggestion serve topped with fresh raspberries or any fresh berries.

vanilla ricotta mousse

PREPARATION TIME 15 MINUTES (PLUS REFRIGERATION TIME) COOKING TIME 15 MINUTES

100g low-fat ricotta cheese
2 x 125g tubs light french vanilla frûche
½ cup (110g) caster sugar
1 teaspoon vanilla essence
1 teaspoon gelatine
½ cup (125ml) water
1 cup (250ml) sweet dessert wine
1 vanilla bean, split

1. Grease four ½-cup (125ml) shallow dishes.
2. Blend or process cheese, frûche, 1 tablespoon of the sugar and essence until smooth. Sprinkle gelatine over 1 tablespoon of the water in cup, stand cup in pan of simmering water, stir until gelatine is dissolved. Stir gelatine through ricotta mixture.
3. Divide mixture evenly among dishes. Cover; refrigerate about 30 minutes or until set.
4. Combine remaining sugar, remaining water, wine and vanilla bean in small pan; stir over heat, without boiling, until sugar dissolves. Bring to a boil; simmer about 5 minutes or until syrup thickens. Remove and discard bean; let syrup cool.
5. Just before serving, turn mousse onto serving plates; serve with wine syrup.

SERVES 4
per serving 2.4g total fat (1.5g saturated fat); 1231kj (294 cal); 8.6g protein; 42.7g carbohydrate; 0g fibre
tips mousse can be made up to 2 days ahead. Store, covered, in refrigerator until required. Make syrup just before serving.

rhubarb and strawberry mousse sponge cake

PREPARATION TIME 50 MINUTES (PLUS CHILLING TIME) COOKING TIME 35 MINUTES (PLUS COOLING TIME)

cooking-oil spray
2 eggs
1 egg white
⅓ cup (75g) caster sugar
1 teaspoon vanilla essence
⅓ cup (50g) self-raising flour
¼ cup (30g) almond meal

MOUSSE

4 stems fresh rhubarb (250g), chopped coarsely
2 tablespoons caster sugar
2 tablespoons water
250g strawberries
½ cup (100g) low-fat ricotta cheese, sieved
100g packaged low-fat cream cheese
3 teaspoons gelatine
2 tablespoons water, extra
2 egg whites
1 tablespoon caster sugar, extra

1. Preheat oven to 180°C160°C fan-forced. Coat deep 22cm round cake pan with cooking-oil spray; line base with baking paper.
2. Beat eggs, egg white, sugar and essence in small bowl with electric mixer until thick and creamy.
3. Gently fold in sifted flour and almond meal. Pour mixture into pan; bake in moderate oven about 25 minutes or until just firm. Cool on wire rack.
4. Meanwhile, make mousse.
5. Split cold cake into 2 layers. Cover base and side of 20cm springform tin with foil. Place one cake layer in tin, pour mousse over cake, top with remaining layer of cake. Cover with plastic wrap; refrigerate several hours or overnight.
6. Remove cake from tin, dust with sifted icing sugar and decorate with extra berries, if desired.

MOUSSE place rhubarb, sugar and water in small saucepan, simmer, uncovered, until rhubarb is soft, stirring occasionally; cool. Blend or process rhubarb mixture with strawberries, ricotta and cream cheese until smooth; transfer to large bowl. Sprinkle gelatine over extra water in jug, stand in small pan of simmering water, stir until dissolved. Stir into rhubarb mixture. Beat egg whites in small bowl with electric mixer until soft peaks form; gradually add extra sugar, beat until dissolved. Fold egg white mixture into rhubarb mixture in two batches.

SERVES 8
per serving 7g total fat (2.6g saturated fat); 759kj (181 cal); 8.6g protein; 21.3g carbohydrate; 2.3g fibre
tip recipe best made a day ahead. Store, covered, in refrigerator.

blackberry pudding

PREPARATION TIME 20 MINUTES COOKING TIME 30 MINUTES (PLUS COOLING AND REFRIGERATION TIME)

3 eggs
½ cup (110g) caster sugar
1 tablespoon cornflour
¾ cup (110g) self-raising flour
1 teaspoon butter
¼ cup (60ml) boiling water
⅓ cup (75g) caster sugar, extra
½ cup (125ml) water
300g frozen blackberries
500g frozen mixed berries
¼ cup (80g) blackberry jam

1. Preheat oven to 180°C/160°C fan-forced. Grease 25cm x 30cm swiss roll pan; line with baking paper.
2. Beat eggs in small bowl with electric mixer until thick and creamy. Gradually add sugar, one tablespoon at a time, beating until sugar is dissolved after each addition. Transfer to large bowl.
3. Fold triple-sifted flours into egg mixture. Pour combined butter and boiling water down side of bowl; fold into egg mixture. Pour mixture into pan; bake, uncovered, about 15 minutes. Cool in pan.
4. Meanwhile, place extra sugar and the water in medium saucepan; bring to a boil. Stir in fruit; return to a boil. Reduce heat, simmer, uncovered, about 3 minutes or until fruit thaws. Strain over medium bowl; reserve syrup and berries separately.
5. Turn cake out onto board. Line 1-litre (4-cup) pudding basin with plastic wrap, extending wrap 10cm over side of basin. Cut circle from cake slightly smaller than top edge of basin using tip of sharp knife; cut second circle exact size of base of basin from cake. Cut remaining cake into 10cm pieces. Place small cake circle in base of basin and use pieces to line side of basin. Pour ⅔ cup of the reserved syrup into small jug; reserve. Fill basin with berries; cover with remaining syrup, top with large cake circle. Cover pudding with overhanging plastic wrap, weight pudding with saucer; refrigerate 3 hours or overnight.
6. Stir jam and 2 tablespoons of the reserved syrup in small saucepan until heated through. Turn pudding onto serving plate; brush with remaining reserved syrup then jam mixture. Serve with whipped cream, if desired.

SERVES 6
per serving 3.6g total fat (1.3g saturated fat); 1250kj (299 cal); 7.2g protein; 60.7g carbohydrate; 5.9g fibre

blackberry pudding

balsamic strawberries with black pepper wafers

balsamic strawberries with black pepper wafers

PREPARATION TIME 15 MINUTES (PLUS STANDING AND REFRIGERATION TIMES) COOKING TIME 5 MINUTES

750g strawberries, halved
¼ cup (55g) caster sugar
2 tablespoons balsamic vinegar
¼ cup (35g) plain flour
2 tablespoons caster sugar, extra
1 egg white
30g butter, melted
½ teaspoon vanilla extract
½ teaspoon freshly ground black pepper

1. Preheat oven to 180°C/160°C fan-forced. Line oven tray with baking paper.
2. Combine strawberries, sugar and vinegar in bowl. Cover; refrigerate 1 hour.
3. Meanwhile, using wooden spoon, beat flour, extra sugar, egg white, butter and extract in small bowl until smooth.
4. Place one level teaspoon of the wafer mixture on tray; using back of spoon, spread mixture into 8cm circle. Repeat with remaining wafer mixture, allowing 2cm between each wafer. Sprinkle each wafer with black pepper; bake, uncovered, about 5 minutes or until browned lightly. Cool 15 minutes.
5. Serve strawberry mixture with wafers.

SERVES 4
per serving 6.4g total fat (4.1g saturated fat); 862kj (206 cal); 5.1g protein; 32.3g carbohydrate; 4.5g fibre

pavlovas with fresh berries

PREPARATION TIME 35 MINUTES COOKING TIME 1 HOUR

3 egg whites
¾ cup (165g) caster sugar
1 teaspoon vanilla essence
200g carton low-fat vanilla fromage frais
500g fresh berries
icing sugar

1 Preheat oven to 120°C/100°C fan-forced. Line oven tray with baking paper, mark four 8cm circles on paper.
2 Beat egg whites in small bowl with electric mixer until soft peaks form. Gradually add sugar, beating until dissolved after each addition; fold in essence.
3 Spread a rounded tablespoon of meringue mixture over each circle. Spoon remaining mixture into piping bag fitted with medium fluted tube. Pipe around edge of each round.
4 Bake, uncovered, about 1 hour or until pavlovas are dry and crisp.
5 Divide fromage frais among pavlovas, top with half the berries; dust with icing sugar. Blend or process remaining berries until smooth, serve with pavlovas.

SERVES 4
per serving 0.3g total fat (0.1g saturated fat); 1004kj (239 cal); 8.9g protein; 51g carbohydrate; 2.9g fibre
tip meringue can be prepared a day ahead; store in airtight container. Assemble pavlovas just before serving.

vanilla panna cotta with berry compote

PREPARATION TIME 15 MINUTES (PLUS REFRIGERATION TIME) COOKING TIME 10 MINUTES

2 tablespoons boiling water
2 tablespoons honey
1 vanilla bean
2 teaspoons gelatine
1½ cups (380g) yogurt

BERRY COMPOTE
2 cups (300g) frozen mixed berries
¼ cup (40g) icing sugar

1 Combine the water and honey in small heatproof jug. Split vanilla bean in half lengthways; scrape seeds into jug then add pod. Sprinkle gelatine over honey mixture; stand jug in small saucepan of simmering water. Stir until gelatine dissolves; cool 5 minutes. Discard pod.
2 Combine honey mixture and yogurt in small bowl; stir until smooth. Strain into four ½-cup (125ml) moulds. Cover; refrigerate 3 hours or overnight.
3 Meanwhile, make berry compote.
4 Turn panna cotta onto serving plates; serve with berry compote.

BERRY COMPOTE cook berries and sugar in medium saucepan, stirring occasionally over low heat, uncovered, about 5 minutes or until berries just soften. Transfer mixture to small bowl; cool 10 minutes. Cover; refrigerate until required.

SERVES 4
per serving 3.3g total fat (2.1g saturated fat); 727kj (174 cal); 7.2g protein; 28.6g carbohydrate; 1.7g fibre
tip wipe the outsides of panna cotta moulds with a hot cloth to make turning them onto plates easier.

mini lemon yogurt cakes with syrup

PREPARATION TIME 10 MINUTES COOKING TIME 15 MINUTES

The combination of lemon, yogurt and poppy seeds lends an eastern Mediterranean accent to these morsels.

⅓ cup (50g) self-raising flour
¼ cup (55g) caster sugar
1½ tablespoons cornflour
¼ teaspoon bicarbonate of soda
1 teaspoon poppy seeds
1 egg yolk
¼ cup (70g) yogurt
½ teaspoon finely grated lemon rind
1 teaspoon lemon juice
10g butter, melted

LEMON SYRUP

1 medium lemon (140g)
¼ cup (55g) sugar
¼ cup (60ml) water

1. Preheat oven to 180°C/160°C fan-forced.
2. Sift flour, sugar, cornflour and soda into small bowl; stir in seeds, yolk, yogurt, rind, juice and butter.
3. Drop rounded teaspoons of mixture into baby patty cases on oven tray. Bake, uncovered, 10 minutes.
4. Meanwhile, make lemon syrup.
5. Drizzle or brush hot lemon syrup over hot cakes.

LEMON SYRUP using vegetable peeler, remove rind from lemon; shred peel finely. Juice the peeled lemon; place 2 teaspoons of the juice (reserve remainder for another use) in small saucepan with shredded rind, sugar and the water. Stir over heat, without boiling, until sugar dissolves. Boil, uncovered, without stirring, about 5 minutes or until mixture thickens slightly; transfer to small heatproof jug.

MAKES 30
per cake 0.6g total fat (0.3g saturated fat); 119kj (28 cal); 0.4g protein; 5.5g carbohydrate; 0.2g fibre

lemon cakes with passionfruit syrup

PREPARATION TIME 10 MINUTES COOKING TIME 25 MINUTES

You will need about six passionfruit to make this recipe. The thin-skinned purple-black variety will yield much more pulp than the thicker-skinned panama passionfruit.

1¼ cups (185g) self-raising flour
½ cup (110g) caster sugar
2 teaspoons finely grated lemon rind
1 egg, beaten lightly
40g butter, melted
2 tablespoons skim milk
¾ cup (210g) low-fat yogurt
1 cup (250ml) water
1 teaspoon cornflour
½ cup (125ml) passionfruit pulp
2 tablespoons finely sliced lemon rind

1. Preheat oven to 180°C/160°C fan-forced. Grease eight holes of a 12-hole (⅓ cup/80ml) muffin pan.
2. Combine flour in medium bowl with ¼ cup of the sugar and grated rind. Add egg, butter, milk and yogurt; stir until just combined. Divide mixture among pan holes.
3. Bake, uncovered, about 25 minutes. Stand cakes in pan 5 minutes; turn out onto wire rack.
4. Meanwhile, combine the water and remaining sugar in small saucepan. Stir over heat until sugar dissolves; bring to a boil. Reduce heat, simmer, uncovered, without stirring, 10 minutes. Stir in blended cornflour and passionfruit until mixture boils and thickens. Strain into small heatproof jug; discard seeds. Stir in sliced rind; cool.
5. Serve lemon cakes with passionfruit syrup.

MAKES 8
per cake 5.1g total fat (3g saturated fat); 841kj (201 cal); 5.3g protein; 33.1g carbohydrate; 3.2g fibre
tip lime rind can be substituted for lemon rind.
serving suggestion scatter each serving plate with fresh berries, such as blueberries or raspberries.

apple and cinnamon cakes with lemon syrup

PREPARATION TIME 20 MINUTES COOKING TIME 50 MINUTES

¼ cup (60ml) water
¼ cup (50g) brown sugar
1 medium unpeeled red apple (150g), sliced thinly
40g low-fat margarine
⅓ cup (75g) caster sugar
1 egg, beaten lightly
¼ cup (60ml) low-fat milk
¾ cup (105g) self-raising flour
¼ teaspoon ground cinnamon
1 medium lemon (140g)
½ cup (110g) caster sugar, extra
¼ cup (60ml) water, extra
1 cinnamon stick

1. Preheat oven to 180°C/160°C fan-forced. Grease four ⅔ cup (160ml) moulds.
2. Cook the water and brown sugar in medium saucepan, stirring, until sugar dissolves. Add apple; cook, stirring, about 10 minutes or until most of the liquid evaporates and apples have caramelised. Spoon into moulds.
3. Beat margarine, caster sugar and egg in small bowl with electric mixer until thick and pale. Stir in milk, flour and cinnamon; pour into moulds. Bake, uncovered, about 20 minutes or until cooked when tested. Turn onto wire racks to cool.
4. Using a vegetable peeler, peel a 10cm strip of rind from lemon. Combine lemon strip, 1 tablespoon lemon juice, extra sugar, extra water and cinnamon stick in small saucepan; stir over heat until sugar dissolves. Simmer, uncovered, about 12 minutes or until thick and syrupy. Discard cinnamon stick and lemon rind.
5. Serve cakes with warm lemon syrup.

SERVES 4
per serving 5.7g total fat (1.2g saturated fat); 1641kj (392 cal); 5.2g protein; 82.1g carbohydrate; 2.2g fibre
tip cakes can be made up to 1 day ahead; store in airtight container. Syrup can be made up to 1 week ahead; store, covered, in refrigerator. Reheat before serving.

apple ginger shortcake

PREPARATION TIME 15 MINUTES (PLUS REFRIGERATION TIME) COOKING TIME 40 MINUTES (PLUS COOLING TIME)

You will need 1 passionfruit for this recipe.

1¼ cups self-raising flour (185g)
1 tablespoon cornflour
2 tablespoons caster sugar
40g monounsaturated or polyunsaturated margarine
2 egg whites
1 tablespoon lemon juice, approximately
2 tablespoons icing sugar
2 teaspoons ground cinnamon

APPLE GINGER FILLING

425g can pie apples
1 tablespoon passionfruit pulp
1 teaspoon finely chopped glacé ginger
1 teaspoon finely grated lemon rind

1 Preheat oven to 180°C/160°C fan-forced. Grease 20cm round sandwich pan; line base with baking paper.

2 Sift flour, cornflour and sugar into large bowl; rub in margarine. Stir in egg whites with enough juice to make ingredients cling together (or process all ingredients until mixture forms a ball). Cover; refrigerate for 30 minutes.

3 Roll three-quarters of the pastry on floured surface until large enough to line base and side of pan.

4 Make apple ginger filling; spread over base. Fold pastry edge over filling; lightly brush edge with water.

5 Roll out remaining pastry to a 20cm round; place over filling. Press edges to seal. Bake, uncovered, about 40 minutes or until lightly browned. Cool on wire rack.

6 Sprinkle with combined sifted icing sugar and cinnamon to serve.

APPLE GINGER FILLING combine ingredients in medium bowl.

SERVES 8
per serving 4.4g total fat (0.6g saturated fat); 684kj (163 cal); 3.3g protein; 27.7g carbohydrate; 1.7g fibre
tip recipe can be made a day ahead. Store, covered, in refrigerator.

french meringues with berries

PREPARATION TIME 30 MINUTES COOKING TIME 30 MINUTES

2 egg whites

1 teaspoon lemon juice

½ cup (110g) caster sugar

⅓ cup (50g) shelled pistachios, chopped finely

200g tub low-fat strawberry frûche

75g fresh raspberries

75g fresh blueberries

1. Preheat oven to 120°C/100°C fan-forced. Line three oven trays with baking paper; trace twelve 5.5cm circles onto each sheet of baking paper.
2. Beat egg whites and juice in small bowl with electric mixer until soft peaks form. Add sugar, in batches, beating until dissolved after each addition.
3. Spread meringue thinly over circles on paper, sprinkle with nuts; bake, uncovered, about 30 minutes or until crisp. Cool in oven with door ajar.
4. Divide frûche among 18 of the meringues, decorate with raspberries and blueberries; top with remaining meringues. Decorate with extra berries, if desired.

MAKES 18

per meringue 1.5g total fat (0.2g saturated fat); 232kj (55 cal); 1.9g protein; 8.8g carbohydrate; 0.6g fibre

tip meringues can be made up to 3 days ahead; store in airtight container. Assemble just before serving.

zucchini and kumara cake

PREPARATION TIME 35 MINUTES COOKING TIME 50 MINUTES (PLUS COOLING TIME)

cooking-oil spray

3 eggs

½ cup (100g) firmly packed brown sugar

½ cup (75g) self-raising flour

2 teaspoons ground ginger

⅓ cup (40g) almond meal

10g butter or margarine, melted

1 tablespoon boiling water

½ cup (70g) finely grated zucchini

½ cup (65g) finely grated kumara

TOPPING

1 large (150g) zucchini

½ small (125g) kumara

½ cup (110g) caster sugar

⅓ cup (80ml) water

1. Preheat oven to 200°C/180°c fan-forced. Coat deep 20cm round cake pan with cooking-oil spray; line base and side with baking paper.
2. Beat eggs and sugar in medium bowl with electric mixer until thick and creamy. Gently fold in sifted flour and ginger, nuts, butter and water. Fold in zucchini and kumara.
3. Spread mixture into pan; bake, uncovered, about 35 minutes.
4. Meanwhile, make topping.
5. Serve cake decorated with syrupy vegetables from topping mixture and dusted with a little sifted icing sugar, if desired.

TOPPING peel zucchini thickly, cut skin into thin strips (reserve zucchini flesh for another use). Cut kumara into thin strips. Stir sugar and water in small saucepan over heat, without boiling, until sugar is dissolved. Add zucchini and kumara, simmer, uncovered, 10 minutes; remove vegetables from syrup, cool on tray.

SERVES 8

per serving 6.3g total fat (1.5g saturated fat); 906kj (216 cal); 5.1g protein; 36.2g carbohydrate; 1.6g fibre

tip cake can be made a day ahead. Store in airtight container.

creamed rice with rhubarb and raspberries

PREPARATION TIME 10 MINUTES COOKING TIME 1 HOUR

The Greeks invented the partnership of rice and milk for dessert. They call it rizógalo; we call it seriously good comfort food.

1 litre (4 cups) skim milk
⅔ cup (150g) caster sugar
½ cup (100g) calrose rice
500g rhubarb, trimmed, chopped coarsely
¼ cup (55g) caster sugar, extra
200g raspberries

1. Combine milk and sugar in medium saucepan; bring to a boil. Stir in rice; reduce heat, simmer, covered, about 1 hour or until rice is creamy, stirring occasionally with wooden spoon.
2. Meanwhile, cook rhubarb and extra sugar in large saucepan over low heat, stirring, about 10 minutes or until rhubarb is tender.
3. Layer creamed rice and rhubarb mixture in serving dishes, finishing with rhubarb; sprinkle with raspberries.

SERVES 4
per serving 0.8g total fat (0.3g saturated fat); 1736kj (415 cal); 13.5g protein; 89.2g carbohydrate; 6.9g fibre
tips any berry – boysenberries, blackberries, strawberries – can be substituted for the raspberrries. A pinch of grated nutmeg or ground cardamom can be added to the creamed mixture.

satsuma plum clafouti

PREPARATION TIME 15 MINUTES COOKING TIME 40 MINUTES

Sometimes called indian blood plum, the large plum used in this recipe has a distinctive dark-red to purple fibrous flesh, is extremely juicy and pleasantly sweet, and is the plum most frequently canned.

1½ cups (375ml) low-fat custard
¼ cup (35g) self-raising flour
1 egg yolk
2 egg whites
825g can whole plums, drained, halved, seeded
2 teaspoons icing sugar

1. Preheat oven to 180°C/160°C fan-forced.
2. Combine custard, flour and egg yolk in medium bowl.
3. Beat egg whites in small bowl with electric mixer on highest speed until soft peaks form; fold gently into custard mixture. Pour into 24cm-round ovenproof pie dish.
4. Pat plums dry with absorbent paper; arrange plums, cut-side down, over custard. Place pie dish on oven tray; bake, uncovered, about 40 minutes or until firm.
5. Just before serving, dust with sifted icing sugar.

SERVES 4
per serving 2.4g total fat (1g saturated fat); 969kj (232 cal); 7.2g protein; 45.7g carbohydrate; 1.6g fibre
tip canned apricots or peaches can be substituted for plums.
serving suggestion serve with a scoop of low-fat ice-cream.

crepes with vanilla cream and raspberries

PREPARATION TIME 15 MINUTES (PLUS STANDING TIME) COOKING TIME 15 MINUTES

¾ cup (105g) plain flour
1 tablespoon caster sugar or powdered artificial sweetener
½ teaspoon ground ginger
1 egg
1¼ cups (310ml) low-fat milk
cooking-oil spray
100g raspberries

VANILLA CREAM

50g packaged low-fat cream cheese
2 tablespoons low-fat sour cream
2 teaspoons icing sugar
1 teaspoon vanilla essence

1. Sift flour, sugar and ginger into bowl, gradually stir in combined egg and milk; beat until smooth. Cover; stand 30 minutes.
2. Coat heated crepe pan with cooking-oil spray, pour ¼ cup (60ml) batter into pan; cook until lightly browned underneath. Turn crepe, brown other side. Repeat with remaining batter. You will need eight crepes in total.
3. Make vanilla cream.
4. Serve crepes with cream and raspberries.

VANILLA CREAM combine all ingredients in bowl; mix well.

SERVES 4
per serving 7.8g total fat (4.1g saturated fat); 931kj (223 cal); 9.7g protein; 28.2g carbohydrate; 2.3g fibre
tip recipe can be made a day ahead. Store separately, covered, in refrigerator. Crepes can be frozen.

apple and cinnamon pancakes with maple syrup

PREPARATION TIME 20 MINUTES COOKING TIME 20 MINUTES

Maple syrup, the processed sap of the maple tree, has a natural affinity with apple. Maple-flavoured syrup or pancake syrup, made from cane sugar and artificial maple flavouring, is not an adequate substitute.

1 cup (150g) self-raising flour
¼ cup (50g) firmly packed brown sugar
½ teaspoon ground cinnamon
½ cup (125ml) skim milk
1 egg yolk
½ cup (110g) canned pie apple, chopped coarsely
2 egg whites
2 granny smith apples (300g), peeled, cored, cut into wedges
2 tablespoons brown sugar, extra
200g low-fat vanilla ice-cream
2 tablespoons maple syrup

1. Combine flour, sugar, cinnamon, milk, egg yolk and canned pie apple in large bowl.
2. Beat egg whites in small bowl with electric mixer on highest speed until soft peaks form; fold gently into apple mixture.
3. Heat medium frying pan; pour ¼-cup batter into pan for each pancake. Cook until browned both sides; repeat with remaining batter. You will need eight pancakes in total.
4. Cook apple wedges and extra sugar over low heat in same pan, stirring, until apple caramelises.
5. Divide pancakes among serving dishes. Top with apple mixture then ice-cream; drizzle with maple syrup.

SERVES 4
per serving 3.4g total fat (1.5g saturated fat); 1545kj (369 cal); 9.8g protein; 76.5g carbohydrate; 3.3g fibre
serving suggestion a flavoured ice-cream, such as toffee crunch or butterscotch, can be used instead of plain vanilla; omit the maple syrup if you use a flavoured ice-cream.

ricotta pancakes

PREPARATION TIME 20 MINUTES COOKING TIME 15 MINUTES

- 1 cup (150g) white self-raising flour
- 1 cup (160g) wholemeal self-raising flour
- ⅓ cup (75g) caster sugar
- 1 cup (200g) low-fat ricotta cheese
- 1½ cups (375ml) low-fat milk
- 2 egg whites
- cooking-oil spray

1. Sift flours and sugar into large bowl, whisk in cheese and milk. Beat egg whites in small bowl until soft peaks form; fold into ricotta mixture.
2. Coat frying pan with cooking-oil spray; pour ½ cup (125ml) of mixture into pan, spread to 14cm round; cook over low heat until browned on both sides. Repeat with remaining mixture. You will need eight pancakes in total.
3. Serve pancakes with a tablespoon of maple syrup, fresh berries and 2 small scoops of low-fat ice-cream per person, if desired.

SERVES 4
per serving 6.5g total fat (3.2g saturated fat); 1825kj (436 cal); 19g protein; 75.8g carbohydrate; 5.9g fibre

ricotta pancakes with vanilla-flavoured quince

PREPARATION TIME 25 MINUTES (PLUS STANDING TIME) COOKING TIME 2 HOURS 45 MINUTES

- 2 small quinces (400g)
- 1 vanilla bean
- 3 cups (750ml) water
- 1½ cups (330g) caster sugar
- ¾ cup (150g) ricotta cheese
- 2 eggs, separated
- ½ teaspoon vanilla extract
- 1 tablespoon caster sugar, extra
- 2 tablespoons milk
- 2 tablespoons self-raising flour
- 10g butter

1. Peel and core quinces; cut each into four slices widthways.
2. Halve vanilla bean lengthways, place in medium saucepan with the water and sugar, stirring, until sugar dissolves; bring to a boil. Add quince; reduce heat, simmer, covered, about 1½ hours. Uncover; simmer, stirring occasionally, about 1 hour or until quince is tender and syrup rosy-pink in colour. Discard vanilla bean.
3. Meanwhile, beat cheese in medium bowl with electric mixer until smooth; beat in egg yolks, vanilla, extra sugar, milk and flour until smooth. Stand mixture 15 minutes.
4. Beat egg whites in small bowl until firm peaks form; fold egg whites, in two batches, into cheese mixture.
5. Melt butter in large frying pan; using 2 tablespoons of batter for each pancake, cook two pancakes at a time, uncovered, until bubbles appear on the surface. Turn; cook until browned lightly. Remove pancakes from pan; cover to keep warm. Repeat process with remaining batter. You will need eight pancakes in total.
6. Place two pancakes on each serving plate; top each with a slice of quince, drizzle with syrup.

SERVES 4
per serving 9.3g total fat (5g saturated fat); 2075kj (496 cal); 8.4g protein; 98.6g carbohydrate; 5.4g fibre

passionfruit soufflés

PREPARATION TIME 10 MINUTES COOKING TIME 15 MINUTES

You will need 4 large passionfruit for this recipe.

1 tablespoon caster sugar
2 egg yolks
⅓ cup (80ml) fresh passionfruit pulp
2 tablespoons cointreau
½ cup (80g) icing sugar
4 egg whites
2 teaspoons icing sugar, extra

1. Preheat oven to 180°C/160°C fan-forced. Grease four 1-cup (250ml) ovenproof dishes. Sprinkle inside of dishes evenly with caster sugar; shake away excess. Place dishes on oven tray.
2. Whisk yolks, passionfruit pulp, liqueur and 2 tablespoons of the icing sugar in large bowl until mixture is combined.
3. Beat egg whites in small bowl with electric mixer until soft peaks form. Gradually add remaining icing sugar; beat until firm peaks form. Gently fold egg white mixture, in two batches, into passionfruit mixture.
4. Divide mixture among prepared dishes; bake, uncovered, about 12 minutes or until puffed and browned lightly. Serve immediately, dusted with extra sifted icing sugar.

SERVES 4
per serving 2.5g total fat (0.7g saturated fat); 773kj (185 cal); 5.4g protein; 31.6g carbohydrate; 2.8g fibre

apricot and honey soufflés

PREPARATION TIME 15 MINUTES COOKING TIME 30 MINUTES

¼ cup (55g) caster sugar
4 apricots (200g)
¼ cup (60ml) water
2 tablespoons honey
4 egg whites

1. Preheat oven to 200°C/180°C fan-forced. Lightly grease six ¾-cup (180ml) ovenproof dishes; sprinkle inside of dishes with a little of the sugar, place on oven tray.
2. Place apricots in small heatproof bowl, cover with boiling water; stand 2 minutes. Drain; cool 5 minutes. Peel and seed apricots; chop flesh finely.
3. Place apricot in small saucepan with the water, honey and remaining sugar; bring to a boil. Reduce heat, simmer, uncovered, about 10 minutes or until apricots soften to a jam-like consistency.
4. Beat egg whites in small bowl with electric mixer until soft peaks form. With motor operating, gradually add hot apricot mixture, beating until combined.
5. Spoon mixture into dishes; bake, uncovered, about 15 minutes or until browned lightly. Serve immediately.

SERVES 6
per serving 0.1g total fat (0g saturated fat); 366kj (87 cal); 2.6g protein; 19.6g carbohydrate; 0.7g fibre

cheese-filled crepe triangles with caramelised oranges

PREPARATION TIME 25 MINUTES (PLUS REFRIGERATION TIME) COOKING TIME 30 MINUTES

You will need 1 lemon, 4 passionfruit and about 6 small oranges for this recipe.

1½ cups (300g) ricotta cheese
2 teaspoons caster sugar
2 teaspoons lemon juice
¼ teaspoon ground cinnamon
¾ cup (110g) plain flour
1 tablespoon caster sugar, extra
1 egg
1⅓ cups (330ml) no-fat milk
1 teaspoon vegetable oil
1 tablespoon coarsely chopped fresh mint

CARAMELISED ORANGES

1kg small oranges
¼ cup (60ml) water
½ cup (55g) caster sugar
⅓ cup (80ml) passionfruit pulp
1 tablespoon lemon juice

1. Place cheese in muslin-lined strainer or colander set over large bowl. Cover then weight cheese with an upright saucer topped with a heavy can. Drain overnight in refrigerator; discard liquid.
2. Mix drained cheese in medium bowl with sugar, juice and cinnamon. Cover; refrigerate until required.
3. Place flour and extra sugar in medium bowl; gradually whisk in combined egg, milk and oil until batter is smooth. Strain into large jug. Cover; refrigerate 30 minutes.
4. Meanwhile, make caramelised oranges.
5. Pour 2 tablespoons of the batter into heated greased 18cm frying pan; cook crepe until browned lightly both sides. Repeat process with remaining batter. You will need 12 crepes in total.
6. Spoon equal amounts of the cheese mixture onto a quarter section of each crepe; fold crepe in half over filling and then in half again to enclose filling and form triangular parcels. Divide filled crepes among serving plates; top with equal amounts of caramelised oranges and mint.

CARAMELISED ORANGES remove peel and pith from oranges over small bowl to save juice; slice oranges thinly. Stir the water and sugar in medium saucepan, without boiling, until sugar dissolves; bring to a boil. Boil, uncovered, without stirring, about 5 minutes or until mixture begins to brown. Add passionfruit, lemon juice and reserved orange juice; cook, stirring occasionally, until any pieces of toffee dissolve. Cool 10 minutes; stir in orange slices.

SERVES 4
per serving 11.6g total fat (6.1g saturated fat); 1770kj (423 cal); 18.8g protein; 60.7g carbohydrate; 7.5g fibre

crepes and strawberries with caramelised cointreau sauce

PREPARATION TIME 15 MINUTES (PLUS REFRIGERATION TIME) COOKING TIME 30 MINUTES

Cointreau is a colourless orange-flavoured liqueur. You can replace it with grand marnier, triple-sec or brandy.

¾ cup (110g) plain flour
½ cup (110g) sugar
1 egg, beaten lightly
1⅓ cups (330ml) skim milk
1 teaspoon vegetable oil
¼ lime
1 teaspoon low-fat dairy-free spread
2 tablespoons cointreau
¼ cup (60ml) water
500g strawberries, halved

1. Combine flour and 1 tablespoon of the sugar in medium bowl, gradually whisk in combined egg, milk and oil until mixture is smooth. Strain batter into large jug, cover; refrigerate 30 minutes.
2. Meanwhile, push fork into skin-side of lime. Melt spread in large frying pan; cook remaining sugar, stirring with lime wedge, until sugar caramelises. Remove from heat; stir in liqueur and the water. Return to heat; bring to a boil. Reduce heat, simmer, uncovered, until mixture reduces by half. Add strawberries; stir gently until well coated then remove from heat.
3. Pour 2 tablespoons of batter into small heated greased frying pan; cook crepe until browned lightly both sides. Repeat with remaining batter to make 12 crepes in total.
4. Serve crepes warm, filled with strawberries in sauce.

SERVES 6
per serving 2.2g total fat (0.5g saturated fat); 799kj (190 cal); 5.3g protein; 34.7g carbohydrate; 0.9g fibre
tips stirring the sugar with lime wedge gives a slight lime flavour to the sauce. Orange juice can be substituted for cointreau for a non-alcoholic alternative.

pink grapefruit soufflés

PREPARATION TIME 30 MINUTES COOKING TIME 25 MINUTES

⅓ cup (75g) caster sugar
⅓ cup (50g) plain flour
¾ cup (180ml) skim milk
1 tablespoon finely grated pink grapefruit rind
¼ cup (60ml) pink grapefruit juice
1 teaspoon grenadine
40g low-fat dairy-free spread
3 egg yolks
5 egg whites

1 Preheat oven to 220°C/200°C fan-forced. Grease six ¾-cup (180ml) ovenproof dishes. Sprinkle base and side of dishes with a little of the sugar; place on oven tray.

2 Place remaining sugar with flour in medium saucepan, gradually whisk in milk; cook, stirring, until mixture boils and thickens. Whisk in rind, juice, grenadine and spread; remove from heat.

3 Transfer mixture to large bowl. Whisk in egg yolks, one at a time.

4 Beat egg whites in small bowl with electric mixer until soft peaks form. Fold a quarter of the egg white mixture into grapefruit mixture; fold in remaining egg white mixture.

5 Spoon mixture into dishes; bake, uncovered, about 15 minutes or until browned lightly.

SERVES 6
per serving 5.2g total fat (1.2g saturated fat); 653kj (156 cal); 6.3g protein; 21.7g carbohydrate; 0.4g fibre
tip grenadine is a non-alcoholic syrup made from pomegranate juice; bright red in colour, it's used to colour and flavour drinks and desserts. You can also find a pomegranate syrup in Middle-Eastern food shops which can be substituted for the grenadine. It has a much tarter flavour, but would work well with the grapefruit in this recipe. Alternatively, you could use raspberry cordial or topping instead of the grenadine to enhance the pink colour.
serving suggestion serve dusted with icing sugar.

low-fat parties

lamb fillo triangles

PREPARATION TIME 30 MINUTES COOKING TIME 20 MINUTES

From the Greek word meaning leaf, fillo means paper-thin sheets of dough, which give the crunch and pleasure of pastry without the kilojoules.

2 cloves garlic, crushed
1 teaspoon ground cumin
1 teaspoon ground coriander
¼ teaspoon ground cinnamon
1 tablespoon pine nuts
250g lean lamb mince
2 tablespoons sultanas
1 tablespoon coarsely chopped fresh coriander
1 tablespoon coarsely chopped fresh mint
16 sheets fillo pastry
cooking-oil spray
1½ cups (420g) low-fat yogurt
½ cup finely shredded fresh mint

1. Cook garlic, spices and pine nuts in medium heated frying pan 1 minute or until fragrant. Add lamb; cook, stirring, until lamb is browned and cooked through. Add sultanas, coriander and chopped mint; stir until just combined. Cool 5 minutes.
2. Preheat oven to 200°C/180°C fan-forced. Oil oven tray.
3. Brush one sheet of the fillo lightly with water; layer with second sheet of fillo. Cut lengthways into thirds. Place 1 tablespoon of the lamb mixture at bottom of one narrow edge of fillo pieces, leaving a 1cm border. Fold opposite corner of fillo diagonally across the filling to form a triangle; continue folding to end of fillo piece, retaining triangle shape. Place on oven trays, seam-side down; repeat with remaining fillo and filling to make 24 triangles in total.
4. Coat triangles with cooking-oil spray; bake, uncovered, about 10 minutes or until browned lightly.
5. Serve fillo triangles with combined yogurt and shredded mint.

SERVES 8
per serving 5.8g total fat (1.9g saturated fat); 899kj (215 cal); 13.5g protein; 26.8g carbohydrate; 1.2g fibre
tip triangles can be prepared ahead. Store uncooked, covered, in freezer. No need to thaw before baking; just place on oven trays and cook until browned.
serving suggestion to make this a more substantial meal, serve it with a greek salad made with low-fat fetta cheese.

lamb fillo triangles

fresh rice paper rolls with prawns

fresh rice paper rolls with prawns

PREPARATION TIME 25 MINUTES COOKING TIME 5 MINUTES

You will need 1 medium carrot and a quarter of a small wombok for this recipe.

24 cooked medium prawns (650g)
1 cup (80g) finely shredded wombok
½ cup (120g) coarsely grated carrot
2 tablespoons chopped fresh mint
2 tablespoons coarsely chopped fresh coriander
12 x 16cm rice paper rounds

DIPPING SAUCE

⅓ cup (75g) caster sugar
¼ cup (60ml) white vinegar
¼ cup (60ml) water
2 teaspoons fish sauce
2 fresh red thai chillies, sliced thinly
1 tablespoon coarsely chopped fresh coriander

1 Shell and devein prawns. Combine wombok, carrot, mint and coriander in medium bowl. Place one rice paper round in medium bowl of warm water until softened slightly; lift sheet carefully from water. Place on board; pat dry with absorbent paper.

2 Place a twelfth of the wombok mixture in centre of rice paper round; top with two prawns. Fold in sides; roll to enclose filling. Repeat with remaining rice paper rounds, wombok mixture and prawns.

3 Just before serving, make dipping sauce. Serve rolls with sauce.

DIPPING SAUCE stir sugar, vinegar and the water in small saucepan over heat until sugar dissolves; bring to a boil. Remove from heat, stir in sauce and chilli; cool. Stir in coriander.

MAKES 12 ROLLS
per roll 0.3g total fat (0.1g saturated fat); 268kj (64 cal); 6.2g protein; 9.2g carbohydrate; 0.6g fibre
tip cover rolls with a damp towel to help prevent the rice paper from drying out.

mussels with chilli-lime sauce

PREPARATION TIME 10 MINUTES

32 cooked mussels, on the half shell

CHILLI-LIME SAUCE

¼ cup (60ml) sweet chilli sauce
1 tablespoon tequila
⅓ cup (80ml) lime juice
1 tablespoon finely chopped fresh coriander

1 Loosen mussels in shell.

2 Make chilli-lime sauce.

3 Divide sauce among mussels; serve cold.

CHILLI-LIME SAUCE combine ingredients in medium jug.

MAKES 32
per mussel 0.1g total fat (0g saturated fat); 38kj (9 cal); 0.5g protein; 1.1g carbohydrate; 0g fibre
tip chilli-lime sauce can be made ahead. Store, covered, in refrigerator.

tzatziki

PREPARATION TIME 10 MINUTES

2 lebanese cucumbers, seeded, coarsely grated
¾ cup (200g) yogurt
1 clove garlic, crushed

1 Combine ingredients in small bowl.

MAKES 1 CUP
per tablespoon 0.5g total fat (0.3g saturated fat); 54kj (13 cal); 0.8g protein; 1.2g carbohydrate; 0.3g fibre

beetroot dip

PREPARATION TIME 10 MINUTES

2 medium beetroot (350g), grated finely
⅓ cup (80g) light sour cream
1 teaspoon red wine vinegar

1 Combine ingredients in small bowl.

MAKES 1 CUP
per tablespoon 1.3g total fat (0.9g saturated fat); 105kj (25 cal); 0.7g protein; 2.5g carbohydrate; 0.8g fibre

baba ghanoush

PREPARATION TIME 10 MINUTES (PLUS REFRIGERATION TIME) COOKING TIME 35 MINUTES (PLUS COOLING TIME)

2 small eggplants (460g)
⅓ cup (80g) low-fat plain yogurt
1 tablespoon lemon juice
2 cloves garlic, crushed
1 teaspoon tahini
1 teaspoon ground cumin
½ teaspoon sesame oil
2 tablespoons finely chopped fresh coriander

1 Preheat oven to 200°C/180°C fan-forced.

2 Halve eggplant lengthways; place on oven tray. Bake, uncovered, about 35 minutes or until tender. Cool; remove and discard skin.

3 Blend or process eggplant with remaining ingredients until smooth. Cover; refrigerate about 30 minutes.

SERVES 4
per serving 2.1g total fat (0.5g saturated fat); 209kj (50 cal); 2.7g protein; 4.7g carbohydrate; 2.9g fibre
tip baba ghanoush can be made 3 days ahead. Store, covered, in refrigerator.

ricotta and green olive dip

PREPARATION TIME 10 MINUTES

½ cup (120g) low-fat ricotta cheese
¼ cup (30g) seeded green olives, finely chopped
1 clove garlic, crushed
¼ cup finely chopped fresh chives
¼ cup finely chopped fresh flat-leaf parsley
1 teaspoon finely grated lemon rind
1 tablespoon lemon juice

1 Combine ingredients in small bowl.

MAKES 1 CUP
per tablespoon 1g total fat (0.6g saturated fat); 75kj (18 cal); 1.2g protein; 1g carbohydrate; 0.2g fibre

cornichon dip

PREPARATION TIME 10 MINUTES

2 tablespoons cornichons, drained, chopped finely
2 green onions, chopped finely
1 tablespoon capers, drained, chopped finely
¾ cup (150g) low-fat cottage cheese
2 teaspoons dijon mustard
1 tablespoon finely chopped red capsicum

1 Combine ingredients in small bowl.

MAKES 1 CUP
per tablespoon 1.5g total fat (0.2g saturated fat); 100kj (24 cal); 1.2g protein; 1.6g carbohydrate; 1.1g fibre
tip French for gherkin, cornichons are a very small variety of pickled cucumber. Traditionally served as an accompaniment to pâté or as a condiment to salads..

honey soy wings

PREPARATION TIME 10 MINUTES COOKING TIME 30 MINUTES

16 small chicken wings (1.3kg)
⅓ cup (115g) honey
½ cup (125ml) salt-reduced soy sauce
3 cloves garlic, crushed
1 tablespoon grated fresh ginger

1. Preheat oven to 220°C/200°C fan-forced.
2. Cut wings into three pieces at joints; discard tips. Combine chicken with remaining ingredients in large bowl.
3. Place chicken mixture, in single layer, in large shallow baking dish; brush any remaining marinade over chicken. Bake, uncovered, turning occasionally, about 30 minutes or until chicken is browned and cooked through.
4. Serve hot.

MAKES 32
per wing 1.4g total fat (0.4g saturated fat); 205kj (49 cal); 6.1g protein; 3.1g carbohydrate; 0.1g fibre
tip wing tips can be used to make chicken stock.

ginger vegetable gow gees with dipping sauce

PREPARATION TIME 1 HOUR COOKING TIME 30 MINUTES

Gow gee wrappers are found packaged in the refrigerated section of Asian grocery stores as well as in some supermarkets. Wonton or spring roll wrappers can be used instead.

cooking-oil spray
1 small red capsicum (150g), chopped coarsely
1 small kumara (250g), grated
1 small buk choy (150g), chopped finely
2 green onions, chopped finely
2 teaspoons grated fresh ginger
1 clove garlic, crushed
1 cup (80g) bean sprouts, chopped
1 tablespoon chopped fresh mint
40 gow gee wrappers

DIPPING SAUCE
1 tablespoon low-salt soy sauce
2 teaspoons lime juice
2 teaspoons sugar
¼ teaspoon sambal oelek

1. Coat frying pan with cooking-oil spray; cook capsicum, kumara, buk choy, onions, ginger and garlic, stirring, until vegetables are just tender. Stir in sprouts and mint.
2. Place a rounded teaspoon of mixture on centre of each wrapper. Brush edges with water, gather together in centre, press firmly to seal.
3. Place gow gees in single layer in steamer; cook, covered, over simmering water for 20 minutes.
4. Make dipping sauce; serve with gow gees.

DIPPING SAUCE combine all ingredients in bowl; mix well.

MAKES 40
per gow gee 0.2g total fat (0g saturated fat); 92kj (22 cal); 0.9g protein; 4.3g carbohydrate; 0.4g fibre
tip gow gees and sauce can be prepared 3 hours ahead. Store separately, covered, in refrigerator.

chicken gow gees

PREPARATION TIME 30 MINUTES (PLUS REFRIGERATION TIME) COOKING TIME 10 MINUTES

Gow gee wrappers are found packaged in the refrigerated section of asian grocery stores as well as in some supermarkets. Wonton or spring roll wrappers can be used instead.

400g lean chicken mince
2 green onions, chopped finely
2 cloves garlic, crushed
2cm piece fresh ginger (10g), coarsely grated
¼ teaspoon five-spice powder
½ cup (50g) packaged breadcrumbs
1 tablespoon hoisin sauce
2 tablespoons coarsely chopped fresh coriander
1 tablespoon coarsely chopped fresh thai basil
1 egg
24 gow gee wrappers

SWEET CHILLI DIPPING SAUCE

⅓ cup (80ml) sweet chilli sauce
¼ cup (60ml) red wine vinegar
¼ cup coarsely chopped fresh coriander

1. Using hand, combine chicken, onion, garlic, ginger, five-spice, breadcrumbs, sauce, herbs and egg in large bowl. Roll level tablespoons of the mixture into balls; place balls on tray. Cover; refrigerate 30 minutes.
2. Meanwhile, make sweet chilli dipping sauce.
3. Brush one wrapper with water; place one chicken ball in centre of wrapper. Fold wrapper over to completely enclose chicken ball. Pleat edge of wrapper along join; repeat process with remaining wrappers and chicken balls.
4. Place gow gees, in single layer, about 1cm apart in baking-paper-lined steamer fitted over large saucepan of boiling water; steam, covered, about 8 minutes or until gow gees are cooked through.

SWEET CHILLI DIPPING SAUCE place ingredients in screw-top jar; shake well.

SERVES 4
per serving 7.3g total fat (1.9g saturated fat); 1363kj (326 cal); 28g protein; 36.1g carbohydrate; 2.7g fibre

oysters with chilli-lime dressing

PREPARATION TIME 10 MINUTES

24 oysters

CHILLI-LIME DRESSING

½ tespoon finely grated lemon rind

¼ cup (60ml) lime juice

2 teaspoons sugar

1 kaffir lime leaf, shredded

2 fresh small red thai chillies, sliced thinly

1 tablespoons peanut oil

1. Make chilli-lime dressing.
2. Divide dressing among oysters.

CHILLI-LIME DRESSING place ingredients in screw-top jar; shake well.

MAKES 24
per oyster 1.8g total fat (0.4g saturated fat); 96kj (23 cal); 1.3g protein; 0.4g carbohydrate; 0g fibre

oysters with green olive paste

PREPARATION TIME 10 MINUTES

24 oysters

GREEN OLIVE PASTE

½ cup (60g) seeded green olives

2 teaspoons olive oil

¼ cup (60ml) red wine vinegar

2 cloves garlic, quartered

2 tablespoons pine nuts, toasted

2 teaspoons coarsely chopped fresh lemon thyme

1. Make green olive paste.
2. Divide paste among oysters; sprinkle with thyme.

GREEN OLIVE PASTE blend or process ingredients until mixture forms a paste.

MAKES 24
per oyster 1.5g total fat (0.2g saturated fat); 96kj (23 cal); 1.4g protein; 0.9g carbohydrate; 0.1g fibre

oysters with lemon-garlic dressing

PREPARATION TIME 10 MINUTES

24 oysters

LEMON-GARLIC DRESSING

2 teaspoons finely grated lemon rind

¼ cup (60ml) lemon juice

2 cloves garlic, crushed

1 tablespoon olive oil

1 tablespoon finely chopped fresh chives

1 Make lemon-garlic dressing.

2 Divide dressing among oysters.

LEMON-GARLIC DRESSING place ingredients in screw-top jar; shake well.

MAKES 24

per oyster 1g total fat (0.2g saturated fat); 63kj (15 cal); 1.3g protein; 0.2g carbohydrate; 0.1g fibre

oysters with tomato-capsicum salsa

PREPARATION TIME 10 MINUTES

24 oysters

TOMATO-CAPSICUM SALSA

2 small vine-ripened tomatoes (60g), seeded, chopped finely

1 small red onion (100g), chopped finely

1 small green capsicum (150g), chopped finely

¼ cup (60ml) tomato juice

¼ cup (60ml) lemon juice

1 teaspoon tabasco sauce

1 tablespoon olive oil

2 cloves garlic, crushed

1 Make tomato-capsicum salsa.

2 Divide salsa among oysters.

TOMATO-CAPSICUM SALSA combine ingredients in small bowl.

MAKES 24

per oyster 1g total fat (0.2g saturated fat); 75kj (18 cal); 1.4g protein; 0.6g carbohydrate; 0.2g fibre

grilled swordfish and snow pea skewers

PREPARATION TIME 20 MINUTES COOKING TIME 10 MINUTES

You will need 24 bamboo skewers; soak them in cold water for at least an hour before use to prevent splintering or scorching.

400g swordfish steak

24 large snow peas (120g)

2 teaspoons tabasco sauce

¼ cup (60ml) lemon juice

2 tablespoons olive oil

1 Remove skin and bones from fish; cut fish into 24 long thin slices. Thread each slice, with one snow pea, on a skewer; brush with half of the combined remaining ingredients.

2 Cook skewers, in batches, on heated oiled grill plate (or grill or barbecue), brushing constantly with remaining tabasco mixture, until fish is browned lightly and cooked as desired. Serve hot.

MAKES 24
per skewer 1.9g total fat (0.3g saturated fat); 138kj (33 cal); 3.6g protein; 0.3g carbohydrate; 0.1g fibre
tip uncooked fish and snow peas can be skewered up to 4 hours ahead. Store, covered, in refrigerator until required.

sashimi stacks

PREPARATION TIME 30 MINUTES

Use the freshest, sashimi-quality fish you can find. Salmon sold as sashimi has to meet stringent guidelines regarding its handling and treatment after leaving the water. We suggest you seek local advice from authorities before eating any raw seafood.

½ lebanese cucumber (65g), seeded

½ medium avocado (125g)

400g piece sashimi salmon

1 teaspoon wasabi paste

4 green onions, quartered lengthways

½ sheet toasted seaweed (nori), cut into 1cm strips

2 teaspoons toasted sesame seeds

2 tablespoons japanese soy sauce

1 Cut cucumber and avocado into long thin strips.

2 Cut salmon into 32 thin slices.

3 Place 16 slices of the salmon on serving platter; spread each with a little wasabi then divide cucumber, avocado and onion among slices. Top each stack with one remaining salmon slice.

4 Wrap seaweed strip around each stack; sprinkle each with sesame seeds. Serve sashimi stacks with soy sauce.

MAKES 16
per serving 3.3g total fat (0.7g saturated fat); 217kj (52 cal); 5.3g protein; 0.3g carbohydrate; 0.3g fibre
tip use scissors to cut the seaweed into strips.

prawn wontons with sweet chilli sauce

PREPARATION TIME 45 MINUTES COOKING TIME 20 MINUTES

1kg medium uncooked prawns
3 green onions, chopped coarsely
1 tablespoon grated fresh ginger
1 clove garlic, quartered
1 tablespoon lime juice
1 tablespoon finely chopped fresh vietnamese mint
1 tablespoon finely chopped fresh thai basil
40 wonton wrappers
1 egg, beaten lightly
½ cup (125ml) sweet chilli sauce

1. Shell and devein prawns.
2. Blend or process prawns, onion, ginger, garlic and juice until mixture forms a paste. Stir in mint and basil.
3. Place 1 heaped teaspoon of prawn filling in centre of each wonton wrapper. Brush edges with egg; pinch edges together to seal.
4. Place wontons, in batches, in single layer in bamboo steamer; cook, covered, over wok of simmering water about 10 minutes or until wontons are cooked through.
5. Serve wontons with chilli sauce.

MAKES 40

per wonton 0.4g total fat (0.1g saturated fat); 150kj (36 cal); 3.7g protein; 4.2g carbohydrate; 0.2g fibre

tips you can deep-fry wontons in vegetable oil, in batches, until browned all over. Uncooked wontons are suitable to freeze for up to 3 months. There's no need to defrost them. Remove from freezer and cook in covered bamboo steamer for 15 minutes or until cooked through.

serving suggestion serve steamed wontons either using the bamboo steamer as a tray or sit each wonton on a porcelain chinese soup spoon, drizzle with sweet chilli sauce then pass around on trays to guests.

oven-baked spring rolls

PREPARATION TIME 30 MINUTES COOKING TIME 20 MINUTES

Named because they are usually served on the first day of the Chinese New Year (early in the Northern Hemisphere's spring), spring rolls are a perennially popular appetiser. Here, they're baked instead of deep-fried, reducing the kilojoule count dramatically. You will need half a small wombok for this recipe.

4 dried shiitake mushrooms
5 green onions, sliced thinly
1 clove garlic, crushed
1 teaspoon grated fresh ginger
1 medium red capsicum (200g), sliced thinly
2 cups (160g) finely shredded wombok
⅓ cup (65g) canned bamboo shoots, drained, sliced thinly
1 tablespoon light soy sauce
1 tablespoon sweet chilli sauce
½ teaspoon fish sauce
¼ cup finely chopped fresh coriander
1 cup (80g) bean sprouts
15 sheets fillo pastry
cooking-oil spray

CHILLI SOY DIPPING SAUCE

¼ cup (60ml) light soy sauce
¼ cup (60ml) sweet chilli sauce
2 tablespoons lime juice
1 teaspoon sugar
1 tablespoon finely chopped fresh coriander
1 fresh red thai chilli, chopped finely

1 Place mushrooms in small heatproof bowl; cover with boiling water. Stand 20 minutes or until tender; drain. Discard stems; slice caps thinly.

2 Preheat oven to 200°C/180°C fan-forced. Oil oven tray.

3 Heat large oiled frying pan; cook onion, garlic and ginger, stirring, until onion softens. Add mushrooms, capsicum, wombok, bamboo shoots and combined sauces; cook, stirring, until wombok just wilts. Remove from heat; stir in coriander and sprouts. Drain away excess liquid.

4 Cut fillo sheets in half. Coat one piece fillo with cooking-oil spray; fold in half crossways. Coat again with cooking-oil spray; turn fillo so folded edge is on your right and one short side faces you. Place 1 tablespoon of the vegetable mixture 2cm from bottom edge of fillo. Fold in sides; roll bottom to top to enclose filling. Repeat with remaining pieces fillo and filling. You will make 30 rolls in total.

5 Place rolls on oven tray. Bake, uncovered, about 15 minutes or until rolls are browned lightly.

6 Make chilli soy dipping sauce. Serve rolls with dipping sauce.

CHILLI SOY DIPPING SAUCE combine ingredients in small bowl.

MAKES 30
per roll 0.4g total fat (0.1g saturated fat); 155kj (37 cal); 1.4g protein; 6.6g carbohydrate; 0.6g fibre
tip you can vary the vegetables in the filling to suit your personal taste.

skewered lemon prawns

PREPARATION TIME 15 MINUTES (PLUS REFRIGERATION TIME) COOKING TIME 5 MINUTES

Soak bamboo skewers in cold water for at least 1 hour before use to prevent splintering or scorching.

1.5kg uncooked large king prawns

¼ cup (60ml) olive oil

1 tablespoon grated lemon rind

1. Remove heads and legs from prawns, leaving shells intact. Gently pull veins from each prawn, from head end. Cut along the length of the prawn on the underside, without cutting all the way through. Thread prawns onto skewers.
2. Place prawns in shallow dish, pour over combined oil and rind; sprinkle with freshly ground black pepper. Cover; refrigerate for 3 hours.
3. Cook prawns on heated barbecue, flesh-side down, until browned lightly. Turn; cook until just cooked through.
4. Serve prawn skewers with lemon wedges, if desired.

SERVES 8
per serving 7.4g total fat (1.1g saturated fat); 602kj (144 cal); 19.2g protein; 0g carbohydrate; 0.1g fibre

tikka prawns with raita

PREPARATION TIME 20 MINUTES COOKING TIME 10 MINUTES

24 uncooked large king prawns (1.2kg)

¼ cup (70g) tikka paste

1½ cups (420g) yogurt

¼ cup finely chopped fresh coriander leaves

½ teaspoon ground cumin

1. Shell and devein prawns, leaving tails intact.
2. Combine paste and ½ cup of the yogurt in small bowl.
3. Cook prawns, in batches, on heated oiled grill plate (or grill or barbecue), brushing with paste mixture, until just changed in colour.
4. Meanwhile, combine remaining yogurt in small bowl with coriander and cumin.
5. Serve prawns hot with raita.

MAKES 24
per prawn 1g total fat (0.1g saturated fat); 134kj (32 cal); 5.3g protein; 0.2g carbohydrate; 0.3g fibre
per tablespoon raita 0.3g total fat (0.2g saturated fat); 50kj (12 cal); 0.9g protein; 1.3g carbohydrate; 0g fibre
tip uncooked prawns can be marinated and raita made a day ahead. Store separately, covered, in refrigerator.

salmon tartare

PREPARATION TIME 30 MINUTES

Salmon sold as sashimi salmon has met stringent guidelines regarding its treatment since leaving the water, so you can be guaranteed of its quality and that it's safe to eat raw.

250g sashimi salmon, chopped finely
1 small red onion (100g), chopped finely
2 tablespoons lemon juice
2 teaspoons prepared horseradish
1 tablespoon drained capers, chopped finely
2 tablespoons finely chopped fresh chives
1 packet (80g) mini toasts
¼ cup (65g) crème fraîche
40 small fresh dill sprigs

1. Place salmon, onion, juice, horseradish, capers and chives in medium bowl; toss gently to combine.
2. Divide salmon tartare among mini toasts; top each with crème fraîche and a dill sprig. Serve cold.

MAKES 40
per toast 1.2g total fat (0.5g saturated fat); 92kj (22 cal); 1.5g protein; 1.4g carbohydrate; 0.1g fibre
tip tartare ingredients can be chopped up to 3 hours ahead of combining. Store separately, covered, in refrigerator until required.

tarragon and lime scallops

PREPARATION TIME 15 MINUTES COOKING TIME 10 MINUTES

You will need 24 bamboo skewers; soak them in cold water for at least an hour before use to prevent splintering or scorching.

24 scallops (500g), without roe
2 tablespoons coarsely chopped fresh tarragon
1 tablespoon lime juice
1 tablespoon olive oil
3 limes

1. Rinse scallops under cold water; dry with absorbent paper.
2. Combine scallops with tarragon, juice and oil in medium bowl.
3. Cut each lime into eight wedges. Thread one scallop and one lime wedge on each skewer.
4. Cook skewers, in batches, on heated oiled grill plate (or grill or barbecue) until scallops are cooked through. Serve hot.

MAKES 24
per skewer 0.9g total fat (0.2g saturated fat); 84kj (20 cal); 2.5g protein; 0.2g carbohydrate; 0.2g fibre
tip uncooked scallops and lime wedges can be skewered up to 4 hours ahead. Store, covered, in refrigerator until required.

steamed sweet chilli prawn dumplings

PREPARATION TIME 20 MINUTES COOKING TIME 5 MINUTES

500g medium uncooked prawns
2 tablespoons sweet chilli sauce
2 green onions, sliced thinly
1 clove garlic, crushed
1 teaspoon grated fresh ginger
2 tablespoons coarsely chopped fresh coriander
1 teaspoon finely chopped fresh lemon grass
24 gow gee wrappers

1. Shell and devein prawns; chop finely.
2. Combine prawn, sauce, onion, garlic, ginger, coriander and lemon grass in medium bowl.
3. Place 1 heaped teaspoon of the prawn filling in centre of each gow gee wrapper; brush edges with water. Fold wrapper in half to enclose filling; pinch edges together to seal.
4. Place dumplings, in batches, in single layer in bamboo steamer. Cook, covered, over wok of simmering water about 5 minutes or until dumplings are cooked through.

SERVES 6
per serving 0.9g total fat (0.2g saturated fat); 472kj (113 cal); 11g protein; 14.9g carbohydrate; 1.1g fibre
tip wonton wrappers can be used as an alternative to gow gee wrappers.
serving suggestion serve drizzled with extra sweet chilli sauce and a small bowl of soy sauce for dipping.

glossary

ALLSPICE also known as pimento or Jamaican pepper; so-named because is tastes like a combination of nutmeg, cumin, clove and cinnamon – all spices. Is available whole (a pea-size dark-brown berry) or ground, and used in both sweet and savoury dishes.

ALMONDS flat, pointed ended nuts with pitted brown shell enclosing a creamy white kernel which is covered by a brown skin. Available blanched, flaked, slivered and ground.

ARTICHOKES

globe large flower-bud of the thistle family; having tough petal-like leaves, edible in part when cooked.

hearts tender centre of the globe artichoke. Artichoke hearts can be harvested fresh from the plant or purchased in brine canned or in glass jars.

jerusalem neither from Jerusalem nor an artichoke, this crunchy tuber tastes a bit like a fresh water chestnut and is related to the sunflower family.

BAKING POWDER a raising agent consisting mainly of two parts cream of tartar to one part bicarbonate of soda (baking soda). The acid and alkaline combination, when moistened and heated, gives off carbon dioxide which aerates and lightens the mixture during baking.

BEANS

black also known as turtle beans or black kidney beans, they are an earthy-flavoured dried bean completely different from the better-known Chinese black beans (which are fermented soy beans). Most used in Mexican, South and Central American, and Caribbean cooking, especially soups and stews.

borlotti also called roman beans, they can be eaten fresh or dried. Borlotti can also substitute for pinto beans as they are similar in appearance – both are pale pink or beige with darker red spots. They can be used for Mexican frijoles refritos (refried beans), and in soups and salads.

broad also known as fava, windsor and horse beans, these are available dried, fresh, canned and frozen. Fresh and frozen, they are best peeled twice (discarding both the outer long green pod and the beige-green tough inner shell).

butter cans labelled butter beans are, in fact, cannellini beans. Confusingly butter is also another name for lima beans, sold both dried and canned; a large beige bean having a mealy texture and mild taste.

cannellini small white dried bean similar in appearance and flavour to other *Phaseolus vulgaris* varieties great northern and navy or haricot beans. Sometimes sold as butter beans.

green sometimes called french or string beans (although the tough string they once had has generally been bred out of them), this long fresh bean is consumed pod and all.

haricot similar in appearance and flavour to other small dried white beans such as great northern, navy and cannellini; sold dried, good in soups and casseroles.

sprouts also known as bean shoots; tender new growths of assorted beans and seeds germinated for consumption as sprouts. The most readily available are mung bean, soy bean, alfalfa and snow pea sprouts.

BEETROOT also known as red beets; firm, round root vegetable. Can be eaten raw, grated, in salads; boiled and sliced.

BROCCOLINI a cross between broccoli and chinese kale, is milder and sweeter than broccoli. Each long stem is topped by a loose floret that closely resembles broccoli; from floret to stem, broccolini is completely edible. Although broccolini looks somewhat like asparagus, these vegetables are not related.

BUK CHOY also known as bak choy, pak choi, chinese white cabbage or chinese chard, has a fresh, mild mustard taste; use stems and leaves, stir-fry or braised. **Baby buk choy**, also known as pak kat farang, Shanghai buk choy, chinese chard or white cabbage, is small and more tender than buk choy. Its mildly acrid, distinctively appealing taste has brought baby buk choy to the forefront of commonly used Asian greens.

BURGHUL also called bulghur wheat; hulled steamed wheat kernels that, once dried are crushed into various size grains. Used in Middle-Eastern dishes such as kibbeh and tabbouleh.

CAYENNE PEPPER a thin-fleshed, long, extremely hot dried red chilli, usually purchased ground; both arbol and guajillo chillies are the fresh sources for cayenne.

CELERIAC tuberous root with brown skin, white flesh with celery-like flavour.

CHEESE

bocconcini from the diminutive of boccone meaning mouthful, is the term used for walnut-sized, baby mozzarella, a delicate, semi-soft, white cheese traditionally made in Italy from buffalo milk. Spoils rapidly so must be kept under refrigeration, in brine, for 1 or 2 days at most.

brie often referred to as the 'queen of cheeses', brie originated in France but is now manufactured locally. Smooth and voluptuous, brie has a bloomy white rind and a creamy centre which becomes runnier as it ripens.

cheddar the most common cow milk 'tasty' cheese; should be aged, hard and have a pronounced bite. For our lower-fat versions we used one with no more than 20% fat.

fetta Greek in origin; a crumbly textured goat or sheep milk cheese with a sharp, salty taste. For our lower-fat versions we used one with an average fat content of 15%.

goat made from goat milk, has an earthy, strong taste; available in both soft and firm textures, in various shapes and sizes, sometimes rolled in ash or herbs.

gorgonzola a creamy Italian blue cheese having a mild, sweet taste; good as an accompaniment to fruit or to flavour sauces etc.

haloumi a firm, cream-coloured sheep milk cheese matured in brine; somewhat like a minty, salty fetta in flavour, haloumi can be grilled or fried, briefly, without breaking down.

mozarella soft, spun-curd cheese; originated in southern Italy where it is traditionally made from water buffalo milk. Cow milk versions of this product commonly known as pizza cheese are now available. It has a low melting point and wonderfully elastic texture when heated and is used to add texture rather than flavour. For our lower-fat versions we used one with a fat content of 17.5%.

parmesan also called parmigiano, parmesan is a hard, grainy cow milk cheese which originated in the Parma region of Italy. The curd is salted in brine for a month before being aged for up to two years in humid conditions. Parmesan is mainly grated as a topping for pasta, soups and other savoury dishes, but it is also delicious eaten with fruit.

CHICKPEAS also called garbanzos, hummus or channa; an irregularly round, sandy-coloured legume used extensively in Mediterranean and Latin cooking.

CHILLI available in many different types and sizes. Use rubber gloves when seeding and chopping fresh chillies as they can burn your skin. Removing seeds and membranes lessens the heat level.

bottled, hot red whole small red chillies in a vinegar and salt solution.

chipotle hot, dried, smoked jalapenos, available in cans.

green generally unripened Thai chillies but sometimes different varieties that are ripe when green, such as habanero, poblano or serrano chillies.

hot sauce we used a hot Chinese variety made from bird's-eye chillies, salt and vinegar. Use sparingly, increasing the quantity to your taste.

jalapenos fairly hot green chillies, available in brine bottled or fresh from specialty greengrocers.

paste every Asian cuisine has its own chilli paste, and each is different from the next. Vietnamese chilli paste is quite hot, Indonesian sambal oelek (chilli with ginger, oil and garlic) has a medium heat or, for less heat, mild sweet Thai chilli sauce, made with vinegar and sugar.

serrano hot and savoury Mexican chilli; available in cans.

sweet chilli sauce a comparatively mild, thin Thai sauce made from red chillies, sugar, garlic and vinegar; used as a condiment more often than in cooking.

CHINESE BARBECUED DUCK traditionally cooked in special ovens, this duck has a sweet-sticky coating made from soy sauce, sherry, five-spice and hoisin sauce. It is available from Asian food stores.

CHINESE BROCCOLI also called gai lan, kanah, gai lum, chinese broccoli and chinese kale; appreciated more for its stems than its coarse leaves. Can be served steamed and stir-fried, in soups and noodle dishes.

CHOCOLATE

choc bits also called chocolate chips and chocolate morsels; available in milk, white and dark chocolate. Made of cocoa liquor, cocoa butter, sugar and an emulsifier; hold their shape in baking and are ideal for decorating.

compounded best used for dipping and coating.

melts discs of compounded chocolate ideal for melting and moulding; available in milk and white chocolate.

CHOY SUM also known as pakaukeo or flowering cabbage, a member of the buk choy family; easy to identify with its long stems, light green leaves and yellow flowers. Is eaten, stems and all, steamed or stir-fried.

COCONUT

cream is obtained commercially from the first pressing of the coconut flesh alone, without the addition of water; the second pressing (less rich) is sold as the milk. Available in cans and cartons at supermarkets.

desiccated unsweetened, concentrated, dried finely shredded coconut.

milk not the juice found inside the fruit, which is known as coconut water, but the diluted liquid from the second pressing from the white meat of a mature coconut (the first pressing produces coconut cream). Available in cans and cartons at supermarkets.

CORNFLOUR also called cornstarch; used as a thickening agent.

COUSCOUS a fine, grain-like cereal product, originally from North Africa; made from semolina.

CUCUMBER

lebanese short, slender and thin-skinned; this variety is also known as the European or burpless cucumber.

telegraph long and green with ridges running down its entire length; also known as continental cucumber.

CUSTARD POWDER instant powdered mixture used to make pouring custard; similar to North American instant pudding mixes.

DAIKON sweet, fresh flavour. The daikon's flesh is crisp, juicy and white, while the skin can be either creamy white or black. It can range from 6 to 15 inches in length with an average of 2 to 3 inches. Some exceptional daikon are as fat as a football. Choose those that are firm and unwrinkled. Refrigerate, wrapped in a plastic bag, up to a week. Daikon radishes are used raw in salads, shredded as a garnish or cooked in a variety of ways; it is also called the giant white radish.

DHAL an Indian term that describes both legumes, dried peas and beans, and the range of spicy stew-like dishes containing them.

CREME FRAICHE a naturally fermented cream (minimum fat content 35%) having a velvety texture and tangy taste.

EGGPLANT also known as aubergine; belongs to the same family as tomatoes, chillies and potatoes. Ranging in size from tiny to very large and in colour from pale green to deep purple, eggplant has an equally wide variety of flavours.

FRISEE also known as curly endive; a curly-leafed green vegetable, mainly used in salads.

GALANGAL also known as ka, a rhizome with a hot ginger-citrusy flavour; used similarly to ginger and garlic as a seasoning and as an ingredient. Sometimes known as Thai, Siamese or Laos ginger, it also comes in a dried powdered form called laos. Fresh ginger can be substituted for fresh galangal but the flavour of the dish will not be the same.

GINGER

fresh also called green or root ginger; the thick gnarled root of a tropical plant. Can be kept, peeled, covered with dry sherry in a jar and refrigerated, or frozen in an airtight container.

ground also known as powdered ginger; used as a flavouring in cakes, pies and puddings but cannot be substituted for fresh ginger.

GLUCOSE SYRUP also known as liquid glucose, made from wheat starch; used in jam and confectionery and available at health food stores and supermarkets.

GOW GEE PASTRY spring roll or egg pastry sheets or wonton wrappers can be substituted.

GREMOLATA A garnish usually made of minced parsley, lemon peel and garlic, but can also include breadcrumbs. Can be sprinkled over dishes or used as a coating for meat.

GROUND NUTS we used packaged commercially ground nuts in our recipes, unless otherwise specified.

HERBS we have specified when to use fresh or dried herbs. We used dried (not ground) herbs in the proportion of one to four for fresh herbs; use 1 teaspoon dried herbs instead of 4 teaspoons (1 tablespoon) chopped fresh herbs.

basil generally there are three types of fresh basil used in our recipes: **holy** (also known as kra pao or hot basil) is different from Thai basil (horapa) and the familiar sweet basil used in Italian cooking; has an almost hot, spicy flavour similar to clove, and is used in many Thai dishes, especially curries. It is also used to treat indigestion and stimulate the appetite. Can be distinguished from horapa by the tiny 'hairs' on its leaves and stems. **Thai** (also known as horapa), is different from holy basil and sweet basil in both look and taste. Having smaller leaves and purplish stems, it has a slight licorice or aniseed taste, and is one of the basic flavours that typify Thai cuisine. **Sweet** used extensively in Italian dishes and is one of the main ingredients in pesto.

chives related to the onion and leek, with subtle onion flavour. **Garlic chives** (also known as Chinese chives), are strongly flavoured, have flat leaves and are eaten as a vegetable, usually in stir-fries.

coriander also known as pak chee, cilantro or chinese parsley; bright-green-leafed herb with a pungent flavour. Often stirred into or sprinkled over a dish just before serving for maximum impact. Both the stems and roots of coriander are also used in Thai cooking; wash well before chopping. If roots are unavailable, use two stems per root instead.

parsley, flat-leaf also known as continental parsley or Italian parsley.

sage pungent herb with narrow, grey-green leaves; slightly bitter with a slightly musty mint aroma. Refrigerate fresh sage wrapped in a paper towel and sealed in a plastic bag for up to 4 days. Dried sage comes whole, crumbled or ground. It should be stored in a cool, dark place for no more than three months.

thyme a basic herb of French cuisine is widely used in Mediterranean countries to flavour meats and sauces. A member of mint family, it has tiny grey-green leaves that give off a pungent minty, light-lemon aroma. Dried thyme comes in both leaf and powder form. Dried thyme should be stored in a cool, dark place for no more than three months. Fresh thyme should be stored in the refrigerator, wrapped in a damp paper towel and placed in a sealed bag for no more than a few days. **Lemon thyme** if unavailable, you can use fresh thyme with a dash of lemon zest.

veitnamese mint not a mint at all, but a pungent and peppery narrow-leafed member of the buckwheat family. Not confined to Vietnam, it is also known as Cambodian mint, pak pai (Thailand), laksa leaf (Indonesia), daun kesom (Singapore)... and rau ram in Vietnam! It is a common ingredient in Thai foods, particularly soups, salads and stir-fries. If unavailable, substitute with equal parts mint and coriander (cilantro).

KAFFIR LIME also called magrood, leech lime or jeruk purut; wrinkled, bumpy-skinned green fruit of a small citrus tree originally grown in South Africa and Southeast Asia. Give Thai food a unique aromatic flavour; usually only the zest is used. It's leaves look like two glossy dark green leaves joined end to end, forming a rounded hourglass shape. Used fresh or dried in many Asian dishes and used like bay leaves or curry leaves, especially in Thai cooking. Sold fresh, dried or frozen, the dried leaves are less potent so double the number called for in a recipe if you substitute them for fresh leaves. A strip of fresh lime peel may be substituted for each kaffir lime leaf.

LEMON GRASS a tall, clumping, lemon-smelling and tasting, sharp-edged grass; the white lower part of the stem is used, finely chopped, in cooking.

LENTILS (red, brown, yellow) dried pulses often identified by and named after their colour.

LIGHT CORN SYRUP an imported product available in some supermarkets, delicatessens and health food stores. Made from cornstarch, it is a popular ingredient in American cooking for frostings, jams and jellies.

LOW-FAT DAIRY-FREE SPREAD we used a polyunsaturated, cholesterol-free, reduced-fat diet spread made of vegetable oils, water and gelatine having 2.35g of fat per 5g.

MACADAMIA native to Australia, rich and buttery nut; store in the refrigerator because of its high oil content.

MAILBU coconut-flavoured rum

MAPLE SYRUP a thin syrup distilled from the sap of the maple tree. Maple-flavoured syrup or pancake syrup is not an adequate substitute for the real thing. Maple-flavoured syrup is made from sugar cane and is also know as golden or pancake syrup.

MAYONNAISE we prefer to use whole egg mayonnaise in our recipes.

MILK we used full-cream homogenised milk unless otherwise specified.

buttermilk sold alongside fresh milk products in supermarkets and is commercially made, by a method similar to yoghurt. Despite the implication of its name, it is low in fat and is a good substitute for dairy products such as cream or sour cream, good in baking and salad dressings.

sweetened condensed from which 60% of the water had been removed; the remaining milk is then sweetened with sugar.

evaporated unsweetened canned milk from which water has been extracted by evaporation.

skim use milk with 0.1% fat content.

MIXED PEEL candied citrus peel.

MOLASSES a thick, dark brown syrup, the residue of sugar refinement. Available in light, dark and blackstrap varieties it has a slightly bitter taste. An essential ingredient in American cooking, molasses is used in gingerbread, shoofly pie and Boston baked beans.

MUSHROOMS

button small, cultivated white mushrooms with a mild flavour.

caps slightly larger and with a stronger flavour than buttons, caps, sometimes called cups, are firm textured and ideal for soups, pies and casseroles.

dried porcini the richest-flavoured mushrooms, also known as cèpes. They are expensive but due to their strong flavour, only a small amount is required. Need to be soaked before use.

dried shiitake also known as donko or dried Chinese mushrooms; have a unique meaty flavour. Sold dried; rehydrate before use.

field the correct name for mushrooms found growing wild on forest floors. Australian varieties include the Australian cepe or slippery jack and the saffron milk cap.

flat large, flat mushrooms with a rich earthy flavour, ideal for filling and barbecuing. They are sometimes misnamed field mushrooms which are wild mushrooms.

oyster also known as abalone; grey-white mushroom shaped like a fan. Prized for their smooth texture and subtle, oyster-like flavour.

shiitake when fresh are also known as chinese black, forest or golden oak mushrooms; although cultivated, have the earthiness and taste of wild mushrooms. Are large and meaty; often used as a substitute for meat in some Asian vegetarian dishes. When dried, they are called donko or dried chinese mushrooms; rehydrate before use.

swiss brown light to dark brown with full-bodied flavour also known as roman or cremini. Button or cap mushrooms can be substituted.

MUSTARD

dijon a pale brown, distinctively flavoured fairly mild French mustard.

french plain mild mustard.

mild english less pungent version of traditional hot English mustard.

seeded also known as wholegrain. A French-style coarse-grain mustard made from crushed mustard seeds and dijon-style French mustard.

NOODLES

asian also known as stir-fry, hokkien and singapore noodles; fresh wheat noodles resembling thick, yellow-brown spaghetti needing no pre-cooking before being used.

fresh egg also known as ba mee or yellow noodles; made from wheat flour and eggs, and sold fresh or dried. Range in size from very fine strands to wide, thick spaghetti-like pieces as thick as a shoelace.

fried crispy egg noodles packaged (commonly a 100g packet) already deep-fried.

soba thin spaghetti-like pale brown noodle from Japan made from buckwheat and varying proportions of wheat flour.

somen extremely thin dried wheat noodle from Japan; can be made with egg, then is called tamago somen.

udon available fresh and dried, these Japanese broad white wheat noodles are similar to the ones in homemade chicken noodle soup.

vermicelli also known as sen mee, mei fun or bee hoon. These are used throughout Asia in spring rolls and cold salads; similar to bean threads, only they're longer and made with rice flour instead of mung bean starch. Before using, soak the dried noodles in hot water until they're soft (about 15 minutes), then boil them briefly (from 1 to 3 minutes) and rinse with hot water. You can also deep-fry the dried noodles until they're crunchy and then use them in Chinese chicken salad, or as a garnish or bed for sauces.

OIL

cooking spray we use a cholesterol-free cooking spray based on canola oil.

grapeseed oil from grape seeds.

olive made from ripened olives. Extra virgin and virgin are the first and second press, respectively, of the olives and are considered the best; extra light or light is diluted and refers to taste not fat levels.

peanut pressed from ground peanuts; most commonly used in Asian cooking because of its capacity to handle high heat without burning.

sesame made from roasted, crushed, white sesame seeds; a flavouring rather than a cooking medium.

vegetable any oils sourced from plants rather than animal fats.

ONIONS

green also called scallion or (incorrectly) shallot; an immature onion picked before the bulb has formed, having a long, bright-green edible stalk.

red also known as Spanish, red Spanish or Bermuda onion; a sweet-flavoured, large, purple-red onion.

shallots also called French shallots, golden shallots or eschalots; small, elongated, brown-skinned members of the onion family. Grows in tight clusters similar to garlic.

spring crisp, narrow green-leafed tops and a round sweet white bulb larger than green onions.

PASTA

ditali, ditalini tiny, very short tubes of macaroni, often used in minestrone.

farfalle bow-tie shaped short pasta; sometimes known as butterfly pasta.

gnochhi Italian 'dumplings' made of potatoes, semolina or flour; can be cooked in boiling water or baked with cheese or sauce.

pappardelle in Bologna, these are also called larghissime, which means 'very wide'. They are the widest ribbon and can cut either straight or saw-edged.

penne translated literally as 'quills'; ridged macaroni cut into short lengths on the diagonal.

risoni small rice-shape pasta; very similar to another small pasta, orzo.

PASTES some recipes in this book call for commercially prepared pastes of various strength and flavours, ranging from the mild Tikka and medium Madras to the Fiery Vindaloo. Use whichever one you feel suits your spice-level tolerance best.

harissa sauce or paste made from dried red chillies, garlic, oil and sometimes caraway seeds.

shrimp also called kapi, trasi and blanchan; a strong-scented, very firm preserved paste made of salted dried shrimp. Used as a pungent flavouring in many South-East Asian soups and sauces. It should be chopped or sliced thinly then wrapped in foil and roasted before use.

tandoori consisting of garlic, ginger, tamarind, coriander, chilli and spices.

thai red curry consisting of red onion, red chilli, soy bean oil, garlic, galangal, lemon grass, shrimp paste, citrus peel, salt, coriander seed and citric acid.

tikka a mild paste consisting of chilli, coriander, cumin, lentil flour, garlic, ginger, oil, turmeric, fennel, pepper, cloves, cinnamon and cardamom.

vindaloo a fiery hot/sour flavour consisting of coriander, cumin, turmeric, chilli, ginger, garlic, tamarind, lentil flour and spices.

PATTY-PAN SQUASH also called crookneck or custard marrow pumpkins; a round, slightly flat summer squash being yellow to pale green in colour and having a scalloped edge. Harvested young, it has firm white flesh and a distinct flavour.

PEARS

beurre bosc sweet, juicy dessert pear with a long tapering neck and greenish-brown skin which changes to cinnamon-brown skin when ripe. Ideal cooking pear, particularly for long cooking such as poaching or baking.

corella miniature dessert pear up to 10cm long.

nashi also called Japanese or Asian pear; a member of the pear family but similar in appearance to an apple.

PECANS native to the United States; golden-brown, buttery and rich. Good in savoury as well as sweet dishes; especially good in salads.

PEPITAS dried pumpkin seeds.

PINE NUTS also known as pignoli; not in fact a nut but a small, cream-coloured kernel from pine cones.

PITTA also known as Lebanese bread. This wheat-flour pocket bread is sold in large, flat pieces that separate into two thin rounds. Also available in small thick pieces called pocket pitta.

POLENTA a flour-like cereal made of dried corn (maize) sold ground in several different textures; also the name of the dish made from it.

POTATOES

congo purple flesh, small, elongated, sweet, mealy; good boiled and in salads.

sebago white skin, oval; good fried, mashed and baked.

desiree oval, smooth and pink-skinned, waxy yellow flesh; good in salads, boiled and roasted.

kipfler small, finger-shaped, nutty flavour; great baked and in salads.

new potatoes also known as chats; not a separate variety but an early harvest with very thin skin; good unpeeled steamed, eaten hot or cold in salads.

pontiac large, red skin, deep eyes round, white flesh, good grated, boiled and baked.

idaho also called Russet Burbank; russet in colour, fabulous baked.

pink-eye small, off-white skin, deep purple eyes; good steamed and boiled, great baked.

PRESERVED LEMON whole or quartered salted lemons preserved in a mixture of olive oil and lemon juice are a North African specialty usually added to casseroles and tagines to impart a rich, salty-sour acidic flavour. They're available here from good food shops and delicatessens. Rinse preserved lemon well under cold water before using.

QUINCE yellow-skinned fruit with hard texture and astringent, tart taste; eaten cooked or as a preserve.

RAITA yogurt that is whipped and seasoned with salt, pepper and one or two various spices, usually sour or piquant in flavour. Has other ingredients added to it and is served as a condiment with the main meal; possesses cooling properties to help temper the heat of a curry.

READY-ROLLED PUFF PASTRY packaged sheets of frozen puff pastry, available from supermarkets.

RICE

arborio small, round grain rice well-suited to absorb a large amount of liquid; especially suitable for risottos.

basmati a white, fragrant long-grained rice. It should be washed several times before cooking.

calrose a medium-grain rice that is extremely versatile; can substitute for short- or long-grain if necessary.

jasmine fragrant long-grained rice; white rice can be substituted but will not taste the same.

koshihikari small, round-grain white rice. Substitute short-grain rice and cook by the absorption method.

ROCKET also known as arugula, rugula and rucola; a peppery-tasting green leaf which can be used similarly to baby spinach leaves, eaten raw in salad or used in cooking.

SAMBAL OELEK also ulek or olek; is a salty paste made from ground chillies and vinegar.

SAUCES

black bean a Chinese sauce made from fermented soy beans, spices, water and wheat flour, and is much used in stir-fry cooking.

char siu a Chinese barbecue sauce made from sugar, water, salt, fermented soybean paste, honey, soy sauce, malt syrup and spices. Available at most supermarkets or Asian food stores.

fish made from pulverised salted fermented fish (most often anchovies); has a pungent small and strong taste. There are many versions of varying intensity, so use according to your taste.

kecap manis called sieu wan in Thai, sold here usually under this more familiar Indonesian/Malaysian name. A dark, thick sweet soy sauce used in most Southeast Asian cuisines. Depending on the brand, the soy's sweetness is derived from the addition of either molasses or palm sugar when brewed.

SAVOY CABBAGE large, heavy head with crinkled dark-green outer leaves; a fairly mild tasting cabbage.

SEAFOOD

atlantic salmon originally from Atlantic coastal waters, now farmed widely. Available whole or as steaks, cutlets or fillets.

balmain bug crustacean; a type of crayfish.

barramundi an Aboriginal word, barramundi means 'river fish with large scales'. Wild barramundi, found in both coastal and fresh waters in the tropical northern half of Australia, weigh an average 4kg; farmed barramundi are an average 400g in weight. 'Baby' barramundi (often referred to as 'plate-size'), also farmed commercially, are a firm, moist white fish best served whole.

calamari a type of squid.

scallops a bivalve mollusc with fluted shell valve; we use scallops having the coral (roe) attached.

SPATCHCOCK a small chicken (poussin), no more than 6 weeks old, weighing a maximum 500g. Also, a cooking technique where a small chicken is split open, then flattened and grilled.

SPICES

chermoulla spicy Moroccan mixture of freshly ground spices including coriander, cumin and paprika. This paste may be covered with a thin layer of olive oil to preserve it.

fenugreek hard, dried seed usually sold ground as an astringent spice powder. Good with seafood and in chutneys, fenugreek helps mask unpleasant odours.

five-spice powder a fragrant mixture of ground cinnamon, cloves, star anise, sichuan pepper and fennel seeds.

garam masala a blend of spices, originating in North India; based on varying proportions of cardamom, cinnamon, cloves, coriander, fennel and cumin, roasted and ground together. Black pepper and chilli can be added for a hotter version.

MASALA literally meaning blended spices; a masala can be whole spices, a paste or a powder, and can include herbs as well as spices and other seasonings. Traditional dishes are usually based on and named after particular masalas.

SPINACH also called English spinach and (incorrectly) silverbeet. Tender green leaves are good uncooked in salads or added to soups, stir-fries and stews just before serving.

STAR ANISE a dried star-shaped pod whose seeds have an astringent aniseed flavour; used to favour stocks and marinades.

STARFRUIT also called carambola, five-corner fruit or Chinese star fruit; pale green or yellow colour. It has a clean, crisp texture; flavour may be either sweet or sour, depending on variety and when picked. There is no need to peel or seed it and they're slow to discolour. Avoid any with brown specks or streaks.

STRAWBERRIES we used 250g punnets of strawberries.

SUGAR we used coarse, granulated table sugar, also known as crystal sugar, unless otherwise specified.

brown an extremely soft, fine granulated sugar retaining molasses for its characteristic colour and flavour.

caster also known as superfine or finely granulated table sugar.

demerara small-grained golden-coloured crystal sugar.

icing also known as confectioners' sugar or powdered sugar; pulverised granulated sugar crushed together with a small amount cornflour added.

palm also called nam tan pip, jaggery, jawa or gula melaka; made from the sap of the sugar palm tree. Light brown to black in colour and usually sold in rock-hard cakes; substitute it with brown sugar if unavailable.

pure icing also called confectioners' sugar or powdered sugar.

SUGAR SNAP PEAS also known as honey snap peas; fresh small pea which can be eaten, whole, pod and all, similarly to a snow peas.

SUMAC a purple-red, astringent spice grind; adds a tart, lemony flavour to dips and dressings and goes well with barbecued meat. Can be found in Middle-Eastern food stores. Substitute: ½ teaspoon lemon pepper + 1/8 teaspoon five-spice + 1/8 teaspoon all spice = ¾ teaspoon sumac.

TAT-SOI also called rosette, pak choy, tai gu choy and chinese flat cabbage; a variety of buk choy, developed to grow close to the ground so it is easily protected from frost. Its dark green leaves are cut into sections rather than separated and used in soups, braises and stir fries.

TOMATOES

cherry also called Tiny Tim or Tom Thumb tomatoes, small and round.

egg also called plum or Roma, these are smallish, oval-shaped tomatoes much used in Italian cooking or salads.

paste triple-concentrated tomato puree used to flavour soups, stews, sauces and casseroles.

puree canned pureed tomatoes (not tomato paste). Substitute with fresh peeled and pureed tomatoes.

teardrop small pear-shaped toamtoes.

truss small vine-ripened tomatoes with vine still attached.

TREACLE thick, dark syrup not unlike molasses; a by-product of sugar refining.

VINEGAR

balsamic originally from Modena, Italy, there are now many balsamic vinegars on the market ranging in pungency and quality depending on how, and how long, they have been aged. Quality can be determined up to a point by price; use the most expensive sparingly.

brown malt made from fermented malt and beech shavings.

cider made from fermented apples.

rice a colourless vinegar made from fermented rice and flavoured with sugar and salt. Also called seasoned rice vinegar. Sherry can be substituted.

rice wine made from fermented rice with no additives.

sherry natural vinegar aged in oak according to the traditional Spanish system, mellow wine vinegar named for its colour.

white made from spirit of cane sugar.

WHOLE EGG MAYONNAISE commercial mayonnaise of high quality made with whole eggs and labelled as such. Must be refrigerated once opened.

WOMBOK also known as chinese cabbage, Peking or napa cabbage, or petsai. Elongated in shape with pale green, crinkly leaves; is the most common cabbage in South-East Asia. Can be shredded or chopped and eaten raw or braised, steamed or stir-fried.

WORCESTERSHIRE SAUCE a thin, dark-brown spicy sauce used as a seasoning for meat, gravies and cocktails and as a condiment.

ZA'ATAR dry blend of roasted sesame seeds, wild marjoram, thyme and sumac; available in Arabic specialty shops.

conversion chart

Wherever you live, you'll be able to use our recipes with the help of these easy-to-follow conversions. While these conversions are approximate only, the difference between an exact and the approximate conversion of various liquid and dry measures is minimal and will not affect your cooking results.

dry measures

metric	imperial
15g	½oz
30g	1oz
60g	2oz
90g	3oz
125g	4oz (¼lb)
155g	5oz
185g	6oz
220g	7oz
250g	8oz (½lb)
280g	9oz
315g	10oz
345g	11oz
375g	12oz (¾lb)
410g	13oz
440g	14oz
470g	15oz
500g	16oz (1lb)
750g	24oz (1½lb)
1kg	32oz (2lb)

liquid measures

metric	imperial
30ml	1 fluid oz
60ml	2 fluid oz
100ml	3 fluid oz
125ml	4 fluid oz
150ml	5 fluid oz (¼ pint/1 gill)
190ml	6 fluid oz
250ml	8 fluid oz
300ml	10 fluid oz (½ pint)
500ml	16 fluid oz
600ml	20 fluid oz (1 pint)
1000ml (1 litre)	1¾ pints

length measures

metric	imperial
3mm	⅛in
6mm	¼in
1cm	½in
2cm	¾in
2.5cm	1in
5cm	2in
6cm	2½in
8cm	3in
10cm	4in
13cm	5in
15cm	6in
18cm	7in
20cm	8in
23cm	9in
25cm	10in
28cm	11in
30cm	12in (1ft)

oven temperatures

These oven temperatures are only a guide for conventional ovens. For fan-forced ovens, check the manufacturer's manual.

	°C (Celsius)	°F (Fahrenheit)	Gas Mark
Very slow	120	250	½
Slow	150	275 – 300	1 – 2
Moderately slow	160	325	3
Moderate	180	350 – 375	4 – 5
Moderately hot	200	400	6
Hot	220	425 – 450	7 – 8
Very hot	240	475	9

measuring equipment

The difference between one country's measuring cups and another's is, at most, within a 2 or 3 teaspoon variance. (For the record, one Australian metric measuring cup holds approximately 250ml.) The most accurate way of measuring dry ingredients is to weigh them. When measuring liquids, use a clear glass or plastic jug with the metric markings. (One Australian metric tablespoon holds 20ml; one Australian metric teaspoon holds 5ml.)

how to measure

When using graduated metric measuring cups, shake dry ingredients loosely into the appropriate cup. Do not tap the cup on a bench or tightly pack the ingredients unless directed to do so. Level top of measuring cups and measuring spoons with a knife. When measuring liquids, place a clear glass or plastic jug with metric markings on a flat surface to check accuracy at eye level.

Note: North America, NZ and the UK use 15ml tablespoons. All cup and spoon measurements are level.

We use large eggs having an average weight of 60g.

index